The PARROT in HEALTH and ILLNESS

A magnificent female Red-tailed Black Cockatoo (*Calyptorhynchus magnificus magnificus*). Her posture and plumage are indicators of her obvious vigor. *Bill Wegner, Malibu Exotics*

The PARROT in HEALTH and ILLNESS

An Owner's Guide

BONNIE MUNRO DOANE

Illustrations by Martha Vogel

HOWELL BOOK HOUSE

New York

Maxwell Macmillan Canada
Toronto

Maxwell Macmillan International
New York   Oxford   Singapore   Sydney

This book is dedicated to
the loving memory of

Michael Munro Doane, LCpl, USMC
and
Richard Michael Brockschmidt

Semper Fidelis

Howell Book House
Macmillan Publishing Company
866 Third Avenue
New York, NY 10022

Maxwell Macmillan Canada, Inc.
1200 Eglinton Avenue East, Suite 200
Don Mills, Ontario M3C 3N1

Macmillan Publishing Company is part of the Maxwell Communication Group of Companies.

Library of Congress Cataloging-in-Publication Data
Doane, Bonnie Munro.
    The parrot in health and illness: an owner's guide / Bonnie Munro Doane.
       p.   cm.
    Includes bibliographical references and index.
    ISBN 0-87605-826-8
    1. Parrots—Diseases.   2. Parrots—Health.   I. Title.
SF994.2.P37D63   1991
    636.6'865—dc20   90-20692

Macmillan books are available at special discounts for bulk purchases for sales promotions, premiums, fund-raising, or educational use. For details, contact:

                    Special Sales Director
                    Macmillan Publishing Company
                    866 Third Avenue
                    New York, NY 10022

10 9 8 7 6 5 4 3 2 1

Printed in the United States of America

Contents

The Eclectus parrot *Eclectus roratus* is of great interest because of its sexual dimor-
phism. The male shown here is typically green with an orange upper mandible. The hen
is red and blue with a black beak. When the Eclectus was first discovered, it was
thought that the two sexes were different species.
Photo courtesy Richard Schubot, Avicultural Breeding and Research Center

Foreword

Birds are being heralded as the pet of the 1990s. The current pet bird population has been estimated to be at least 12.9 million (AVMA, 1988), which is truly an underestimate. Nonetheless, the population has increased by more than 20 percent since 1983.

Why have birds become so popular? Several reasons can be cited.

- Life-style changes. Birds are basically a "low maintenance" pet. High-density housing makes it difficult to maintain a dog or cat, and many housing units place restrictions on cats and dogs but usually not on birds.
- Increased availability. Nationwide, more pet stores are carrying birds, and the number of larger birds available is increasing. Pet shops dealing exclusively in birds are more common. Increased success in raising birds domestically and by hand is a major reason for their greater availability.
- Hand-raising. For years, imported birds were the only source of larger birds in the United States. These birds were usually wild and aggressive young adults or mature birds that required extreme patience in taming, which did not always occur. Hand-raised birds are tamer, calmer, less likely to carry exotic diseases. Most important, they are already "bonded" to people, making them more affectionate and hence more desirable pets. They are also much more expensive than other pets, since the maintenance process is labor intensive.
- The nature of birds. Birds have been kept as pets for thousands of years. Their coloration, songs, antics, and companionship make them ideal pets. They need to socialize, and because of this need, they develop a

rewarding relationship with their owners. People who keep birds only as "ornaments" or as "trendy" pets are missing out on the true beauty of a relationship with a pet bird.

For avian veterinarians such as myself these are exciting times. We are seeing increasing numbers of birds in our practice, with a greater percentage of domestically hand-raised babies. Avian medicine is undergoing an information explosion. Long gone are the notions that "a sick bird is a dead bird" or that the treatment for a sick bird consists of heat and a little whiskey in the water. Our understanding of bird diseases, nutrition, and husbandry has increased dramatically as veterinary schools are developing avian medicine courses and active avian research is being conducted worldwide. Hence our sophistication and effectiveness in the treatment of avian diseases continually improve.

One of the greatest frustrations that face avian veterinarians is that by the time a bird owner/breeder brings a sick bird in for treatment the disease is well advanced, making treatment difficult if not impossible. The disturbing statistics are that only 7.6 percent of bird-owning households sought veterinary care in 1987, compared to 78 percent of dog owners and 60 percent of cat owners (AVMA, 1988). It is not that birds are so hardy that they are rarely sick; rather, recognition of disease may be so difficult and the understanding of basic bird husbandry so poor that proper care is not provided.

Unfortunately, most bird owners do not provide their pets with the proper nutritional requirements for optimal health and resistance to infection. Merely providing fresh seed and clean water is not enough. Also, many owners do not provide basic health care, which includes yearly physical examinations and physical examinations of all new birds before they are placed with other birds in the home or aviary.

An owner's failure to recognize illness in its early stages is a vexing problem. Most people can tell when a dog or cat is sick but cannot do so with a bird. The failure to recognize illness in birds is not a matter of negligence by bird owners but, rather, their unfamiliarity with the subtle signs of early disease. When addressed promptly, most diseases can be treated effectively.

What further complicates matters is that birds hide their illnesses because that is part of their natural defenses. In the wild a bird that is obviously sick will be subject to predator attack or harassed by other birds. Therefore, a bird that has been sick and ruffled all day may perk up when someone walks into the room in order to appear normal, in an effort to mask its illness. When a bird is no longer able to effectively conceal its illness, it is usually seriously ill.

Quite frequently new owners are given scant information at the time of purchase as to the proper care of a bird and may think that little is required. Such a scenario sets the stage for tragedy. It is truly heartbreaking when illness or death occurs to one of these lovely animals that could have been prevented if their needs had been better understood. One does not want to learn about bird care the hard way, through mistakes that are made. With hand-raised baby birds the outcome can be even more tragic because they are especially dependent on their owners and are even more susceptible to disease if inadequate care is provided.

These problems can be overcome through proper education of the bird owners. This can be provided through avian veterinarians, breeders, pet store professionals, or books on bird care. However, up to this time it has been difficult to find substantial information on bird care written in an understandable fashion for the serious bird fancier. The sources have been either too basic or written for the veterinarian. This book bridges the gap and is the long-awaited reference book that bird owners need.

Through her exhaustive research and desire to provide information on the cutting edge of avian medicine, the author has produced a work that will be of great value to anyone seriously concerned about providing quality care for his or her birds. This book is not a substitute for proper veterinary care; rather, it is a literate, intelligent source of information relating to avian medicine/bird care to encourage proper husbandry practices. The bird owner will learn what precautions can be taken to reduce the risk of disease and how to recognize it if it does occur. *The Parrot in Health and Illness* will be a welcome addition to the library of any bird fancier and will surely be a frequently used reference for many years to come.

PETER SAKAS, D.V.M.
Visiting Lecturer
College of Veterinary Medicine
University of Illinois

Hispanolan Conures (*Aratinga chloroptera chloroptera*)

Preface

As LITTLE AS fifteen years ago, a sick bird was a dead bird. All too often owners of an avian companion were faced with the sudden and unaccountable loss of their pet through illness. All too often breeders of exotic birds were faced with the loss of valuable breeding stock. All too often, if breeders were fortunate enough to obtain viable young, either the parents or the breeders were unable to raise the infants to maturity. All these circumstances were accepted as regrettable but commonplace.

However, the explosion of knowledge concerning avian husbandry, physiology, medicine, pharmacotherapeutics, nutrition, breeding strategies, and psittacine pediatrics has been nothing short of astonishing. Fifteen years ago a veterinarian specializing in exotic birds was himself a *rara avis*. Today many veterinarians are specializing in avian medicine, and their numbers continue to grow at a comfortable and comforting pace. Veterinary schools are beginning to add courses to their curricula that deal specifically with the exotic companion bird, and students in many of these schools are now able to experience a clinical rotation covering the care of exotic birds.

Today's avian veterinarian has an armamentarium of knowledge, tools, and techniques that was undreamed of fifteen years ago. These include not only highly effective medications, such as the new broad-spectrum antibiotics and antifungal medications, but also techniques such as electrocardiography, radiology, microsurgery, and electroencephalography.

Indeed, we have come a very long way since Robert Stroud, the "Bird Man of Alcatraz," published his book *Stroud's Digest on the Diseases of Birds* in 1943. Stroud states in the introduction: "The road [to the knowledge of avian therapeutics] stretches into the dim future, far beyond the accomplishments of any single lifetime, but if in this book I have been able to point the direction and inspire others to carry on from the point where I have left off, I shall consider my efforts worthwhile.'' Yes, we have come a long way from the time when Stroud's recommended treatment of avian conjunctivitis was a salve containing yellow oxide of mercury. One feels he would have been pleased and gratified by our great progress in the field of avian pathophysiology and medicine.

However (and hereby hangs the tale), all these wonderful advancements, all this knowledge, will do little for the sick bird unless its owner is a concerned, informed health care consumer on behalf of his pet. The owner is the bird's first line of defense against illness. It is the owner who first notes the change that may be the harbinger of illness. It is the owner who must make the decision to contact the avian veterinarian. Owners must equip themselves, before the fact of illness, to make these observations and decisions. The responsibility is theirs. The most brilliant diagnostician in the world, using the most skilled treatment, cannot save a bird whose owner has waited too long.

It is for these reasons that this book has been written. The material is presented, not to create self-educated veterinarians, but to familiarize the bird owner with health and illness alike. Indeed, self-treatment of one's bird, triggered by initiative, ignorance, ego, and a regrettable reluctance to give veterinarians their just due, usually lead to lamentable conclusions. An informed pet-care consumer can be both the bird's first defense against illness and its medical adviser's intelligent, effective partner in the bird's care.

Caring for such pets is a great responsibility and an even greater privilege. They did not ask to live with us. In many cases they have been removed from their native homes, their flocks, their mates, and their offspring. They have endured the hardships and terror of exportation, quarantine, strange food, and stranger surroundings. And for those tough, gallant individuals who survive, most come to our homes and eventually give us not only their tolerance but also, miraculously, their love. It is a humbling thing to comprehend. Can we do less than give them the best of which we are capable—not only in our affection for them, but in commitment to their health and longevity?

Baby Cockatiel (*Nymphicus hollandicus*), age 12 days

1

Selecting an Avian Veterinarian

SELECTING A VETERINARIAN specializing in bird care is one of the most important decisions you will make regarding your bird's health. Needless to say, this should be done before an illness occurs. It should also be noted that your bird needs an *avian* veterinarian, as not all veterinarians are skilled in the care of birds.

The best way to make your veterinarian's acquaintance, and familiarize the veterinarian with the bird and owner, is through the annual physical examination. There are many good reasons for such a course of action. A primary reason is that it provides your bird with preventive care. Just as with human health care, prevention is always preferable to treatment of an existing illness. It also allows the veterinarian to detect any subclinical, inapparent illness and treat it before it becomes serious or even life-threatening.

During the annual physical, the doctor can collect clinical facts pertinent to your specific bird while its health status is normal. Such data will include a complete blood count, a packed cell volume, cultures of material from the choana and cloaca, and a psittacosis titer. Your veterinarian may also add serum chemistries to this list. A fecal flotation will be performed to check for intestinal parasites. A Gram stain of the fecal material may reveal an abnormally large number of Gram-negative bacteria. Your veterinarian may also request a full-body radiograph of your bird. (Laboratory work, its meaning and implications, will be discussed in greater depth later in this section.)

In addition to obtaining the laboratory data, your veterinarian will give the bird a complete physical examination. This will include observation of the bird's eyes, ears, nose, and mouth, and an evaluation of the condition of the feathers, feet, beak, and skin. Palpation of the entire body, including the abdomen, will be performed. The veterinarian will also listen to your bird's heart, lungs, and air sacs with a pediatric stethoscope. All these findings will allow the veterinarian to formulate a picture of what is normal for *your* bird. These data will be invaluable should your bird become ill at a later time. Your veterinarian will then be able to compare the results of your bird's normal data with the data obtained at the time of illness. In this way, a diagnosis may be arrived at more quickly and with greater accuracy.

Bringing your bird in for an annual physical examination provides the veterinarian with an opportunity to make appropriate suggestions geared toward helping you provide better daily care for your bird. Perhaps your bird's diet could be improved. Maybe the sandpaper perches should be removed and replaced with something healthier for your bird's feet. Possibly your bird would benefit by more regular nail trimming or physical exercise.

The annual physical provides you, the owner, with an opportunity to meet and evaluate the veterinarian and staff. Subsequent physicals will allow you to continue to build rapport with and confidence in the bird's medical adviser. Having met your bird's doctor and staff, you will have access to a group of health-care professionals who are familiar with you and your bird. This can be a tremendous comfort when questions concerning your bird's health and behavior arise. You will feel more comfortable making that necessary phone call if you already know the people who will respond on the other end.

How do you go about locating an avian veterinarian? You should talk with other bird owners and breeders. Who do they recommend? What have been their personal experiences and feelings about their avian veterinarians? If you already have a veterinarian who you comfortably trust with other pets such as dogs and cats but who does not see birds, ask him or her for a recommendation. You can also contact your local veterinary medical society and request a list of doctors in your area who specialize in bird care. In the United States, the following three organizations also can provide you with information:

Association of Avian Veterinarians
P.O. Box 299
East Northport, NY 11731
(516) 757-6320

American Animal Hospital Association
P.O. Box 768
Mishawaka, IN 46544
(219) 256-0280

American Veterinary Medical Association
930 North Meacham Road
Schaumburg, IL 60196
(312) 885-8070

The source from which you purchased your bird may also be able to advise you in this capacity. However, you should be cautious when evaluating any recommendations. On the one hand, if the seller's facilities are clean, the stock healthy, and the personnel knowledgeable, their advice can probably be accepted. On the other hand, if the converse is true, it would be best to look elsewhere for a recommendation.

EVALUATING THE AVIAN VETERINARIAN

Having decided upon an avian veterinarian, and having made an appointment for your bird, what criteria should you use to evaluate your experience when you arrive? Basically, there are four areas that should receive your critical attention: the physical environment and equipment, the doctor and staff, the matter of fees, and after-hours care.

Physical Environment and Equipment

Your first contact will be with the receptionist when you telephone to make an appointment. He or she should sound friendly and be helpful. You should feel welcomed into the practice. At no time should you feel that your call has created a nuisance or inconvenience for the receptionist.

When you arrive, your registration should be pleasant and expedited as quickly as possible. In many practices, it is usual for the client to be given a form to fill out covering pertinent client data such as name, address, telephone number, and so forth. The form may also ask you to check from among a list of symptoms those you feel are pertinent to your bird if it is visiting the doctor due to illness rather than for a routine physical. The form should also include a place for biographical data about your bird, such as age, sex (if known), species, where and when purchased, number of other birds in house, how long owned, and their species.

You should be ushered into the examination room within fifteen to twenty minutes of your scheduled appointment. Although unforeseen emergencies sometimes arise that require immediate attention from the doctor and resultantly throw the day's schedule into a state of chaos, the majority of visits should not require an extended wait.

The appearance of the waiting room itself should come under scrutiny. Is it clean, light, and airy? Are there any unpleasant odors? Are there comfortable accommodations for the waiting client and pet? If the practice sees dogs and cats in addition to birds, is there a separate waiting area for birds to minimize their stress? How about reading material? Is it current and timely? Are there magazines and journals of interest to you in your role as a bird owner? Are there extra touches such as pictures on the walls and plants in the windows that would indicate the pride and interest of the staff in their working environment?

With regard to the equipment, there are basic requirements for any hospital dealing with exotic birds. It may not be possible for you to observe how the

The reception area in a modern avian veterinary hospital.   *M. Vogel*

Avian veterinary clinic and patients in exam room.   *M. Vogel*

hospital is equipped when you are there with your bird. However, most veterinarians are proud of their establishments and are happy to provide a tour when it is convenient for the staff. A veterinarian who is unwilling to do this is probably undeserving of your confidence and trust.

What do you look for when inspecting the hospital? The hospital should have a well-stocked pharmacy. The laboratory should contain a refrigerator, microscope, centrifuge, Bunsen burner, and incubator, as well as other small articles needed for the performance of basic laboratory work. There should be a radiograph machine. The hospital should contain holding cages and incubators for hospitalized birds, equipped with sources for heat, humidity, and oxygen. If at all possible, there should be separate rooms for treatment and for surgery. A separate surgical theater allows for control of an aseptic environment in which *sterile* surgery may be performed. All operating room personnel should wear caps, gowns, masks, and shoe covers while in the operating room. A newly sterilized instrument pack should be used for each surgical case. In this respect, the hospital should be equipped with both an autoclave and means for cold sterilization of instruments.

An anesthesia machine should be in evidence. Pertinent to this is the type of anesthesia used by the veterinarian. In the United States, isoflurane is the preferred agent for inhalation anesthesia. It is expensive, but its safety when used with birds, and its low hepatotoxicity relative to the human staff, make it preferable by far to anything else available for this type of anesthesia. Be sure to ask your veterinarian what anesthetic agent he or she uses; if it is not isoflurane, ask for an explanation.

The Doctor and Staff

It goes without saying that the veterinarian and staff should be articulate, neat, and well groomed. How does your bird's doctor handle the patient in the examination room? The veterinarian should be firm, but gentle. After all, even the toughest little Amazon parrot is a fragile creature. Does the doctor possess the confidence and skill to restrain a large, possibly angry bird? Even the most ferocious, affronted macaw will have medical needs that cannot be addressed until the large-beaked, uncooperative patient has been restrained for examination and treatment. Beware of any practitioner (or assistant) who appears frightened by the beak, the wildly dilating eye, the raised crest, or the extended wings of an angry psittacine.

Is your veterinarian willing to hear your questions and answer them? All of us have questions, from the brand-new, first-time bird owner to the breeder possessing many years of experience. Can the doctor answer your questions in language you can understand, based on *your* level of experience with birds, without being patronizing?

Occasionally, a very sick bird does not respond to treatment. It is at this point that the competent, concerned practitioner will seek a second opinion. It is wise to ascertain your veterinarian's policy on this point.

Is your bird's doctor compassionate? This falls into an area of value judgment on the owner's part. However, most of us can perceive when we are in the presence of compassion. And just as easily, we certainly feel its lack. Suffice it to say that if you perceive a sense of coldness, distance, or indifference, examine your feelings carefully and do not dismiss them as "imagination" or "just me." You may be correct in your estimation of that person's lack of compassion. If you determine that you are dealing with such a person, seek another medical adviser for your bird. Your pet deserves and needs every ounce of care and compassion it can get, even when it is well. When the bird is sick, this becomes doubly true.

Fees

While most of us would agree that the doctor, the facility, and the care the bird receives are of paramount importance, the matter of expense remains an important consideration. Acquaintances in your community can often supply information about fee levels that are "customary and usual" in given instances. For example, what does Doctor A charge for an office call, a nail clip, a wing trim, a routine physical examination—as opposed to Doctor B or C? Such information may influence your choice of practitioners even before you make your initial appointment. Fees should not be the primary motivating factor in making that choice, however.

Ask the receptionist about the hospital's fee-payment policy. Are services to be paid at the time service is rendered, or does the hospital routinely do billing? If pet insurance is available in your area and you carry it for your bird, will the hospital complete the necessary insurance forms or will you be expected to do so? If you have medical insurance for your bird, will the hospital wait for payment by the insurance company, or will they wish payment from you (in which case *you* will be the one to wait for reimbursement)?

It is also important to determine the hospital's policy concerning large, unexpected emergency bills. It is understandable that in such a situation one may not be immediately able to fully pay what could be a sizable fee. Most veterinarians understand this and are willing to work out a payment schedule with their clients. Indeed, many animal hospitals offer the use of credit cards, not only for emergency situations but also for payment of routine visits.

It is becoming more common to provide the client with a written estimation of fees in situations where prolonged hospitalization, numerous treatments, surgery, and the like are anticipated. This helps the client determine what the cost of the care is likely to be. However, it is important to remember that an estimate is merely that—an *estimate*. The situation may change suddenly with any ill creature, causing the entire care plan to be revised. In such cases, your veterinarian should contact you to discuss your bird's care and the treatment alternatives available. Remember that the fee estimate is a courtesy to you. Even though your veterinarian will try to make it as complete as possible, it will not be exact. The client should not feel cheated if the final fee turns out to be higher than anticipated, particularly if he has been informed of the bird's ongoing progress and the subsequent financial ramifications.

After-Hours Care

There is one final area to consider when selecting an avian practitioner: after-hours and weekend emergency care. Some veterinarians take their own clients' off-hour emergency calls. This is true especially if there are two or more doctors in the practice, thereby allowing an equitable rotation of this duty. In such cases, the practitioner will often employ an answering service to screen calls and forward emergency cases so that he or she may contact the client by telephone and determine whether the bird should be seen immediately.

Some veterinarians do not take their own emergency calls during off-hours. Instead, they refer their clients to an emergency veterinary service. Such services are actual animal hospitals, fully equipped to handle emergency problems. They are generally open all night and throughout the weekend. The important fact to determine about this kind of service is whether or not a veterinarian skilled in the treatment of birds will be available. If so, this will be a good emergency resource for the bird owner. If not, the owner should look for a veterinarian who takes emergency calls, or for an emergency service that employs an avian veterinarian. Unfortunately, many potentially grave situations arise at exactly those times when one's doctor is unavailable. You will wish to have a backup service that provides the same excellent care to your bird that it receives during regular office hours.

It should be obvious that a veterinarian who has made no provision for emergency care during off-hours should be avoided.

TRANSPORTING YOUR BIRD TO THE VETERINARIAN

A little planning can make your trip to the veterinarian much less stressful for you and your bird. (In this section we will discuss preparations for a planned visit. Transportation of a critically ill bird or one with a life-threatening condition will be discussed in Chapter 4, "Emergency First Aid.")

A few words of warning: Never take your bird to the veterinarian unconfined. Animal practitioners have a term for owners who bring their birds in on their shoulder: "the Long John Silver syndrome." For whatever reason, be it ego or ignorance, such owners selfishly fail to consider the dangers implicit in this mode of transport for the bird. There are many stories of birds that have been frightened by traffic noises, dogs, strange surroundings, and the like and have flown in panic to serious injury or death. Such incidents are doubly tragic in that with a little intelligence on the bird owner's part the accidents need never have happened.

The avian veterinarian must rely on the nature of droppings as a barometer of a bird's health. When visiting the veterinarian always take the cage paper for the evaluation. Use waxed paper to wrap the cage paper for its entire length and width and folded as one unit. In this way, the droppings are preserved for the veterinarian but are easy to transport.   *M. Vogel*

The first item for consideration is the type of container to use to carry the bird. If the bird is small, take it in its customary cage. If the bird resides in a very large cage of the type used to house cockatoos and macaws, or if it is kept in an aviary, then you will need a pet carrier. A cardboard box might suffice, but it is better to use a carrier made of material strong enough to resist a parrot's powerful beak. The author strongly recommends the type made of polyvinyl material, such as those used by airlines to transport pets. They are strong, and easily cleaned and disinfected.

Regardless of what you use, be sure to cover the carrier with a towel or sheet. This provides some protection from cold weather. It also provides the bird with privacy, limits its vision, and thereby lessens the stress it might otherwise experience. The towel or sheet also provides some protection against aerosol droplet contamination from exposure to other sick birds while in the waiting room.

When using a container other than the bird's normal cage, place a low perch inside. If the bird is weak, it might be better to cover the floor of the carrier with an old towel. This will allow a better purchase for the bird's feet. It will also provide some additional insulation if the weather is cold.

When using a carrier, you will also need to take the cage liner that has been used in the normal cage for the past twenty-four hours. It is extremely important for the veterinarian to be able to observe the bird's twenty-four-hour dropping production, as the droppings can provide much significant information about the bird's health status. Place a layer of waxed paper on the side of the liner on which the droppings have fallen to prevent their obliteration when you fold the cage paper to take it with you.

When using a carrier rather than the cage, you will also need to take along a sample of the bird's food. This is especially important if the bird is ill. Many illnesses arise from poor nutrition, or from food that has been improperly prepared or left in the cage too long.

When using the cage as the transport container, remove all toys and loose items that could ricochet and cause injury. Leave only one perch, preferably placed low in the cage. Remove the water dishes. Food containers may remain, partially filled with whatever the bird normally eats. Leave the cage liner in place so the droppings may be examined. Do not clean the cage. The veterinarian will gain valuable clues to illness, if present, from observing your bird's daily living environment. After inspecting the cage, the veterinarian may make suggestions about future husbandry, if the cage's condition warrants this.

Make every attempt to reassure the bird during its trip. Speak often and reassuringly. Drive carefully and avoid sharp turns and sudden stops. If your car is equipped with a radio, play some soothing music on low volume. If the weather is cold, preheat the car before placing the bird inside. If the weather is hot, requiring the use of air conditioning, be sure to place the bird out of the direct blast of cold-air vents.

IMPORTANT QUESTIONS TO ANSWER

Before your visit, make a list of any questions you wish to ask. Also list any medications your bird has been given, including vitamins.

During your visit, the veterinarian will take a complete history of your bird. In addition to providing information about your bird's diet and any medication it is taking, be prepared to answer the following questions. They fall into three general categories.

1. Biographical data: age (if known); sex (if known); length of ownership; where purchased; other birds in house (species, length of ownership, any very recently acquired; caging: as pairs, singly, in multiple bird flights, indoor or outdoor caging).

2. Behavioral data: eating habits (type of food eaten, easy or difficult acceptance of new food items); activity level (daily activity routine, any changes in activity level); placement of bird's cage in home (high activity area, isolated from family and other pets); time spent out of cage, or with family; breeding history, if applicable; relationship with various family members.

3. If bird is sick: main complaint; symptoms (nature, when first noticed, status: same, better, worse); other birds ill; other family members ill; exposure to toxins (fumes, for example, polyfluorocarbons; plants; cleaning supplies; ingestion of carpet or other fabric fibers; lead: stained glass ornaments, paint); previous medical problems (drugs used and bird's response to them); attempt at home treatment (what was attempted, length of time attempted); treatment by another veterinarian (drugs used, bird's response to them).

VETERINARY OFFICE ETIQUETTE FOR THE BIRD OWNER

A good part of the foregoing material has been devoted to your veterinarian's responsibility to your bird and to you. But what of your responsibility to your veterinarian? There is indeed a code of etiquette the health-care consumer should bear in mind when dealing with a bird's health care adviser. Any relationship is a two-way interaction. Taking the following suggestions to heart will help ensure that your relationship with your veterinarian will be long, happy, and advantageous to your bird.

Do not expect a diagnosis and treatment plan to be provided for your bird over the telephone. This is unfair to the bird and to the veterinarian. No matter how skilled the doctor, if your bird is sick, it must be seen. The general symptoms sick birds exhibit do not allow a specific diagnosis over the telephone. The bird will need a hands-on examination and, very likely, laboratory testing of some type.

When asking your veterinarian questions, be as succinct and clear as

Computerized serum chemistry analyzer.   *M.Vogel*

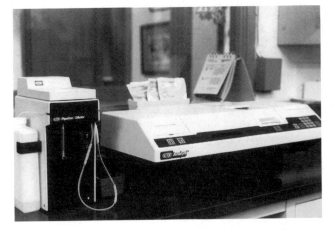

This computerized machine allows in-house identification of pathogens that have grown out on culture plates incubated for 24 hours.   *M. Vogel*

The binocular microscope with second microscope attached to allow viewing of one slide by two persons. The primary unit (right) is also equipped with an attachment allowing slides to be photgraphed.
M. Vogel

possible. Do not ramble, bringing in material not pertinent to the question at hand. Other clients and patients are waiting, and deserve the courtesy of being seen on time, just as you were.

Observe customary office hours for routine procedures, such as obtaining wing and nail clips, picking up special food or medications, or dropping off samples of any type. It is unfair to expect the hospital staff to open earlier or close later to accommodate your schedule. Emergencies are, of course, a different situation—but remember that the staff works hard and deserves to go to their homes and families on time.

Respect your veterinarian's training and expertise. He or she is a health care professional with many years of education, obtained at great expense. Regrettably, many people withhold from their veterinarians the respect they accord their physicians because "after all, he's just an animal doctor."

When your bird is ill and you are frustrated, frightened, and possibly angry that recovery is not as speedy as you had hoped, try not to blame the doctor and staff. They want your pet to recover as badly as you do. Indeed, every veterinary hospital probably has its own story of a devoted, caring doctor or attendant staying up all night with a critically ill animal, or taking an animal home on Sunday (a time when most hospitals are minimally staffed) so that the pet could continue to receive the care and observation it needed. Once you have placed your trust in a veterinarian, leave it there, unless you have irrefutable evidence that your trust has been betrayed. Your veterinarian has enough to deal with in attempting to heal your pet, without also having to deal with a hostile client. Show that you are willing to be an intelligent partner in your bird's health care, not an adversary. Having a good working partnership with your veterinarian will benefit your bird. Indicate your willingness to listen and understand what is happening to your pet. This will be greatly appreciated by the veterinarian.

When any animal is ill, alternative treatment plans are often available. Sometimes one of these alternatives is a conservative plan using medication and a "wait and see" attitude. Many times the practitioner will feel a more vigorous approach is justified. Be very clear in your mind about the ramifications of all the alternatives your veterinarian proposes—not only in terms of cost, but in regard to expected outcomes. It is the doctor's job to present to you the relative merits of each plan. The final decision is yours. Therefore, if against your veterinarian's advice you elect a less expensive treatment plan with less chance of success, be prepared to accept the consequence. If your bird fails to recover completely, or dies, refrain from blaming the veterinarian. Remember that the choice was yours, and abide with the outcome. This situation is unfortunate, but there is much to be learned from it. Apply your hard-won knowledge the next time it becomes necessary, so that a happier ending will result.

Finally, pay your bills in a manner consistent with hospital policy. Many of us have had the experience of losing a beloved pet after much expense has been incurred providing the care it required. Paying the fee in these circumstances can be one of the loneliest experiences a pet owner can have, because there is no pet to bring home, returned to full health and vitality. It may be natural to feel some anger and resentment, but remember that with any living creature, especially a sick one, there can be no guarantees. Think of the kindness, concern, and compassion you received when your pet was ill. Think of the skill and dedication with which it was treated. No one desired more to return a healthy pet to you than did your veterinarian and the attending staff. Wanting to save an animal and being unable to do so is one of animal health-care practitioners' worst frustrations. They share your sadness and grief. To paraphrase an old saying, their skilled labor was worthy of your hire, so do not begrudge it.

The above suggestions may seem unusual to the reader, but they are based upon the actual experience of dealing with clients in the animal hospital setting. The client who is welcomed with open arms is the one who is courteous, civil, and an informed pet health-care consumer. If you are such a client, both your input regarding your bird and your presence will always be welcome.

Umbrella Cockatoo (*Cacatua alba*)

2

The Well Bird

CHARACTERISTICS OF A HEALTHY PARROT

A healthy parrot is one of nature's loveliest creations, a joy to the eye and a delight to the mind—especially if it is conversant! This chapter will discuss the characteristics of the well bird, and how an owner proceeds to keep his bird healthy. The importation-quarantine process and its meaning to a bird's health will also be briefly discussed.

Let us begin with the external appearance of a healthy parrot. Its eyes should be bright and clear. There should be no exudate of any kind, nor should there be any sores around the lid margins or facial skin if the bird is of a species that possesses this characteristic. There should be no redness or thickening of the eyelids.

The nares (nostrils) should likewise be free of any drainage, and should not appear plugged. The feathers surrounding the nares should not appear matted or stained. If this is the case, it is likely that nasal discharge has been present in the not too distant past.

The beak should be smooth and free from defects. It should be well formed, allowing the bird to obtain and swallow its food properly. There should be no evidence of scaliness that might indicate the presence of mites, especially in budgerigars (see Chapter 5).

The feathers should be glossy and full. At no time should the bird exhibit bald patches or areas where only the undercoat of down feathers is present. Birds recently out of quarantine will often have a poorly clipped wing. Wing and tail feathers may appear ragged or broken. These things will have occurred due to overcrowding during the import-quarantine process and will be rectified at the next molt. It is important to note that when a parrot molts, at no time does it lose more than a few feathers from any area of its body. This is a protective mechanism to allow the bird to escape from predators in the wild. A partially bald bird is exhibiting signs of disease or undue psychological stress. Such a bird should be seen by the veterinarian. If contemplating the purchase of such a bird, the advice is: *Do not*.

The parrot's feet should possess their full complement of toes, two pointing backward and two pointing forward on each foot. They should be smooth, with no evidence of scaliness, which indicates mite infestation. Each toe should have a toenail, although sometimes a bird will be missing a nail due to trauma sustained in the wild or during the import-quarantine process. If this is the case, the toe should be well healed, with no drainage or scabbing present. Indeed, neither of these conditions should be apparent anywhere on the feet or legs.

The healthy parrot will tuck one or the other of its feet up off the perch, especially when relaxed and resting. However, a consistent reluctance to use a foot, whether perching or walking, should be called to the veterinarian's attention. Likewise, the use of a foot accompanied by limping or obvious inability to bear full weight should also be investigated.

The vent should be clean, with no dried fecal matter or urates present on the surrounding feathers.

A dropping consists of three components: feces, urates, and urine. The fecal portion is solid, formed in a tubular wormlike shape, light to dark green in appearance. The urates comprise the solid waste produced by the kidneys. They are irregularly wrapped about the feces, rather pasty in consistency, and white in color. The urine is the liquid part of the dropping and is essentially clear in color. There are variations in the normal stool, particularly in regard to the amount of liquid present. Under unusual stress, such as a trip to the veterinarian, the dropping will contain a large amount of urine in proportion to feces. This is normal and represents the "flight or fight" reflex. When the bird is frightened it will immediately evacuate the cloacal contents in preparation for flight from perceived danger; this will include the urine content of the dropping, the liquid part of which under ordinary circumstances should have been partially absorbed by the colon. This is a normal dropping given the situation of temporary stress. Another variation of the normal dropping is the large ratio of liquid urine to feces when a bird's diet is very high in water content, as when many fruits and vegetables are consumed. A hand-raised baby's formula has a high water content, thus resulting in more liquid droppings; this is also normal given the food eaten.

The important thing to remember when observing droppings is the overall appearance of the twenty-four-hour sample. One or two droppings that vary from normal are no cause for concern. A whole day's worth of atypical droppings merits a call to the veterinarian. (A more complete discussion of droppings, their normal and abnormal variations, and their meaning will be found in Chapter 3.)

Next we turn to the characteristics of a normal parrot relative to its level of activity. Naturally, each bird's normal activity and routine will vary slightly from another's. This is in part dependent upon the schedule of the family with which it lives. However, all healthy parrots have the following attributes in common. They appear bright, alert, and inquisitive. A large amount of time is given to preening, vocalizing, playing, and performing comfort activities (such as wing stretching and wing flapping). A tame bird will frequently solicit its family's attention in a variety of ways, such as bowing the head for a comfortable scratch, making frequent eye contact combined with vocalization, or begging to be let out of its cage. Depending on the species, an aviary bird with a mate will spend a great deal of time in close or approximate contact with the mate, soliciting allo-preening and/or allo-feeding, nest-box inspection, and so forth. Allo-preening and allo-feeding are behaviors between any two birds (not necessarily a true pair), in which mutual feeding and/or preening occur.

Contrary to popular opinion, a good appetite is not necessarily a sign of good health. A bird may, and usually does, eat up until a few hours before its death. This largely involuntary activity is a protective mechanism peculiar to birds that allows them to present an appearance of normality to their flockmates. An ill bird draws predators and represents a threat to the flock's safety. Such a bird will be driven away by its congeners. Therefore, an appearance of normality allows the sick bird to remain within the flock and the safety it provides. Because of this, it is essential to know if the bird is actually eating. Be sure to observe whether the bird is merely cracking seed or is actually ingesting the kernel it has hulled out. Be sure that food is not just scattered on the cage bottom, but that the bird is actually swallowing food. Periodic weight checks using a gram scale or by palpating the bird's breast muscles will help ensure that the bird is "ingesting as well as messing."

In regard to daily activity level, the following is fairly representative of a parrot's usual routine. Parrots tend to be very active in the early morning when they have first awakened. Eating, vocalizing, and playing tend to be at their height during this time. Late mornings are often devoted to bathing, preening, and other desultory activity. The period from noon to midafternoon is usually a time for snoozing or quiet contemplation. Late afternoon is again a very active time. Eating and vocalization are high on the parrot's agenda. Evening will be a quiet time in preparation for night roosting and sleep for the aviary bird. For the tame bird, it may be a time of further activity, as its family is home for the day and has time to spend with it.

The important thing to note about the daily routine is to learn what is normal for your bird. Any marked, consistent deviation from a bird's personal schedule should alert you to possible trouble.

Another area concerning the normal, healthy parrot is its breeding success, where applicable. A healthy parrot, provided it has a mate of the opposite sex, appropriate housing and nesting facilities, proper light (both type and duration), and good nutrition should produce viable young. Obviously, there are many subtle variables that cause a pair of birds to mate and go to nest. If great attention has been given to all the factors that have been shown to lead to reproductive success and no success has been attained, then either one or both birds may have a health problem. On the other hand, a pair that consistently produces viable, healthy young may be judged to be in good health.

KEEPING YOUR PARROT HEALTHY

Given that one is in possession of a healthy bird, how does one keep it that way? There are five equally important areas the owner must consider to achieve this goal: nutrition, hygiene, safety, daily observation, and psychological health.

Nutrition

A balanced diet similar to a human health food diet has been found to benefit your parrot friend. The exclusive use of a seed diet invites malnutrition and its sequelae of disease.

Water should be fresh daily. As a precaution, run the water faucet at least three minutes to flush the line prior to filling your bird's water dish. The reason for this is that *Pseudomonas* bacteria live in the clean water pipes. They are not harmful to humans, but are potential sources of disease for the parrot. By running the water for at least three minutes, you are flushing out the line and accessing water from the main pipes where water has flowed all night, thereby preventing bacterial buildup.

Vitamin powder should be sprinkled on soft food for your bird. Putting vitamins in the water has two disadvantages. First, it allows the water to become a perfect medium in which harmful bacteria can thrive. Second, many parrots, especially those whose native homeland is semiarid, do not drink large quantities of water. They will not, therefore, receive great benefit from vitamins placed in their cage water source.

A cautionary note: When placing additives in food or water, be sure that the supplements are not preventing the bird from drinking or eating. Birds are notoriously suspicious about anything that gives their food a slightly different appearance. They may avoid food or water to which anything new has been added. Whenever such measures have been instituted, observe the bird very carefully for the first few days to make sure it is not starving itself or refusing to drink.

One area of nutrition has frequently been a nightmarish source of frustration to the conscientious parrot owner. This is the problem of how to convert a "sunflower seed junkie" to a balanced, healthy diet. Oftentimes the owner is fully aware of what constitutes a good diet for his pet, but the bird refuses to cooperate.

There are several factors that contribute to this dilemma. First, the parrot (indeed, any bird) is by nature suspicious of anything new or different, including food items. This instinctive behavior allows it to stay alive in the

A group of beautiful, well-kept parrots reflects thoughtful care. The birds are a male Eclectus parrot, a Scarlet Macaw (*Ara macao*), a rare Red-fronted Macaw (*Ara rubrogenys*) and an Umbrella Cockatoo (*Cacatua alba*).
Photo courtesy Richard Schubot, Avicultural Breeding and Research Center

19

wild. Second, the parrot literally may not *recognize* new foods as food. Third, the owner, after having tried for three or four weeks to convert his stubborn friend to the joys and benefits of a nutritious diet, may well give up in frustration. The owner may not realize that it often takes as long as a year to effect the desired conversion—not a matter of weeks.

The following suggestions may assist the owner in providing a good diet that the parrot actually *eats*—instead of relegating to the cage or living room floor. In working toward the goal of a sound diet for your bird, be prepared for wasted food. There is going to be a lot of it. However, a year's worth of wasted fruit and vegetable will still not cost as much as treating serious disease in your parrot resulting from nutritional deficiency, so grit your teeth, ignore the waste, and be of good heart.

The parrot's suspicion of anything new has two implications for the owner. First, when introducing new food in the food bowl, it is wise to use small pieces. Second, any change attempted must be *gradual*. Very small amounts of the new food should be added to the accustomed food; increase the amount only as the bird accepts it. Never change the content of the food bowl all at once. It is possible that the bird will quite literally starve if such a radical change is made. Remember that a bird's metabolic rate is very high, making it extremely dangerous for a bird to go without food for even a day in a small species, two days at the most in the larger species.

In order to assure yourself that the bird is eating, you must monitor it very carefully in the following ways. First, observe your bird in the physical act of eating and actually swallowing food. Second, monitor the number and size of droppings. What goes in must come out. If your bird's droppings (both number and size) remain normal, you can be assured that it is eating. If the number and amount decrease, its food intake is down. If such is the case, back off. You are probably attempting the change in diet too rapidly to suit the bird's sense of caution. The third thing you must do is monitor its weight, either by palpating the breast or by daily weight checks. Although this is easily accomplished with a tame bird, it is more difficult with a wild or semi-tame one. Nevertheless, it should be done.

If using the palpation method, the bird's pectoral muscles should remain as they were before the dietary changes were instituted. If you are weighing your bird, you must use a gram scale. Any decline in weight, however small, over a three-day period, indicates that the bird is not eating enough to satisfy its metabolic needs and maintain weight. In this situation, you must make available an increased amount of the food to which the bird is accustomed and temporarily decrease the amount of the new, strange food.

A note of caution is appropriate here. Weaning a bird onto a new diet is stressful. Stress is a major agent in causing a previously subclinical problem to break into full-blown illness. Therefore, if you have any reason to believe that the bird is ill (for example, a continuation of weight loss, or continued decrease in number or size of droppings—even after the usual diet has been reinstated), have the bird checked by your veterinarian immediately.

There are a variety of strategies with which you can accomplish the conversion to a better diet. One of the ways the author has had a great deal of success is with the use of various vegetable sprouts. Even the pickiest cockatoo will accept and relish these after a few days, provided they are mixed into the seed dish in very gradually increased amounts. In the area where the author lives, packaged sprouts can be obtained from the produce section of the grocery store. The best results have been obtained with sprouted wheat, or a mixture of mung beans, azuki, and lentil sprouts (labeled three-bean mix). In the author's experience, sprouts such as radish or alfalfa have not worked nearly as well in tempting a bird to sample its first new food offering.

If you are unable to purchase sprouts from the grocery store, you may wish to sprout your own seed. An excellent guide is *The Bean Sprout Book*, by Gay Courter (1972). If attempting to do your own sprouting, follow directions exactly; sprouts are a great medium for bacterial growth if care is not taken to prevent it.

Once the bird is used to having sprouts mixed in with its seed, other new foods may be added judiciously. The author has successfully used a mixture of fresh, dark green and yellow vegetables coarsely chopped in the food processor or blender. Fruits can be prepared in the same way. A tablespoon of sprouts, one each of vegetable mixture, fruit mixture, seed, and ground dog chow are combined. The entire mash is then sprinkled with a vitamin/mineral supplement. The addition of *each* component should occur *only* after the bird is accepting the previous additions well. Remember, this may take many weeks, so be patient.

One of the advantages of using such a mash is that each new component closely resembles the previous addition. This helps to negate the visual aspect of newness and strangeness. Another advantage is that fruit and vegetable mixes can be prepared separately in large quantities and frozen for convenience. The disadvantage of such a mash is that it spoils easily. To prevent this, the author offers the mash for an hour in the morning, then removes and refrigerates the remainder, offering it again for an hour or two in the evening. Since birds are accustomed to eating twice a day in the wild, this schedule is not upsetting to them and provides all the daily nutrition and calories needed.

However, many people wish to leave something for their birds to nibble on throughout the day. This usually takes the form of fruit and vegetables. This is fine, provided that spoilage is guarded against. But how do you get the bird to accept these offerings? Again, use *small* pieces if they are to be placed in a food bowl. Another, perhaps easier way to get your bird to sample new goodies is to take advantage of its sense of curiosity and penchant for playing and gnawing. Tying an ear of corn, a banana, an apple, a bunch of grapes to its cage—or hanging them by means of a chain—provides it with a toy. At first your bird will probably ignore it, but in a day or two it will no doubt attempt to chew the new addition as if it were a piece of wood. This method not only gives the bird the opportunity to taste the new food, but also provides a play activity—a type of occupational therapy, so to speak. This is an excellent way of helping your bird become accustomed to new foods. A chicken drumstick also can be used. Most birds adore them, even to the point of cracking the bone and extracting the marrow.

Other foods that serve the double purpose of introducing healthy dietary additions plus providing play activity are whole green beans, peas in the pod, uncooked pasta, nuts, whole hard-boiled eggs (for large birds such as cockatoos and macaws), hands of fresh ginger, and stick cinnamon. Once your imagination is engaged, the possibilities are almost endless.

Another approach to the introduction of new food that works well with the tame bird is to bring it to the table and let it sample a little bit of whatever is there (no alcohol, please). The author's husband is owned by JB, a Blue-Crowned Amazon that shares his evening meal every night. A separate little plate is prepared containing samples of the family's meal. Since JB always immediately wants whatever his human is eating, he has been successfully introduced to a wide variety of healthy foods in this way.

Another possibility for introducing your bird to new food involves "junk food." This method should be used cautiously, and as a last resort for the bird that stubbornly refuses all your dietary blandishments after a period of at least two to three months. The object is to get the bird to realize that there are other pleasing taste sensations in this world besides the sunflower seeds to which it is so loyally attached. In this situation, the occasional offering of a potato chip, french fry, cheese curl, a cube of pound cake, or the like will sometimes convince the bird that what you are offering is good. It may then be more willing to accept your next offering, even if it should be (Heaven forbid!) a nutritional tidbit.

Sometimes just placing a picky eater next to a parrot that eats well proves successful. Some years ago, the author acquired a Moluccan Cockatoo named Willy. When Willy took up residence with the family, he made acquaintance with Molly, an Umbrella Cockatoo that had been in the author's possession for about one and a half years. Molly had accepted the mash mentioned earlier in this chapter but refused all cut-up fruits and vegetables with the exception of corn on the cob. Willy, on the other hand, ate everything that was not nailed down. Because Willy and Molly enjoyed each other's company, they spent a great deal of time together and had access to each other's open cages. Molly watched Willy eat fruit and vegetables, literally by the pint. Before long, Molly began to sample some of those previously unacceptable food offerings. At the time of this writing, Molly heartily consumes everything from plum tomatoes to cantaloupe. Parrots are imitative creatures, not only with respect to vocalization, but also behavior. Taking advantage of this trait when you are attempting to convert a bird to a well-balanced diet may pay unexpected dividends!

Much has been printed lately about the pelleted diet. It has the advantage of being easy to prepare and resistant to spoilage. However, in the author's experience, it is not eaten with enjoyment by parrots that are accustomed to much variety in their daily diet. Most pelleted diets taste chalky and bland. When thinking of changing a bird's diet to one consisting of pellets, consider that, beside providing nourishment, food has an occupational therapy value to birds. Rummaging through the day's offering of mash, fruit, and vegetables is an event

Pet birds are typically social and enjoy being at the center of activity. Here a budgerigar (*Melopsittacus undulatus*) and a Timneh African Gray Parrot (*Psittacus erithacus timneh*) share their owner's dinner.

Pet birds are sought the world over for the brightness they bring to a home and the pleasure people derive from their company.   *M. Vogel*

in which the author's parrots take daily delight. Having pellets, and only pellets, in the bowl day after day is a pretty unexciting prospect for a bird. The author therefore suggests that the pellet diet be supplemented with fruit and vegetables for both the visual interest and mental stimulation they provide. A good combination is 80 percent pellets and 20 percent "people food."

In addition, *no* pelleted diet has been proven scientifically to be "complete." We simply do not know at this time what "nutritionally complete" means for any given parrot species. It stands to reason, therefore, that no one pelleted product can satisfy the nutritional requirements of any and all parrot species. The owner should be aware of this before deciding to wean a bird to a diet consisting exclusively of pelleted food. If the owner does choose such a diet, it must again be reiterated that "gradual" is the watchword when effecting the change.

Another factor to consider is the bird's physiological status at any given time. The bird's need for protein is increased during the molt, while breeding or rearing young, and during times of illness. The owner should be aware of this and be prepared to supply a pellet formulated for such needs. Extra protein can also be provided by cooked meat or legumes and by dairy products such as low-fat cheese, powdered skimmed milk, low-fat cottage cheese, and yogurt.

Hygiene

Proper hygiene is very important in maintaining your parrot's health. There is nothing more heartbreaking and less excusable than to see a parrot, a creature of light and air, sitting in a filthy cage littered with spoiled food, large accumulations of droppings, and a water cup coated with slime. The effect of this kind of abuse and neglect is tragic: eventually, and without question, the bird will die. At this time in our history, when conservation is not only morally imperative but necessary for survival, finding a bird (or any animal, for that matter) in such a condition is unspeakably evil.

When a bird lives out its life span in the wild, it is able to remove itself from its discarded food, its own excrement. When a bird is living in captivity, it is the owner's responsibility to keep the parrot's environment and immediate surroundings clean. A bird is a fastidious creature, much like a cat in this respect. But unlike a cat, which can use a litter box, cover its excreta, and walk away, the bird is unable to tidy its cage. The *very least* in the way of hygiene that your parrot requires is that its cage liner be changed daily and its food and water bowl be washed every day and replenished with fresh food and water.

In discussing the concept of cleanliness for your parrot, the following is extremely important to grasp. Your bird comes from an environment *totally* different from the one in which it lives with you. Although a bird is able to withstand the bacteria found in its wild environment, its body has no experience in providing immunity to the bacteria commonly found in the so-called civilized environment. And this includes the bacteria that are natural and normal on and in you—its owner! The things we see no harm in, such as water from the tap (mentioned earlier), a kiss on the beak, a piece of food offered from which the owner has already bitten a piece—all these situations are potentially harmful for your parrot. As the bird's owner, you must be aware of these things and learn to guard against them.

Let us first consider the bird's cage. The cage liner should be changed daily. Newspaper is still the best material to use for this purpose. It is cheap, easily available, and allows good visualization of droppings. Changing the liner daily prevents accumulation of droppings and the disease potential they represent. It also prevents the buildup of old food. Spoiled food material represents a harmful source of bacterial contamination. By changing the cage liner daily, the owner becomes cognizant of the normal characteristics of the bird's droppings. The importance of this has already been mentioned.

Perches, toys, and other such items that have been soiled need to be cleaned on an "as needed" basis. It is extremely unwise to procrastinate when such chores are needed.

Once a week, the cage should be stripped, thoroughly washed to remove food particles and other soiling, and then disinfected. Most disinfecting agents are not effective when organic matter is present (such as food and droppings). This is why such soiling must be removed *first* with soap and water before applying the disinfectant. After the disinfectant has been applied, it is a good idea to let it remain on the cage for at least thirty minutes, then rinse it away thoroughly. Most disinfectants are harmful when ingested, so take pains that not even a trace remains. Some effective disinfectants are Lysol, One-Stroke-Environ, Chlorox, Betadine, and Wavecide-O1. If these are unavailable to you, ask your veterinarian for the names of some good alternatives.

Never use a secondhand cage without first cleaning and disinfecting it, and throwing away all wooden items such as perches. You have no way of knowing if the former occupant was ill. To avoid the above precautions is to invite disaster.

The one best way to be sure that a previously used cage is safe to use is to have it cleaned by a commercial steam-cleaning company, such as those that steam-clean car engines. This will assure you that the cage has been rendered sterile and free of all previous pathogens.

You will need to repaint the cage if it had a painted finish prior to the cleaning process. This is easily accomplished using a *nontoxic* spray paint. With regard to the paint finish on any cage, never buy or use a cage unless you are positive that the paint is lead-free and nontoxic.

The next topic to consider is the condition of the food and water bowls. They should be cleaned daily with hot water and soap. All food containers should be disinfected at least once a week. It is a good idea to have two sets of bowls for each bird—one for the wash and one to use.

Water should be replaced at least once daily, as should food—including seeds. Food dropped into the water bowl, vitamins added to the water, or droppings in the water all provide a rich growth medium for bacteria. Within twenty-four hours the parrot will be drinking from a veritable bacterial stew. Avoid this at all costs. Placing the food and water bowls on opposite sides of the cage will help prevent food contamination of water. Placing the food and water receptacles away from overhead perches will likewise help prevent fecal contamination. With some of the smaller and less destructive parrots, covered food and water cups may be used.

Food preparation is another area requiring great care. Wash all fruits and vegetables thoroughly to avoid the ingestion of pesticides by your bird. Wash your own hands before preparing your parrot's meals. Never use any food that is less than top quality. You would not enjoy eating a rotten banana or wilted spinach. Neither does your bird.

It is a good idea to microwave or bake dry products such as seed, monkey chow, or dog kibble to help destroy potential pathogens that may be present. Place the items on a shallow container to a depth of one inch. Microwave on high for five minutes, or bake in a 350°F oven for ten minutes.

Any moist food should be removed from the cage after two hours, possibly sooner in very hot weather. Whole fruit and vegetables may be left in the cage for longer periods of time, as they do not spoil as readily as those that have been cut up. However, all such items should be removed at the end of the day.

In regard to your bird's personal hygiene, allowing him to bathe is extremely important. Regular bathing confers a sheen and neatness to the feathers that are not otherwise obtained. The psychological benefits are also great. In the author's home, bath time is one of the highlights of the day for the birds. Their enjoyment is so manifest that even if other health benefits did not accrue, bathing would still be an important part of the bird-care routine.

A plant mister, filled with warm water, seems to be the best way to accomplish a bird's bath. However, some birds enjoy a shallow pan of water in which to bathe. Others enjoy the use of the kitchen sink. One young gentleman of the author's acquaintance takes his Mealy Amazon into the shower with him every morning.

When bathing your parrot, it is important to do it early enough in the day to allow thorough drying before evening. Be sure the bird is not exposed to drafts while bathing and drying off.

When sources of bacterial contamination are being considered, one needs to take into account the possibility of passing infection from the owner to the bird. Although there has been little research in this area, current thinking tends to confirm that this may be more than a remote possibility. Christine Davis cites a case where a Green-Winged Macaw was infected with *Streptococcus* by its owner, resulting in the bird's death. It would seem a wise precaution, then, to avoid excessive handling of your bird if you are ill. Take special care not to sneeze in your bird's face, and wash your hands before handling it. *Never* allow your bird to eat from your mouth or ingest food you have already had in your mouth, even if you are healthy. Even a kiss on the beak is unwise if you are "under the weather." In short, take the same precautions to prevent the spread of illness to your bird that you would take to prevent the same to family members.

Another way in which your bird can become ill is by fomite transmission

Parrot species typically love water and most will relish being sprayed with water from a plant mister. *M. Vogel*

An adult male Blue-fronted Amazon (*Amazona aestiva aestiva*) housed in the type of parrot cage in wide general use. *M. Vogel*

27

of pathogens. A fomite is an object on which bacteria and viruses can "hitch a ride" from the source of infection to another potential victim. You can carry germs to your bird on your hair, on your clothing, on your shoes, on dirty feeding utensils—the list is almost endless. Therefore, if you have been to a pet shop, visited a friend who has a bird—in fact, been anywhere there is even a possibility of having contacted an ill bird—use strict precautions before handling your own bird. At the very least, wash your hands and change your shoes and clothing. If you have been in contact with obviously sick birds, shower, shampoo, and use a nail brush before contacting your birds.

Of course, birds can transmit illnesses among themselves. Any bird showing signs of illness should be segregated from the rest of the birds, in another part of the house. Do not allow its food and water bowls to come in contact with those of other birds in the home. When caring for your birds, do whatever needs to be done for the sick bird *last*. Then use appropriate personal hygiene to eliminate the possibility of carrying germs back to your healthy birds. You may even want to set aside a separate set of clothing, or a coverall, to wear only when caring for the sick bird.

This brings up the critical area of introducing a new bird into an already established collection. One of the most important measures you will ever take to protect your bird's health will be to quarantine every new bird for a minimum of thirty days before placing it with your "old" bird. Ideally, the new bird should have a complete physical examination, including appropriate laboratory work, before ever entering your home. This procedure should be repeated at the end of the thirty-day period; if the new bird gets an "all clear" from your veterinarian, then it can be placed with your other birds. During the time the new bird is in isolation, the hygiene precautions discussed above should be followed rigorously.

Safety

Applying common sense will go a long way in protecting your bird from the hazards present in every home. The author has found that a good attitude to take is the same as one would adopt if there were a young toddler in the home. Every parent has discovered the need for "eyes in the back of the head" when there is a young child present. This same dedication to accident prevention is needed when birds are present.

Placement of the cage within the home is important. It should not be situated directly in front of a window, where the bird may be subjected to drafts. In addition, when the sun's rays shine through glass, even in the winter, they are intensified, and this could lead to serious overheating of the bird. Placement of the cage *near* a window presents no danger, however, and your bird will thoroughly enjoy its view.

In summer, be sure that the window screens fit tightly. Many birds have flown through open windows, never to return. If your bird is allowed freedom from its cage, be sure it does not chew on screens or framework. Large birds can chew their way through a screen; small birds are surprisingly capable of escaping in this way, too. Caution and supervision are always the watchwords when your avian friend is unconfined.

While your bird is confined to its cage, it will greatly appreciate a supply of toys to occupy its mind and beak. Be sure to check the safety of any toy given to your bird. Toys should have no parts that can be removed and swallowed. They should never be suspended from the cage by string. Use chain or rawhide for this purpose. The chain itself should be of a gauge that will not allow the bird to catch a toe or nail.

Never use a toy that contains lead. A popular toy for budgies is a plastic penguin with a lead-weighted base. Although safe enough for a very small bird, toys of this type are easily dismantled by any bird larger than a cockatiel, thereby exposing the bird to a harmful source of lead.

There are many kinds of wooden chew toys on the market that will provide hours of fun and beak exercise. Be sure, though, that they are unfinished. Varnish and paint are harmful when ingested. Some of these have small bells attached. These should be removed, or the toy avoided altogether. It is all too easy for a bird to catch a nail or beak in the slits of such bells.

There are many inexpensive, safe, and easy to obtain items the owner can provide for use as toys. A brief list follows, but a little imagination plus an eye to your bird's safety will doubtless allow the owner to expand the list.

Uncooked pasta (small, colored pasta; manicotti shells; pieces of lasagna)
Stick cinnamon
Portion of a hand of fresh ginger
Whole (unshelled) hard-boiled eggs
Pine cones
Beef ''jerky'' sticks (manufactured for dogs)
Dog biscuits
Dried hot peppers
Sugar cane
Nuts (for example, walnuts, Brazil nuts, pecans, almonds; they should be precracked for all but large cockatoos and macaws)

A few words of caution are in order concerning the above suggestions. All fruits and vegetables should be well washed. Any soft food offered as toys, such as hard-boiled eggs, should be removed after two hours to avoid spoilage. Any fruit, such as plums, apricots, peaches, and apples, should have the pit or seeds removed first, since they contain hydrocyanic acid (prussic acid).

If fresh sugar cane is offered, it must be *thoroughly scrubbed* first. All moldy ends must be removed, as well as any dark or reddish-colored portions. Sugar cane has a high sugar content and spoils easily. After preparation, refrigerate or freeze the extra pieces. Remove unused portions from the cage at the end of the day.

It is of great benefit to any bird to be allowed out of its cage for supervised play. The psychological benefits are immeasurable, and the bird benefits physically as well. However, the average home presents many opportunities for accidents. You must learn to be aware of these and guard against them.

If you bird is free-flighted and allowed out for exercise, be sure all doors and windows are closed. It is a good idea to lock all outside doors to prevent someone from coming in unexpectedly and allowing the bird to escape. Draw all window shades or draperies to keep the bird from flying into windows in the mistaken assumption that it is flying through an open area. Mirrors should be covered for this same reason.

A bird with clipped wings is much less likely to fly out an open window, or into an uncovered cooking pot, a sink full of water, or a toilet bowl. Never allow your bird into the kitchen while food preparation is in progress.

If you insist upon leaving your bird full-flighted, be sure all doors are closed and toilet lids secure, and prevent access to the kitchen area.

Toxins in the Home: Homes are rife with potential toxins that could sicken or kill your bird. Among the more dangerous hazards are cleaning supplies, plants, leaded glass ornaments, and nonstick cookware.

Many cleaning supplies emit fumes that are harmful to your bird. When using them, be sure your bird is confined to another area of the house. Provide adequate ventilation, and follow label directions carefully. A special mention is necessary concerning flea products. *Never* use them in your home without first consulting your avian veterinarian. Many are extremely harmful to birds.

Margaret Petrak (1982) cites a fatality due to the use of spray starch. According to Petrak, the owner was using a spray starch containing 2 percent fluoropolymer. Two parrots were in the room where she was ironing. Within a little over three hours, both birds were dead. This is a sad example of how the use of a seemingly innocent product can have unexpected and devastating consequences.

Plants in the home present another hazard. Many birds enjoy "pruning" their owners' potted plants, and in so doing can become gravely ill. Greg Harrison (1986), Gary Gallerstein (1984), and R. Dean Axelson (1984) all have cited extensive lists of plants known to be toxic to birds. Such a list is also included in Chapter 4 of this book. The reader would do well to consult these sources. If there is any question about the safety of a plant not included in these sources, contact the botany department of the local college or university for advice. Agricultural extension services are frequently available in many localities, and they can prove to be a good source of information about plant toxicities.

Leaded glass ornaments, with their jewellike colors and fanciful designs, are very popular decorations. Unfortunately, they are as attractive to parrots as they are to us. The lead solder used in such ornaments can be lethal to your bird, so place all such items far out of its reach.

Much of the paint used in older homes contains lead, as does the plaster. Care must be taken to prevent ingestion of such lead sources by your bird.

Only within the past two or three years have the hazards of nonstick cookware entered the aviculturist's awareness (Sakas, 1986). (These utensils

A free-flying parrot and a sliding glass door do not mix. Parrots colliding with windows are a common cause of injury in the home. *Peter Sakas, D.V.M.*

Coated drip pans make kitchen clean-up easier, but the fumes released from such pans under normal use will kill birds in the home. *Peter Sakas, D.V.M.*

bear various tradenames, such as Teflon, Supra, or Silverstone.) The active ingredient in such cookware is polytetrafluorethylene. When overheated, potentially lethal fumes are released. Such cookware, for all its convenience, cannot be recommended for homes in which birds are residing. This same chemical is often a component of self-cleaning ovens and range drip pans. Check with the manufacturer before purchasing these items.

HUMAN DANGERS: Small children can also be another source of potential danger to your bird. Children are often untutored (or unheeding of instruction) concerning the treatment a bird should receive. Some are unable to resist poking, teasing, or otherwise taunting a bird. Supervision, and immediate intervention when required, are necessary when children are present.

Unfortunately, many adults will engage in the same juvenile behavior—something the author finds doubly offensive in a person who should know better. Be aware that the occasional adult guest may seek to ply your bird with alcoholic libations, as well as unwanted attention. Swift intervention is definitely called for in such a situation.

OTHER DANGERS: Other sources of potential danger are electric cords, fireplaces, and legbands. If your bird has a legband, have your veterinarian remove it. *Never* attempt to remove it yourself. Removal requires special tools and your veterinarian's skill to avoid breaking the bird's leg. All too often a legband can become caught on the cage or other object, resulting in serious, sometimes mutilative injury to the bird. An Eclectus Parrot known to the author caught its legband on its cage. When the owner returned, he found the bird in a welter of blood and barely alive—the bird had chewed its foot off in an attempt to regain its freedom.

Obviously, the list of potential hazards to your bird could go on ad infinitum. Suffice it to say that a truly caring attitude on the owner's part, coupled with common sense, will go far in keeping a companion bird healthy.

Daily Observation

Daily observation of your bird is the next area of consideration. It should become a habit to observe your bird daily for overall appearance and changes in activity level and appetite. Droppings should be carefully inspected each day when the cage papers are changed. Davis recommends daily weights be taken, until you have at least six months' to a year's worth of data. After this point, weighing once every two or three days should be adequate. A gram scale should be used. If the bird shows a weight loss, however slight, over a three-day period, it needs to be seen by the veterinarian. Many veterinarians feel that consistent weight loss may be one of the only measurable signs of early illness.

Daily palpation of the bird's breast muscles will also give the owner a good idea about the bird's health. If muscle mass appears to remain the same over time, this is one indication of good health. Obesity will sometimes be noted and is a real health hazard. Both weight loss and obesity need to be checked by your avian veterinarian.

Psychological Health

A bird may be the recipient of the best physical husbandry in the world, but if its owner has not cared for the bird's mental health, that bird will be a deprived, sad creature. Birds are flock animals, just as dogs are pack animals. This biological fact has important implications for the bird owner. To ignore it imperils the bird.

Your bird needs social interaction with you and other family members. It needs supervised time out of its cage to play, to be social, perhaps to join its family at supper, watch television, or go for a ride in the car. Parrots are extremely intelligent creatures and require the stimulation of change and social interaction. When your bird must be confined to its cage, be sure it is supplied with appropriate toys and a supply of chewing material. If you are going to be out of the house, leave the radio or television on for its entertainment. The author's birds are very fond of "Sesame Street," the PBS program for children. Watching this colorful, musical show is a great treat for them.

The foregoing applies mainly to family pets. The requirements of the aviary-kept or breeding bird are slightly different. In these situations, the other birds in the aviary will supply the requisite companionship. If the bird is a breeding bird, it will have a happy, fulfilling life with its mate, raising their little ones.

In an aviary setting, the owner will bear great responsibility in the areas of housing, nutrition, health care, and the like. But the responsibility to provide personal companionship to the birds will be less than with a house pet. However, having a keeper with whom the birds feel comfortable and trust will greatly enhance their mental health, and ultimately their reproductive success to some degree.

Much has been written on how to meet the psychological needs of parrots in captivity. It is not the author's intent to reiterate this material here. Rather, the author wishes to leave the reader with this thought: Owning a bird is like having a baby or toddler in one's home. If owners devote the same time, concern, and love to the well-being of their bird that they would for a child, they will be successful in providing the safe, loving, stimulating environment their bird needs to attain its full potential as an unrivaled companion who will very likely be with its owner for a lifetime.

IMPORTATION AND QUARANTINE

Some readers may possess a parrot that is recently out of quarantine. Others may contemplate purchasing such a bird in the near future. These individuals, indeed all parrot owners, need to be aware of certain facts about the importation and quarantine process. They are not all palatable, but such facts have great bearing on your bird's health.

Birds captured in the wild and imported to this country undergo unbelievable stress, both physical and psychological. Usually birds are collected and kept in holding areas prior to being taken to the point from which they are shipped. These holding areas are often pits dug in the ground. Often, too, the birds endure very primitive methods of transportation to the shipping point, such as horseback, mule, or camel.

The care of the birds from time of capture to entry into the quarantine station is usually very poor. Water and food are often contaminated and/or inappropriate. Overcrowding is the rule and sanitation is often nonexistent.

Very often young babies, sometimes four weeks of age or less, are removed from their nest and forced to endure the rigors of import and quarantine. This is a time in their lives when their immune systems are not yet fully functional, and warmth and regular feeding are paramount to survival. Needless to say, many birds do not survive. Walter Rosskopf and Richard Woerpel (1987b) state that 803,873 birds were imported into the United States in 1983. Of that number, 40,054 were dead on arrival and 92,768 died during quarantine—making it obvious that once a bird reaches the quarantine facility, its troubles are not over. Conditions of overcrowding and minimal sanitation may be present. The author learned from an excellent source a sad story involving birds that died in a quarantine facility and were left for their cage mates to scavenge.

The food there is strange and frequently unacceptable to the birds. Chlortetracycline-treated pellets are the primary food source, given to treat psittacosis. The success of this food is limited, however, because many birds refuse to accept it. As a result, many birds released from quarantine have subclinical or clinical psittacosis. Another problem is that birds are held in quarantine for only thirty days, while the recommended treatment period for psittacosis is forty-five days. (See Chapter 5 for a complete discussion of psittacosis and its treatment.)

Because quarantine systems exist not for the health of the imported birds but to protect the poultry industry in the United States from Newcastle disease and avian influenza, medical care for birds with existing illness is often a low priority. It can be readily seen that in any given facility, the major thrust is to release birds that are free of the abovementioned conditions. Whether or not the bird is sick from any other cause is not a concern of the U.S. Department of Agriculture. Thus, because of the economics involved, there is little incentive for a station operator to treat such illnesses. To be sure, there are quarantine station owners who are caring and committed to the health of their avian charges, but just as surely there are those who are not.

A bird newly released from quarantine probably harbors some kind of illness, many times on the inapparent, subclinical level. Such birds may be purchased and brought into their new homes, only to succumb weeks or months later. This is heartbreaking for the owner and tragic for the bird.

The quarantine system does not guarantee a healthy bird. If you purchase a bird from this source, be sure to have the bird checked immediately by an avian veterinarian. And be prepared for extra medical expense, as it is extremely likely that the bird will have one or more health problems requiring attention.

Timneh African Gray (*Psittacus erithacus timneh*)

3

The Sick Bird

BEHAVIORAL AND PHYSIOLOGICAL ASPECTS INFLUENCING AVIAN ILLNESS

Detecting illness in your avian friend is much more difficult than in one's dog or cat. Nevertheless, it can be done.

Every bird owner should learn how to determine when their avian charge is ill, as early in the process as possible. At this point expert avian veterinary care has the best chance of dealing effectively with the disease process. To do this owners must be familiar with the signs of avian illness, both those that are fairly obvious and those that are more subtle. This also requires that they have intimate knowledge, informed by love and concern, of their individual bird's habits and behavior. Otherwise they may fail to observe those subtle changes in behavior that are often the harbingers of worse to come. An owner should never say, "Oh, that's nothing much. I must be imagining things." Likewise, an owner should never be afraid of "running to the doctor for no good reason." It is much better to be safe than sorry. There would be fewer dead birds if more bird owners would take more seriously the small deviations in the personal routine of their birds, and would take less seriously what their veterinarians will think of them for presenting a bird for "such a small reason."

It is helpful if the bird owner understands why illness is sometimes difficult to detect in birds. Birds are unique in their manifestation of illness. The first reason was discussed in Chapter 2: The bird presents to its flock an appearance of health for as long as it can to avoid being driven away because of the attraction of predators to a sick animal.

The second reason is the elimination of undesirable genes from the flock gene pool (Rosskopf and Woerpel, 1987c). Birds, for the most part, reside in flocks. A hierarchical "pecking order" is established, with the strongest individuals at the top of the flock's social organization. Ostensibly, these birds have the choice of the best mates, best food, and best nesting sites. In this way, their reproductive success is enhanced and their genes continue to exist in their offspring. Conversely, weaker members of the flock are harassed, often affecting their reproductive success. Fewer of their genes will be passed to successive generations. A bird weakened by illness, and perceived to be so by flock members, will be killed or driven out, thus preventing the passage of possibly defective genes.

In light of the above, it becomes obvious that it is to the bird's advantage to conceal illness. This is not a consciously determined behavior. Rather, it is instinctive, and determined by long evolutionary history. As a result, birds are able to compensate for an astonishingly long time for damage done to a single or several body systems as a result of illness. When ill, birds *are physiologically able to compensate for a far longer time than mammals*. What this means is that the bird's organ (or organs) may be damaged beyond repair when the first "noticeable" symptoms appear. There are less obvious, earlier signs that the bird owner may note if informed and observant. If a bird's illness is treated at an early stage, its chances for recovery are usually much greater.

In addition to the above, there are other reasons that make it difficult to detect illness in a bird. Birds are able to harbor dangerous disease organisms, sometimes for years, without exhibiting symptoms or laboratory evidence of infection. Such birds may also shed these organisms—in their feces, for example—thus becoming a source of infection for other birds.

This carrier state may exist for several reasons. The bird may have been exposed, over a period of months or years, to a constant, low-level dose of the disease-causing germs. In this situation, the bird's immune system will have been stimulated to produce antibodies that probably destroyed most of the foreign invaders. Oftentimes, some of these germs escape destruction, living in the bird's body in numbers too few to cause full-blown illness. This is a carrier state. If the bird becomes stressed, its immune system becomes much less efficient and antibody production will drop. The germs are then able to multiply unhindered. Finally the bird "breaks" with an illness, sometimes after having appeared perfectly healthy for years.

Stress may be caused by chronic malnutrition, molting, sudden changes in diet, breeding activity, rearing young, attainment of puberty, debilitating illness of another kind, trauma (such as fracture or laceration), change of environment, or the loss of a mate or beloved owner. The causes of stress are myriad, but the reader can begin to see why the avoidance of stress is so important in maintaining a bird's health.

According to Don Harris (1984), at least one of the following criteria must be present in order to detect disease in a bird. The agent must: (1) "make the bird physically and visibly ill; (2) cause some alteration in the bird's blood or

A flock of White-tailed Black Cockatoos (*Calyptorhynchus funereus baudini*), in their native Australian habitat. The environment of a wild bird is a major contributing factor to its continued health.
Bill Wegner, Malibu Exotics

An adult female Blue-crowned Amazon (*Amazona farinosa guatemalae*). In the home, a bird is safe from many of the threats of the wild, but other hazards exist against which it must be guarded.
M. Vogel

tissue that can be detected by currently available laboratory methods; (3) be shed from the bird in large enough numbers so the agent itself can be visualized and identified." However, as Harris states, "Unfortunately, diseases can, at times, infect birds without meeting any of these stipulations."

In addition, laboratory methods themselves may not be available or accurate enough, in some cases, to allow disease detection and diagnosis. Tests may be available that are sometimes, but not always, helpful. There are other tests that are useful in broadly screening a bird for a category of illness, but cannot specifically tell the practitioner the exact identification of the causative agent. A Gram stain is a good example of this. A Gram stain of fecal material can indicate the presence of Gram-negative bacteria in a bird's gastrointestinal tract, but it cannot identify which type of the many Gram-negative bacteria (for example, *E. coli, Salmonella, Klebsiella, Pseudomonas*) is the culprit. In order to do this, the veterinarian must make a culture of the bird's fecal material to identify the specific bacterium, and determine whether it is a harmful type.

Practicality and economics also play their part in the difficulty of identifying causative disease organisms in birds. It is not often practical to test a bird for all the possible causes of disease, nor could most owners afford it. Therefore, the veterinarian and owner must collaborate to determine which tests will most likely yield the answers sought.

SIGNS AND SYMPTOMS OF THE SICK BIRD

For the following lists of symptoms, the author is indebted to "Avian Axioms," a tape prepared by Richard W. Woerpel, D.V.M. This tape (see the Bibliography) cannot be too highly recommended. It contains a wealth of information for aviculturists.

Dr. Woerpel has divided his list of signs and symptoms into two categories: obvious signs and subtle signs.

Obvious Signs of Illness

Inactivity
Eyes closed most of the time
Feathers fluffed all the time
"Droopy" wings
Low, almost horizontal, posture on perch
Falling off perch
Talking and other vocalization stops
Eating stops
Noticeable and noisy breathing
Frequent sneezing
Discharge from nose
Tail bobbing with each breath ("tail-pumping")

Perching with neck extended and beak grasping wire of cage (the bird does this to straighten its breathing passages to make breathing less effortful)

Vomiting or regurgitating

Vent soiled or pasted

Feathers are being lost and not replaced

Bleeding

Subtle Signs of Illness

Weight loss

Swellings on bird's torso

Changes in water consumption

Changes in routine and habits

Change in droppings

Change in overall activity level

Decrease in preening activity

In addition to the above signs and symptoms, the author would add the following:

Frequent flicking of the head

Regression to infantile behavior in young hand-fed birds that had previously moved smoothly and uneventfully to fledging and weaning, and had begun to take on adult behavior characteristics

Other problems the owner may observe that certainly warrant immediate examination by the veterinarian are:

A swelling anywhere on the bird's body (in addition to swelling on the torso mentioned above)

Self-mutilation of feathers, wing-web, feet, or legs

The bird remaining on the bottom of the cage

Any one of the above signs should alert the owner that the bird is in need of medical attention. Naturally, things such as swelling, mutilation, hemorrhage, or occupying the cage bottom require *immediate* attention. But do not procrastinate over other signs. Any of them need to be checked—not within a week's time, but within the next twenty-four to forty-eight hours.

OBSERVANCES OF DROPPINGS

In determining the normality (or lack thereof) of droppings, it is important to grasp the following concept: normal droppings *vary* in color, consistency, and diet when the bird is healthy; when the bird is ill, the droppings are *consistently* abnormal.

Although previously discussed in Chapter 2, it is worthwhile to reiterate here the appearance of the normal dropping. The dropping has three components:

1. *Feces*: solid, tubular in shape, light to dark green in color
2. *Urates*: pasty, light cream to white in color, irregularly wrapped about the feces
3. *Urine*: clear liquid portion of the dropping, when normal has no odor

Diarrhea and Polyuria

The owner will need to be able to distinguish between diarrhea and polyuria (excessive urine in the dropping). True diarrhea is not common in the parrot dropping. It can occur from time to time, but it is far more common to see polyuria. True diarrhea produces soft, unformed feces. The polyuric dropping is extremely watery. The increased water content is urine—the fecal material remains normal in shape, color, and consistency.

There are several causes of polyuria: virus infections, stress, kidney disease, tumors, poisoning, food allergies, and diabetes mellitus. It is normal for a bird whose diet contains a large number of high water-content foods, such as fruits and vegetables. Cockatoos seem to have polyuria frequently.

Walter Rosskopf states in his "Analysis of Pet Bird Droppings" that the polyuria of cockatoos is psychogenic (of mental origin) in cause, rather than organic (caused by disease). He cautions, however, that this diagnosis can be made only after all the possible disease causes have been eliminated.

As discussed in Chapter 2, excitement or a sharp, temporary stress can cause polyuria. Infections that cause an increase in body temperature may cause a bird to drink more water, therefore increasing the urine content of the dropping. Lead poisoning causes polyuria in cockatiels and most other species except Amazons. Amazon parrots exhibit hemoglobinuria (blood in the urine) with this condition. Certain foods with high salt content cause the bird to drink and urinate more (cheese or salty snack foods, for example). Polyuria also occurs in birds that refuse all food (anorexia) for whatever reason. According to Sayle (1986), large amounts of water are lost in this condition due to the breakdown of body tissues for energy.

Although diarrhea is less common than the excessively watery stool, there are many causes for it. The reader should note that diarrhea (or, for that matter, polyuria) is *not* a disease, it is a *symptom* of disease.

Spoiled food is a common cause of diarrhea. If a parrot has swallowed a foreign object, diarrhea can occur. Stress is often a cause. Other possible causes of diarrhea are sudden dietary changes, illness affecting all the bird's body systems, viral diseases such as *Reovirus* and Newcastle disease, chemical poisoning, inflammation of the liver and/or pancreas, abdominal hernia, and chronic malnutrition.

It is possible for birds to overeat grit, especially if they are ill. The gizzard may become impacted, resulting in diarrhea. Sometimes fecal material will be retained in the intestines, becoming rock hard. This irritates the delicate intestinal lining, causing diarrhea.

A very soft "cow pie" stool is frequently seen in cockatiels with a *Giardia*

Normal parrot droppings.
Peter Sakas, D.V.M.

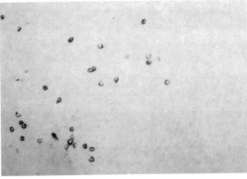

Normal budgie droppings.
Peter Sakas, D.V.M.

Normal droppings from a bird fed a primarily pelleted diet. With this diet, the fecal portion of the droppings will be brown, compared with the green coloration of the feces of a bird fed a seed diet.

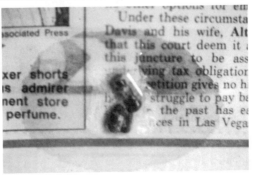

In polyuria the droppings will show a large ring of liquid urine surrounding urates and normally formed feces.
Peter Sakas, D.V.M.

infection. Self-mutilation, feather picking, and screaming are often associated with giardia in this species. An owner with a cockatiel with the above signs should have the bird checked immediately.

Owners of a breeding hen in whom egg laying is imminent, or has just been completed, will notice that her droppings are larger and the fecal component soft and somewhat shapeless ("cow pie" stool). This is normal for a hen in this situation and not a cause for concern. The owner may further note that the hen's droppings at this time have a slight odor. This, too, is normal.

It is also normal for the first dropping of the morning to be a large "cow pie" stool. Many birds do not empty the cloaca when they sleep. So, first thing in the morning, they produce a very large dropping in which the fecal content is somewhat soft and unformed. The author's African Gray Parrot does this, producing some truly spectacular results. Certain of her macaws have also followed this pattern. The stools will return to normal volume and consistency for the remainder of the day.

According to Sayle (1986), strong odor of the stool, especially in Amazons, is often associated with chronic cloacal papillomalike problems.

Color and Texture Variations

Let us now examine the color variations in feces that indicate abnormality. Blood in the stool can be caused by a number of problems. Some of the more common are blood-clotting problems, intestinal infections, poisoning, liver disease, malnutrition, or excessive stress. Sometimes, rather than bright red blood in the stool, the owner may see a tarlike stool. This is from bleeding in the upper gut. The blood is digested as it passes down the intestinal tract, thus yielding its tarlike appearance. Sayle states that blood in the stool may also be associated with impending egg laying. The owner must also bear in mind that blood on the surface of the stool may be from the oviduct, testicles, kidneys, or cloaca.

A bird with bright, "pea green" urates probably has severe liver disease. This bright chartreuse stool is often seen in birds having sustained liver damage as a result of psittacosis.

A white or clay-colored "popcornlike" stool may indicate digestive problems of some type. Rosskopf feels this may indicate pancreatitis. Sayle states that the cause of such a stool is yet unknown, but that it may be attributable to kidney disease, candidiasis, or giardiasis, as well as inflammation of the pancreas. Other authorities feel such a stool may be the result of exocrine pancreatic insufficiency.

A stool that is lumpy in appearance is usually related to incomplete digestion resulting from a lack of digestive enzymes. Incomplete digestion may also be due to parasitic infection of the gut, infection of the ventriculus or proventriculus, pancreatic problems, or other gut infections.

The passing of whole seeds or other undigested food may be a result of giardiasis, especially in cockatiels. It may also be due to a hypermotile intestine (similar to spastic colon in humans). In macaws, it certainly indicates the possibility of macaw wasting syndrome. Such a bird should be taken to the veterinarian immediately.

Mucus in the stool may indicate the presence of infection in the intestinal tract or other digestive difficulties, such as gut irritation or abdominal masses.

The owner may see what appears to be blood in the stool, but that is in reality pigment from dietary items the bird has eaten. Foods such as carrots, pomegranates, and cherries will cause the feces to be red temporarily. Blueberries and blackberries will, in like manner, produce a purple-bluish color in the feces. Usually, the stools following will be the conventional green color, unless the bird is munching on these items throughout the day. The passage of food through the digestive tract is remarkably rapid. Within thirty minutes of eating an item, the bird may be eliminating the waste products of that food in the stool.

Variations in the Urine and Urates

We will now turn our attention to abnormal variations in the urine portion of the dropping. Blood in the urine (hematuria) may be seen in lead poisoning, especially in Amazon Parrots. Kidney disease is also a cause of bloody urine.

Green pigmented urine may be an indication of severe liver disease. Psittacosis is one disease that produces liver damage, although there are many others that may also do so. Yellow-colored urine also indicates liver problems.

One may also note color abnormalities in the urates. Greenish or yellowish urates may be due to liver disease. Sayle (1986) states that large doses of vitamin A (carotene) may cause changes in the color of the urates.

LABORATORY WORK

The parrot owner will find it helpful to have some knowledge of various laboratory tests and procedures. In this section, some of the more commonly used tests will be described, as well as a few of the more unusual ones. The emphasis will be upon what these tests are and why they are performed. For convenience, entries will be presented alphabetically.

ACTH STIMULATION TEST: This test is used to determine the functional status of the bird's adrenal glands. There are two adrenal glands, each located on top of a kidney. The adrenal gland is divided into two parts: the outer layer (cortex) and the inner portion (medulla). Both parts manufacture substances needed for various body functions. The adrenal cortex manufactures, among other things, glucocorticoids, which are involved with protein and carbohydrate metabolism.

ACTH is the abbreviation for adrenocorticotropic hormone—a pituitary hormone that stimulates the adrenal cortex to produce its various hormones. The ACTH stimulation test measures the concentration of corticosterone, one of the types of glucocorticoids, before and after the administration of a test dose of ACTH. If the adrenal cortex is normal, one would expect the production of corticosterone to fall within the normal range following administration of ACTH. If the adrenal cortex is compromised in some way by disease, the production of corticosterone after a dose of ACTH will be either greater or less than normal, depending upon the disease present. For example, in adrenal insufficiency, no elevation of corticosterone is seen after ACTH stimulation. In Addison's disease, very low levels are found after ACTH administration. In Cushing's syndrome, elevated corticosterone levels are frequently seen before and after an ACTH dose.

If the ACTH stimulation test is recommended for your pet, it will be performed in the following way. First, a small sample of blood will be obtained to get a baseline reading of the level of corticosterone in the blood. After this, the dose of ACTH is administered. One to two hours later, another blood sample will be taken, and its corticosterone level determined and compared to that of the first sample. It can then be seen how the adrenal cortex responded to the stimulating effect of ACTH.

ALKALINE PHOSPHOTASE (AP): Alkaline phosphotase is an enzyme, made primarily in the bone, liver, and placenta. The alkaline phosphotase test is used mainly as one indication of liver and bone disease. According to Terry Campbell (1987), it is not a very good test for determining liver disease in birds. However, Campbell feels that it *is* a fairly good indicator of bone problems. He states that AP levels are increased with bone fractures, osteomyelitis (bone infection), hyperparathyroidism (overactive function of the parathyroid glands, which are involved in metabolism of calcium and phosphorous), and in normal bone growth (occurring in the young, growing bird). Campbell also states that AP levels are higher, normally, in egg-laying hens.

The AP level is determined by obtaining a blood sample and measuring the alkaline phosphotase component of the blood serum.

ASPARTATE AMINOTRANSFERASE (AST), OR SERUM GLUTAMIC-OXALOACETIC TRANSAMINASE (SGOT): This enzyme is present in many body tissues (heart, liver, skeletal muscle, kidney, brain, pancreas, spleen, and lungs). Following the injury or death of cells, it is released into the blood. Any disease process that affects the above tissues will cause a rise in the AST/SGOT levels in the blood.

Because AST/SGOT occurs in several body tissues, it is not liver specific. Nevertheless, it is used as an indicator of liver disease, especially in the absence of illness that would cause damage to other body tissues. Its elevation can indicate disease in tissues other than the liver. Campbell (1987) states that an elevation of AST/SGOT occurs most commonly in caged birds as a result of liver disease; the most common cause of elevation in raptors is skeletal muscle injury.

AST/SGOT levels are determined by drawing a blood sample and measuring the amount of AST/SGOT present. This test is the preferred indicator of liver function.

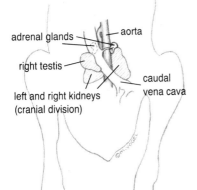

adrenal glands — aorta

right testis —

left and right kidneys
(cranial division)

caudal
vena cava

**Location of adrenal glands in a
male parrot.**

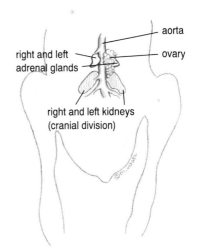

aorta

right and left
adrenal glands

ovary

right and left kidneys
(cranial division)

**Location of adrenal glands in a
female parrot**

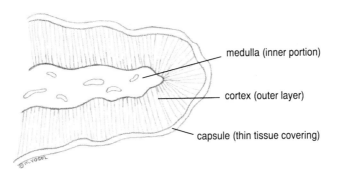

medulla (inner portion)

cortex (outer layer)

capsule (thin tissue covering)

Microscopic cross section of adrenal gland

BARIUM SERIES (CONTRAST STUDY): This is a variation of the plain radiograph, or X ray. It is used to determine the position, filling, and peristaltic movement of the digestive tract. It is helpful in formulating a diagnosis when the veterinarian suspects that a foreign object in the gut, a tumor, or some other disease process is affecting the digestive tract.

When performing a barium X-ray series, the bird is given an oral dose of barium sulfate. This material shows up extremely well on X ray, giving greater contrast to areas of the gastrointestinal (GI) system that would be difficult to see on a plain X ray. The barium passes through the GI in the same manner as ordinary food and water. As it does, it outlines the entire GI tract, including any abnormalities that may be present within the gut. It may also indicate displacement of the gut by masses outside the GI tract proper.

By X-raying the bird before the barium has been given and at regular intervals as the barium passes on through the gut, the veterinarian is able to obtain a complete picture of the functional status of the entire digestive tract.

BILIVERDIN: This substance, in birds, is the end product of the breakdown of old red blood cells. It is removed from the system by the liver, where it is excreted into the bile.

A rise in the blood serum level of biliverdin may indicate excessive breakdown of red blood cells (hemolytic anemia), or disease in the liver, which prevents the normal removal of biliverdin from the bloodstream. Therefore, biliverdin levels are checked if there is a question of the above problems. It may be also associated with kidney failure. Occasionally, the urates in the dropping will be greenish in color, indicating the presence of biliverdin. Severe liver disease, hemolytic anemia, or starvation may be causes for this symptom (Campbell, 1987).

The biliverdin level is determined by examining the serum portion of a blood sample.

BIOASSAY: This is a technique whereby the effects of a disease-causing organism or a chemical substance are tested on one or several living animals or birds. In avian medicine, it is applied primarily in a flock situation or laboratory testing.

The "sentinel bird" test involves placing several healthy birds from a disease-free source next to birds suspected of disease. The sentinels are observed very closely for a period of at least three weeks. Should any of the sentinels die, they are necropsied (autopsied) to determine the cause of death. A good example of this technique is the use of cockatiels as sentinel birds by breeders who have groups of newly imported conures. Conures are often infected with Pacheco's disease. Although they themselves are fairly resistant to this viral liver ailment, it is quickly fatal to most other species of parrot. Oftentimes a sentinel bird is used by breeders with mixed collections of parrots who wish to assure themselves that any conures being introduced are Pacheco's free. The sudden death of such a sentinel bird, coupled with necropsy results, gives timely warning and avoids much grief and economic loss.

BONE MARROW TEST: In this test, the bird's bone marrow is examined to see if the bird has a blood disorder. The clinician examines material from the bone marrow to determine if the marrow is functioning normally and producing red and white blood cells. This test can diagnose leukemia, anemia, invasion of cancer into the bone marrow, or toxic states preventing normal blood cell production.

The bone-marrow sample is usually taken from the top (head) of the bird's shin bone. This area is cleaned well with a surgical cleansing agent. A needle is then inserted into the bone marrow and a small portion of it is aspirated (sucked into the syringe). An anesthetic is normally used for this procedure, as it can cause great discomfort. The material thus obtained is placed on slides, stained appropriately, and examined under the microscope.

CALCIUM LEVEL (SERUM CALCIUM): Calcium has many vital uses in the body. Besides being a vital component of the skeleton, calcium is necessary for proper muscle contraction, heart function, blood clotting, transmission of nerve impulses, and egg laying. Most calcium is stored in the skeleton.

Sometimes a bird will have too much calcium circulating in its blood as a result of an excess of vitamin D_3. Too little calcium is sometimes seen in African Grey Parrots (cause unknown), resulting in convulsions. Kidney disease can cause low calcium. Poor nutrition is a notorious cause of low calcium levels, often resulting in egg binding in laying hens. Low calcium levels may also result in bones that break with abnormal ease (pathological fractures).

In order to determine calcium levels, a blood sample is drawn and the serum portion checked for circulating calcium levels.

CAT SCAN: CAT is the abbreviation for computerized axial tomography. This is a sophisticated type of radiograph (X ray), originally developed to investigate brain problems (Squire, 1982). However, it can be used for any part of the body. One of the advantages of the CAT scan is that it can obtain greater resolution between soft tissues (brain, tumor, blood, other body fluids) than with conventional radiography, thereby aiding the clinician in making a diagnosis. In some cases, a dye (usually containing iodine and sodium) is injected intravenously to allow greater contrast and ease of visualization to the area being studied.

At present, CAT scans are not commonly used in avian medicine, but they will no doubt be increasingly utilized in the future.

CHOLESTEROL AND FATTY ACIDS: Cholesterol and fatty acids are present in muscles, red blood cells, and cell membranes. They are used in the manufacture of hormones, among other things. Since the liver is involved in the manufacture of chemical substances using cholesterol, the measurement of cholesterol and fatty acids is one indicator of liver function. Such measurements are also affected by age, heredity, and nutrition. Increases in cholesterol are associated with starvation and excessive levels of dietary fat (Campbell, 1987). High levels of cholesterol may also indicate a risk of arteriosclerosis (hardening of the arteries) and heart disease.

Cholesterol and fatty acid levels are determined by examination of a serum sample.

COMPLETE BLOOD COUNT (CBC): This is a commonly used test, and it will be the rare bird that visits its veterinarian without having this done on at least one occasion. Blood is examined routinely because it provides information about total body function, either directly or indirectly. This is because the blood is the one body fluid that comes in contact with every part of the body.

Both the blood cells themselves, and the fluid in which they are suspended (serum), are examined. The owner may hear two terms used for the liquid portion of blood: *serum* and *plasma*. Serum is the fluid portion of the blood after it has been allowed to clot and the red cells have been removed. Plasma is the fluid portion of the blood in which the blood cells are suspended. It still contains the clotting elements (that is, fibrinogen).

The CBC gives valuable information about the bird's condition, response to treatment, and prognosis (predicted outcome of disease). It gives information about the health of the red and white blood cells, thrombocytes (needed for blood clotting), possible toxic reactions, function of the bone marrow, and a wealth of other valuable information.

The CBC actually encompasses several separate tests.

Red Blood Cell Count: The function of the red blood cells is to carry oxygen to the body's cells. An increase in red blood cell counts can indicate a variety of problems, including acute poisoning, severe diarrhea, and dehydration. A decrease in red blood cell counts can indicate hemorrhage, anemia of various types, and disease of the bone marrow.

White Blood Cell Count: White blood cells have two main functions: to fight invasion of foreign organisms and to manufacture, transport, and distribute antibodies. Examination of the total white cell count gives information about the diagnosis and prognosis of disease, especially one caused by infection.

Differential White Cell Count: There are several types of white blood cells, each with its own special function. Examination of the relative number of each type, and comparison of these numbers with each other and the total white cell count, yields information about whether an infection is acute or chronic, whether the bird is a victim of parasites, whether blood cancers (leukemia, for example) are present, whether the bird is affected by allergies or stress—to name just a few conditions.

Hemoglobin: Hemoglobin is the oxygen-carrying component of the red blood cell. A measurement of the amount of hemoglobin gives information about the oxygen-carrying capacity of the blood. An increase in the hemoglobin can indicate dehydration and heart problems, and is also seen in severe burns. A decrease in hemoglobin may indicate, among

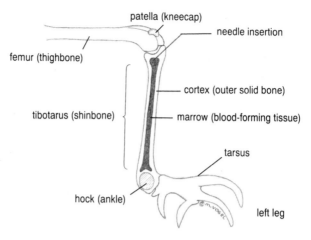

Bone-marrow aspiration

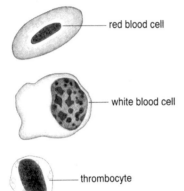

— red blood cell

— white blood cell

— thrombocyte

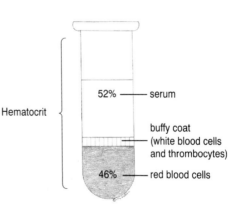

Hematocrit

Hematocrit

51

other things, anemia, liver problems (such as psittacosis), hemorrhage, and a reaction to various poisons.

Red Blood Cell Indices: These measurements are used to define the size of the red blood cells and their hemoglobin content. They are extremely useful in distinguishing among the various types of anemias.

Packed Cell Volume (Hematocrit): This is another measure of the oxygen-carrying capacity of the blood. It is expressed as a percentage of red cells in a given volume of whole blood.

Stained Red Cell Examination: In this examination, a thin film of blood is placed on a slide, appropriately stained, and examined microscopically. In this way, the presence of red blood cell parasites can be discovered. This test also allows the clinician to observe any abnormalities present in the cells (for example, any abnormally high number of immature red blood cells, a condition associated with some types of anemia).

Thrombocyte Count: Thrombocytes are responsible for normal blood clotting. They also play a role in fending off the invasion of foreign organisms and substances. A decrease in thrombocytes may indicate blood problems, severe infection, or some types of blood cancer.

Serum Protein: The serum portion of the blood contains many different protein molecules, some of which are involved in the making of antibodies; they also serve as a source of nutrition for body tissues. Examination of the various protein components in the blood serum gives information on the bird's nutritional status, liver function, state of hydration, and detect the presence of chronic disease (tuberculosis, for example).

Plasma Color: The color of a bird's plasma may reveal factors about its health. Normally, plasma is clear and rather yellowish in the normal bird. Egg-yolk peritonitis may color the plasma a rather creamy orange. The plasma of birds with liver disease, or on a high-fat diet, may exhibit a thick, creamy color and consistency. Other diseases may alter the normal color and consistency of a bird's plasma.

In order to perform a CBC, a blood sample will be needed. Blood can be obtained by clipping a toenail, or by directly removing it from the bird's vein with a sterile needle. Three veins are commonly used for this purpose: the medial metatarsal, found on the top of the foot; the ulnar, found at the "inner" elbow of the wing; or the jugular, in the bird's neck.

CREATININE PHOSPHOKINASE (CPK): This enzyme is found primarily in the heart and skeletal muscle. These organs contain a high amount of CPK. Because of this, CPK levels are good indicators of damage to muscle tissue. (Fischbach, 1984; Woerpel and Rosskopf, 1984b). They also are used to determine possible damage to the heart. Elevated levels of CPK are also seen in disorders of the nervous system, as well as in cases of lead toxicity, psittacosis, and bacterial septicemia (Campbell, 1987).

CULTURE AND SENSITIVITY: This test is commonly used for birds suspected of having a bacterial infection. A bacterial culture is obtained by propagating microorganisms or living tissue cells in special media that are conducive to their growth. To accomplish this, a sterile swab of the body fluid in question (pus, drainage from sinuses, fecal material, for example) is obtained and streaked on a laboratory plate. This plate is a shallow, flat receptacle filled with blood agar, Levine EMB agar, or MacConkey agar. These substances provide the nourishment that allows the suspected bacteria to grow. The culture plate is placed in an incubator overnight. By the next day, bacterial growth is usually apparent. If little growth has occurred, the organism may be restreaked onto a different growth medium or placed in a special broth and incubated for another twenty-four-hour period. Thus, the culture process allows the specific bacteria infecting a bird to be identified.

Some bacteria need special culture techniques in order to grow in numbers large enough to allow identification, but the basic principles remain the same. Special techniques are also required for the growth of fungi.

Once the offending organism has been identified, the next step is to determine its sensitivity to various antibiotics. Sensitivity is a given bacterium's ability to be killed by one or more of the antibiotics tested. To test for sensitivity, antibiotic-impregnated paper discs are placed on the surface of the culture plate on which the bacteria are growing. After a period of time, the plates are observed for bacterial "kill off." This is manifested by a clear zone around one or more of the antibiotic discs, indicating that the bacteria are unable to live and grow in the presence of that particular antibiotic.

Not all bacteria are killed by all antibiotics. Your veterinarian will choose the most effective antibiotic for a bird with an infection, based on the results of culture and sensitivity testing.

CYTOLOGY: Cytology is the study of cells—their anatomy, physiology, pathology, and chemistry. It can provide much valuable information about the disease process being examined. And, because only a very small sample of cells is needed, it does not produce further trauma to already compromised tissue.

Exfoliated cells (cells that have been sloughed from their underlying tissues) are examined for a number of reasons. The number of cells present and their type are noted. The detection and diagnosis of cancer can be made by cytologic study (for example, the Pap smear to detect cervical cancer in women), and techniques allowing the sexing of birds can be done using cytology (Prus and Schmutz, 1987). Cytology also gives information on the nature of infectious processes—whether they are acute or chronic.

Cells from virtually any part of the body may be examined: crop, sinuses, trachea, air sacs, abdomen, cerebrospinal fluid, oral cavity, lungs, skin, joint capsules, and abdominal organs such as the spleen or liver. The cells may be obtained in several ways. In an exposed area of the body, as in an open wound, a swab or scraping of the area will be taken and its contents spread on a slide. Sometimes a slide will be pressed directly to the area in question in order to obtain the needed cells. This is called an impression smear. If cell samples are

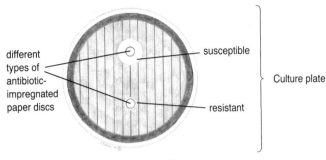

different types of antibiotic-impregnated paper discs

susceptible

resistant

Culture plate

Culture plate showing antibiotic sensitivity

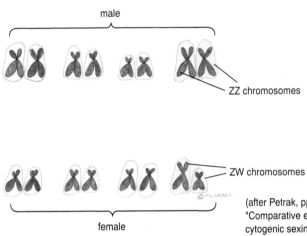

male

ZZ chromosomes

ZW chromosomes

female

(after Petrak, pp. 23-24: + Prus + Schmutz)
"Comparative efficiency and accuracy of surgical and
cytogenic sexing in psittacines," in *Avian Diseases* 31:2

Cytology: chromosome sexing

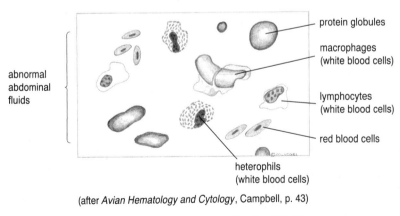

protein globules

macrophages
(white blood cells)

lymphocytes
(white blood cells)

red blood cells

abnormal
abdominal
fluids

heterophils
(white blood cells)

(after *Avian Hematology and Cytology*, Campbell, p. 43)

Cytology: abnormal abdominal fluid

needed from an inaccessible area of the body (fluid in the abdomen, for example), a sterile needle and syringe will be utilized to aspirate the necessary sample. If samples are needed from the crop or trachea, sterile saline will be instilled into these areas and then removed by sterile syringe and tubing. The saline solution will then contain numbers of cells that can be examined.

ELECTROCARDIOGRAM (EKG OR ECG):   This is a recording of electrical impulses of the heart onto special graph paper. Electrodes are usually placed on each wing and leg, after the bird has been restrained. In some cases, birds are anesthetized for this procedure. Michael Miller (1986) feels that, if at all possible, the bird should be awake.

The EKG may be recommended for a bird suspected of having heart problems.

ELECTROENCEPHALOGRAM (EEG):   Using this technique, the electrical activity of the brain is amplified and recorded on special graph paper, then analyzed. The procedure consists of placing electrodes on the surface of the scalp. EEG studies have been performed on domestic fowl in order to measure the effects of drugs or environmental stress on avian subjects (Benzo, 1986). The EEG is used to diagnose conditions such as epilepsy, brain tumors, brain abscesses, intracranial hemorrhages, and death of brain tissue.

At present, the EEG is not much used in avian medicine, though it will no doubt become more common as a diagnostic tool in the future.

ELECTROMYOGRAM (EMG):   This test detects abnormalities of the muscles due to faulty nerve stimulation and problems with nerve conduction. A needle electrode is inserted into the muscle to pick up muscle electrical activity. This electrical activity is then recorded onto special graph paper in the same manner as an EKG or EEG.

Ronald Lyman (1986) states that nerve problems requiring the use of the EMG are rare in birds and are usually either the result of trauma or of totally unknown origin (idiopathic).

ENDOSCOPY: This is a minor surgical procedure that allows the veterinarian to see inside the bird's body by means of a fiberoptic instrument. This instrument consists of a long, narrow, flexible tube with a lighted mirror-lens system attached. The light for the mirror-lens system is supplied by the optic fiber in the tube. This tube is inserted directly into the body cavity the veterinarian wishes to examine. If the abdomen is examined, the procedure is called a laparoscopy; if the joint is examined, it is called arthroscopy (examination of the trachea and bronchi, bronchoscopy; examination of colon, proctoscopy—and so forth).

Endoscopy is probably most familiar to parrot owners as the procedure known as surgical sexing. In addition to facilitating diagnosis, endoscopy is used to obtain tissue for biopsy (removal of small pieces of tissue for microscopic examination).

FECAL SMEAR: This demonstrates whether intestinal parasites are present in the bird's stool. A small amount of feces is spread on a slide and examined under the microscope. The eggs of intestinal parasites can be discovered in this way, as can be bacteria, fungi, and protozoa.

FLUORESCENT ANTIBODY TEST (FA): This test is used to diagnose various bacterial and viral infections. Clinton Lothrop and Greg Harrison (1986) state that it is a helpful adjunct to the diagnosis of Pacheco's disease, eliminating the need to isolate the virus in eggs or cell cultures in order to identify it.

The principle of the FA test involves bringing together a bacteria or virus (grown on culture plates, or placed as a smear on a microscope slide) and the antibody effective against the suspected organism. This antibody is tagged with a fluorescent dye. If the organism reacts to the antibody being used in the test, it will form a precipitate (clump) with the antibody when the two are mixed together. This precipitate, when examined under ultraviolet light, is luminous. Since the tagged antibody is known to be *specific* for *only* one kind of organism, an identification of the unknown organism can then be made.

GLUCOSE, BLOOD: Every living creature has a specific amount of sugar (glucose) in the blood. Too much or too little indicates various disease problems. A decrease in the expected amount of blood glucose may indicate malnutrition, starvation, liver problems (psittacosis, Pacheco's, for example), and septicemia, among other things. An increase in the expected amount of blood sugar may indicate diabetes mellitus or an abnormal amount of stress. Lewandowski et al. (1986) state that certain diets and hyperthermia (higher than normal body temperature) may cause increases in the blood glucose level. They also state that blood glucose may be elevated during the breeding season.

Blood glucose is determined by examining the serum portion of a blood sample.

GLUCOSE, URINE: See Urinalysis.

GRAM STAIN: This commonly used test is an extremely important way to determine the nature of the bacteria suspected of causing infections in birds. A sample of feces, pus, or other body discharges is smeared on a microscope slide. The specimen is then stained (dyed) using a specific procedure called the Gram method. It involves (1) initial dyeing with gentian or crystal violet; (2) washing off the violet dye and flooding the smear with iodine; (3) washing off the iodine and then applying alcohol to the smear; and (4) applying the final dye—safranin (Fischbach, 1984).

The treated bacteria will fall into one of two major groups. The first are called Gram positive, because they retain the dark blue or violet of the first dye used. The second group is Gram negative. These bacteria do not retain the violet color of the first dye, and are therefore "negative" in this sense. The Gram-negative bacteria retain the color of the second dye used—safranin. They are colored light red or pink.

Distinguishing between these two groups is of major importance in determining the agent causing the infection. Gram-positive bacteria are generally not considered to cause disease in birds, with the exception of a few organisms such as beta-hemolytic *streptococcus*. Gram-negative bacteria are *not* considered normal to a bird's microscopic flora and are therefore able to cause serious infection.

HEMATOLOGY: This term describes the study of blood and blood-forming tissues. See Complete Blood Count.

LACTASE DEHYDROGENASE (LDH): LDH is an enzyme found in skeletal muscle, the lungs, and the liver. LDH elevation is used as an indicator of liver problems, soft tissue injury, and abnormal destruction of red blood cells. According to Campbell (1987), the expected normals for this enzyme vary widely in healthy birds, making it somewhat less reliable than other available tests for the determination of liver disease. Lewandowski et al. (1986) agree with this conclusion.

LDH level is determined by examining the serum portion of a blood sample.

PACKED CELL VOLUME (PCV): See Complete Blood Count.

PHOSPHORUS, SERUM: The ways in which calcium and phosphorus work in the body are closely tied together. Lewandowski et al. (1986) feel that our present knowledge of these processes in the bird are not well enough known to make serum phosphorus determinations a useful diagnostic. Nevertheless, Campbell (1987) feels that elevated serum phosphorus levels may indicate kidney disease. He further states that decreased levels may be seen in intestinal diseases that interfere with the absorption of phosphorus from the gut into the bloodstream.

Serum phosphorus levels are determined by examining the serum portion of a blood sample.

POTASSIUM, SERUM: Potassium is a major component of the fluid inside the cells of all living creatures. It is extremely important in the conduction of nerve impulses and muscle function—including heart muscle. It plays a large role in the balance of fluid in and around the cell in body tissues and in the bloodstream. It is also important in the regulation of the acid-base balance of the body (the mechanism whereby the acidity and alkalinity of the body fluids are kept in a state of equilibrium). An increase in serum potassium levels may be seen in kidney disease, adrenal gland disease, and shock (Campbell, 1987).

Serum potassium levels are determined by examination of the serum portion of a blood sample.

PSITTACOSIS TESTING: This is done routinely during physical examination of a new bird by many veterinarians. It is also done if the clinician suspects that a bird has psittacosis (Chlamydiosis).

There are several ways of testing for psittacosis. The first method involves examining a blood sample for the possible presence of antibodies against the organism that causes psittacosis; this is called a chlamydia titer, psittacosis titer, or psitt titer. The results are given as a titer, a titer being defined as the highest dilution of blood serum (suspected of containing psittacosis antibodies) that will react with a laboratory-standardized dose of *C. psittaci*. A positive reaction indicates that the bird is infected with C. psittaci, or has been in the past. If the bird is actively ill, at least two blood samples taken three weeks apart will be tested during the bird's illness and the results compared. (Daft et al., c. 1986). If the second sample shows a titer higher than the first (at least four-fold), the bird definitely has psittacosis (Gerlach, 1986b).

Another method used to diagnose psittacosis involves the use of chicken embryos. A small amount of material taken from a culture of the bird's feces is inoculated into a six-day-old chicken embryo. The chicken embryos will die if the fecal culture material contained a *C. psittaci* infection. Chicken embryos can also be inoculated with blood or tissues from birds suspected of having psittacosis.

A third method of diagnosis consists of preparing smears of nasal discharges on a microscope slide, and then staining and examining the material for evidence of *C. psittaci*. In a similar fashion, material from diseased organs found on necropsy can be placed on slides and examined.

According to Michael Paster (1983b), if feces are being examined for the presence of *C. psittaci*, it is necessary to use serial droppings over a period of several days, as the organism may not be shed in the droppings consistently. He also recommends that a bird that has been treated for psittacosis be retested at three- and six-month intervals following treatment. (The bird will not shed Chlamydia in the feces while it is being treated with antibiotics).

RADIOGRAPH: The radiograph, or X ray, is a basic tool in the formulation of a diagnosis in a variety of diseases. It is customary to X-ray the bird's entire body, as most birds will easily fit into the dimensions of standard X-ray film. Two pictures are routinely taken: the bird lying on its side (lateral view) and on its back (ventro-dorsal view). In some instances, more than two films will be taken. This is dependent upon the bird's suspected condition and the degree of additional information needed.

Because complete immobility is required to obtain a useful radiograph, the bird is positioned on a restraint board. Very often, the veterinarian will briefly anesthetize the bird to ensure the patient's cooperation—unless, of course, there is a danger that anesthesia will compromise an already sick bird.

SENTINEL BIRD: See Bioassay.

SERUM CHEMISTRY: This term denotes the examination of the blood serum for a variety of components. One blood sample can be used for a variety of tests

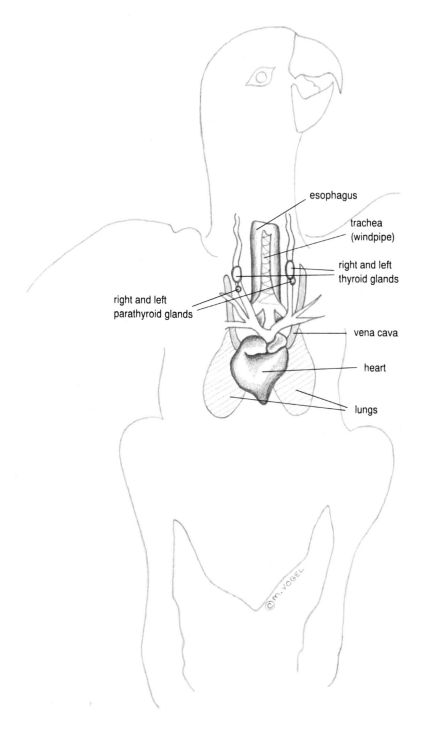

esophagus

trachea
(windpipe)

right and left
thyroid glands

right and left
parathyroid glands

vena cava

heart

lungs

©M. VOGEL

Normal thyroid/parathyroid anatomy

59

(for example, determination of levels of potassium, protein, sodium, LDH, AST/ SGOT, and so forth).

SERUM PROTEIN: See Complete Blood Count.

SODIUM, SERUM: Sodium is an extremely important element in maintaining the body's function. Its jobs are very similar to that of potassium (see Potassium, Serum). A decrease in serum sodium may indicate kidney or adrenal gland problems. Increased serum sodium levels are caused by dehydration, such as that resulting from prolonged and severe diarrhea, or water deprivation.

Paster (1983b) states that serum sodium levels may also rise with excessive dietary salt intake. However, according to Frances Fischbach (1984), it is generally agreed that when an organism is in a state of health, the "level of sodium is kept constant within narrow limits despite wide fluctuations in dietary intake." It is difficult to see, therefore, how dietary salt intake could increase serum sodium levels, at least in a healthy bird.

Serum sodium levels are determined by examination of the serum portion of a blood sample.

T4 TEST: T4 (thyroxine) is a hormone manufactured by the thyroid gland, from whence it is released into the bloodstream. It can be measured to provide one indication of the functional status of the thyroid glands. A single test is not significant, but must be repeated in order to provide a more complete assessment of thyroid status. See Thyroid Stimulating Hormone Test.

THYROID STIMULATING HORMONE (TSH) TEST: This test measures thyroid function. It can help the veterinarian determine whether the thyroid gland is overactive or underactive.

To perform this test, TSH is used. A blood sample is drawn and the T4 component is measured. A dose of TSH is then given. After the TSH has been given, a period of time is allowed to elapse (four to six hours). A second blood sample is then drawn, the T4 content measured, and then compared with that of the first blood sample.

A decrease in T4 from the expected normal can be seen with hypothyroidism (underactive thyroid gland function), inflammation of the thyroid gland, iodine deficiency (caused by too little iodine in the diet), and tyrosine deficiency (tyrosine is an amino acid present in some kinds of protein; it is needed in the manufacture of thyroxine).

According to Woerpel and Rosskopf (1984b), no true hyperthyroid cases have been found by them among their avian patients. They further state that of all birds they examined for thyroxine, cockatoos had the highest normal readings. Amazons, conures, and African Grays had consistently lower normal readings.

URIC ACID: Uric acid results from the metabolism of protein, and is excreted in the urine. A small amount is excreted in the feces. Excessive uric acid production occurs in any condition where there is a great deal of cell breakdown (cells contain protein), in gout, and in kidney disease, which prevents normal excretion of uric acid. Increased amounts of uric acid are found in cases of starvation (because the bird's body is digesting its own protein for energy) and massive trauma. Elevated uric acid levels may also result from lead poisoning and some types of cancer. Paster (1983b) states that decreased uric acid levels are found during ovulation.

Uric acid levels are determined by examining the serum portion of a blood sample.

URINALYSIS: This test consists of an examination of the urine/urate portion of the bird's dropping for several of its components: appearance and color, specific gravity, pH, protein, glucose, ketones, blood (frank), red and white blood cells, casts, crystals, and bacteria.

Collection of the urine is facilitated by allowing the bird to deposit its droppings on a smooth, water-impervious surface such as plastic wrap or aluminum foil. The urates and urine are then recovered by aspiration with a syringe and needle.

Walter Rosskopf, in his "Analysis of Pet Bird Droppings," notes that urinalysis is a very helpful diagnostic tool, especially in kidney infection. Rhonda Sayle (1986) feels that urinalysis is somewhat less helpful because the urate/urine component of the dropping is contaminated by feces, thereby obscuring the true nature of the urine. A further qualification has been made by Woerpel and Rosskopf (1984b), who state that when the urine is examined for the presence of various cells, it must be borne in mind that the origin of these cells may be from the reproductive or digestive tracts, cloaca, or kidneys. Nevertheless, urinalysis remains a valuable screening test in the opinion of many avian practitioners.

Urine is examined for the following components:

Appearance and color: Avian urine normally is rather cloudy. Normal colors of urine include clear, shades of yellow, straw colored, greenish white, or light green. These colors are normally very faint. Water-soluble vitamin B-complex colors the urine yellow (Woerpel and Rosskopf, 1984b).

Specific gravity: This is a measure of the kidney's ability to concentrate urine. Specific gravity readings are obtained by comparing a given weight of urine against the same weight of distilled water (the specific gravity of which is 1.000). Since urine contains not only water but minerals, salts, and other compounds as well, its specific gravity will be greater than water. A decrease in the urine specific gravity indicates that the kidney is allowing too much water to be excreted, usually due to infection. An increase in specific gravity may be due to diabetes mellitus, or excessive water loss from the body, as may occur with prolonged vomiting, diarrhea, or high fever.

pH: This symbol expresses the strength of the urine as either a dilute acidic or basic (alkaline) solution. It is an indicator of the kidney's ability to maintain the correct hydrogen ion concentration in blood and tissues. pH values are expressed on a scale of 1 through 14: 7.0 is considered neutral; a pH value of less than 7.0 indicates an acidic solution, while a pH value greater than 7.0 indicates a basic solution. The normal urine pH for companion birds is 6.0–8.0. Acidic urine may reflect diarrhea, starvation, uncontrolled diabetes mellitus, or severe respiratory problems. Basic urine may reflect urinary tract infections or kidney disease.

Protein: About 90 percent of normal bird urine will show a trace of protein (Woerpel and Rosskopf, 1984b). This may be due to the contact of urine with the feces in the dropping. More than a trace of protein, especially if noted in two or more urine samples from a sick bird, may indicate kidney disease. Above-normal amounts of protein in the urine may also be due to fever, trauma, abdominal tumors, or obstructions.

Glucose: A small amount of glucose (sugar) is seen in many bird urine specimens, probably for the same reasons that trace amounts of protein are seen. High dietary intake of sugar may also cause a temporary, normal rise in the amount of glucose found in the urine. An abnormally high level of glucose in the urine may indicate the presence of diabetes mellitus. It is generally felt that such a finding should be followed up with an examination of blood glucose levels. This is thought to be a more accurate indicator for diabetes in a bird (Woerpel and Rosskopf, 1984b).

Ketones: Ketones result from the burning of fats in the body for fuel. Ordinarily, the body uses carbohydrates for fuel, but when this process is disturbed by disease, as in diabetes, the body burns fats as an alternative. Therefore, ketones are sometimes found in the urine of a bird severely ill with diabetes.

Blood, frank: Frank (obvious) blood in the urine is an abnormal finding. It indicates hemorrhage from the digestive tract, reproductive tract, cloaca, or kidneys. In Amazon Parrots, it is a classic symptom of lead poisoning.

Red and white blood cells: These are often seen in small numbers in normal urine. Abnormally high numbers of red blood cells may indicate disease in the urinary tract, or may also be due to problems in the gut, reproductive tract, or cloaca. According to Fischbach (1984), this may also occur in cases of trauma or aspirin ingestion. Excessive numbers of white blood cells in the urine also indicate infection in one or more of the above-mentioned systems.

Casts: A urine cast is essentially a molded replica of various cells in the urinary tract (including kidneys), or of red or white blood cells. They are made of waxy substances or protein materials. Their presence usually indicates urinary tract infection.

Crystals: Crystals in the urine are microscopic and formed from urates. It is normal to find many of these in bird urine.

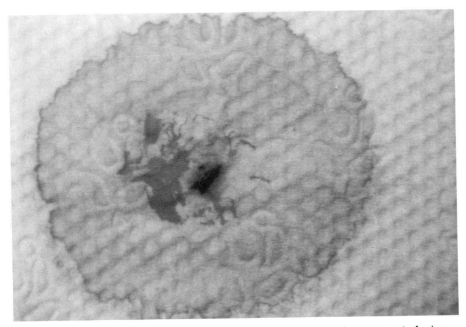

The droppings of a bird suffering from lead poisoning will show a large amount of urine, tinted brownish-red from kidney damage (hematuria).   *Peter Sakas, D.V.M.*

The droppings of birds suffering from psittacosis characteristically show bright green urine.
Peter Sakas, D.V.M.

Bacteria: It is normal to find small numbers of bacteria in bird urine, probably due to contamination of the urine by feces. However, high numbers of bacteria are not normal and are an indication that the bird needs closer examination for possible infection.

WATER DEPRIVATION TEST: This test is done to determine the kidney's ability to concentrate urine. Urine contains many dissolved substances. Almost all substances found in the blood are also found in the urine, but the amounts are higher per given volume of urine than for the same volume of blood. The reason for this is that it is the job of the kidneys to remove from the bloodstream any substance in excess of the body's need for that particular substance. We refer to the kidney's ability to perform this function as its ability to concentrate. In some diseases, the kidneys produce a very dilute urine. In other diseases, a very concentrated urine is produced.

The water deprivation test is performed by withholding water for twelve hours and then measuring the urine specific gravity at the end of that time. It is sometimes performed if a bird is suspected of being a psychogenic water drinker. It may also be recommended as an aid to diagnosis in certain types of kidney disease.

X RAY: See Radiograph.

THE USE AND ABUSE OF ANTIBIOTICS AND OTHER MEDICATIONS

Antibiotics

"Antibiotics" is a term with which all of us are familiar. To many, it means "cure." These drugs are so commonly used that, generally speaking, most people fail to respect them as the potent, sometimes dangerous, drugs they really are. Nor is there a general understanding of their limitations.

The following are some common misconceptions about antibiotics:

1. There is no difference among antibiotics. They are all pretty much the same, and one kind will do the job as well as another.
2. Antibiotics cure everything—including virally caused disease.
3. An antibiotic only has to be administered until the symptoms are gone.
4. Antibiotics are 100 percent safe—they can cause no damage to the body.
5. If a bird is sick, all it needs is an antibiotic—all those fancy tests really aren't necessary.

These misconceptions often create unrealistic expectations about the outcome of an illness and inhibit the owner's understanding about what can and cannot be reasonably expected when antibiotics are employed.

Before continuing on, there are three rules concerning drugs—any drug, including antibiotics—that readers should engrave upon their minds:

1. All drugs are toxins.
2. All toxins are drugs.
3. All drugs are poisons at the right time and dose (Clipsham, 1987).

Owners should *never*, under any circumstance, treat their birds with *any* drug without first consulting an avian veterinarian. Severe problems, including death, may result from such ill-advised action.

Antibiotics are defined as any variety of natural or synthetic substance that inhibits the growth of or destroys microorganisms. The microorganisms referred to in this definition are bacteria. Antibiotics do not cure or inhibit viruses, for the most part. Owners often expect that if their birds are ill with an infection, an antibiotic should be routinely prescribed. If the infection is caused by a virus rather than a bacteria, an antibiotic will not help. The reason for this is that viruses live *inside* the body's cells. Many antibiotics do not penetrate the inside of cells and therefore cannot come in contact with the virus. In this situation, antibiotics cannot be effective.

There are two general categories of antibiotic: bacteriocidal and bacteriostatic. Bacteriocidal antibiotics kill bacteria. Bacteriocidal antibiotics include penicillins, cephalosporins, and aminoglycosides. Bacteriostatic antibiotics slow the growth of, but do not kill, bacteria. They rely on body defenses to eliminate bacteria. If the body defenses are weakened, bacteriostatic drugs may not be effective. Bacteriostatic antibiotics would include erythromycin, tetracycline, and chloramphenicol.

Antibiotics produce their results by blocking some process in the bacterium necessary for its survival. One way this may be accomplished is that the antibiotic disrupts the bacterial cell wall, causing its collapse. Another way that an antibiotic may work is to affect the bacterial cell membrane in such a way as to cause leakage of vital cell fluids. Yet a third way that antibiotics function is to affect, in various ways, the genetic function and integrity of the bacterium, thus killing it or preventing its normal function.

Not all antibiotics work equally well in all parts of the body. A good example of this is the "blood-brain" barrier. This is a mechanism that exists to protect the brain from assault and damage by foreign substances in the bloodstream. Unfortunately, it has this effect on many antibiotics as well. Only a relative few of them cross from the blood into the brain tissue. This is one reason why infections of the central nervous system can be so difficult to treat effectively.

Another situation that may render the antibiotic ineffective, or less effective than usual, is the accumulation of large amounts of dead tissue, or pus. It takes much longer for the antibiotic to penetrate these areas than in only mildly inflamed tissue.

The route of administration affects the performance of antibiotics. Some may be given orally. Others are inactivated by the enzymes in the digestive tract and therefore must be given by injection.

Still another issue that must be considered is toxicity. Some antibiotics have harmful effects on the kidneys. An example of this is gentamycin. Streptomycin is known to cause hearing loss in some individuals. Chloramphenicol can cause dose-related anemias. These examples are not mentioned in order to create an "antibiotic phobia" in the reader; rather, it is hoped that the reader will realize that antibiotics, like all drugs, can be harmful when misused. In order to use them safely, an avian veterinarian's knowledge and experience are needed.

There are several concepts concerning the use of antibiotics that the reader will find useful to know. They help explain why the inappropriate use of an antibiotic can slow or prevent a bird's recovery. They also elucidate the necessity of giving the bird the *exact* dose prescribed, at the *right* time, and for the *required length* of treatment. The problem of antibiotic resistance can also be better understood.

In the following discussion, it will first be helpful to understand something of a bird's biology at the "microorganism level." In all living creatures, birds included, the body is populated by a host of beneficial bacteria and other microscopic organisms. They live on skin, in hair, in the mouth, in the digestive tract, even on the eyeball. Over the millennia of evolution, each species has developed a resistance to the disease-causing potential of such organisms and, in fact, have developed mutual relationships of benefit with them. For example, bacteria in a given species' digestive tract can actually help in the breakdown and digestion of food. Microscopic mites living on the skin of some species scavenge dead skin cells.

These beneficial microorganisms perform yet another invaluable service that can perhaps best be understood from an ecological viewpoint. In any ecosystem, whether it be a forest, a tropical lagoon, or a bird's body, the creatures inhabiting a given environment have been adapted through evolution to fit perfectly into their given niches. They fit "lock and key" into their environments. Because they function so effectively in their specific situations, and have evolved a mutually beneficial relationship with them (or their host, if one speaks of the bacterial population—flora—of a living creature), they thrive in great numbers and *preclude* other organisms new to that environment from gaining a foothold and flourishing.

This is precisely what occurs in the bird's body. Its beneficial bacteria fill all the available ecological niches in its body and *prevent* harmful bacterial from gaining entrance and thriving. Thus, a bird's normal bacterial flora constitutes an effective defense mechanism against infection.

Now, in this context, what happens if a bird is given an antibiotic not suited to its particular problem? What often happens is that the indiscriminately used drug actually destroys the "good" bacteria, leaving the door wide open for marauding bacteria to set up housekeeping and do their worst. Furthermore, it often happens that the antibiotic that was so carelessly used will not be effective against the newly established hordes.

The next difficulty is that of bacterial resistance to an antibiotic. How does

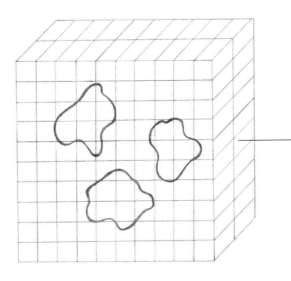

Bacteriostatic drugs
prevent further
germ growth.

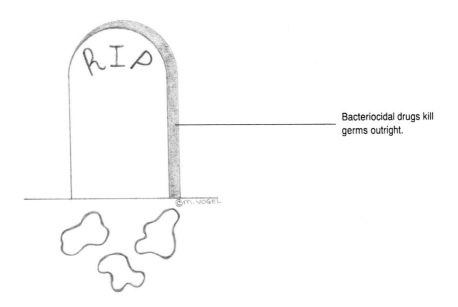

Bacteriocidal drugs kill
germs outright.

Bacteriostatic versus bacteriocidal drugs

it happen? At the outset, it should be realized that not one bacterium or hundreds of bacteria are being treated; quite literally, it must fight billions of them. In such a huge population, mutations are bound to occur. When a mutation occurs, a permanent change in that organism's genetic material has been effected. If this change has allowed it to survive the onslaught of the antibiotic being used in treatment, it has become better suited to its specific environment. Its offspring will inherit this resistance to that particular antibiotic. In turn, they will pass on these resistant genes to *their* offspring. Those bacteria that have not evolved a particular antibiotic resistance will not survive to pass on their genes to offspring. In this way, antibiotic-resistant bacteria populations evolve. The more frequently a particular antibiotic is used, the greater the chance that resistant bacterial mutations will occur, by virtue of the fact that the bacteria have been repeatedly exposed to it and are being given greater opportunity to "learn" survival in its presence, by genetic means. This is Darwin's "survival of the fittest" theory in microcosm: It is just as effective with bacteria and viruses as it is with elephants, monkeys, orchids, and all other living creatures.

It is further interesting to note that resistance may be transferred to other species of bacteria (Harris, 1984). When this occurs, the antibiotic becomes totally useless as a weapon against either of the bacteria involved.

In light of these facts, it is easy to see why antibiotics should not be used indiscriminately. In the first place, the antibiotic may be only mildly effective, killing off sensitive bacteria and leaving the resistant ones to multiply and form resistant populations. Second, the more frequently an antibiotic is used, the greater the chance that resistant bacteria will evolve. These two factors have seriously concerned the medical community for years: There is a real fear that bacteria will develop resistance more quickly than new antibiotics can be developed, leaving animals and humans alike without effective tools with which to fight them. Another reason that dictates judicious use of antibiotics is the bodily harm they can do in untutored hands; the wrong dose, delivered for an incorrect period of treatment time, and delivered the wrong way, can cause severe illness and may result in death.

This leads us to the three cardinal rules for administering an antibiotic to any creature, including Homo sapiens:

1. Give the *correct dose*.
2. Give it at the *correct time*.
3. Give it for the *entire* length of time prescribed.

Why is this so vitally necessary? In order to understand, it is helpful to know what happens when an antibiotic is given. The requisite condition allowing an antibiotic to be effective is the achievement of *sustained, consistent* blood levels of said drug. To accomplish this, one must give the antibiotic as prescribed. If directions indicate a dose every four hours, this does *not* mean in the morning, at noon, later afternoon, and bedtime. It means *every four hours around the clock*. If this is not done, blood concentration of the antibiotic will fall during the night, giving the bacteria time to "catch breath" and commence multiplying again.

Giving the correct dose is essential. To give less than the amount prescribed will fail again to obtain adequate blood levels of the antibiotic. Only sensitive bacteria will be killed, allowing resistant ones to multiply and form resistant populations.

The medication must be given in the correct way. If your bird has been given a liquid antibiotic and you have been instructed to give the bird one milliliter (ml) by mouth, *do it*. Do not put the medication in the bird's drinking water because it is easier. The bird will never ingest enough medication to do any good.

Give the antibiotic for the entire length of time prescribed. Do not stop when symptoms disappear and your bird looks better. If you do, the infection will return. The first few doses will kill the weak bacteria immediately. A few more will kill the slightly stronger bacteria. At this point, many, observing their bird's improvement, stop the medication. But the error is this: the strongest bacteria still survive, and they will continue to multiply. The illness will thus return. Only administration of the antibiotic for the full treatment time will kill the strongest bacteria and achieve a cure.

How, then, does one know which antibiotic is needed, how much to give, when to give it, and for how long? The answer is simple: Your avian veterinarian is the *only* person qualified to make these judgments. He will do a culture and sensitivity test to determine what bacteria are causing the problem and which antibiotic is most effective. He will combine this information with his knowledge of your bird, and with other laboratory work that has been performed. For example, if serum chemistries indicated that your bird had kidney problems, he would not prescribe an antibiotic known to be toxic to the kidneys—even if sensitivity testing indicated it to be the most effective for the pathogen in question. Using informed judgment, he would choose a safer medication.

Prescribing an antibiotic, or any medication, is not merely a matter of formula. Much knowledge and experience are needed. For this reason, when your bird has an infection, do not rely on the advice of your next-door neighbor, best friend, breeder, or pet shop.

Other Medications

There are many preparations on the market designed for the sick bird. It is even possible to buy erythromycin and tetracycline without a doctor's prescription. Studies have shown that both of these antibiotics are useless in treating most common infectious agents of birds (Harris, 1984). Indeed any over-the-counter (OTC) medication for birds is suspect. In the first place, the vast majority of bird owners are not qualified to diagnose their bird's illnesses. This, of course, makes an effective treatment plan impossible. In the second place, OTC medications contain very few active ingredients and therefore are ineffective. They fall into the category of placebos. They make owners feel better because they falsely believe they are "doing something" to help their sick bird. All they are really doing is wasting life-saving time by not taking the bird to a qualified avian veterinarian. All too often, when bird owners elect to self-treat their bird, it is too late to save it by the time they realize that they have failed.

Some owners are tempted to medicate their birds with their own prescriptions. This should *never* be done, for all of the above reasons. In addition, many medications prescribed for dogs, cats, and humans are toxic to birds when given in doses strong enough for people and other animals.

Never give alcohol to a sick bird. Alcohol is poisonous to birds. It is a depressant, not a stimulant. When given to an ailing avian, alcohol will further depress an already weakened system. This is particularly true if the bird has suffered a head injury or shock due to trauma—for example, flying into a window or mirror. In addition, alcohol is extremely dangerous to a bird's liver.

A final word of caution about medications. Never use an ointment unless prescribed by your bird's veterinarian; when it is prescribed, follow directions exactly. Ointments are dangerous to birds because they are compounded with an oil base. Oil coats a bird's feathers, rendering them unfit to carry out their function of insulation and body temperature regulation. Birds frequently die of hypothermia (lowered body temperature) as a result of ointment use. Such an example can be seen when shore birds are coated with oil as a result of oil spills. Thousands of unfortunate birds have died of hypothermia in situations such as this.

SICK AND CONVALESCENT CARE

In the interval of time between when you notice that your bird is ill and its appointment with the veterinarian, there are a number of things you can do to make your bird more comfortable and increase its chances of recovery. These things are also basic to the convalescent care of your bird, once it is home and under the treatment plan outlined by its medical adviser.They fall into the following categories:

Warmth
Rest and freedom from stress
Nutrition
Conscientious monitoring
Isolation
Special husbandry

Warmth

A sick bird needs warmth. Arthur Freud (1982) states that the importance of warmth can rarely be overestimated. In some cases birds too ill to leave their cage bottoms are able to climb back onto their perches within a few hours of raising the ambient air temperature to the requisite level.

An infrared lamp mounted
above the cage of a sick bird
will raise the ambient air temperature—an important factor
for recovery.   *M. Vogel*

An intensive care unit in an avian veterinary hospital.   *M. Vogel*

The immediate environmental temperature should be raised to 80°–90°F for a sick bird. *Always* place a thermometer in or very near the cage so the temperature can be accurately gauged and adjusted as needed. A bird that is too hot will hold its wings away from its body and pant. One too cold will sit in a huddled position with fluffed feathers. When using a heat source exterior to the cage, place it on one side, rather than directly over the cage. In this way, the bird will be provided with a cooler area in which to move if it becomes too warm. The temperature can be raised in several ways:

1. Place a heating pad underneath the cage and wrap the cage on three sides and top with towels. This works well with a small cage, but is not adequate for a very large cage, such as those for cockatoos and macaws. The heating pad may also be fixed to the side of the cage, taking care that the bird is unable to chew it. An alternative to covering the cage with towels is to wrap the cage on the top and three sides with plastic wrap.

2. An aquarium (ten- to fifteen-gallon size) with screen covering may be placed on a heating pad and wrapped top and sides with towels. This works well for smaller birds.

3. An electric blanket, suspended on *all* sides by a cradle device, works well for larger cages. It is *absolutely essential* to keep the blanket away from the reach of inquisitive beaks.

4. Suspend a 75- or 100-watt light bulb six to twelve inches from the side of the cage or aquarium. It is recommended by Joel Pasco (1983) and Amy Worrell (1986a) that a *green, red, or blue bulb* be used. In this way, heat may be supplied throughout the night without disturbing the bird's rest.

5. An infrared light may be used several feet from the cage.

Rest and Freedom from Stress

Rest is as important for the sick bird as for the sick person. Some guidelines are:

1. Place the cage in a quiet part of the house.
2. Avoid unnecessary handling.
3. Keep other pets and children away.
4. Keep the cage partially covered, as mentioned above, not only to retain warmth but to provide privacy.
5. Provide *twelve hours* of sleep in a darkened, quiet room.

Nutrition

Sick birds frequently refuse to eat. Because of their high metabolic rates, birds will soon starve if they cannot be persuaded to take nourishment—this is

Aviculture and veterinary science have developed sophisticated procedures for artificially feeding and medicating birds. With better understanding of parrot anatomy and physiological requirements of birds, we can hand-raise birds from the nest, as with the Rose-breasted Cockatoo (right). The Major MItchell's, or Leadbeater's, Cockatoo (below) is older and more advanced but still works with the syringe. The rubber tip helps avoid beak injury in feeding applications. Medication can be delivered in the same way. *Bill Wegner, Malibu Exotics*

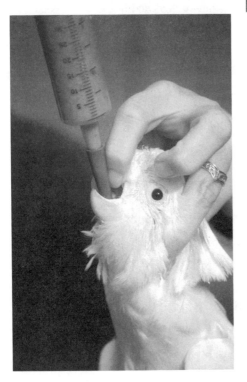

absolutely essential. The aim is twofold: to provide an adequate amount of calories and to provide an adequate state of hydration.

Hand feeding or spoon feeding a tame bird or a hand-raised baby is often a good approach if the bird refuses to take food from its dishes. Feeding by syringe or dropper may also be good alternative if the bird is too weak to take food from your hand. If this method is used, always use a plastic implement. Glass is easily broken by a bird's beak, with the potential for serious damage. Occasionally, a bird will need to be fed by tube directly into the crop. If this should be necessary, your veterinarian will demonstrate the method and supervise your first attempts. *Never* try this by yourself without having been taught how to do it properly. The risks of forcing formula or fluid into the bird's trachea and lungs are considerable. It is also possible to puncture the delicate crop.

A word needs to be said about grit. Many authorities today feel that grit is totally unnecessary to a parrot's digestive process. However, if you still offer grit to your bird, remove it if the bird is ill. Sick birds frequently overeat it. This leads to an impaction in the crop, or farther down in the digestive tract, and may result in the bird's death.

In the matter of food selection for a sick bird, what the bird will eat determines what is offered. In this situation, attempting a balanced diet is secondary; that can be reinstituted when the bird has regained health. The main concern is getting sufficient calories into the bird. If it loves pizza, give it pizza. If it dotes on sunflower seeds, provide them (hulled, if the bird is too weak to crack them on its own). Many birds adore peanut butter, and this makes a good invalid food because it is high in calories and protein. In short, any favorite food with which you can tempt your ailing friend should be tried.

Offering food warm often increases its palatability for the sick bird. A warm mash, such as the one mentioned in Chapter 2 or one of your own devising, may appeal to the ailing bird. The author feels that the texture of such an offering somewhat approximates that regurgitated to the bird as an infant by its parents (or fed by surrogates). Since all creatures regress emotionally to some degree when ill, a familiar food with the familiar texture of infancy may well be acceptable to your parrot because of its association with early comfort and well-being. After all, when we humans are ill, we enjoy nursery foods such as hot milk, chicken noodle soup, or rice pudding—probably more than at other times when we are feeling healthy and vigorous.

There are various ways of providing adequate fluid intake to the sick bird. If it is able to drink from its bowl, you may wish to use fruit juice instead of water (orange and cherry flavors seem to appeal). Chicken or beef broth may be used if your bird will accept it. The idea here is to provide fluid, plus the extra calories and nourishment that plain water cannot afford. Of course, any of these fluids may be given via dropper or syringe, if necessary.

J. A. Stunkard (1984) gives a good formula for a ''quick energy electrolyte'' mixture:

1. Mix one pint of water and one pint of Gatorade.

Tube feeding is used on adult birds that will not eat on their own. *Peter Sakas, D.V.M.*

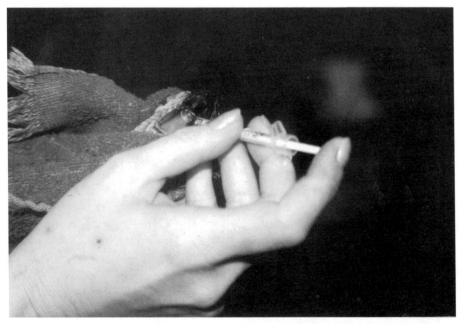

A disposable syringe (minus the needle) is an efficient means of administering oral medication. Towel restraint is used, and the technician's hand is positioned to be out of reach of a protesting beak! *Peter Sakas, D.V.M.*

2. Add the following:

 1 teaspoon honey or Karo syrup
 1 level teaspoon baking soda
 1 level teaspoon table salt

He cautions that the ingredients must be measured with care, or serious diarrhea can result. This formula is especially helpful for a dehydrated bird.

Conscientious Monitoring

Careful observation of the sick bird's droppings is required. Daily weights on a gram scale should be taken. These items are fully discussed in Chapter 2 and elsewhere in this chapter.

Isolation

If your bird becomes ill, place its cage in another part of the house. This provides it with peace and quiet and also protects your other birds from disease transmission. Isolation precautions as outlined in Chapter 2 should be followed.

Special Husbandry

Often, sick birds are too weak to remain on their perches. They then will occupy the cage floor. Be sure that all food and water dishes are placed within easy reach of the bird, as it will not be able to climb to its accustomed perch to eat. Sprinkling seed or other favorite food on the cage floor may also encourage the bird to eat. Extra precautions are needed in this circumstance to ensure that your bird and its food do not become soiled with droppings.

Other Precautions

In addition to the above care, which is basic and necessary for any sick bird, there are two additional problems sometimes encountered in the sick bird that the owner can take steps to alleviate. One of these is diarrhea. Joel Pasco (1983) recommends that fruits and vegetables be limited in this situation. He also suggests that cooked rice is a good choice for birds with this condition. The author would add that white rice is the only rice that should be used, and it should be prepared without salt or other seasonings.

The other problem is that of respiratory problems causing the bird mild discomfort. In addition to the plan of treatment prescribed by your avian veterinarian, you may wish to use a steam vaporizer. Pasco states that the steam may be directed into the covered cage for twenty minutes, three times a day, and that Vicks vaporizer may be used in the water of the vaporizer. Be extremely careful that you do not burn your bird when using this method. The author has found the "cool-mist" vaporizer to be just as effective. A decongestant such as Vicks can be added to the water in these humidifiers as well, and there is no risk of steam-cooking your bird.

Be sure to keep your bird's nostrils free of drainage or exudate. Gentle cleansing with wet cotton balls or tissue may suffice. If the drainage is viscous, an infant-type rubber bulb syringe can be used to aspirate the offending material.

It cannot be overemphasized that the above material has been presented in order to help owners make their bird more comfortable and to increase the bird's chances of a swift and uneventful recovery. These are *not* substitutes for a veterinarian's care, but serve to enhance whatever treatment plan the doctor has determined for your bird.

HOW TO MEDICATE A BIRD

Sooner or later, you will be faced with the task of medicating your bird. It can be quite a challenge, especially if you are dealing with an untamed one.

The most common methods of administering medicine are in the drinking water, directly into the mouth, topically to an injured or diseased area, and by injection. If your veterinarian has prescribed a medication for your bird, it will be your job to give it (unless the bird has been hospitalized). If the medicine does not get into the bird, it will do no good.

The first item of business in giving your bird medicine is to be comfortable with its proper restraint. Hopefully, you will have an assistant. But if you do not, don't despair. It is possible to restrain and medicate a bird by yourself, with the exception of giving injections. Before catching and restraining your bird, lay out all necessary medicines, implements, etc. In order to minimize stress, you will want to restrain your bird for as short a period as is necessary to get the job done.

It is recommended that the towel method of restraint be used. Gloves are clumsy for the wearer and often very frightening for the bird. The use of gloves may also result in a previously tame bird becoming hand shy.

In order to restrain the bird, it is first necessary to get it out of the cage, if it is not tame enough to come onto your hand. (If the bird is tame, take it to a restricted space, such as a corner of the bathroom, set the bird on the floor, and towel it there.) It is often helpful to darken the room, when removing a bird from its cage—first taking note of its position in the cage.

Take the towel in one hand, slowly approaching the bird from behind. Using a smooth, rapid motion, grasp the bird (using the towel) behind the jaws, thus immobilizing its head and beak. With the other hand, quickly place the towel over its back and grasp it about the fleshy part of its tail and legs. *Never* grab a bird around its abdomen, or hold it in such a grasp. Birds do not have diaphragms, but breathe with their abdominal muscles. If these muscles are restricted, the bird will suffocate.

Once the bird has been caught, gently work its feet free from the perch or cage wires and remove it from the cage. At this point, the rest of the towel can be loosely wrapped around its wings to prevent flapping.

If you are alone, the bird can be cradled against your body for greater stability and security. The bird will be lying in the palm of your hand with its head movement restricted by your grasp under its jaws. If you have a helper, you can transfer the bird, again being sure that its head is firmly and gently restrained and that the rest of its body remains immobilized as described.

When removing a bird from its cage, it is a good idea to first remove all toys, extra perches, and food and water bowls. This will give you more room to maneuver.

Water Medication

This method does not require that you restrain your bird. Your job will be to place the medicine in the water as directed by the veterinarian. In order to encourage your bird to drink, restrict its intake of fresh fruits and vegetables, which are high in water content. You want your bird to get its water from the water dish. A diet of seed and medicated water will not harm the bird for a few days. If not medically contradicted, salty snacks such as a potato chip or pretzel will encourage the bird to drink. Likewise, fruit juice or a touch of syrup or Kool-Aid may encourage it to drink, as well as help to mask unpalatable medicines.

There are disadvantages to placing medication in the water. The first is that the medication may not remain in suspension in the water. The second is that the bird may refuse to drink water to which medicine has been added. The third disadvantage is that some birds do not drink much water. Examples of such birds are cockatiels, budgerigars, and other such avian species that are primarily desert dwellers and have adapted evolutionarily to low water consumption. In any of the above situations, the result is that the bird will not be able to maintain adequate, consistent blood levels of the prescribed medication and will receive no benefit from it.

Oral Medications

Medication is often prescribed that must be given by mouth. This requires that the patient be restrained, being sure that a firm, gentle grip under the mandible is maintained. Tip the bird's head *slightly* backward. Approach the beak from the side, squirting the medicine *up and over* the tongue. Placing the medication in the mandible under his tongue will only result in it being dribbled out and not swallowed. Slight pressure at the jaw, where the upper and lower beak join (the commissure) will allow you to force the bird's mouth open gently.

An ingenious method of delivering oral medication is described by Arthur Freud (1982). A wooden dowel, six to eight inches in length, is drilled with holes large enough to accommodate the medicine dropper. The dowel is presented to the bird, who, being a parrot, will grab it. One of the holes is then aligned

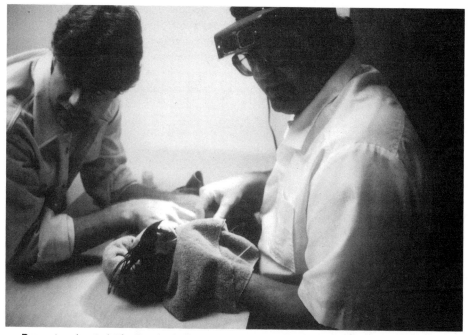

Proper towel restraint for the physical examination of a Black Palm Cockatoo.

Peter Sakas, D.V.M.

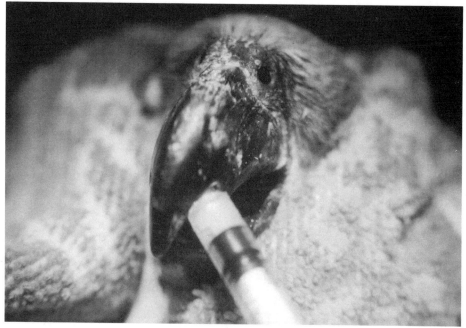

A closeup view of the delivery of oral medication via syringe.

Peter Sakas, D.V.M.

with the open beak, the medicine dropper inserted through it, and the medication is squirted into the patient's mouth. Although not effective for a small bird because of the beak size, it works well for Amazon Parrots on up.

Fairly often, when giving an oral medication, one will observe the medicine bubbling out the bird's nostrils. Do not be alarmed. You are not suffocating or drowning it. This phenomenon occurs when the bird aspirates the medication through the choanal slit on the roof of the mouth into its nostrils. The medication is confined to these areas only and does not mean the patient has sucked the medicine into its lungs.

Injections

Occasionally, the owner may have to give medication by injection. Your veterinarian will show you how to do this. *Never* attempt this procedure without first having been taught how to do it properly.

Injections are usually given in the breast muscle. It is important that you have actually introduced the needle into the muscle and not into the feathers. In order to facilitate this, it is helpful to dampen the feathers around the injection site with sterile water or alcohol, so that the skin may be more easily seen. Warm the alcohol or water slightly so that cold liquid contacting the bird's warm skin will not cause the bird any unnecessary discomfort.

Once the needle has been inserted into the muscle, pull back on the plunger slightly. If blood appears in the barrel of the syringe, you have placed the needle in a blood vessel. If this should occur, withdraw the needle *without* injecting the medication, and try again.

When giving an injection, use a quick "dart-throwing" type of hand motion. Discomfort will be greatly minimized in this way. Placing the needle against the skin and shoving it in causes unnecessary pain.

After the injection has been given, massage the injection site rapidly but gently. This will greatly enhance the absorption of the medication into the bird's body.

As with injections in human beings, use clean technique. Wash your hands before the procedure. *Never* reuse a needle or syringe. The object is to cure the patient, not introduce it to further infection and illness.

Topical Medications

These are medications prepared as salves, ointments, and creams. They are used externally on wounds, skin, for eye problems, and the like. They should never be used without a veterinarian's prescription. When prescribed, follow the directions explicitly. As mentioned previously, ointments can ruin a bird's feathers, severely compromising their insulation qualities and resulting in hypothermia and even death. So use great caution. Apply only the *smallest* amount necessary to do the job.

Whichever method you use, remember that a quick, gentle delivery of medication is the one that stresses the bird the least. Do not become discouraged if your first attempts are not completely successful. With practice comes skill. Without perseverance, your bird will not receive its medicine and cannot recover. So don't give up. You and your bird will both have cause to be glad of your persistence.

Jardine's Parrots (*Poicephalus gulielmi gulielmi*). The male bird is at the right.

4

Emergency First Aid

INTRODUCTION

If you keep enough birds long enough, eventually an emergency will arise. It seems inevitable that regardless of the amount of intelligent care and concern lavished on your collection, some situations arise that require the bird owner to take immediate, sometimes life-saving action.

The purpose of this chapter is to prepare bird owners for such an eventuality. The topics are arranged alphabetically for quick reference. Readers should familiarize themselves with the contents of this chapter in a general way. This will aid in locating a topic more quickly should the need arise. Readers should also be familiar with the general principles of care of the sick and convalescent bird, as discussed in Chapter 3.

All readers must realize that the suggestions contained in this chapter in no way eliminate the need for veterinary care for the patient, which should be obtained as soon as possible. Indeed, all the situations discussed require veterinary attention within twenty-four hours. Some, such as bleeding, poisoning, and acute respiratory problems, require care as soon as it is possible to transport the patient safely. The emergency care outlined for these various conditions is presented in order to help the owner minimize further damage to the bird and keep it alive long enough to obtain qualified avian veterinary care.

It is extremely important to reiterate here that birds hide illness. Minor changes in behavior and/or appearance that indicate illness are often missed. They escalate to major, emergency problems. According to Walter Rosskopf and Richard Woerpel (1987a), many avian emergencies are, in actuality, the end result of long-standing chronic illness.

EMERGENCY PROBLEMS

ACUTE RESPIRATORY PROBLEMS: Signs of labored breathing may include any or all of the following: open-mouthed breathing, frequent sneezing, wheezing or clicking sounds, tail bobbing, or a constantly outstretched neck. In addition, the bird may exhibit nasal discharges and the area around the eyes may be swollen. It may regurgitate, shiver, and have a decreased appetite, loose droppings, weight loss, lethargy, weakness, ruffled feathers, or a swollen abdomen.

All respiratory symptoms should be treated as urgent and the bird should be taken to the veterinarian at the *earliest possible time*. Follow the guidelines in Chapter 3, on care of the sick and convalescent bird. The use of a vaporizer is highly recommended.

AIR SAC RUPTURE: The bird is equipped with a series of air sacs located inside its body: in the neck area (cervical air sacs), in the chest (thoracic air sacs), and in the belly (abdominal air sacs). These structures are part of the bird's breathing system and help it extract oxygen from the air in a highly efficient manner. They also help provide the lightness and buoyancy needed for flight.

Occasionally, one of these air sacs will rupture—usually as the result of injury. When this happens, air will leak from the sac and accumulate under the bird's skin. This condition is known as subcutaneous emphysema. This air accumulation must be removed, otherwise there is the danger that the tear in the air sac will enlarge. Susan Clubb (1983b) recommends that the skin over the swelling be cleansed with a disinfectant and incised with a small pair of sterilized scissors. A tiny cut is made in the skin, allowing the air to escape. Alternately, a sterile needle and syringe may be used for this purpose.

The above process may need to be repeated several times. According to Rosskopf and Woerpel (1987a), air sacs usually repair themselves within two weeks. However, if the owner sees no improvement within twenty-four to forty-eight hours using the above treatment, the bird should be seen by an avian veterinarian. Surgical repair, supplemented by antibiotic therapy, may be necessary.

Keep the bird warm and quiet. Follow the guidelines for care of the sick and convalescent bird, as discussed in Chapter 3.

ANOREXIA: Anorexia is defined as the loss of appetite. The bird may be experiencing a decline in the amount eaten and in its enthusiasm with which food is taken, or it may refuse food altogether. Either situation is serious. A bird's metabolic rate is very high, requiring constant nutritious food intake. A large bird that has not eaten in twenty-four hours should be seen immediately by an avian veterinarian. In very small birds, such as budgerigars, cockatiels, lovebirds, and the like, a period of twelve hours without food requires that the bird be seen. Waiting twenty-four hours before having a small bird seen by a veterinarian might prove fatal. A small bird's metabolic rate is so high that it will rapidly exhaust all body reserves in an attempt to maintain its body temperature and physiologic activity level, if it is not constantly replenishing its reserves by eating.

In the period before the veterinarian's examination has been accomplished, implement the guidelines outlined in Chapter 3 on care of the sick and convalescent bird. Particular attention should be given to the suggestions relative to tempting an anorexic bird to eat.

BLEEDING: Blood anywhere on the bird, or found splattered on cage, perches, and other accouterments, requires immediate investigation and steps to stop the bleeding. The circulating volume of blood in even the largest bird is small. Therefore, birds can ill afford even a small blood loss.

The first step is to determine the source of the bleeding. It should be stated at the outset that *blood from the nose or mouth cannot be halted by any first aid method available to the owner. The bird should be transported to the veterinarian as soon as possible.*

When applying first aid for bleeding:

1. Always handle the bird gently and calmly.
2. Always observe the bird for at least one hour after the bleeding has stopped to make sure that it has not restarted.
3. If bleeding has not stopped after one hour of treatment, take the bird to the veterinarian immediately.
4. If any signs of listlessness, weakness, paralysis, or breathing difficulty are noted, take the bird to the doctor immediately.
5. If bleeding continues, necessitating a trip to the veterinarian, try to have another person drive so that you can continue to apply pressure to the bleeding area.

Bleeding from the beak may result from trauma such as a fight or flying into some object. It may also occur as a result of an improper attempt to trim the beak. Pack styptic powder into the bleeding area. If you have none available, cornstarch, baking soda, flour, or boric acid will also work. Direct pressure using a finger or gauze pad may also be necessary. If all else fails, searing the area with a red-hot needle may be tried. Keep the bird warm and quiet.

A blood feather is a feather in the process of growing in. It still has a nerve and blood supply. Occasionally a blood feather may be broken as a result of trauma or rough handling. Such a feather must be pulled completely out or it will continue to bleed, resulting in the bird's death. Use sturdy tweezers or a pair of needle-nosed pliers. Grasp the feather firmly and pull it out, always applying pressure in the direction in which the feather is growing. Take care not to tear the feather follicle. Such damage could prevent the regrowth of any subsequent new feathers. If blood is seen oozing from the feather follicle after the feather has been removed, apply styptic powder or use direct pressure with finger or gauze pad. Keep the bird quiet and warm. Continue to observe for further bleeding.

Cuts, abrasions, and bite wounds are usually a result of trauma, but may sometimes result from self-mutilation. Stop the bleeding first, using gentle pressure with a clean cloth or gauze pad. Dirt and feather debris may be gently removed with fine tweezers. Then, if the lesion is minor, cleanse the area gently with a 3 percent hydrogen peroxide solution, chlorhexidine (Nolvasan), or Betadine.

Keep the bird warm and quiet. Follow the guidelines for care of the sick and convalescent bird. Observe for shock or signs of wound infection. If either of these should occur, the bird should be seen without further delay by the veterinarian.

If there is even the smallest doubt as to the seriousness of the injury, stop the bleeding and have the bird seen by a veterinarian immediately.

One type of wound is considered a genuine emergency, no matter how small. This is a *cat bite*. Cats transmit with their bites a bacterium called *Pasteurella*. Birds are very susceptible to it and may die within twenty-four hours of Pasteurella septicemia. Therefore, lose no time in transporting any bird that has suffered a cat bite to the veterinarian, where it can receive appropriate antibiotic therapy.

Bleeding from the nails is treated in the same manner as bleeding from the beak. Pack the nail with a blood-clotting agent. Direct pressure may also be necessary. Keep the bird quiet and warm. Observe for at least an hour afterward to make sure that the bleeding has not recommenced.

Bleeding from the feet can be treated by using a clotting agent and applying direct pressure. Gentle cleansing is in order if it can be accomplished without restarting the bleeding. A word of caution is necessary here. Because the foot is a weight-bearing appendage, with the toes constantly being flexed and extended, it is extremely difficult to stop bleeding from the foot for any length of time. The bird must be watched constantly to be sure bleeding has not recommenced. If this is the case after one or two attempts to stop the bleeding, the bird should be taken promptly to the veterinarian, where a pressure bandage can be applied. Keep the bird warm and quiet. If it has difficult perching, follow the guidelines for special husbandry in Chapter 3 in the section on care of the sick and convalescent bird.

Conure Bleeding Syndrome is a condition suffered by various conure species. It is characterized by repeated nosebleeds and/or bleeding from the respiratory or digestive systems. The cause of this syndrome is unknown, although it is variously thought to be either virally caused or the result of a diet low in calcium and vitamin K (Rosskopf and Woerpel, 1987b). There is nothing that can be done at home for such a bird and it should be seen by an avian veterinarian immediately.

BLOOD IN THE STOOL: The reader may wish to review the section in Chapter 3 on interpretation of droppings. Blood in the stool, whether it be bright red or tarlike in color and consistency, always indicates a serious condition. The bird should be seen as soon as possible by an avian veterinarian. In the meantime, follow the guidelines in Chapter 3 for care of the sick and convalescent bird.

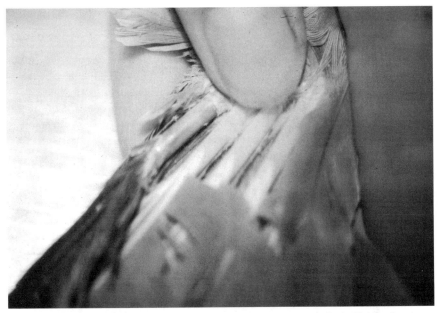

Blood feathers are so named because while growing they are supplied with blood vessels and nerves. Severing such a feather will result in hemorrhaging.

Peter Sakas, D.V.M.

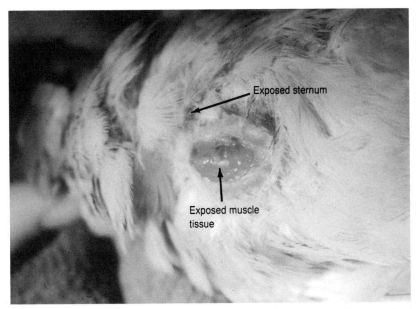

Exposed sternum

Exposed muscle tissue

Exposed breastbone (sternum) due to trauma. Such injuries are most often sustained by birds with improperly trimmed wings that cannot maintain balance and suffer falls from perches.

Peter Sakas, D.V.M.

BREATHING PROBLEMS: See Acute Respiratory Problems. Also, Cessation of Breathing.

BURNS: Burns may be caused by flame, electricity, hot grease or water, or by chemical means such as strong acids or bases (alkalis). An example of an acid would be hydrochloric (muriatic) acid; of a base, household chlorine bleach.

The following suggestions are for mild, superficial burns only. Any severe burn, no matter how small, should be seen immediately by an avian veterinarian.

According to Robert Kirk and Stephen Bistner (1969), the seriousness of burns may be estimated as follows:

> Group I: Superficial—variable damage to skin; swelling, redness, and blisters. Feathers may be singed but remain attached.
> Group II: Partial thickness—much more loss of skin than in Group I. Severe redness and swelling; dry, tan crust will follow. Feathers may remain intact; skin will slough off before healing can occur.
> Group III: Full thickness—entire skin destroyed. Feathers fall out. Lesion may be black or pearly white. Healing will not occur without grafting.

The following guidelines are suggested by Gary Gallerstein (1983):

1. Spray or flush the area with cool water.
2. If the burn has been caused by an acid, apply a thin coat of baking soda paste to the area.
3. If the burn has been caused by a base, the area can be treated with vinegar.
4. *Never* use ointment or butter on a burned area.

When caring for any burn, follow the guidelines for care of the sick and convalescent bird. Watch it carefully. If there is any tissue sloughing, or any indication whatsoever that the bird is experiencing shock, it should be seen immediately by an avian veterinarian.

Symptoms of shock are as follows:

Feathers fluffed
Listlessness
Rapid breathing
Weakness
Skin of legs and feet cool to touch
Unconsciousness

If any of the above are noted, take great pains to keep the bird warm and quiet while transporting it to the veterinarian.

If the burn has been caused by hot grease, sprinkle the area liberally with flour or cornstarch before rinsing with cool water (always being careful to keep these substances out of the bird's eyes and nose). This will make it easier to rinse away the grease from the burn, and will also prevent the grease from further contaminating the bird's feathers.

Follow the guidelines in Chapter 3 on care of the sick and convalescent bird.

CAT BITES: See Bleeding.

CESSATION OF BREATHING: According to Rosskopf and Woerpel (1987a), in the past, once a bird's heart had stopped beating, it was felt that nothing could be done. However, the authors cited have had several cases in which they were able to restore heart function and respiration in such situations. They have found that blowing into the bird's nostrils while holding its mouth shut has sometimes revived the patient. This is followed by the administration of oxygen and respiratory-stimulating drugs. They have also found intracardiac massage and intravenous administration of cardiac-stimulating drugs to be of help if the heart stops beating a second time, after the initial measures have been instituted.

For this kind of emergency, one needs the immediate, skilled help of an avian veterinarian if there is to be any chance at all for the bird's ultimate survival. However, owners who find themselves with a bird that has stopped breathing have nothing to lose and everything to gain by the immediate institution of artificial respiration. If someone can quickly take them to the veterinarian, resuscitation efforts can be continued en route.

CONVULSIONS: A convulsion consists of waves of involuntary spasms of the muscles. Legs, wings, head, feet, and body will jerk and twitch. The bird may lose consciousness. It will fall from the perch and may appear disoriented, even after the convulsion is over. According to Scott McDonald (1986), these episodes may last from several seconds to one or two minutes. The causes of seizures may include poisoning, nutritional deficiency, epilepsy, and infectious disease (bacterial, fungal, viral, and parasitic origin).

The care required is aimed at (1) keeping the bird safe during the actual convulsion and (2) preventing a recurrence (any forceful stimulus may trigger another episode).

1. If the bird is in its cage, remove all perches, food and water dishes, and toys.
2. If the bird is out of its cage, place it in a box padded with a towel.
3. After the convulsion is over, cover the cage to provide a dim environment.
4. Avoid all loud noises.
5. Keep the bird warm.
6. *Do not* attempt to give any medication.
7. *Do not* attempt to place any object in the bird's mouth.
8. Seek avian veterinary care immediately.

CROP BURNS: This occurs in babies being hand-fed, the result of too hot formula. The damage may not be apparent for one to two weeks following the

initial injury. At this time, the owner may note a foul odor, or food dribbling out through the neck. An opening in the neck can usually be seen upon inspection. Keep the bird warm and quiet and transport to the veterinarian immediately.

CROP EMPTYING PROBLEMS: These difficulties usually fall into one of three categories: crop impaction, sour crop, or crop stasis (loss of crop function, resulting in failure to empty). To some extent, all three conditions may be interrelated, especially in the case of a hand-fed baby parrot.

Where a hand-fed baby is concerned, an underlying bacterial or fungal problem is commonly the cause. Such an infection will create inflammation of the crop lining. The contents will empty sluggishly or not at all. The material thus retained will begin to ferment, hence the name "sour crop." If the crop contents remain for a long enough time, they will harden, causing a firm obstruction, or crop impaction. Crop impaction may also occur from the overeating of grit, or ingestion of a foreign object. A crop that has ceased functioning is then said to be static, hence the condition of crop stasis. In an adult bird, crop stasis may be caused by bacterial or fungal infection, frequently as a result of eating spoiled food.

In any of these three related problems, the owner may note a sour smell emanating from the bird's mouth. In a baby, you may observe that the crop fails to empty. When gently felt with the fingers, the crop may have a lumpy, hard consistency. The bird may regurgitate. In addition, it may present a fluffed, lethargic appearance.

There are several approaches to dealing with crop-emptying problems. For sour crop, Gallerstein (1984) recommends the use of Maalox or Di-Gel given orally, the dosage being the same as listed for Pepto-Bismol or Kaopectate (see Diarrhea). These preparations will soothe the irritated crop lining and help neutralize the acids produced by the fermentation of food in the crop. Gallerstein states that this treatment should be followed by a bland diet for several days.

In the matter of crop impaction, Gallerstein recommends giving a few drops of mineral oil in the mouth, waiting for a few minutes, then gently massaging the crop to break up the obstruction. He advises that if this procedure has been successful, it be followed by administration of Di-Gel or Maalox, and the feeding of a soft, bland diet for a few days.

Many breeders manually empty the crop in baby birds whose crops fail to empty, or which exhibit symptoms of sour crop. This is done by holding the bird so that the head is tilted downward, then gently expressing or "milking" the food from the crop. The bird should be allowed to rest frequently and *great care* should be taken to prevent choking. This procedure is very dangerous, with tremendous risk of aspiration. It *cannot* be recommended.

Some breeders use a feeding tube, with a syringe or suction bulb attached, that is inserted into the crop to aspirate the crop contents. This can be extremely risky, as it is easy to puncture the inflamed and delicate crop lining as well as the esophagus. Also, the tube can easily become clogged with food and fail to function.

Vomiting in a budgerigar. Note sticky, clumped feathers around beak and forehead.
Peter Sakas, D.V.M.

Distended crop on a cockatiel. Normally the crop should not be visible even immediately after the bird has eaten. *Peter Sakas, D.V.M.*

Crop fistulas will occur in young, hand-fed birds fed a too-hot formula. The result is burns and tissue sloughing clear through the chest wall.
Peter Sakas, D.V.M.

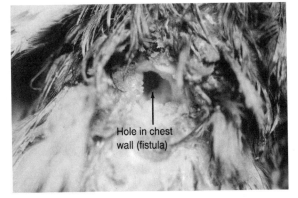

Hole in chest wall (fistula)

It is the author's opinion that any bird with a crop-emptying problem should be seen immediately by an avian veterinarian, rather than any attempt at first aid being made by the owner. There are several reasons for this:

1. Few bird owners have the skill to attempt successfully the manual emptying of a bird's crop.
2. In the case of crop impaction (especially in adult birds that may have swallowed a foreign object), manipulation of the crop could result in tears or punctures.
3. Any crop-emptying problem is usually caused by or accompanied by underlying infection.

Temporarily removing the crop contents or giving medication to soothe the crop can at best give only temporary relief. The bird requires the skill of an avian veterinarian and follow-up administration of appropriate antibiotics or antifungal medication.

DEHYDRATION: This condition is seen in birds that have suffered prolonged bouts of regurgitation/vomiting, diarrhea, or refusal to take food and liquid. Symptoms include weakness and depression. In severe cases, the eyes may appear sunken; the legs, feet, and wing tips feel cool to touch; and ridging of the skin over the sides of the toes may be present. This is a genuine emergency. Keep the bird warm and quiet and take it to an avian veterinarian without delay.

For birds that are reluctant to take fluids, but are taking *some* liquid, the suggestions outlined in Chapter 3 in the section on care of the sick and convalescent bird may be tried. Watch the bird closely and do not delay veterinary treatment if your attempts to increase the bird's fluid intake are unsuccessful.

DIARRHEA: Diarrhea is a symptom of underlying illness, not a disease. The following suggestions are made to forestall dehydration and make the bird more comfortable. Follow the guidelines for care of the sick and convalescent bird found in Chapter 3 and take the bird to an avian veterinarian as soon as possible, certainly within twenty-four to forty-eight hours, depending on the severity of the diarrhea and your success in alleviating it. In addition, remove fresh fruits and vegetables from the bird's diet, along with grit. Feed a bland, nonirritating diet. Joel Pasco (1983) suggests cooked rice, if the bird will accept it. Peanut butter and canned baby foods (chicken noodle, oatmeal/banana, etc.) may also be used, as well as baby pablum.

According to Gallerstein (1984), Kaopectate or Pepto-Bismol can be given, in the following dosages:

Budgerigars: 1–2 drops every four hours
Cockatiels: 2–3 drops every four hours
Amazons: 12–20 drops every four hours (0.6–1.0 cc)
Macaws and cockatoos: 20–40 drops every four hours (1–2 cc)

EARTHQUAKE SYNDROME: This syndrome is described by Rosskopf and Woerpel (1987). A series of earthquakes and aftershocks in southern California recently caused a great number of emergency avian trauma cases. These were the result of the birds flying in panic against the cage wires during these upheavals. Injuries included serious bruising, especially in wing tips, chest, and abdomen. Such birds need to be kept warm and quiet and seen by the veterinarian as soon as possible. The authors cited also recommend the use of a night light for several days after the earthquake to reassure birds and provide light should further geological disturbances occur.

EGG BINDING: This is a potentially life-threatening situation. If an egg is lodged against the bones of a hen's pelvis, the bird's kidneys could be crushed, causing the hen to go into shock and die. Another serious consequence arises from the compression of the outlets from the ureters (tubes conducting the urine from the kidneys to cloaca) and large intestine, thus making it impossible for the bird to urinate or pass feces. This situation can also cause the bird's death. Aside from the damage caused by mechanical blockage from the unpassed egg, the hen may exhaust herself in the attempt to lay her egg, which may also cause her death.

The signs that may indicate that the hen is egg bound are as follows (in a hen known to be laying or on the point of laying):

Weakness
Abdominal swelling
Squatting and straining
Paralysis or weakness in one or both legs
Breathing difficulty
Fluffed feathers
Appearance of egg at outlet of cloaca
Red mass of tissue protruding from cloaca

Any one or more of the above signs may be present. In addition, the owner may note the hen on the bottom of the cage in an obvious state of exhaustion, or the bird assuming a low, crouching posture on the perch.

Such a bird should be caught up very gently. Place the bird in a warm, steamy environment such as a bathroom in which the tub or shower has been allowed to run. Alternatively, the bird may be placed in a hospital cage with the heat adjusted to 85° to 90°F and the humidity adjusted to 60 percent. If neither of these alternatives is available, use a steam vaporizer directed into the bird's cage (being careful not to steam cook her) and use heating pads, electric blankets, light bulbs, or infrared lamps to increase the ambient air temperature (see Chapter 3 on care of the sick and convalescent bird). Clubb (1983b) suggests the use of wet toweling on the cage floor to increase humidity. This should be quite effective if a heating pad is being used *underneath* the entire cage. These wet heat treatments should be done intermittently for fifteen-to thirty-minute periods per treatment.

In addition, the hen will need a quick, easily available source of calcium, which no doubt has been seriously depleted in fruitless muscular contractions to expel her egg. She should also be supplied with calories to increase her energy level and combat exhaustion. Clipsham (1988b, 1988d) recommends the following preparations:

1. Dried milk or ground cuttlebone dissolved in water to which a few drops of white Karo syrup have been added (granulated sugar can substitute for the Karo syrup)
2. Neo-calglucon syrup (available from your pharmacist)
3. D-Ca-Phos powder dissolved in water (available from Fort Dodge Laboratories, 800 Fifth Street N.W., Fort Dodge, IA 50501)

The above treatments should be continued for no longer than twelve hours for a large bird, three to four hours for a small bird. If the egg has not been passed in that time, veterinary care should be sought without further delay.

FOREIGN OBJECT IN THE EYE: Occasionally a bird will get something in its eye, usually a piece of seed chaff. Placing a very small amount of sterile opthalmic ointment or sterile KY Jelly (available over the counter at most pharmacies) will do an excellent job of soothing irritated tissues and "floating" the offending object out. If the bird has experienced no relief in two to three hours, do not delay taking it to the veterinarian. The object may need to be removed with forceps and the bird placed on a follow-up course of antibiotics to guard against possible infection.

FRACTURES: According to Clubb (1983b), the most common sites for fractures are the humerus (upper arm or wing bone) and the radius and ulna (lower arm or wing bones). These are followed by fractures of the tibiotarsal bone (shin bone) and femur (upper leg, or thigh bone). Fractures are usually the result of trauma of some kind—flying into a mirror or window, fights with pets or other birds, or rough handling by its human companions.

There are basically three kinds of fractures: simple, compound, and comminuted. A simple fracture consists of a broken bone that does not protrude through the skin. A compound fracture consists of a broken bone that protrudes through the skin, often with extensive soft tissue damage. A comminuted fracture is a bone broken in many pieces; it may also be compound, but not necessarily. In addition, you may also hear the term "green stick fracture." This is a bone that is essentially cracked, but not broken all the way through. Such fractures often occur in a spiral fashion, usually as a result of the direction in which the traumatic stress has been brought to bear upon the injured extremity.

The primary object in treating a bird with a fracture is to prevent further damage, especially to surrounding soft tissue, nerves, and blood vessels. To this end:

1. Wrap the bird loosely with soft toweling to prevent movement of wings and legs.

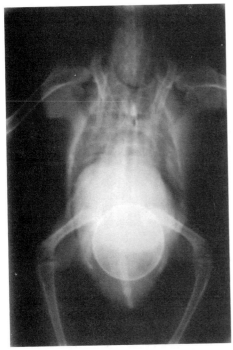

Front view X ray of an egg-bound hen.
Peter Sakas, D.V.M.

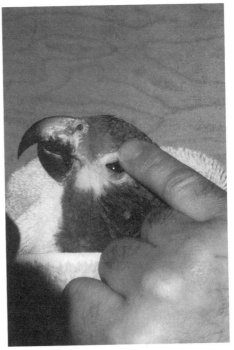

Physical examination of eyelid and eye in a Red-lored Amazon (*Amazona a. autumnalis*). *Peter Sakas, D.V.M.*

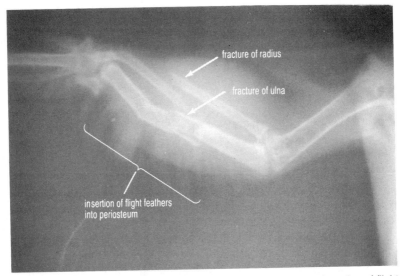

fracture of radius

fracture of ulna

insertion of flight feathers into periosteum

Fracture of both bones in lower wing (radius and ulna). Also, note insertion of flight feathers directly into bone covering (periosteum). This differs from body feathers, which have their origin in the skin. *Peter Sakas, D.V.M.*

95

2. Keep the bird warm and quiet.
3. Transport to the veterinarian immediately.

Never attempt to set a fracture yourself. Not only can more tissue damage be created, but your chance of making a functional repair that allows the bird full use of the injured extremity is so slight as to be nonexistent. A skilled avian veterinarian is required for this.

HEATSTROKE: Heatstroke occurs when the bird has been subjected to excessive heat, rendering its normal heat-regulating mechanisms useless. Placing the bird's cage in direct sun without shade or water, or leaving it in a humid, hot building or a car parked in the sun are all ways a bird may develop heatstroke. According to Sheldon Gerstenfeld (1981), old or fat birds are especially prone to heatstroke. Young babies are also at risk due to their immature temperature-regulating mechanisms.

If unable to rid its body of excessive heat in the usual ways, such as moving to a cooler place, panting, holding its wings away from its body, and drinking water, the bird will develop an abnormally high, exceedingly dangerous body temperature. The chance of death in such a situation is great, as is permanent brain damage due to death of brain cells by excessive body heat. The signs of heatstroke are heavy panting; outstretched wings; a fixed, staring expression; slobbering; profound weakness; hot, dry skin; and collapse.

The overriding concern in the first aid of heatstroke is to lower the bird's body temperature *immediately*. This can be accomplished in several ways:

1. Spray the feathers with alcohol (keep it away from the bird's face) or cold water. Be sure the feathers are wet right down to the skin.
2. Place the bird in an air-conditioned room or in front of a fan.
3. Immerse the bird's feet in cold water; or place cold water, a few drops at a time, in the bird's vent with a syringe or dropper to help lower internal temperature rapidly.
4. If the bird is conscious, allow it to drink—or give it manually—a *few* drops of water at a time.

There is always the danger of shock following heatstroke. Observe the bird carefully. When its panting has lessened and it appears more alert and comfortable, wrap it *loosely* and comfortably to prevent chill, keep it quiet, and take it to the veterinarian *immediately*.

LEG BAND PROBLEMS: Quite frequently birds catch their leg bands on cage wires. Leg bands also can become constrictive, thus causing obstruction in blood circulation to the foot, swelling, and tissue damage or death. These kinds of problems are genuine emergencies, and the bird should be taken to the veterinarian immediately. Never attempt to remove a leg band yourself. The risk of causing further tissue damage or breaking the bird's leg is very great.

If the bird has caught its leg on the cage wire, *do not attempt to disentangle*

Leg bands should be watched carefully for any sign of constriction. A too-tight leg band resulted in this damaged, swollen foot. Note also areas of dead tissue.

A bird suffering from heatstroke is in very great danger and its body temperature must be reduced quickly if the victim is to survive. Wetting the affected bird with cold water to the skin is one way to help an affected bird.   *M. Vogel*

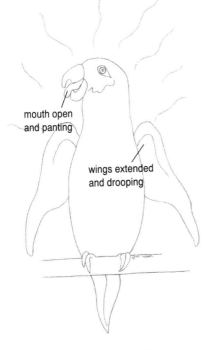

mouth open and panting

wings extended and drooping

The signs of overheating

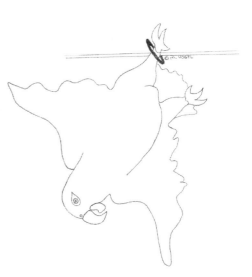

This bird's leg band has been caught on a cage wire. Constant watchfulness is necessary for mishaps of this kind in order to avoid more serious injury.

it. Have someone support the bird so as to lessen further strain on the already damaged leg and foot. With a pair of heavy wire cutters, cut the offending wire loose from the cage. Immediately transport the bird to the veterinarian for removal of the leg band and wire.

If the bird's leg and foot have become constricted by its leg band, take the bird to the veterinarian immediately.

Once the bird has been treated appropriately and is home recuperating, watch its leg and foot carefully. Birds often develop constricting scabs in this kind of injury. Such a scab can restrict blood flow as effectively as a constrictive leg band. If this should occur, the scab will have to be loosened, requiring another trip to the veterinarian.

Loss of Appetite: See Anorexia.

Night Fright: Nocturnal episodes of panic, flailing, and subsequent injury to wing tips, chest, and head have been observed by many avian veterinarians. These night panics seem most common in cockatiels, especially lutinos (Sakas, personal communication; Rosskopf and Woerpel, 1988). Rosskopf and Woerpel hypothesize that in the case of the the Lutino Cockatiel, this mutation may genetically lack the "locking mechanism" that allows the bird to remain secure on its perch while sleeping; the result is a loss of balance and panic in dark surroundings.

Other birds besides cockatiels may experience night frights and subsequent injury resulting from cage or aviary wires and various objects in their enclosures. Sudden noises, earthquakes, and the presence of such predators as cats, raccoons, opossums, or dogs may also contribute to the problem.

The use of a night light in the bird room or aviary will help the bird reorient itself quickly and without harm. Making outdoor aviaries secure against unwanted nocturnal visitors is also desirable. The immediate presence of a familiar owner and soft, soothing words are also of great benefit in calming birds that have experienced night fright.

Any bird that has sustained injuries resulting in bleeding, bruising, or fractures should receive immediate first aid or the attention of an avian veterinarian, depending upon the extent and severity of the injury.

Not Breathing: See Cessation of Breathing.

Oil Contamination of Feathers: Oil contamination of feathers poses a serious threat to birds because of the real danger of chilling and subsequent death. In order for the insulating properties of the feathers to be restored, all traces of oil must be removed.

The author suggests that the first step in the de-oiling process be a thorough dusting of the bird with cornstarch or flour. This will absorb a great deal of the offending substance, making it easier to wash off in subsequent steps. Take great care to keep the oil absorbative out of the bird's eyes and nose. A good way to accomplish this is to use a pillowcase, if the bird will tolerate it. Have someone assist you, so as to help with necessary restraint. Place a good amount of cornstarch or flour in the pillowcase, and encase the bird up to its neck. Then shake the oil absorbative over the bird's entire body—in much the same manner as you would dredge meat. Once the flour or cornstarch has been evenly distributed over the bird's body, it should remain on for at least thirty minutes to allow for the most complete absorption of oil. After this has been accomplished, gently brush off the excess material.

You are now ready to wash the bird. Fill a sink with warm water to a depth of three to four inches. Have at hand a mild detergent such as Dawn, plenty of soft towels, a blow dryer such as used in hair styling and drying, and an assistant. A sink spray attachment is also helpful.

Have your assistant restrain the bird. Gently wet its body, and apply a moderate amount of shampoo to the feathers. Distribute the shampoo over the bird's body, *working always with the direction of feather growth*. Be sure the feathers are wet and soaped right down to the skin. Rinse the soap away, again in the direction of feather growth, being sure no soap residue is left on the skin. Blot the bird dry with toweling. Finish the drying by using the blow dryer set at a comfortable temperature and placed a reasonable distance from the bird's body.

Allow the bird to rest in a very warm room or heated cage. Observe it carefully for any signs of shock (see Burns). If any such signs are noted, keep the bird warm and quiet and transport it to the veterinarian without delay.

If oil contamination is severe, the above process may need to be repeated over a period of several days. The author advises that the bird not be subjected to the procedure more than once in a twenty-four-hour period. Such a bird will, of course, need to be kept warm and every attention will need to be given to its nutritional and psychological status.

ON BOTTOM OF CAGE: Birds go to the bottoms of their cages and remain there because they are too sick and too weak to be anyplace else. A bird in this condition is usually very close to death, the result of a longstanding, undetected illness.

Take the bird to its veterinarian without delay. In the meantime, keep it warm and quiet and try to get the bird to take nourishment if this can be done without unnecessary stress (see Chapter 3 on the care of the sick and convalescent bird).

POISONING: Birds are curious creatures. If allowed the freedom of the house, unsupervised, it is more than likely that eventually the bird will ingest a harmful substance. In addition, birds are very sensitive to harmful fumes produced by household cleaning materials, paint, nonstick cooking surfaces (Teflon and Silverstone), flea products, aerosol insect repellents, and other such products. Faulty kerosene heaters, gas stoves and furnaces, and wood-burning fireplaces and stoves are also a source of fume poisoning.

There are basically two types of poisoning: poisoning due to ingested (eaten) materials, and poisoning due to inhalation (breathing) of fumes. In addition, the bird may have skin contact with poisonous or irritating materials.

First aid is divided into two sections: what to do when the veterinarian is immediately available, and procedures to follow when there is no veterinary care to be had. Tables 4-1 through 4-4 are provided to help owners treat their bird *if no veterinary care is available*. Extreme care must be taken when dealing with poisonings because first aid for one kind of poisoning is often absolutely contraindicated in another type.

Suspect poisoning if a potentially poisonous substance has been in use, or available to, your bird; if you observe a foreign substance on the bird's feathers;

TABLE 4-1. Common Poisonous Substances That Are Acids, Alkalis, or Petroleum Products

Dishwasher detergent	Oven cleaner
Drain cleaner	Paint remover
Floor polish	Paint thinner
Furniture polish	Shoe polish
Gasoline	Toilet bowl cleaner
Kerosene	Wax (floor or furniture)
Lye	Wood preservative

Source: Sheldon Gerstenfeld, *The Bird Care Book* (Reading, Mass.: Addison-Wesley, 1981).

TABLE 4-2. Sources of Lead Poisoning

Air rifle pellets	Galvanized chicken wire
Antiques	Glass ornaments (leaded)
Base of lightbulbs	Hardware cloth
Batteries	Lead-framed doors, windows
Bird toys (weighted)	Mirror backing
Bonemeal products	Paint (old)
Bullets and shotgun shot	Plaster (old)
Chronic exposure to leaded gasoline fumes	Putty
Costume jewelry	Sheetrock
Curtain weights	Solder
Dolomite	Unglazed ceramics
Fishing sinkers	Zippers (some types)
Foil from wine and champagne bottle seals	

Source: Adapted from Greg J. Harrison and Linda R. Harrison, eds., *Clinical Avian Medicine and Surgery* (Philadelphia: W. B. Saunders, 1986); and Peter Sakas, "Household Dangers to Pet Birds," Niles Animal Hospital, 7278 N. Milwaukee Avenue, Niles, IL 60648.

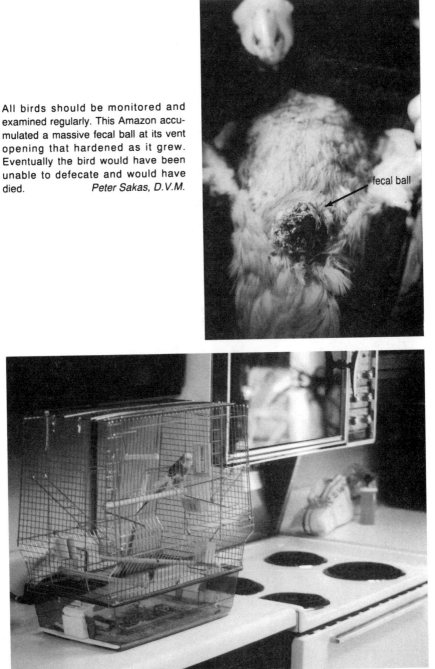

All birds should be monitored and examined regularly. This Amazon accumulated a massive fecal ball at its vent opening that hardened as it grew. Eventually the bird would have been unable to defecate and would have died.   *Peter Sakas, D.V.M.*

fecal ball

The kitchen may be a congenial spot for people, but it can be lethal for birds. Heat and the fumes of cooking, gas, or the new coated cookware will kill birds very quickly.

Peter Sakas, D.V.M.

TABLE 4-3. Common Household Poisons

Acetone	Lighter fluid
Ammonia	Linoleum (contains lead salts)
Antifreeze	Model glue
Ant syrup or paste	Mothballs
Arsenic	Muriatic acid
Bathroom bowl cleaner	Mushrooms
Bleach	Nail polish
Boric acid	Nail polish remover
Camphophenique	Oven cleaner
Carbon tetrachloride	Paint
Charcoal lighter	Paint remover
Clinitest tablets	Paint thinner
Copper and brass cleaners	Perfume
Corn and wart remover	Permanent wave solutions
Crayons	Pesticides
Deodorants	Photographic solutions
Detergents	Pine oil
Disinfectants	Plants
Drain cleaners	Prescription and nonprescription drugs
Epoxy glue	Red squill
Fabric softeners	Rodenticides
Garbage toxins	Rubbing alcohol
Garden sprays	Shaving lotion
Gasoline	Silver polish
Gun cleaner	Snail bait
Gunpowder	Spot remover
Hair dyes	Spray starch
Herbicides	Strychnine
Hexachlorophene (in some soaps)	Sulphuric acid
Indelible markers	Suntan lotion
Insecticides	Super Glue
Iodine	Turpentine
Kerosene	Weed killers
Matches (safety matches are nontoxic)	Window cleaners

Source: Adapted from Gary Gallerstein, *Bird Owner's Home Health and Care Handbook* (New York: Howell Book House, 1984); Sheldon Gerstenfeld, *The Bird Care Book* (Reading, Mass.: Addison-Wesley, 1981); and Margaret L. Petrak, ed., *Diseases of Cage and Aviary Birds*, 2nd ed. (Philadelphia: Lea and Febiger, 1982).

TABLE 4-4. Plants Considered Harmful to Birds

Plant Name	Scientific Name	Parts Known to Be Poisonous
Amaryllis	*Amaryllidaceae*	Bulbs
American yew	*Taxus canadensis*	Needles, seeds
Azalea	*Rhododendron occidentale*	Leaves

TABLE 4-4. Plants Considered Harmful to Birds *(cont.)*

Plant Name	Scientific Name	Parts Known to Be Poisonous
Balsam pear	*Memordica charantia*	Seeds, outer rind of fruit
Baneberry	*Actaia* spp.	Berries, roots
Bird of paradise	*Caesalpina gilliesii*	Seeds
Black locust	*Robinia pseudoacacia*	Bark, sprouts, foliage
Blue-green algae	*Schizophyceae* spp.	Some forms toxic
Boxwood	*Buxus sempervirens*	Leaves, stems
Buckthorn	*Rhamnus* spp.	Fruit, bark
Buttercup	*Ranunculus* spp.	Sap, bulbs
Calla lily	*Zantedeschia aethiopica*	Leaves
Caladium	*Caladium* spp.	Leaves
Castor bean (Castor oil plant)	*Ricinus communis*	Beans, leaves
Chalice vine	*Solandra* spp.	All parts
Cherry tree	*Prunus* spp.	Bark, twigs, leaves, pits
Christmas candle	*Pedilanthus tithymaloides*	Sap
Clematis	*Clematis* spp.	All parts
Coral plant	*Jatropha multifida*	Seeds
Cowslip	*Caltha polustris*	All parts
Daffodil	*Narcissus* spp.	Bulbs
Daphne	*Daphne* spp.	Berries
Datura	*Datura* spp.	Berries
Deadly amanita	*Amanita muscaria*	All parts
Death camas	*Zygadenis elegans*	All parts
Delphinium	*Delphinium* spp.	All parts
Dieffenbachia	*Dieffenbachia picta*	Leaves
Eggplant	*Solanaceae* spp.	All parts but fruit
Elephant's ear (Taro)	*Colocasis* spp.	Leaves, stem
English ivy	*Ilex aquafolium*	Berries, leaves
English yew	*Taxus baccata*	Needles, seeds
False henbane	*Veratrum woodii*	All parts
Fly agaric mushroom (deadly amanita)	*Amanita muscaria*	All parts
Foxglove	*Digitalis purpurea*	Leaves, seeds
Golden chain (laburnum)	*Laburnum anagyroides*	All parts, especially seeds
Hemlock, poison	*Conium* spp.	All parts, especially roots and seeds
Hemlock, water	*Conium* spp.	All parts, especially roots and seeds
Henbane	*Hyocyanamus niger*	Seeds
Holly	*Ilex* spp.	Berries
Horse chestnut	*Aesculus* spp.	Nuts, twigs
Hyacinth	*Hyacinthinus orientalis*	Bulbs
Hydrangea	*Hydrangea* spp.	Flower bud
Indian turnip (jack-in-the pulpit)	*Arisaema triphyllum*	All parts
Iris (blue flag)	*Iris* spp.	Bulbs
Jack-in-the-pulpit	*Arisaema triphyllum*	All parts
Japanese yew	*Taxus cuspidata*	Needles, seeds

TABLE 4-4. Plants Considered Harmful to Birds *(cont.)*

Plant Name	Scientific Name	Parts Known to Be Poisonous
Java bean (lima bean)	*Phaseolus lunatus*	Uncooked beans
Jerusalem cherry	*Solanum pseudocapsicum*	Berries
Jimsonweed (thornapple)	*Datura* spp.	Leaves, seeds
Juniper	*Juniperus virginiana*	Needles, stems, berries
Lantana	*Lantana* spp.	Immature berries
Larkspur	*Delphinium* spp.	All parts
Laurel	*Kalmia, Ledum, Rhodo-dendron* spp.	All parts
Lily-of-the-valley	*Convallaria majalis*	All parts, including the water in which they have been kept
Lobelia	*Lobelia* spp.	All parts
Locoweed	*Astragalus mollissimus*	All parts
Lords and ladies (cuckoopint)	*Arum* sp.	All parts
Marijuana	*Cannabis sativa*	Leaves
Mayapple	*Podophyllum* spp.	All parts, except fruit
Mescal bean	*Sophora* spp.	Seeds
Mistletoe	*Santalales* spp.	Berries
Mock orange	*Poncirus* spp.	Fruit
Monkshood	*Aconitum* spp.	Leaves, roots
Morning glory	*Ipomoea* spp.	All parts
Narcissus	*Narcissus* spp.	Bulbs
Nightshades (all types)	*Solanum* spp.	Berries, leaves
Oleander	*Nerium oleander*	Leaves, branches, nectar of blossoms
Philodendron	*Philodendron* spp.	Leaves, stem
Poison ivy	*Toxicodendron radicans*	Sap
Poison oak	*Toxicodendron quercifolium*	Sap
Poinsettia	*Euphorbia pulcherrima*	Leaves, flowers
Pokeweed (inkberry)	*Phytolacca americans*	Leaves, roots, immature berries
Potato	*Solanum tuberosum*	Eyes and new shoots
Privet	*Ligustrum volgare*	All parts, including berries
Rhododendron	*Rhododendron* spp.	All parts
Rhubarb	*Rheum rhaponticum*	Leaves
Rosary pea (Indian licorice)	*Abrus precatorius*	Seeds (seeds illegally imported to make necklaces and rosaries)
Skunk cabbage	*Symplocarpus foetidus*	All parts
Snowdrop	*Ornithogalum umbellatum*	All parts, especially buds
Snow-on-the-mountain (ghostweed)	*Euphorbia marginata*	All parts
Sweet pea	*Lathyrus latifolius*	Seeds and fruit
Tobacco	*Nicotinia* spp.	Leaves
Virginia creeper	*Pathenocissus quinquefolia*	Sap

This Blue-fronted Amazon is chewing on a towel. There is a danger from ingested towel fibers, which could create blockage in the crop or other parts of the bird's digestive tract.

Peter Sakas, D.V.M.

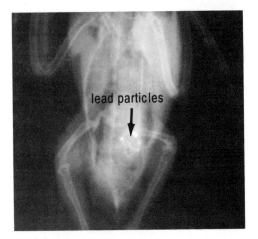

lead particles

This X ray shows lead in the gizzard (ventriculus).

Peter Sakas, D.V.M.

Ruptured neck (cervico-cephalic) air sac in an Umbrella Cockatoo resulting in subcutaneous emphysema.

Peter Sakas, D.V.M.

TABLE 4-4. **Plants Considered Harmful to Birds** *(cont.)*

Plant Name	Scientific Name	Parts Known to Be Poisonous
Western yew	*Taxus breviflora*	Needles, seeds
Wisteria	*Wisteria* spp.	All parts
Yam bean	*Pachyrhizus erosus*	Roots, immature pods

Source: Adapted from American Medical Association Handbook of Poisonous and Injurious Plants (Chicago: American Medical Association, 1985); R. Dean Axelson, *Caring for Your Pet Bird* (Poole-Dorset, England: Blandford Press, 1984); Gary Gallerstein, *Bird Owner's Home Health and Care Handbook* (New York: Howell Book House, 1984); Greg J. Harrison and Linda R. Harrison, eds., *Clinical Avian Medicine and Surgery* (Philadelphia): W. B. Saunders, 1986); and John M. Kingsbury, *Poisonous Plants of the United States and Canada* (Englewood Cliffs, N.J.: Prentice-Hall, 1964).

if you observe the bird chewing or eating harmful substances; or if you find chewed containers or household plants *and* see any of the following symptoms:

Sudden . . .
>vomiting
>diarrhea
>coughing
>loss of appetite
>breathing problems

Unusual thirst
Bloody urine or feces
Redness around the mouth
High-pitched voice
Weakness
Depression
Seizures
Uncoordinated body movements
Tremors
Paralysis
Coma

Regardless of whether veterinary care is or is not immediately available, there are four situations that *require immediate action before any other steps can be taken*:

Cessation of breathing: Apply mouth-to-nose artificial respiration.
Eye contact with poison: Flush with copious amounts of lukewarm water.
Skin contact with poison: Flush area with copious amounts of water.
Shock: Keep bird quiet and warm and transport to veterinarian without delay.

What to Do When Veterinary Care Is Available

1. If bird is overcome by fumes, ventilate the area immediately; if poison has been ingested, remove it to prevent further damage.

2. Keep the bird warm and quiet.
3. Obtain a sample of poison to take to the veterinarian.
4. Transport the bird to medical care immediately.

What to Do When No Veterinary Care Is Available

1. Consult Tables 4-1 through 4-4 to determine what category of poison the bird has ingested.
2. Call the nearest poison control center for information on how to treat the bird (this telephone number can be obtained from the operator or directory assistance).
3. *If the bird has swallowed acid, alkalis, or petroleum products*, make it swallow milk, mixed with Kaopectate or Pepto-Bismol; egg white; or olive oil. These substances will absorb the poison. A slurry of activated charcoal and mineral oil (obtained from your pharmacy) will also help absorb the poison (Gerstenfeld, 1981). *Do not make the bird vomit*—this will cause further damage to the esophagus and respiratory tissues, and could also cause choking and death.
4. *If the bird's mouth and skin appear burned*, apply a paste of sodium bicarbonate for acid burns; use vinegar for alkali burns (Gerstenfeld, 1981).
5. *If the bird has ingested a poison other than alkali, acid, or a petroleum-base product*, induce vomiting; use a mixture of equal parts water and 3 percent hydrogen peroxide *or* a mustard and water solution. Place a small amount at the back of the throat and repeat until regurgitation has occurred (Gerstenfeld, 1981).
6. *If fume poisoning has occurred*, remove the bird from the area immediately and ventilate. Administer artificial respiration if necessary.
7. *Watch for shock*, and treat by keeping the bird warm, quiet, and handling it as little as necessary. If handling is necessary, do not use abrupt movements or change the bird's posture suddenly. If the bird is conscious, encourage it to take small amounts of a high-caloric electrolyte solution (see Chapter 3 on care of the sick and convalescent bird).
8. If the poison cannot be identified, make bird swallow milk, milk of magnesia, egg whites mixed with Pepto-Bismol or Kaopectate, or a slurry of activated charcoal and mineral oil.
9. Even if veterinary care is not immediately available, continue trying to find it—even after treating the bird yourself. The aftereffects of poisoning and shock are ever-present dangers following poisoning.

Suggested Dosages for Egg-white or Activated Charcoal Mixture

Canary or budgerigar: 3–6 drops (0.15–0.3 cc)
Cockatiel or other small parrot: 1/5–2/5 teaspoon (1–2 cc)
Large parrots: 3/5–1/5 teaspoon 3–6 cc (Gallerstein 1984)

POOR APPETITE: See Anorexia.

SEIZURES: See Convulsions

SHOCK: Shock is defined as a syndrome in which the blood flow from the skin, extremities, and internal organs back to the heart is insufficient to maintain normal heart function and blood flow (of freshly oxygenated blood) back into the body. Shock occurs to some degree with every injury. It is particularly serious when it is a result of massive insult to the body, such as hemorrhage, infection, trauma (bites, lacerations, fractures), drug reactions, burns, poisoning, and dehydration.

The signs and symptoms in birds are as follows:

Feathers fluffed
Listlessness
Rapid breathing
Weakness
Skin of legs and feet cool to touch
Unconsciousness

Shock requires immediate attention.

1. Keep the bird quiet and warm.
2. Handle the bird as little as possible.
3. If the bird is quiet and will tolerate it, attempt to get it to take a high-caloric electrolyte solution (see Chapter 3 on sick and convalescent care of the bird).
4. Avoid sudden movements while handling the bird; do not change the bird's posture or position suddenly.
5. Notify veterinarian that you are on your way and transport the bird immediately.

When treating shock, your veterinarian will first provide constant heat, oxygen, fluid therapy (given intravenously or subcutaneously), and corticosteroids (similar in makeup and action to adrenalin). Once the bird is stable, the veterinarian will be concerned with treating the underlying cause of the shock.

SOUR CROP: See Crop-Emptying Problems.

SUBCUTANEOUS EMPHYSEMA: See Air Sac Rupture.

VOMITING/REGURGITATION: These symptoms are not always a sign of illness. Many birds will regurgitate to beloved owners or favorite toys as a sign of affection and courtship. If, however, the regurgitation behavior is accompanied by any signs of illness or other behavior change, the bird should be seen by a veterinarian as soon as possible. This is especially urgent when dealing with baby parrots.

Sometimes the owner will not actually see the bird in the act of regurgitation. However, you may notice that the feathers on the top of its head are sticky and soiled. This happens because birds have a tendency to shake their heads when regurgitating, thus throwing the vomitus over their heads.

Birds can rarely be said to vomit. Regurgitation of crop contents is the rule. The material brought up is undigested crop contents and is usually comprised of mucus, seeds or other food material, and fluid. It will have no appreciable odor if the bird is healthy or in the first stages of illness. In later stages, it may have a sour odor due to fermentation by the bacteria or fungi that have infected the crop. The rare vomitus of a bird will consist of digested or partially digested food. It will usually have an odor because the digestive breakdown of food by bacteria and enzymes will have begun or because of infection or malabsorption problems of underlying disease.

In treating the regurgitating bird at home, first remove any item to which the bird may be displaying courtship behavior. If the bird appears to be in otherwise good condition, a bland diet should be instituted (see Crop-Emptying Problems, also Chapter 3 on care of the sick and convalescent bird). Kaopectate or Pepto-Bismol may also be used (see Diarrhea).

If the bird persists in its regurgitation after twelve to twenty-four hours of treatment, or begins to show weakness or other signs of illness, it should be seen without further delay by the avian veterinarian. (See also Crop Emptying Problems.)

Budgerigar (*Melopsittacus undulatus*)

5

Disease Problems

$\mathbf{T}$HE MATERIAL IN THIS CHAPTER is presented so that the owner may have an up-to-date reference concerning various avian diseases. With the exception of those problems needing immediate care by the owner (discussed in Chapter 4 such as egg binding), these problems require the attention of an avian veterinarian. It is not the intention of the author to provide a treatment guide to avian diseases for the bird owner. Rather, the material contained herein is provided in order to help bird owners become informed partners in their bird's health care should the need arise.

In discussing avian disease, the following format has been used as fully as possible, given the present state of our knowledge:

Name of the disease
Causative agent (What caused the problem?)
Transmission (How did the bird acquire the problem?)
Symptoms
Laboratory work usually done to aid diagnosis
Treatment (What can be done for the problem?)
Prognosis (Will the bird recover fully? Will it recover partially? Will there
     be any lingering problems as a result of the initial disease?)

Preventative measures will also be covered, where possible.

ARTHRITIS: Arthritis is the inflammation of a joint, usually accompanied by pain, swelling, some loss of function of the affected joint, and, frequently, changes in the structure of the joint.

Causative Agent There are several causes of arthritis in the bird:

Aging: This form of arthritis is also called degenerative arthritis or osteoarthritis.

Gout: This condition involves the kidneys. Due to disease or organ failure, the kidneys are unable to excrete urates efficiently, resulting in a buildup of excess urates in the bloodstream and their subsequent deposition in the joints.

Infection: Various bacteria and mollicutes (very small, antibiotic-resistant organisms) can cause infection of joints. Among those implicated are *Streptococcus*, *E. coli*, *Salmonella*, *Pseudomonas*, *Proteus*, *Mycobacterium tuberculosis*, *Mycobacterium avium*, and *Mycoplasma*. Mollicutes are very small organisms, placed between the bacteria and the viruses in classification. They have no cell walls and are therefore resistant to antibiotics, which act on the cell wall. However, because of this lack, they are sensitive to most commonly used disinfectants. Mollicutes survive for only a few hours outside their hosts but can live for up to four days in drinking water, depending on the organism's strain. *Ureaplasma*, *acholeplasma*, and *mycoplasma* comprise the organisms classified as mollicutes.

Trauma: This may include bites, lacerations, or wire punctures. Poor flyers may habitually land on their hocks, thus eventually damaging this joint. Poorly set fractures, which thereby place undue stress on various joints, may cause arthritis.

Poor nutrition: Arthritis of the spine and rib cage may be due to poor nutrition (Altman, 1982).

Transmission Arthritis is not considered a communicable disease. It cannot be transmitted from one bird to another.

Symptoms

Lameness

Inflammation and/or swelling of the joint, sometimes accompanied by increased temperature in the affected limb

Obvious discomfort, often manifested by reluctance to use the affected joint

Loss of function in the affected joint

Laboratory Work

Radiographs: Will indicate abnormalities in the joint characteristic of arthritis. Typical findings may include narrowing of the normal space between bones constituting the joint, abnormal deposition of calcium in the joint, and swelling of the soft tissues surrounding the joint.

Culture and sensitivity: Indicated if infection of the joint is suspected.

Cytology: Examination of the fluid in joint will reveal the presence of various cells that may indicate acute or chronic infection, trauma, or gout.

1. Antibiotics for arthritis caused by infection.
2. Corticosteroids for arthritis of a noninfectious nature (for example, degenerative arthritis). These will reduce inflammation and pain.
3. For gouty arthritis, a diet low in protein to reduce the work load on the kidneys. Allopurinal (Zyloprim) may be given to prevent further deposition of urates in the joint spaces.
4. For obese birds with arthritis, weight reduction programs to lessen the burden on arthritic joints.

Prognosis For the most part, arthritis cannot be cured, only controlled. The exception is arthritis caused by infection. If caught early and treated with appropriate antibiotics, permanent damage can be prevented. Arthritis is a chronic disease that may require medication for the duration of the bird's life. In addition, special attention should be paid to husbandry: perch and food cup placement, special perch padding, and so forth.

ASPERGILLOSIS: This is a fungal disease, primarily of the lower respiratory tract (lungs and air sacs). The trachea, syrinx (voice box), and bronchi may be involved.

Causative Agent The fungus *Aspergillus fumigatus*. This fungus is everywhere in the environment. Birds, mammals, and humans are constantly exposed to its spores. These may be found in soil, rotted wood, aviary dust, and stored seeds and grains. It is found in corncob bedding, and for this reason such material is not recommended for use with parrots. *A. fumigatus* is also a component of the "green" mold seen on bread. It requires warmth, moisture, and protection from drying in order to flourish. Birds kept in crowded, damp situations, without adequate ventilation, often contract aspergillosis. Rotting food, bedding, and soiled utensils are also a potent source of infection.

Birds whose immune systems are not fully functional due to stress are particularly prone to *aspergillosis.* Such birds would include those recently through import/quarantine, those debilitated with other illnesses, victims of chronic malnutrition, or those that have undergone heavy breeding activities in less than peak physical health. Birds living in conditions of very low humidity and very high air dust content may also be at risk of aspergillosis.

Transmission Transmission is by inhalation of airborne spores. The bird must either be exposed to large numbers of spores, or be predisposed to the fungus because of a poorly functioning immune system. Spores may penetrate fresh or incubating eggs, killing the embryo (Patgiri, 1987).

Symptoms The signs and symptoms of aspergillosis are not specifically diagnostic for the disease. The course of illness may range from chronic debilitation with respiratory problems to acute illness and sudden death with few or no symptoms. Some of the following may be noted:

Wheezing (*commonly* heard)

Increased breathing rate, with much lengthened time to regain normal rate after exercise (a frequently noted symptom)

Respiratory gurgling or clicking

Voice changes: reluctance to talk or vocalize, decreased volume, change in tone of voice

Increased urination (polyuria)

Weight loss

Laboratory Work

Radiographs: Will indicate changes in air sacs and lungs.

Endoscopy: Allows visualization of lesions in air sacs, lungs, and trachea.

Hematology: Patients with aspergillosis show an increased number of white blood cells.

Cultures: Often done on material from trachea and/or air sacs. *Aspergillus* can be grown on a special type of growth medium called Sabouroud's agar. Fungus is difficult to grow, even with a special medium. Therefore, a negative culture does not necessarily indicate that the bird is free of *Aspergillus*.

Serology: Examination of the bird's blood serum may indicate the presence of antibodies to *Aspergillus*. However, there is some controversy as to the usefulness of serology in the detection of aspergillosis (Grimes, 1986).

Treatment   The antemortem (before death) diagnosis of aspergillosis is difficult because the symptoms are nonspecific and may indicate any one of a number of respiratory problems. In a bird that has died, necropsy will clearly demonstrate the *Aspergillus* mold growing in the lungs, air sacs, and other affected body organs.

Treatment of aspergillosis is expensive, time consuming, and carries no guarantee of success. The usual regimen consists of surgery to remove the colonies of *Aspergillus* growing in the bird, medication to kill the fungus, and supportive care (such as fluid therapy and tube feeding). Scott McDonald (1984) feels that surgery is probably the single most useful aspect in effecting recovery, in cases where the growth of *Aspergillus* is accessible to surgical intervention.

Medications that can be used (and are often used in combination) include ketoconazole (Nizoral), Amphotericin-B (Fungazone), flucytosine (Ancoban), and rifampicin. These medications may be delivered by injection into muscle, directly into the blood stream, or into the trachea. It is also common to deliver them through nebulization (aerosol therapy).

Good husbandry is essential, not only for the affected bird, but to prevent infection of other birds on the premises. This includes consistent cleanliness, good nutrition, disinfection of cages and aviaries, and the replacement of wooden articles such as perches, which cannot be sterilized.

Prognosis   In general, the outcome of aspergillosis is poor to grave, either with or without therapy (Campbell, 1986). Treatment may prolong life, but relapse and death are common. If therapy does succeed in a cure, the bird may sustain permanent damage to the organ or organs affected, thus becoming prone to problems related to those organs for the rest of its life. Generally speaking, the later in the course of illness treatment is started, the poorer the outlook for recovery.

AVIAN POX: This is a disease of the skin and the mucous membranes of the mouth and upper respiratory tract. The digestive tract may also be involved.

Causative Agent   Avian pox is caused by the virus *Avipoxvirus*, a member of the poxvirus group *Poxviridae*. Other members of this group cause smallpox, molluscum contagiosum in man, myxomatosis in rabbits, canary pox, and pigeon pox. The *Avipoxvirus* can survive in infected soil for up to one and one-half years. It is resistant to drying, humidity, and light, but steam heat kills it easily. Most disinfectants are not effective against it. However, some phenol disinfectants will kill it, especially at room temperature (Gerlach, 1986e).

Transmission   The *Avipoxvirus* lives in the saliva of mosquitoes. A bird is initially infected by a mosquito bite. Once infected, the bird may pass the disease to other birds via close contact and skin lesions through which the virus may pass. The *Avipoxvirus* cannot penetrate whole, healthy skin.

The ritual establishment of a "pecking order," which contributes to fights among birds and consequent skin trauma, is a prime way avian pox spreads in a flock situation. Birds with latent infections, or in a carrier state, shed the virus in feces, flaked skin cells, and feather quills. It has been noted that birds hatched immediately before "mosquito season" are particularly at risk of avian pox, probably because of their immature immune systems. The disease has a late summer and autumn seasonal incidence.

Symptoms   There are five forms of avian pox: cutaneous, diphtheroid, septicemic, coryzal, and tumor. The cutaneous and diphtheritic forms are commonly seen together, and may also be seen in conjunction with the septicemic form.

> *Cutaneous*: This is the most commonly seen form of avian pox. It is also called dry pox. Its lesions affect the unfeathered portions of the bird's skin and are in the form of papules (red, elevated, firm, well-defined sores). Early in the disease the lesions are yellow. They turn dark brown as the disease progresses. After a period of several weeks, the lesions form scabs and drop off, leaving (usually) no scarring.
>
> *Diphtheroid*: This form of avian pox is often called wet pox. Sores, similar to those of cutaneous pox, form in the mouth, throat, syrinx, and on the tongue. Because of the location of these sores, it is often difficult for the bird to eat and, sometimes, to breathe. In extreme cases, the bird may choke to death.
>
> *Septicemic*: This form is very sudden in onset. The sores seen in the

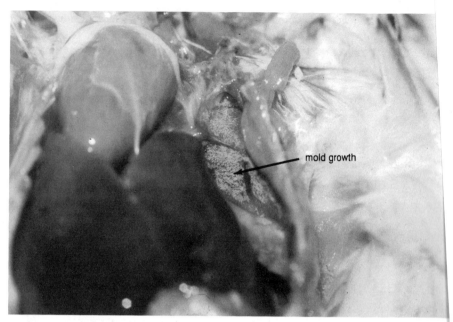

Aspergillus infection of lungs. Note the white mold growth.   *Peter Sakas, D.V.M.*

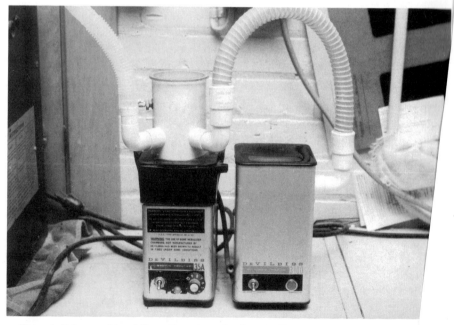

The nebulizing machine delivers fine, aerosolized spray of medication to a bird's lungs air sacs.   *Peter Sakas, D*

cutaneous and diphtheroid forms of avian pox are usually absent in the septic form. The bird appears lethargic, with ruffled feathers. There is a loss of appetite and the tongue and mucous membranes of the mouth may be cyanotic (blue in color, due to lack of oxygen in the blood). Within hours to three days, the bird will die.

Coryza: This form of avian pox has as its hallmark severe inflammation of the nasal membranes. There is copious nasal discharge. Often, there may be involvement of the membranes lining the upper and lower eyelids (conjunctivitis), with the eyelids pasted shut due to discharge.

Tumor: In this form of avian pox, tumors of the skin are the prevalent symptom.

Laboratory Work

Biopsy: Small pieces of tissue taken from skin and mucous membrane lesions may demonstrate evidence of *Avipoxvirus* infection.

Culture: Material taken from birds suffering the septicemic and coryzal forms is inoculated into embryonated chicken eggs. This procedure may demonstrate positive evidence of *Avipoxvirus* infection.

Culture of feces: May be done on apparently healthy birds in order to identify those individuals that are carriers of *Avipoxvirus*. Embryonated chicken eggs are used for this process.

Treatment There is no specific treatment for avian pox. Good husbandry and supportive care are offered while the disease runs its course.

1. Good husbandry, including the exclusion of mosquitoes from the aviary, is extremely important.
2. Vitamin A may be added to food or water.
3. Antibiotics may be prescribed if there is evidence of a secondary bacterial infection; antifungal medications may be given if secondary fungal infections are present.
4. Some veterinarians prescribe a mixture of iodine and glycerol to be applied to skin lesions. This is said to inhibit bacterial and fungal infection of the pox sores.
5. If the eyes are involved, an antibiotic eye salve may be prescribed to soothe the eyes and protect against secondary infectious problems.

Prognosis The prognosis varies, depending upon the form of avian pox the bird is suffering. The bird may recover completely, with no permanent damage. It may make an apparent recovery, only to relapse. In the septicemic form, death is almost inevitable. It causes sudden death in canaries, and is also a scourge in baby and juvenile Blue-fronted Amazons that have been imported. Some kinds of permanent damage due to avian pox include eyelid deformities or depigmentation, inflammation of the cornea or iris, corneal scarring, iris adhesions, scarring of the lining of the eyelids, and permanent drooping of the eyelids (Karpinski and Clubb, 1986).

AVITAMINOSIS A (HYPOVITAMINOSIS A, VITAMIN A DEFICIENCY): This is a condition in which the bird receives far less vitamin A in its diet than is needed for healthy body functioning. Because vitamin A is needed for the health and maintenance of skin (both outside and inside the body), good vision, skeletal development, and reproductive success, any or all of these body systems may be affected to a severe degree by insufficient vitamin A.

It may be surprising to some readers to learn that there is skin (epithelium) on the inside of a bird's body as well as on the outside. Such tissue is found lining nasal cavities, sinuses, mouth, sense organs, blood and lymph vessels, abdominal cavity, kidneys, joint cavities, throat, ear canals, trachea, lungs, bronchi, thyroid and parathyroid glands, large and small intestines, ovaries, testicles, and the thymus gland. So it is not surprising that a lack of vitamin A can manifest itself in many ways, some of them very severe.

The basic mechanisms of avitaminosis A are (1) a weakening of the skin barrier to pathogens such as bacteria, viruses, and fungi; and (2) a failure of the skin to function in its assigned role in the body due to cell changes caused by a lack of vitamin A. The latter particularly applies to the skin *inside* the bird's body.

Vitamin A deficiency is particularly prevalent in all Amazon Parrots.

Causative Agent   This condition is caused by a lack of vitamin A, usually as the result of a dietary deficiency. Seed diets are notorious causes of this problem because they contain virtually no vitamin A. There are some diseases affecting the gut that prevent absorption of and use by the body of vitamin A from dietary sources (tumors, tubercular lesions of the intestine, for example). However, these are rare. The main culprit is a poor diet.

Transmission   This is not an infectious disease, and therefore cannot be transmitted from one bird to another.

Symptoms   The symptoms vary, depending upon the severity of the vitamin A deficiency, its duration, the age of the bird, and the parts of the body affected.

The following are warning signs that vitamin A is seriously lacking in the bird's diet:

Chronic runny nose
Visual impairment that appears to worsen over time
Recurrent *Candida* infections
Frequent sneezing
Poor fertility and/or hatchability

In many cases, the most common symptom is that of sores in the mouth. These are seen on the roof of the mouth, the edges of the choanal slit, and under the tongue. They appear as cheesy, white lumps or plaques. The bird may have difficulty eating and experience a loss of appetite. Where there is sinus and nasal cavity involvement, severe swelling around the eyes may be noted, as well as discharge from the nose and eyes.

This sick budgerigar shows some of the classic symtoms of illness—horizontal posture on the perch, extended neck, and fluffed-out feathers. *Peter Sakas, D.V.M.*

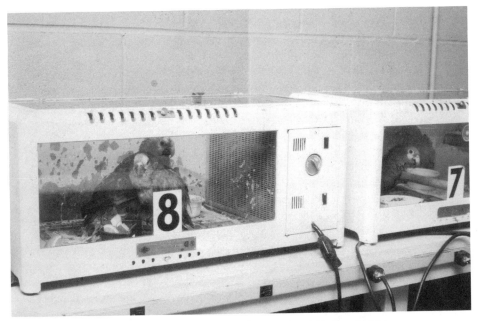

Sick birds often respond well to the environment in premature infant incubators. *Peter Sakas, D.V.M.*

119

If the vitamin A deficiency is severe enough, the lining of the syrinx may become thickened. This thickening will interfere with the free passage of air into the lungs and air sacs, and the bird will experience breathing problems: intolerance to exercise, tail bobbing, lack of stamina, neck stretching, and listlessness.

Vitamin A deficiency may also cause foot problems. It is thought to be a contributing cause of bumblefoot (pododermatitis). Calluses and corns may be a problem, especially in big, heavy-bodied birds such as macaws, whose feet must bear a proportionately larger weight load than those of other birds.

Birds fed a diet deficient in vitamin A may fail to produce fertile eggs, due to low sperm count in the male or defective ova in the hen. Because vitamin A is so essential to the growth and development of embryos, eggs may fail to hatch or newborn chicks may not survive.

In severe, long-standing cases of vitamin A deficiency, the kidney may fail to function properly. Gout may result from such a situation. The kidneys may fail entirely and become unable to eliminate urates and urine.

Laboratory Work

> *Culture and sensitivity*: May be done if secondary bacterial and/or fungal problems are suspected.
>
> *Serum chemistries*: May be done if liver or kidney problems are suspected.

Treatment

> 1. *Vitamin A supplementation*: This may be done orally, with preparations of vitamin A and D_3 If there is gut involvement that would prevent proper absorption of vitamin A, oral preparations cannot be used. In these cases, or with birds having severe and long-standing deficiencies, an injectable preparation of vitamin A and D_3 (Injacom) can be used.
> 2. *Cod-liver oil supplementation*: may be prescribed as a food additive. It is quite effective, but spoils easily. Any food treated with cod-liver oil will need to be discarded after twelve hours.
> 3. *Curettage*: This is the surgical removal of the cheeselike lesions that are sometimes found in the mouths and sinuses of affected birds. This procedure is reserved for those individuals in which such lesions interfere seriously with eating, breathing, or vision.
> 4. *Dietary change*: A complete and lifelong change in diet is absolutely essential for the bird with vitamin A deficiency. Such a change will include the radical diminution of the seed portion of the bird's food, and the inclusion of those foods known to be high in vitamin A content. *Animal sources of vitamin A*: liver and egg yolk; *vegetable sources of vitamin A*: spinach, parsely, broccoli, endive, yams/sweet potatoes, carrots, squash, and red peppers; *fruit sources of vitamin A*: peaches, apricots, cantaloupe, and papaya.

In general, all deep green and deep yellow/orange plant sources contain significant amounts of vitamin A. The avian veterinarian will advise the client in the preparation of suitable diet for the vitamin A–deficient bird.

Prognosis   If the bird is suffering a short-term, uncomplicated vitamin A deficiency, its recovery within three to seven days of therapy should be dramatic. Unfortunately, many birds are the victims of long-standing deficiencies, with secondary bacterial and/or fungal infections and organ involvement. Additional treatment of such conditions will be necessary before the bird can be returned to health. In the case of kidney or other organ involvement, some permanent, irreversible damage may have occurred. The nature of such damage and its implications cannot be generalized, and must be determined for the individual.

BLEEDING CONURE SYNDROME (HEMORRHAGIC CONURE SYNDROME, ERYTHEMIC MYELOSIS):   This condition, is known as BCS, is a malignancy of the red blood cell–forming tissues in the bone marrow. At the time of this writing, it has been reported only to occur in conures; no other species have been diagnosed with this disease. It most often affects young conures, or newborn chicks, although cases have occurred in older birds.

Hemorrhagic Conure Syndrome bears a close resemblance to a disease that occurs in domestic chickens—erythroblastosis.

Causative Agent   This disease is thought to be caused by a virus. For the present, however, this hypothesis remains unproven.

Transmission   Because the infectious origin of BCS has yet to be proven, it cannot be said with any certainty that it is infectious. It is known that the virus that causes the similar disease in chickens can be transmitted through the egg.

Given the above, it is no doubt a wise precaution to isolate any conure suspected of having BCS from other birds in the home and aviary. In view of the fact that egg contamination is at least a possibility, and that newly hatched conure chicks are especially vulnerable to BCS, it would also be advisable to refrain from mixing conure eggs from different clutches if artificially incubating them. Nor would it be wise to mix newborns from different clutches while hand feeding.

Symptoms   One or more of the following symptoms may be noted:

> Nosebleed
> Shortness of breath
> Weight loss
> Intermittent polyuria and/or diarrhea
> Uncoordinated body movements of wings, legs, and head
> Trancelike posture on the perch
> Extreme weakness

Laboratory Work

> *Hematology*: Because this disease affects the bone marrow's ability to produce healthy, mature, fully functioning red cells, several abnormal

findings are routinely found: a highly elevated white blood cell count, a low packed cell volume, or many immature red blood cells circulating in the blood. The latter two findings affect the delivery of adequate oxygen to body cells. It is for this reason that symptoms of weakness and shortness of breath are seen. The cerebellum of the brain is the seat of muscular coordination. If it lacks adequate oxygen, then symptoms of uncoordinated body movements are found.

Serum chemistries: will reveal elevated SGOT and creatinine levels and decreased blood sugar, calcium, and total protein levels.

Bone marrow aspiration: The literature does not record this procedure as having yet been done to facilitate the diagnosis of BCS. However, it is not unlikely that it may be employed in the future (Campbell, 1988).

The above laboratory tests are performed on the living bird. However, much of our knowledge of how BCS affects its victims has been found from necropsies of dead birds. The findings are interesting and some of them are included here:

Abnormal lesions of the bone marrow
Immature, malignant red blood cells in the liver and spleen
Hemorrhage into the lungs and pectoral muscles
Inflammation of the thin membrane encasing the heart (pericardium)
Rupture of the atrium of the heart
Death of some portion of the liver
Pneumonia
Degeneration of the kidney cells

Treatment Some or all of the following may be selected, depending upon the bird and its clinical state when presented to the veterinarian.

Antibiotic injections
Steroid injections
Vitamin B-complex injections
Calcium/phosphorus preparation injections (Calphosan)
Tube feedings and other supportive care, when necessary

Prognosis The outlook for BCS is very grave. Until recently, the disease was invariably fatal. The bird would rally, given treatment, only to succumb when the disease reasserted itself. According to Walter Rosskopf and Richard Woerpel (1985b), many birds can now be saved using a combination of vitamin K and Calphosan. Rosskopf feels that the calcium is the single biggest factor in the success of his treatment of birds with BCS.

BUDGERIGAR FLEDGLING DISEASE (BFD, PARROT PAPOVAVIRUS): This is a virally caused disease of parrot nestlings and fledglings. It occurs most often in hand-fed babies, although occasionally it is seen in the young of parent-fed birds. The disease is a severe one, with death occurring around twenty-one days of

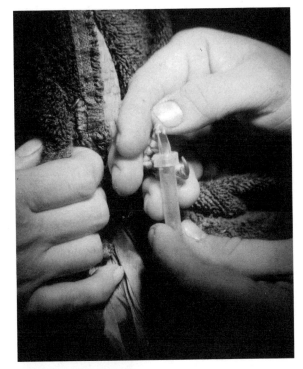

To collect a blood sample, the avian veterinarian will clip a toenail short and take the sample in a small tube called a microtainer.

Peter Sakas, D.V.M.

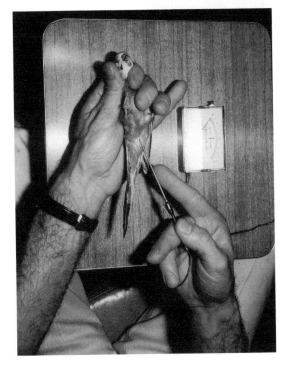

A bird's temperature is taken with an electronic temperature probe. The probe is placed in the bird's vent and the reading appears on the sealed device at right.

T. J. LaFeber

age, with a range of twenty-one to fifty-six days (Gerlach, 1986e). The mortality rate is reported to be approximately 70 percent (Stunkard, 1984). The exact relationship between hand feeding and the occurrence of BFD is not known (Graham and Calnek, 1987).

Birds of many species are affected, although the disease was first noted in budgerigars. Other species documented to have been affected are macaws, Amazons, conures, African Grays, cockatoos, and Eclectus Parrots.

Causative Agent *Papovavirus* is the causative agent. This virus is a member of the family *Papovaviridae*, other members of which cause papilloma infections in various parrot species. The *Papovavirus* is very resistant to heat and freeze-thawing. Most disinfectants are ineffective against it. One-Stroke-Environ is the exception (Gerlach, 1986e; Clubb and Davis, 1984).

Transmission Several routes are thought to be involved in the spread of BFD:

1. Regurgitation of virus-laden crop skin cells of the parents to their offspring
2. Release of feather dust from feather follicles containing the virus, and subsequent inhalation by potential victims
3. Exhalation of virus by infected birds, and subsequent inhalation by potential victims
4. Excretion of the virus from the kidneys via droppings (both oral and respiratory routes are possible here).
5. Transmission of the virus by an infected hen to her eggs. It is felt that a subclinical disease state is also possible, with the bird remaining asymptomatic until stressed, by severe weather or breeding activity, for example (Wainwright et al., 1987).

Symptoms The symptoms of BFD divide themselves into two major groups, which are dependent upon the form the disease takes: peracute (rapidly fatal) or chronic. There is, of course, overlap of symptoms between the two forms. One symptom is considered diagnostic and has great practical value in making a preliminary determination of BFD: feather follicle hemorrhage (Gerlach, 1986e; Clubb and Davis, 1984). The plucking of a feather from a bird with BFD will cause excessive hemorrhage.

The following are symptoms of rapidly fatal BFD:

Reduction in weight gain
Prolonged crop-emptying time
Vomiting
Distended belly
Red skin color
Depression and "glassy" eye appearance
Anorexia and dehydration
Weakness
Breathing difficulty

Areas of hemorrhage under the skin; hemorrhage following feather removal
Death within twenty-four to twenty-six hours

The disease may follow a more chronic course, with birds either recovering or dying. The symptoms are as follows:

Subnormal weight
Maldigestion and slow gut-transit time
Severe polyuria; vent feathers may be stained with urine rather than feces
Secondary yeast infections, usually candidiasis
Abnormal feathering, many times taking the form of retarded growth of tail and contour feathers (in very young birds, lack of, or malformation of down feathers may occur)
Depression
Failure to wean at the normal age for the species

Laboratory Work

Culture: Culture of various materials from infected birds is not always successful except in the case of budgerigars (Gerlach, 1986e). However, Graham has had some success with other species using both chick and budgerigar embryo cells as the culture medium (Graham and Calnek, 1987).
Serology: Using the fluorescent antibody test, it has been possible to detect serum antibodies against *Papovavirus* in infected birds.
Serum chemistries: These will often show elevated liver enzymes, indicating liver involvement and damage.

Treatment   There is no treatment for BFD. The disease runs its course, the birds either dying or surviving. According to Clubb and Davis (1984), the disease appears to be self-limiting.

Prognosis   The prognosis is very grave. Mortality rates range from 30 to 70 percent among young birds with the chronic form. Some may survive. Of these, a certain number will always have feather defects (Wainwright et al., 1987). Some birds surviving to adulthood will become carriers, thus becoming a source of infection of their own young and other birds in the collection or aviary. Other individuals succeed in completely eliminating the virus from their bodies, becoming in all respects healthy birds.
Several methods of controlling BFD in breeding flocks have been employed:

1. Complete depopulation of the aviary, followed by stringent disinfection with a product such as One-Stroke-Environ. In ninety days, new birds are purchased and established in the aviary. The breeding flock remains closed (no introduction of new stock). No visitors are allowed in the breeding aviary.
2. In birds such as budgerigars, which breed all year round, a disruption

of the breeding cycle followed by complete cleaning and disinfection may interrupt the cycle of the virus. (It is thought that, in those parrot species that breed seasonally, this circumstance may break the virus's life cycle and allow for natural control of BFD.)

3. Adult birds that are negative for BFD should not be introduced into an infected aviary. Likewise, healthy babies should not be brought into an infected nursery.

4. When considering the purchase of additional breeding stock, aviculturists should review past breeding records of the birds they contemplate acquiring. Those that have lost young in the pinfeather stage during the past breeding year should not be purchased.

5. Serologic testing of birds being considered should be done before placing them in the breeding aviary.

BUMBLEFOOT (PODODERMATITIS): This is a condition in which the underside of the foot becomes infected. One or both feet may be involved. The infection may occur because of previous injury to the foot (fights, abrasion from sandpaper perches, or overgrown talons that curve around and puncture the foot). Poor nutrition, especially a deficiency of vitamin A, is thought to contribute to the condition. Lack of proper sanitation also causes an increased risk of bumblefoot.

Infection may spread from the initial site to other parts of the foot. It may then spread to the tendons and joints and cause infections in these areas. If the infecting organism gains access to the bloodstream, it may travel to the kidneys and cause damage. When the infection is untreated, generalized ill health and possible death may result.

Causative Agent E. coli and S. aureus are frequently the agents cultured from bumblefoot lesions. Poor nutrition and sanitation and prior foot injury are contributory to bumblefoot.

Transmission Bumblefoot cannot be transmitted, in the usual sense, to other birds. However, if the affected bird is housed with others in conditions of filth and poor nutrition, and contaminates communal perches with drainage from its foot lesions, it is possible that another bird with cuts or abrasions on its feet could also develop bumblefoot.

Symptoms

Swelling and enlargement of the bottom side of the foot
Pain
Lameness
Obvious lesions (in some instances the infection is generalized throughout the tissues of foot [cellulitis], in which case no discreet lesion will be seen).

Laboratory Work Culture and sensitivity of the puslike material from the foot lesions is done to determine appropriate antibiotic therapy.

Hock sores will form on the legs of birds whose cages are fitted with perches of the wrong size or improper material.

Peter Sakas, D.V.M.

In a typical avian hospital, the range of treatment approaches in the intensive care unit will be as varied as the needs of the patients.

Peter Sakas, D.V.M.

Treatment

1. Appropriate oral and systemic antibiotics.
2. Vigorous cleansing of the foot with the appropriate disinfectant.
3. Appropriate perching facilities while the foot heals. Greg Harrison (1986b) states that great success has been had using padded perches soaked in chlorhexidine (Nolvasan). Patrick Redig (1987) suggests foam perching surfaces covered with clean linens and changed daily. Artificial or natural sheepskin also provides a soft, readily cleaned surface that can be affixed to perches.
4. Scrupulous attention to sanitation and nutrition.
5. Application of appropriate topical medication to foot.
6. Surgery to remove any serious abscesses on the foot, followed by bandaging (which must be changed frequently).

Prognosis The prognosis varies with the severity of the infection. Mild to moderate cases respond well to treatment. Severe cases, especially those requiring surgery, are more likely to have less successful outcomes. This is almost entirely due to the fact that the foot must be in constant use while healing occurs. Redig (1987) gives an estimate of four to six weeks postsurgery for those cases where healing occurs in a relatively unimpeded fashion.

In untreated cases, toes or even the entire foot may be lost. Joint and tendon damage may occur, and there may be kidney involvement. Death can be the end of such a sorry progression.

CANCER: See Neoplasm:

CANDIDIASIS: This is usually a fungal disease of the upper digestive tract (mouth, crop, esophagus). The proventriculus and ventriculus may also be affected. The lower intestinal tract is sometimes involved, especially the duodenum (the first part of the small intestine, connecting with the outlet of the gizzard) (Clubb, 1983a). The beak, eyes, skin, lungs, and air sacs are more rarely affected.

Candidiasis is found in all parrot species, but is especially a problem in hand-fed babies. In this age group, it is a common cause of crop impaction and death. Clubb has found that *Giardia* often exists in birds having candidiasis.

Causative Agent The causative agent of candidiasis is *Candida albicans*, a fungus. Occasionally, other *Candida* species are involved in the infection.

C. albicans is found everywhere in the environment. It can also be cultured in small numbers from healthy birds. It is therefore an opportunistic pathogen, able to cause disease only when the bird's immune system has been compromised in some way.

Predisposing factors include:

Extreme youth: Baby birds' immune systems are not fully developed and are therefore less able to fend off an overgrowth of *C. albicans*.
Extended antibiotic therapy, especially of the tetracycline group: These

drugs supply nitrogen in abundance, which *C. albicans* needs in order to flourish (Paster, 1983a). There is also much evidence to indicate that prolonged antibiotic therapy destroys a bird's normal digestive tract flora, thus leaving the body open to *C. albicans* overgrowth. Birds newly out of quarantine, where they have been treated with chlortetracycline-impregnated pellets, frequently are victims of candidiasis.

Vitamin A deficiency: Skin cells weakened by a lack of vitamin A are unable to provide an effective barrier to *C. albicans*.

Moldy food: This is especially common in sprouts of any kind, which may be virtually loaded with *Candida*.

Poor sanitation: Allows the bird's environment to contain abnormally high numbers of *Candida*. The greater the number of pathogens, the greater the bird's exposure and, therefore, the greater its chances of contracting candidiasis.

Immunosuppression: A weak immune system may be caused by a prior and/or coexisting bacterial, viral, fungal, or parasitic disease.

It is interesting to note that *C. albicans* is the organism that causes "thrush" in human infants. In both baby parrots and baby humans, candidiasis is a problem of extreme youth, for the most part. Clubb (1983a) states that young parrots outgrow their tendency to candidiasis as they mature, all other things (such as sanitation, good nutrition, general good health) being equal.

Transmission Candidiasis can be transmitted by improperly cleaned and disinfected feeding implements, and contaminated formula. It is therefore extremely important to practice a high degree of sanitation in the psittacine nursery. Parents feeding their nestlings may also transmit *Candida* to their young via regurgitated food, if they themselves have candidiasis.

Symptoms Symptoms vary with the length of infection, its severity, and the body systems affected. Many times, white, plaquelike mouth lesions will be noted. In hand-fed babies, the breeder may observe delayed or absent crop emptying. According to Terry Campbell (1986a), a general malaise may be the only sign of candidiasis. The following may also be present:

Weight loss or reduced weight (the *Candida* organism interferes with the proper absorption of nutrients by the gut)
Dilated or thickened crop
Frequent regurgitation
Diarrhea
Sudden death (occasional)

In addition, the following less common symptoms may be seen:

Ocular discharge (if the eyes are affected)
Breathing problems (if lungs and air sacs are involved)
Deformity of the beak (*Candida* grows between the horny tissue of the upper beak and the epithelium, thus creating the deformity)

Microscopic examination: Material from mouth lesions and/or feces is examined for presence of *C. albicans*.

Culture: Material from mouth lesions and/or feces may be cultured to detect *C. albicans*.

Insufflation and illumination of the crop: Allows visualization of crop lesions caused by *C. albicans*.

Treatment   One or several of the following may be used by the avian veterinarian in the treatment of candidiasis:

Mycostatin (Nystatin): Antifungal medication

Flucytosine (Ancoban): Antifungal medication

Amphotericin-B location: Antifungal medication for topical use in the mouth

Amphotericin-B ointment: Antifungal medication for topical use in the eyes

Chlorhexadine (Nolvasan): Used in the drinking water in proper dilution, usually for adult birds; can also be added to hand-feeding formula for babies (*Do not* attempt this unless under a veterinarian's direction)

Lactobacillus: To help reestablish normal intestinal flora

Ketoconazole (Nizoral): Antifungal medication, often used for cases that do not respond to the above medications (It is expensive and is often administered by gavage [Clubb, 1983a])

Levamisole: An immune system stimulant

Vitamin A therapy

Supportive therapy: Force feeding, if necessary; antibiotics or other medications if a second disease coexists along with the candidiasis

The approach to treating candidiasis also varies based upon whether a single bird or an entire flock is to be treated. Things to consider are the expense, ease of administration (wild versus hand-fed birds), age of the birds, and degree of stress likely to be caused by the treatment mode being considered. It is important to note that whenever a baby bird is on antibiotics it should also be on prophylactic mycostatin. It is appropriate for the owner to request this of the veterinarian.

Prognosis   The outcome of treatment is dependent upon the length and severity of the infection, the bird's age, other complicating factors (such as another coexisting disease), and the body systems affected. Generally, uncomplicated candidiasis of short standing, and involving only the mouth and crop, is easily cured. If the lower gut is involved, the outlook is not quite as bright. But with aggressive therapy, a cure may well be affected. When the infection involves the skin, beak, lungs, air sacs, or eyes, the outlook is much more guarded.

Prevention of candidiasis is much easier than a cure. Good sanitation is of paramount importance for all birds, but especially in the psittacine nursery.

It may be hard to believe that the tiny bird in these photos will grow up to become the same as the stunning Red-tailed Black Cockatoo shown on the frontispiece of this book. The photo above right shows the bird shortly after birth. Below right, the same bird, with a little growth and starting to "pin out."

Bill Wegner,
Malibu Exotics

Discolored feathers in an Amazon indicating poor nutrition, inadequate caging, and lack of bathing facilities.
Peter Sakas, D.V.M.

131

Thorough cleaning and disinfection of *all* feeding implements after *each* feeding, with a disinfectant such as chlorhexadine, are a must. Each baby should have its own feeding implement. Never save formula from one feeding to the next. If formula is made in large batches, freeze all that will not be used and thaw only enough for each feeding. Putting the formula in ice-cube trays greatly facilitates this. Isolate any baby appearing ill, and care for it after the healthy youngsters have been taken care of, always remembering to wash your hands well.

Provide good nutrition to all birds. Avoid overuse of antibiotics. Some veterinarians now recommend the addition of lactobacillus preparations and antifungal medication on a routine basis to feeding formula. However, this should not be done without first consulting your veterinarian.

CLOACAL PROLAPSE: This is a condition in which a part of the lower intestine (and sometimes the oviduct and one or both ureters) protrudes from the vent opening.

Causative Agent Straining associated with constipation, diarrhea, or egg laying may cause this problem. Any condition that interferes with the sphincter muscles of the vent (these are the muscles that control the opening and closing of the vent) may cause cloacal prolapse. Injury to the nerve supply to the vent sphincter, for example, may cause such a problem. Pat MacWhirter (1987) feels that a tendency to cloacal prolapse may run strongly in some family lines. She therefore advises against breeding birds with a history of this problem.

Transmission This is not an infectious disease and cannot be transmitted from one bird to another.

Symptoms To use Roger Harlin's (1986) very apt description, a cloacal prolapse usually appears to the bird's distressed owner as if "a good portion of the bird may soon be exiting via the 'rear.' " The owner will note a mass of glistening, smooth, pink or reddish tissue protruding from the vent. If the bird lives in a flock situation, its fellow aviary mates may pick at the victim's unfortunate bottom, causing bleeding and infection. Sometimes a prolapsed cloaca may be confused with cloacal papilloma. See Papillomatosis in this chapter for a discussion of this problem.

Laboratory Work None is usually required, as the condition is extremely self-evident. If the avian veterinarian suspects a secondary bacterial infection, a culture and sensitivity test will be done. If surgery is required to correct the condition, then routine serum chemistries and a complete blood count will be done as a part of the presurgical work-up.

Treatment Sometimes, gentle replacement of the prolapsed tissues by the veterinarian, using a lubricated thermometer, will be effective. This is followed by the placement of two small sutures in the vent to hold the tissue in place while it heals, and the original cause of the straining can be determined. If the cloacal prolapse becomes chronic, or the initial prolapse is a severe one, surgery will be required. This is done by making an incision in the bird's abdomen and suturing the cloaca to the abdominal wall.

If, at some time in the future, another abdominal procedure on the bird is contemplated and is to be done by a veterinarian other than the one who performed the cloacal repairs, the new veterinarian should be informed that a cloacapexy has been done previously.

Walter J. Rosskopf, Jr., D.V.M., one of the pioneers of this cloacapexy procedure, reports that birds that have undergone this procedure are apt to "pass wind" (1984c). Owners should be aware that this postsurgical side effect may occur.

Prognosis The chance of recurrence of cloacal prolapse following cloacapexy is moderate. The chance of recurrence following simple manual replacement and suturing is quite high.

CLOSTRIDIUM INFECTION: This is an infection that may cause various problems in birds. It is extremely rare in caged birds, but much more common in waterfowl.

The three forms of clostridium infection are:

Necrotic or ulcerative enteritis: This is a condition in which large portions of the intestine form sores, eventually resulting in tissue death in the gut and, ultimately, death of the bird.

Gangrenous dermatitis: This form of *Clostridium* infection takes place in the skin following small, deep punctures and lacerations. It is rapidly fatal.

Botulism: This infection, also known as limberneck, is caused by the excretion of a potent exotoxin by the *Clostridium* bacterium, within the intestinal tract. (An exotoxin is a poison produced by a bacterium and released into surrounding tissues.)

Causative Agent The above diseases are caused by a member of the *Clostridium* family of bacteria. *Clostridium perfringens* causes ulcerative enteritis; *Clostridium perfringens*, *septicum*, and *novyi* are usually involved in gangrenous dermatitis; *Clostridium botulinum* causes botulism. *Clostridium tetani* cause tetanus, or lockjaw, in humans and other mammals such as horses.

Clostridium species are anaerobic. In other words, they are able to grow only in an environment containing very little, or no, oxygen. They form spores, which unlike the spores of fungi, are primarily a defense mechanism to allow the bacteria to survive under adverse conditions, rather than a routine reproductive mechanism. These spores are very heat resistant and require long exposure to high temperatures to destroy them. They can exist in soil and feces for years. *Clostridia* are Gram positive, though some specific strains appear Gram negative (Washington, 1985). Chemical disinfection is not very effective in eliminating *Clostridia*. Autoclaving materials that will not be destroyed by prolonged high heat and steam is the only sure method for destroying these bacteria. (Autoclaving is a method of sterilization using steam heat at a temperature of 250°F [121°C] for a specified length of time.)

Clostridia are indeed a vicious, dangerous group of bacteria. They cause botulism in humans as well as birds. Botulism is probably one of the most feared bacterial diseases known to man. It has been estimated that one ounce of botulism toxin could exterminate all the people in the United States; a half-pound could kill the entire population of our planet (Smith, 1980).

Transmission Transmission of ulcerative enteritis is presumably the oral route. *The Merck Veterinary Manual* (1986) suggests that a predisposition to this disease may be caused by several factors: rapid change in quantity and quality of food, depressed intestinal mobility, or damage to the intestinal lining by a previous disease such as salmonellosis.

Gangrenous dermatitis is transmitted by the contamination of wounds with one or more *Clostridium* species.

Botulism is caused, not directly by the bacteria, but by the potent, horribly poisonous exotoxin they produce. The route of transmission is oral, through ingestion of protein material containing the exotoxin. Such sources include carrion, plant material, or maggots that have fed on contaminated food.

Clostridium infection cannot be transferred from bird to bird.

Symptoms Necrotic or ulcerative enteritis is usually observed in young birds from two weeks on. Symptoms of acute disease are:

Diarrhea, with or without blood in feces
Increased water intake
Death within a few hours

Symptoms of gangrenous dermatitis are:

Sudden onset of symptoms
Feather loss around affected area of skin
Involved area blue-red or black in color
Affected area swollen
When affected area palpated, a crackling noise can be heard (caused by
   gas formation under the skin by the bacteria)
Pain
Death, usually within twenty-four hours

Symptoms of botulism (limberneck) are:

Limp paralysis of skeletal muscles (hence the name ''limberneck'')
Paralysis of tongue and muscles controlling swallowing
Loss of feathers
Diarrhea
Paralysis of nerve controlling cardiovascular, respiratory, and visceral
   functions (bulbar paralysis)
Death

The culture plate is an invaluable diagnostic tool in avian medicine. Here a technician examines a culture plate that has been placed in an incubator to facilitate bacterial growth and the identification of organisms. *T. J. LaFeber*

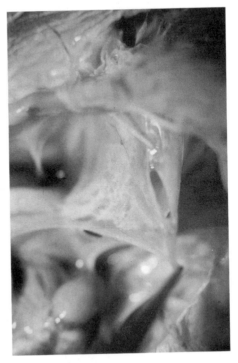

The bacterial growth on this air sac membrane has given it a very cloudy appearance. A healthy air sac membrane has the clarity of transparent cellophane. *Peter Sakas, D.V.M.*

135

Culture: Allows isolation and identification of the organism.

Serology: Identifies presence of *Clostridium* toxins in the blood. Blood serum, and extracts from liver or kidneys can be used. Suspected sources of contamination (such as feed or water) can also be tested for toxins.

Although death is often extremely rapid, and serology and/or culture results are usually not available before this unhappy event occurs, it is still worthwhile and necessary to perform these tests if an entire flock is involved. This will allow concrete identification of the organism and will be helpful in determining preventative measures for birds in the early stages of disease or not yet affected.

Treatment   Treatment usually comes too late. Helga Gerlach (1986a) suggests that when dealing with the ulcerative enteritic form, lincomycin or spiramycin in the drinking water may help; control in nonaffected birds by vaccination with *Cl. perfringens* toxoid is successful but expensive.

For gas gangrene, no effective treatment is known. In humans, amputation of the affected area is done, when possible. The author can find no mention in the literature of this procedure relative to avian patients.

In the case of botulism, it is sometimes possible to effect a cure in the early stages. Gerlach suggests injections of *Clostridium* antitoxin and administration of a laxative to rid the intestine of the botulism exotoxin.

Prognosis   The outcome of any form of *Clostridium* infection is extremely grave. Affected birds usually die, regardless of treatment. Occasional cures are made, but these are the exception.

In the control of *Clostridium* infection, strict sanitation is a must. This is one reason why dirt floors in aviaries are to be avoided. Some aviculturists make a practice of feeding maggots to their breeding stock. If this is done, every effort should be made to determine that the maggots are not contaminated with botulism toxin. If there is the slightest doubt as to the purity of such food material, it should *never* be used.

CNEMIDOKOPTES MITE (SCALY LEG, SCALY FACE MITE):   A mite is a microscopic creature, often parasitic, and belonging to the phylum *Arthropoda*. This group includes crustaceans such as shrimp, crabs, and lobsters. It also includes insects, spiders, scorpions, and ticks. The *Cnemidokoptes* mite affects mainly budgerigars and spends its entire life cycle on its unfortunate avian host. The infestation affects beak, cere, eyelids, feet, legs, and the cloacal opening. Severe, untreated *Cnemidokoptes* infestation seriously damages the growing tissues of the beak, resulting in lifelong beak deformity even if the bird has been cured of the infestation.

It is known that the *Cnemidokoptes* mite is found on healthy, unaffected birds, never causing any symptoms whatsoever (Harrison, 1986b). Other birds become victims of symptom-causing infestation. The cause for this is unknown, although one theory suggests that affected birds have a genetically linked, immune system deficiency that causes them to be susceptible to mite infestation. Other predisposing factors include stress, infection, giardiasis, and low blood protein levels (hypoproteinemia).

Causative Agent   *Cnemidokoptes* mite.

Transmission   All birds are exposed to *Cnemidokoptes* during the feather stage. All birds do *not* become infected, however. At present, *Cnemidokoptes* does not appear to be transmissible.

Symptoms

> Raised, white, crusty lumps on beak, cere, eyelids, legs, feet, vent (frequently these lesions have a honeycombed appearance due to the air holes made in the bird's skin by the mites; occasionally the bird will show signs of mite infestation in the feathered areas of its body)
>
> "Tassels" on legs and feet (the result of overgrowth of skin in the affected areas; this is a very common form of *Cnemidokoptes* infection in canaries)
>
> Malformed beak (may take the form of a "duck bill," excessive elongation of the beak, or "scissoring" of the beak)

Laboratory Work   The diagnosis of *Cnemidokoptes* mite infestation is usually made by physical examination, as the lesions are very distinctive. However, there are some conditions that closely resemble mite infestation (pox virus, infection, food encrusted on the beak, or some skin cancers). If your veterinarian has questions about the symptoms, a skin scraping will be taken and inspected microscopically for evidence of the *Cnemidokoptes* mite (eggs, larvae, adult mites).

Treatment   An injection of Ivermectin is usually very effective in curing the infestation. In some birds, two injections two weeks apart are required. This medication can also be given orally and seems to be as effective as the parenteral route (Clubb, 1986c). A diet high in vitamin A will keep the bird's skin in peak condition and help prevent future problems with *Cnemidokoptes.*

If the bird's beak has been severely affected, periodic trimmings throughout its life will be necessary in order to allow it to eat properly. The initial trimming and reshaping may be done in stages. This is because the bird has accommodated its eating processes to its abnormally shaped beak over a period of time. To reshape its beak suddenly may cause the bird some eating difficulties.

Prognosis   Excellent, with proper treatment.

In terms of prevention, the isolation of affected birds from healthy ones is very important. Good hygiene and sanitation practices will help prevent the spread of *Cnemidokoptes* in the aviary or collection. The affected bird's cage should be thoroughly cleaned and all wooden perches and toys discarded. Your veterinarian may feel the use of an insecticide in the home, bird room, or aviary is necessary and can advise you as to which will be most effective and safe. *Never* use *any* insecticide without first consulting your avian veterinarian.

COLDS: There is no such thing as an avian "cold." This topic has been included to disabuse bird owners of the notion that birds contract colds just as their human owners do. What may appear to the owner as a cold in a bird is actually one of the various forms of upper respiratory tract problems (Stoddard, 1987b).

Causative Agents Infections due to bacterial, viral, or fungal causes are the primary causative agents. Other factors are more in the nature of predisposing factors, some of which serve to leave the door open for infectious pathogens to move in and take over, or to create mechanical breathing problems. Some of these predisposing agents are listed below:

> *Degenerative changes of old age*: An example of this would be cere enlargement in the female budgerigar. This condition often blocks the nostrils, making breathing difficult.
>
> *Anomalies of the upper respiratory tract*: Such an example would be a beak deformity present at birth.
>
> *Nutritional deficiencies*: Vitamin A deficiency in all parrots and iodine deficiency in budgerigars are two examples. Vitamin A deficiency causes skin cells to function suboptimally, thus being unable to provide an effective barrier to germs. Iodine deficiency leads to enlargement of the thyroid gland. This gland then presses on the trachea and syrinx, causing breathing difficulties.
>
> *Metabolic problems*: Liver problems may lead to poor metabolism of food, malnutrition, and susceptibility to germs causing respiratory problems. The parathyroid glands control calcium/phosphorus use in the body; if these glands malfunction, they may cause a condition called "rubber beak." This is common in cockatiels and can cause respiratory problems.

Symptoms

> Increased respiratory rate
> Tail bobbing at rest
> Open-mouth breathing
> Noisy breathing
> Coughing
> Frequent sneezing
> Nasal or ocular (eye) discharge
> Swelling on face, especially in area around eyes
> Swollen eyes
> Change in tone of voice, or loss of voice
> Lethargy
> Ruffled feathers
> Weakness
> Loss of appetite

Laboratory Work Any laboratory work will be dependent on the suspected cause of the upper respiratory problem. Culture and sensitivity testing is routinely done with suspected upper respiratory infections.

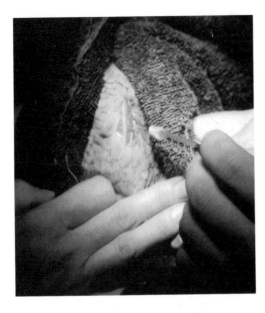

The breast muscle is often the injection site of choice in avian treatment techniques. Note the towel restraint and the angle of the needle in relation to the keelbone (sternum).

Peter Sakas, D.V.M.

There is no mistaking the signs of illness in this Red-lored Amazon. Its eyes are closed and it displays an overall picture of listlessness and depression.

Peter Sakas, D.V.M.

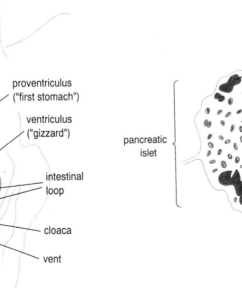

proventriculus ("first stomach")

ventriculus ("gizzard")

intestinal loop

pancreas

cloaca

vent

glycogen-producing cells (alpha)

pancreatic islet

insulin-producing cells (beta)

Location of pancreas in visceral anatomy

Microscopic cross section of pancreas showing pancreatic islet

Treatment The treatment will likewise be dependent upon the cause of the problem. It is extremely necessary for the bird to be checked by the avian veterinarian as soon as a respiratory problem is noted by the owner.

Prognosis Dependent upon the underlying cause of the problem.

DIABETES MELLITUS: This disease is caused by a disorder in the bird's carbohydrate (starch) metabolism. The bird is unable to process and utilize carbohydrates properly for energy. Both insulin and glucagon are necessary for normal carbohydrate utilization in the bird. These substances are manufactured by the pancreas. Insulin allows the body to make and store glycogen (a form of sugar made from the glucose contained in carbohydrates) in the liver, to be used as a future energy store. Glucagon acts to release glycogen from the liver so that it can be broken down into glucose once again and used by the body for energy.

In parrots, unlike humans, glucagon is thought to be the primary glucose-regulating substance in the body. In avian diabetes (excepting carnivorous birds), too much glucagon is made by the pancreas, resulting in an abnormally high blood-sugar level. This is because too much glycogen is being converted to glucose and released into the blood. In many cases of avian diabetes, insulin levels are normal.

The reader may wonder why diabetes is "officially" called diabetes mellitus. This is because there are several forms of diabetes, two of which are the most common: diabetes mellitus and diabetes insipidus. The form commonly known to most people as diabetes is actually diabetes mellitus. *Mellitus* is from the Latin, meaning "sweet." This refers to the high concentration of glucose, or sugar, in the patient's urine. Indeed, doctors in past centuries diagnosed diabetes mellitus in their human patients by actually tasting the patient's urine!

Diabetes insipidus is actually a water-excreting disorder involving both the kidneys and certain pituitary hormones. In this disorder, abnormally large quantities of water are excreted in the urine, resulting in a very low concentration of waste products in the urine. Hence *insipidus*, from the Latin meaning "weak."

Causative Agent An overproduction of glucagon by the pancreas is thought to be the cause of diabetes mellitus in the noncarnivorous bird. This overproduction may be a result of an inherited metabolic defect. Diabetes mellitus has also been reported in cases of pancreatic cancer and kidney tumors. Some of these renal tumors have been found to secrete a glucagonlike substance (Lothrop et al., 1986).

Transmission Diabetes mellitus is not an infectious disease and cannot be transmitted from one bird to another.

Symptoms Classic symptoms of diabetes are excessive thirst and excessive urination. In addition, the bird often eats constantly, but continues to lose weight. This happens because the bird cannot utilize the carbohydrates it eats. Therefore, it feels hungry continually. Weight loss occurs because the bird actually begins

140

to digest its own body fats and proteins as energy sources as it cannot use carbohydrates for this purpose. The by-products of protein and fat breakdown as energy sources are excreted in the urine and create much water loss through the urine as a result. This is why diabetic birds are always thirsty and urinate in abnormally high amounts.

Glucose in the urine and very high glucose blood levels are the other two important findings in the bird with diabetes. Weakness is also often noted as the bird utilizes more and more of its body mass for energy.

Laboratory Work

Serology: Blood glucose levels are determined.
Urinalysis: Urine glucose levels are determined.

In addition, the history obtained by the veterinarian is of extreme importance in making the diagnosis of diabetes. If there are other concurrent problems, appropriate laboratory work will be done for these.

Treatment   The treatment for birds with diabetes, as in humans, is daily injections of insulin. In connection with this, daily determinations of urine glucose content must be made. The day's dose of insulin is determined by this level. Urine can be tested for glucose content using such products as Clinitest or Clinistrips. These are available in any pharmacy.

The owner of a diabetic bird will receive thorough instruction in how to care for the bird by the veterinarian. Such counseling should include how to administer insulin, what side effects to watch for, and how to test the bird's urine. At the time of this writing, Clinton Lothrop et al. (1986) recommend that birds on insulin be allowed free access to food throughout the day, in order to avoid insulin shock. This happens when the bird receives too much insulin, which acts to "burn up" excessive amounts of glucose in the blood, leaving a severe lack of this substance in the blood. The bird will become very weak. It may experience muscle tremors. In severe cases, convulsions, coma, and death may follow. Free access to food will help ensure that the bird always has available enough calories to balance the insulin it has been given. If insulin reaction should occur, the bird (providing it is not comatose) will respond well to sugar given orally.

When giving insulin on a daily basis, it is important to vary the site of injection in the breast muscle. This will avoid damage and scarring at the injection site.

Insulin must always be kept in the refrigerator. The bottle must always be shaken before use, as the insulin settles between uses.

Prognosis   The prognosis varies with each individual, its response to insulin therapy, and the consistency of care given by the owner. In general, birds seem to respond well to treatment. Lothrop cites a case in which a cockatiel had been maintained for three years on insulin. It is entirely possible that a diabetic bird could live out a fairly normal lifespan with adequate treatment and good nursing care.

The author can find no mention in the literature of the following with reference to birds, but humans with diabetes are prone to infections of various kinds. For this reason, it would seem a wise precaution to use excellent sanitation with the diabetic bird, including spotlessly clean perches. Fungal infections such as candidiasis are common in human diabetics. It would therefore also seem wise to provide the diabetic bird with the best possible nutrition, with particular attention to vitamin A content.

EGG BINDING: This is a life-threatening condition caused by the inability of a hen to pass her egg without assistance. It is most frequently encountered in budgerigars, finches, canaries, and cockatiels. Rosskopf and Woerpel (1984) cite a case in which a cockatiel seen by them for egg binding presented with a history of having laid forty eggs in one month. These authors also feel that egg binding is frequently seen in unmated pet birds.

Several serious results may follow egg binding. The hen may die of exhaustion. If the egg is lodged against the pelvic bones, the hen's kidneys could be crushed. If the egg has compressed the ureters and large intestine, she will be unable to pass urine and feces. Compression of blood vessels may cause circulatory collapse and shock. Compression of nerves may result in paralysis of the legs. Most of these conditions will more than likely result in the bird's death.

The process of repeated and fruitless straining may result in uterine rupture, with the consequence that the egg escapes into the abdominal cavity. Frequently, when this happens, the egg is broken and yolk is introduced into the abdomen, resulting in egg-yolk peritonitis. This is a serious problem, especially if not detected immediately.

In his article on egg-laying problems in cockatiels, Gregory Rich (1987) states that the exhausted body store of calcium in the nutritionally compromised hen can result in poor feathering and body condition, an increased susceptibility to infection, increased risk of fractures due to weakened bone structure, and seizures. All this, in addition to the tremendous risk of egg binding!

Causative Agent   The cause of egg binding is multifactorial. Each hen will vary in the specific causes of her egg-binding problem, possessing one or more of the following predisposing factors:

Oversized or malpositioned eggs
Lack of exercise leading to decreased muscle tone
Breeding when not in prime condition
Excessive egg laying, creating abnormally low blood calcium
Uterine infection or damage
Coexisting disease state
Obesity
Malnutrition
Sudden decrease in environmental temperature
Hereditary factors, such as a tendency to lipoma formation in budgerigars,
   or small body size (which may create a narrowed pelvic outlet)

In a side view X ray of an egg-bound hen, the problem-causing egg is clearly visible.
Peter Sakas, D.V.M.

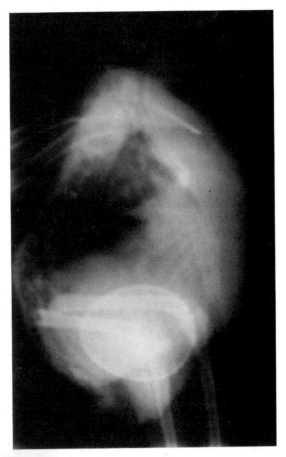

Delivery of egg abdominally in an egg-bound hen—the avian equivalent of Caesarean section. *Peter Sakas, D.V.M.*

The importance of adequate dietary calcium to the breeding hen is well known. Calcium is not only needed for eggshell formation, but also for normal, effective muscular contraction, such as that of uterine muscle contraction when an egg is being expelled. Thus the laying hen with inadequate calcium source will be doubly compromised: she will be prone to soft-shelled eggs and will not have enough muscle power to expel them.

Transmission Egg binding is not an infectious condition, and is therefore not transmissible from one bird to another.

Symptoms Small birds frequently experience a sudden onset of symptoms and also sudden death as a result of egg binding. Larger birds often have a slower onset of symptoms and may survive for a longer period of time before succumbing. Harrison et al. (1986) state that in a small bird such as a finch, the egg must be delivered within an hour of symptom onset, while a bird such as a macaw may remain egg bound for up to twelve hours without danger.

Symptoms are as follows:

Squatting and straining
Generalized weakness
Abdominal swelling
Paralysis or weakness in one or both legs
Breathing difficulty
Ruffled feathers
Appearance of egg at outlet of cloaca
A low, crouching posture on perch (in budgerigars, the hen may be seen to sit on her tail with her legs straddled apart, much like the stance of a penguin; in small birds such as canaries, the stance frequently includes drooping wings and tail tucked under, so that there appears to be a swelling at the base of the tail)
Staying on the cage bottom in an obvious state of exhaustion
Large red lump or swelling under the tail
Periods of straining alternated with nest-seeking behavior

Laboratory Work In addition to the physical examination and history, the veterinarian will take an X ray to confirm the presence of an undelivered egg. A radiograph may also show decreased bone density, indicating that the hen has seriously depleted her stores of body calcium in her attempts to reproduce.

Treatment There are several approaches to the delivery of an unexpelled egg. The choice of treatment method is dependent upon the position of the egg (whether at the cloacal outlet or high up in the oviduct) and the condition of the hen.

1. Heat and humidity
2. Lubrication of the egg if at the cloacal outlet
3. Calcium, multivitamins, and oxytocin injections (Oxytocin is a hormone that stimulates the uterus to contract, thus aiding in the expulsion of the egg)

4. Manual manipulation of the egg to facilitate delivery
5. Small incision to enlarge the cloacal opening (the equivalent of an episiotomy in a human)
6. Hysterectomy, involving an abdominal incision, through which the egg is delivered (the equivalent of a Caesarian section in a human, with the exception that in an avian obstretrical patient the oviduct is usually removed along with the egg; in a human, the uterus is left intact)
7. Immersion of the bird up to the neck in warm water, which acts to relax the hen's muscles so that the egg can be expelled
8. Gentle, warm enema (This serves to relax the hen's muscles, allowing the egg to pass)
9. Fluid therapy if the hen is weak and dehydrated
10. If egg-yolk peritonitis is present, abdominal surgery to clean up the egg yolk (In addition, antibiotic therapy will be required along with other general supportive measures such as fluid therapy and tube feeding)
11. Withdrawal of the egg contents with a needle and syringe introduced through the cloaca or abdomen (depending upon the position of the egg), usually causing collapse of the egg to allow the hen to expel it

Prognosis   All of the above treatments are stressful to the already compromised hen. Some are extremely risky, and the hen may die. Egg binding is an emergency condition, and the sooner the bird receives treatment, the better her chances of survival. The earlier stages of egg binding lend themselves to successful resolution using noninvasive techniques such a heat, humidity, and lubrication of the egg. The more invasive the technique (that is, surgery), the greater the chance of death.

If the hen required treatment for egg-yolk peritonitis, the outlook is guarded. If she recovers, she may have sustained permanent damage to her liver, adrenal glands, or reproductive system. In addition, if pancreatic damage has occurred, diabetes may result (Rosskopf and Woerpel, 1984).

Prevention of egg binding is easier than a cure. Culling of repeat egg binders from the breeding flock will ensure that hereditary factors predisposing egg binding will not be passed to offspring. If the pet bird has a history of egg binding, all stimuli to reproduction should be removed. The owner should not reinforce the bird's sexual behavior. In this way the chances of ovulation will be reduced. It is also helpful to reduce the amount of available light to eight hours per day.

Excellent husbandry is of paramount importance in helping the laying hen achieve reproductive success. Excellent nutrition, adequate exposure to sunlight (which encourages production of vitamin D_3 by the bird, necessary to proper calcium use by the body), and calcium supplementation are all important.

Good sources of calcium include dicalcium phosphorus powder, oystershell, cuttlebone, and dairy products, such as powdered milk and cheese. (The reader should also refer to the section on egg binding in Chapter 4). Robert

Clipsham (1988b) recommends that gray oyster shell be avoided, as it may contain unacceptable levels of lead or other heavy metals; white oystershell is much safer for use with birds.

Clipsham (1988b) states that since the egg yolk is 33 percent fat, the laying hen's diet should be supplemented with the moderate addition of fat. Good sources are egg food, cheese (such as cheddar), or sunflower seeds. Moderation is the watchword here.

Occasionally, birds become repeat egg binders and are refractory to any of the usual treatment protocols. For birds such as these, periodic injections of progesterone may be needed to prevent egg production. Such injections are usually successful in achieving the desired result. However, there are several drawbacks to use of this hormone:

1. It is an incompletely understood medication with regard to effects on the avian patient.
2. The length of time it remains effective in the hen's body varies from bird to bird.
3. It can cause obesity, in itself a predisposing factor in egg binding.
4. It should never be used in birds with a history of liver problems.
5. It should not be used more than three or four times a year (Clipsham, 1988b).

Other common side effects include increased water intake and urination. Frequent administration of progesterone may also cause development of diabetes.

The last resort for the chronically egg-bound hen is a hysterectomy. This procedure was pioneered by Greg J. Harrison, D.V.M., and consists of the removal of the hen's oviduct. This results in the complete and final cessation of all egg laying. The avian hysterectomy is not routinely available because it requires an extremely experienced avian veterinarian and state-of-the-art equipment. Nevertheless, the owners of such a bird, which may be a dear pet or an extremely valuable aviary specimen, may wish to seek out a veterinarian who is able to perform this procedure.

ENTERIC ORGANISM–CAUSED INFECTIONS: The enteric bacteria are common causes of much avian suffering and death. In general, the infections they cause are rapid in onset and frequently fatal. These organisms may, however, cause a more chronic problem.

Enteric bacteria are members of the group *Enterobacteriaceae*. They are Gram negative, and normal to the intestinal flora of mammals (including man), domestic poultry, and insectivorous and carnivorous birds. They are *not* part of the parrot's normal intestinal flora. Enteric bacteria can propagate aerobically (in the presence of oxygen) or anaerobically (in an environment where little or no oxygen is present). They exist everywhere in the environment: soil, plants, and dairy products. Indeed, rodents and wild birds such as starlings, sparrows, and pigeons act as reservoirs for enteric bacteria. When these creatures have

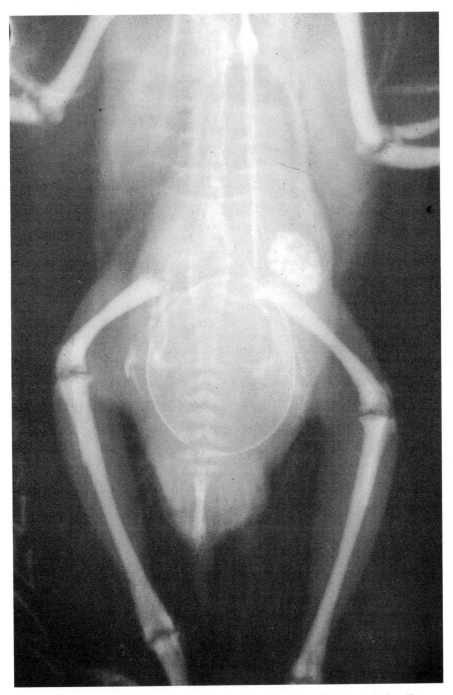

Egg binding must always be regarded as a serious condition. With improper handling, the hen could easily be lost. Fortunately, a variety of techniques are available to bring a crisis to a successful conclusion.   *Peter Sakas, D.V.M.*

access to the aviary, contaminating food, water, and plant material with their feces, they provide a potent source of infection for the aviary inhabitants.

Enteric bacteria are able, given proper conditions, to grow and multiply outside a living host—in soil or water, for example. Most of these harmful bacteria are susceptible to the commonly available disinfectants. The exceptions are those bacteria of the genus *Klebsiella* (Gerlach, 1986a).

Enteric organisms can and do cause a wide variety of illnesses depending upon the organ systems affected. In addition, they may spread throughout the bird's body, causing generalized infection (septicemia) and damage to multiple organ systems. Infections of the gut, lungs, air sacs, bones, skin, liver, and reproductive organs can be caused by enteric bacteria. Infection of the sinuses and nasal cavities (sinusitis and rhinitis, respectively), the membranous sheath covering the heart (pericarditis), the middle ear (otitis media), and brain and spinal cord (encephalomyelitis) are also possible.

Enteric bacteria may be a primary source of disease or may invade an already sick bird, causing a secondary illness.

E. coli is the most commonly isolated pathogenic bacteria in sick birds. R. N. T-W-Fiennes (1982) feels this pathogen to be commonest cause of infectious enteritis in birds. An example of an enteric pathogen causing a secondary disease problem is *Serratia marcescens*. This bacterium is being increasingly implicated in secondary infections of large parrots with debilitating disease, prior antibiotic treatment, or depressed immune systems (Gerlach, 1986a). Interestingly enough, this same organism creates infectious problems in humans having the same difficulties (Smith, 1980).

Most enteric bacteria are capable of causing disease in humans and can be transmitted to them by a sick bird. When caring for such a bird, the owner should take good hygiene precautions to prevent such an occurrence. (See Zoonoses, later in this chapter.)

The severity of enteric bacterial disease in the bird is dependent upon the susceptibility of the bird (that is, the competence of the immune system), the dose to which the bird is exposed (the number of bacteria and frequency of exposure), and the virulence (infectivity) of the bacteria. Among the various species of enteric pathogens are subspecies, or strains. Each strain has slightly different characteristics, such as virulence. Some strains of *E. coli*, for example, are capable of creating overwhelming disease, while others do not cause disease at all.

Causative Agent   There are several species of enteric bacteria capable of causing primary or secondary infection in birds; the most commonly identified in such infections are *E. coli, Salmonella, Pseudomonas, Aeromonas, Yersinia, Pasteurella, Haemophilus, Campylobacter, Klebsiella,* and *Citrobacter*.

Shigella and *Edwardsiella* are also members of the enteric pathogen group, but rarely cause disease in parrots. *Enterobacter, Serratia,* and *Proteus* do cause disease in parrots, but are generally considered to have low disease-causing potential.

Transmission All the enteric bacteria are infectious and can be easily spread from bird to bird, from bird to person, or person to bird, in many cases. Fecal contamination of food, water, perches, cage wires and bottoms, and nestboxes are a major source of infection. Spoiled food and contaminated seed and animal kibble, such as monkey chow, are potent sources of infection. Water contaminated by spoiled food or feces is another source of infection. *Pseudomonas* is notorious for propagating in such conditions.

The bacteria may be spread orally, such as when a bird walks in contaminated feces, then holds food with its foot and eats it. It may also occur through normal preening of the feet. The bacteria may then be passed to babies through regurgitation of crop contents by infected parents. Enteric organisms may also be spread by dissemination in the air of fecal dust or feather dust from infected birds. Potential victims then breathe in the contaminated air. Transmission of bacteria from an infected hen to the egg is also possible.

In addition to being spread from infected bird to potential victim, transmission is also possible by carriers. Such birds have had an enteric illness and have recovered. But they continue to shed the bacteria in their feces and in feather dust, thus remaining a source of infection to other birds, though they themselves remain healthy.

Besides bird-to-bird spread, wild animals and birds acting as reservoirs for enteric bacteria can be sources of infection. Access to the aviary by rodents and wild birds is especially to be discouraged for this reason.

Because enteric bacteria can cause disease in humans as well as birds and animals, owners with such an infection should take precautions to ensure that they do not infect their birds. Hand washing before handling one's birds or preparing their food is absolutely mandatory.

Symptoms Because enteric pathogens can affect a wide array of body systems, or be disseminated generally throughout the bird's body, symptoms vary greatly. Diarrhea is a common presenting symptom when enteric bacteria have invaded the digestive tract. The diarrhea may or may not be bloody. It may also contain varying amounts of mucus.

General symptoms of illness may be the only signs seen. These may be very rapid in onset, or more gradual in their appearance. Such signs would include:

Weakness
Lethargy
Drowsiness
Lack of appetite
Depression
Ruffled feathers

If diarrhea and/or frequent regurgitation or vomiting are present, dehydration will usually result. Signs of dehydration include:

Subtle or more noticeable loss of skin elasticity, as evidenced by "tenting"

of the skin on the foot when pinched by thumb and forefinger (the skin may also appear darkened)
Loss of brightness and "roundness" of the eyes
Coolness of the feet and wing tips
Rapid heart beat
Shock
Coma and/or death

The following may also be noted, alone or in combination with each other and the symptoms described above:

Excessive thirst and excessive urination
Breathing problems
Bird husks seeds but does not eat them
Emaciation
Discharge from eyes and/or nose
Cyanosis (blue color in membranes of mouth)
Overeating of grit
Soiling of vent
Muscle incoordination
Sudden death

Laboratory Work

Gram stain: Performed on feces and/or other body discharges to determine presence of enteric bacteria.

Culture and sensitivity: Often done on feces and/or other body discharges to isolate and identify the organism and its antibiotic susceptibilities.

Serum chemistries: Will determine if organ damage has occurred.

Hematology: Monitors body's immune response to infection; determines whether or not infection is acute or chronic, whether or not anemia is a factor, and bird's general state of nutrition and hydration.

Radiograph: May be done to rule out other causes of disease.

Treatment Treatment will be determined by the severity of infection, its duration, and body systems affected. It may include one, some, or all of the following:

General supportive care: fluid therapy; warmth, humidity; oxygen; tube feedings, if the bird is unable or unwilling to eat; corticosteroids; and vitamin injections

Antibiotics or other chemotherapeutic medications, as indicated by sensitivity testing

Lactobacillus to help repopulate the gut with "friendly" bacteria

Levamisole, a medication that helps boost the bird's immune system

Hyperimmune serum administration, whereby a serum containing antibodies against the enteric pathogen causing the infection is given

A graphic example of severe feather picking. Note the almost completely denuded breast and abdomen of this affected Double Yellow-head Amazon.

Peter Sakas, D.V.M.

The same bird is here being fitted for an Elizabethan collar to discourage feather picking. In treatment the cause should also be determined and corrected.

Peter Sakas, D.V.M.

Prognosis As with the symptoms and treatment of enteric bacterial infections, the prognosis is varied. Cases that are acute and violent in onset commonly end in death. In those cases where symptoms are less violent and more gradual in onset, chances of a happy resolution are much greater. Generally, the very young and very old are more at risk of death than the adult parrot of moderate years. Much depends upon the bird's prior state of health, nutrition, and psychological well-being.

The great majority of enteric bacterial infections are preventable. High standards of hygiene, not only for the bird's environment, but in preparation of food and water, are absolutely necessary. A stress-free environment and nutritious diet are equally important.

Isolation of newly acquired stock will go far in preventing the introduction of disease to the existing flock or collection. Immediate isolation and veterinary care for sick birds will do likewise. Follow-up culture and sensitivity testing for recovered birds will help eliminate carriers. The strict adherence to a rodent-control program in the aviary is of great help in preventing enteric bacterial disease. Designing aviaries to exclude wild birds is also helpful.

For those healthy birds in a flock in which some birds have been diagnosed as having various types of enteric bacterial infections, the prophylactic administration of hyperimmune serum may help prevent the spread of disease.

FEATHER PICKING: "Feather picking is an obsessive destructive behavior pattern of birds during which all or part of their feathers are pulled out, amputated, frayed, or in some other way damaged. This behavior often results in the prevention of normal feather growth and emergence" (Rosskopf and Woerpel, 1987d).

Feather picking is almost exclusively a problem of captive birds. It is rarely seen in wild birds that depend on their feathers for the ability to escape predators. In addition, wild birds are not subject to the boredom and stresses of cage life. They are far too busy searching for food and reproducing to have any need for feather picking as a way of relieving boredom.

The state of a bird's feathers is a good indication of its internal health. "Pretty is as pretty does" can be most aptly applied to the caged parrot.

It is very important for owners to distinguish between feather picking and normal molting. The companion parrot will usually shed occasional feathers throughout the year. Once or twice yearly, it will usually undergo a heavier molt. Such normal events are dependent upon the climate and geography where the bird lives, as well as temperature, amount of light to which it is exposed daily, its species, and its own individuality. At no time during a normal molt should the bird exhibit bald patches.

Hand-fed babies will often present an unkempt appearance because they have not had the opportunity to learn normal preening behavior from their parents. These little ones will benefit from the assistance of their owners in the removal of feather sheaths. If the bird has a cagemate, the cagemate will also help teach it to preen. Frequent gentle misting with warm water will also encourage the youngster to engage in preening activities.

A bird that has picked itself will present a bald or ragged appearance in any area accessible to its beak. If the head presents a picked appearance, such problems as psittacine beak and feather disease become a consideration. If such a bird has a cagemate, the likely possibility is that its bald head is the result of overzealous preening by its avian companion.

Some birds, such as Amazons, African Grays, and macaws, indulge in a self-mutilation syndrome in which the wing webs, groin, or toes may be severely damaged.

Chronic feather picking may lead to other problems due to skin damage and loss of insulation.

Causative Agent   There are many causes of feather picking. They may be roughly divided into three categories: internal, external, and psychological.

Internal causes of feather picking include:

Sexual and/or reproductive problems: Hens, and some cocks, will remove contour feathers from the breast to prepare a brood patch. This allows a more efficient incubation of eggs. Such behavior is normal and will cease when the season's current offspring have been reared. Rosskopf et al. (1986) state that Galahs (Rose-Breasted Cockatoos) will line their nests with feathers. Caged birds without mates experience cyclical hormonal surges that prepare them for courtship and breeding, just as do their wild counterparts. If not allowed to mate, sexual frustration may cause feather picking. This may be a seasonal occurrence that will cease when levels of sex hormones recede to nonbreeding levels. Overzealous preening by a cagemate can also be a cause.

Internal disease problems: (Feather picking may be related to the bird's attempts to alleviate deep body pain.) The disease sources may be bacterial, viral, fungal, parasitic (Giardiasis in cockatiels, intestinal parasites such as tapeworms in African Grays, or blood parasites), or may be caused by tumors of internal organ structures.

Endocrine imbalance problems: Can be induced by imbalances in the adrenal, thyroid, or sexual hormones.

Malnutrition: A diet high in fat and low in calcium and vitamin A will often cause dry skin and subsequent picking. According to Rosskopf et al. (1986), malnutrition can also create mental aberrations that will aggravate the existing physical problem of dry skin and itching. In addition, unhealthy skin predisposes a bird to external parasites and infection, which will further exacerbate feather picking.

Mutilation Syndrome: The reason for this behavior is unknown. It may be due to infection or it may have its origin in underlying internal lesions (Rosskopf et al., 1986; Harrison, 1986a).

External causes of feather picking include:

Feather follicle and/or skin infections by bacteria, fungi, or viruses: Examples of such infections would be: bacterial—*Staphylococcus*, fungal—*Candida*, and viral—*Avipoxvirus*.

External parasites: One example is *Cnemidocoptes* mites in budgerigars. Feather lice are *rarely* ever found in caged birds and are at the very bottom of the list as suspects in cases of feather picking. It is therefore a waste of time to spray birds as a preventative for feather lice. Some of these products are positively unsafe for birds.

There is one group of birds at greater risk of external parasites than birds that have been in captivity for a period of time or are domestically bred. These are the birds that have very recently been imported. Feather lice and mites, as well as feather follicle mites, are seen much more often in this group. (Sakas, personal communication). Feather follicle mites actually live in the feather shaft and can be seen inside the shafts of molted or plucked feathers.

External lesions: Skin tumors, feather cysts, cuts or bruises, fecal matting of feathers, and broken blood feathers.

Psychological factors that may be involved in feather picking include:

Boredom

Unacceptable stress levels

Sexual frustration, a problem with a strong psychological component as well as an internal hormonal one

A bird should never be assumed to pick its feathers because of psychological factors until all other causes have been ruled out by veterinary examination in combination with a thorough history and appropriate laboratory work.

Highly intelligent and emotional birds such as cockatoos, African Grays, and Queen of Bavaria Conures will easily become bored if their environments lack sufficient stimulation. They are also easily stressed by changes in routine; the proximity of a disliked or feared person, pet, or other bird; the loss of a beloved owner (even if only temporary, such as a vacation)—to name a few examples.

Transmission   Feather picking is a behavior and, as such, cannot be transmitted to other birds.

Symptoms   Symptoms are self-evident. The guilty culprit will present a bedraggled and most unaesthetic appearance. As stated previously, a bird exhibiting feather loss and/or damage on the head has either an overzealous cagemate or is suffering from a disease other than feather picking. Such problems might include psittacine beak and feather syndrome, French molt, or *Herpesvirus* or *Adenovirus* infections (Rosskopf et al., 1986).

Laboratory Work   Depending upon the suspected cause of the feather picking, one or many of the following may be advised:

Nearly all birds thought to be feather pickers should have the following tests in order to rule out any underlying disease that may be causing or contributing to the feather picking:

154

After the collar has been applied, the bird becomes accustomed to it and cannot reach its feathers. Ideally, by the time this bird's collar is removed, the feather picking habit will be broken and the cause of it corrected. *Peter Sakas, D.V.M.*

Regular misting will benefit a bird's plumage and will often act against the onset of feather picking. Additionally, the birds love their bath. *M. Vogel*

Hematology
Serum chemistries
Cloacal and choanal Gram stains
Feather-follicle Gram stain
Fecal parasite examination

In addition, some of the following may be done:

Radiograph
Cultures, especially of feather pulp
Biopsy of feather follicles
Serology
Endoscopy

As the bird progresses, repeat follow-up laboratory work may be advised to monitor the bird's response to therapy.

Treatment   Treatment will be dictated by the underlying cause of the feather picking. It may include one, some, or all of the following:

1. The bird may need physical restraint. There are various methods:
   Elizabethan collar: This is a wide, stiff collar fitted around the neck and designed to prevent access of the beak to the feathers. It is frequently used as an adjunct to therapy with chronic feather pickers. This prevents further feather damage while the diagnosis is being made and treatment initiated. Some veterinarians prefer to use an Elizabethan collar only as a last resort.
   Beak notching: This method involves filing the beak in such a way that the bird cannot grasp and damage its feathers. Some veterinarians prefer to use this as a first line of defense. Some prefer to use it as a last resort. It usually is effective in slowing down feather picking. However, repeated beak notching can eventually result in the upper and lower mandibles failing to meet normally, thus making feeding difficult for the bird.
   Feather sprays: These consist of foul-tasting concoctions that are sprayed on the feathers in an effort to discourage feather picking. They are not generally recommended because they mask the underlying cause of feather picking, they are not very effective, and some birds have had adverse reactions to them (Young, 1987). Feather sprays also interfere with normal preening.
2. Bathing may need to be enhanced. Daily misting with warm water encourages normal preening activity and improves the appearance of the plumage.
3. Various medications may be prescribed:
   Antibiotics: Where bacterial infections have caused the feather picking.
   Antiparasitic drugs: Where skin or internal parasites are the causative factor. These might include: Ipropran, for giardiasis; Ivomec, for *Cnemidocoptes* mites; or Droncit, for tapeworms.

Topical medications: Will be prescribed in cases of self-mutilation syndrome, avian pox of the cutaneous type. An example of one such drug would be Zovirax for viral skin lesions. Appropriate antibiotic/cortisone preparations may be prescribed for self-mutilation syndrome.

Progesterone: This sex hormone may be prescribed in some cases of sexually caused feather picking. It can be effective, but does have some side effects of which owners should be aware: thirst, frequent urination, temporary lethargy, weight gain, temporarily lowered resistance to disease, and diabetes (with some types of this medication).

Tranquilizers, such as Valium or phenobarbital: These are rarely used and are reserved for the intractable feather picker in which all else has failed, especially where severe mental aberration has been diagnosed (Rosskopf et al., 1986).

Antidepressant medications: Cathy Johnson (1987a) believes that the emotionally aberrant behavior observed in feather pickers (fear, inappropriate and misplaced aggression, inability to cope with captivity) may be due to depletion of certain chemicals in the brain responsible for transmitting nerve impulses in the brain, and increased levels of corticosteroids in the bloodstream. She has begun to work with antidepressants as a way of treating what she believes to be an underlying physiological cause of feather picking. At the time of this writing, much work remains to be done before a determination of long-term efficiency in the treatment of feather picking with these drugs can be made.

4. Psychological "tender loving care" may be needed. This is a very large and important area. The reader is encouraged to review the section on psychological health in Chapter 2. One or more consultations with a *qualified* psittacine behaviorist may be of great value in establishing an effective program to stop feather picking. It should always be remembered that parrots are intelligent, emotional creatures. In any attempt to relieve the psychological causes of feather picking, owners should give great thought to the quality and quantity of time spent with the bird, as well as the comfort, security, and appropriate stimulation inherent in the bird's immediate environment.

5. Dietary changes may be required. *All* parrots should have a well-balanced, nutritious diet. This is doubly important for the feather picker. Not only should the diet be adequate from the nutritional standpoint, but it should also provide visual, textural, and taste variety as well. This kind of "recreational" food intake cannot be overemphasized. (See the section on nutrition in Chapter 2.)

Prognosis As with many other avian disease problems, the treatment outcome for the bird that mutilates its plumage is dependent upon the response to therapy of the underlying cause. In many cases of feather picking, there is not a single cause, but several underlying conditions that must be dealt with.

For individuals that pick because of infectious or dietary problems, there is a good chance for a successful outcome, providing treatment is rigorous, appropriate, and the treatment protocol faithfully adhered to by the owner.

Birds suffering from internal tumors may or may not make a good recovery, this being dependent upon the success of the surgical or medical procedures required to remove the growth.

Birds that feather pick as a result of stress and/or boredom have a guarded outlook. Chronic and habitual feather picking may be very difficult to cure, and require a serious commitment on the owner's part for an extended period. Some birds are never cured of this habit, regardless of the owner's commitment and the excellence of veterinary care and guidance.

FRENCH MOLT: French molt is a condition found in young budgerigars that are at the point of fledging, or have been out of the nest for a few days. It is characterized by the breaking or loss of the primary flight and tail feathers. In severe cases, the secondary flight feathers may be lost. In the most extreme cases, the bird may lose all its feathers. Occasionally, birds are so mildly affected that the problem goes undetected.

Feathers so affected are lost symmetrically. Those that are fully grown are not lost. Only those still developing are involved in French molt. Birds afflicted with French molt never regain normal feathering, and are often called creepers or runners because of their inability to fly.

Outbreaks are frequently sudden and unexpected. French molt usually appears toward the end of breeding season, often in third nests. The youngest in the clutch seems to be most often the victim, but not invariably. The disease sometimes strikes at random regardless of the youngster's birth order in the clutch. According to T. Geoffrey Taylor (1982), once such an outbreak has occurred, it will continue with increasing severity throughout the remainder of the breeding season. If this should occur, the breeding cycle must be interrupted for six months, after which time the problem will usually not reappear.

Taylor has noted some interesting findings with regard to affected birds: The crop contents of chicks from pairs that previously produced French molters had less protein than that of chicks from pairs producing only healthy chicks. Also, birds with French molt had abnormal blood findings: low PVC; anemia; red blood cells that were abnormally fragile and had a shorter life-span; bone marrow with an excessive amount of normal blood cell–producing tissue (hyperplastic bone marrow); and bone marrow unable to supply red blood cells fast enough for normal body requirements, even with a hyperplastic bone marrow, thus contributing to the bird's anemia.

Taylor cites a study by Schofield in which the following findings were made:

1. No evidence of feather mites or other parasite in birds affected with French molt
2. No evidence of skin infections or other skin lesions in affected birds

Optimum health and condition in most pet birds will be strongly advanced by providing the bird with an interesting, stimulating environment. As an example, this budgerigar enjoys a spacious cage and many toys serving as outlets to occupy its interest. *M. Vogel*

Giardia (single-celled organism)

3. Poor development of quill keratin (keratin is the tough, protein substance in hair, nails, feathers, and horny body tissues)
4. Large amounts of hemorrhage in the quill pulp, which has a rich blood supply
5. A decreased rate of growth of flight feathers compared to that of normal birds

When using the term "French molt," one must be careful of the exact syndrome to which it is being applied. In the United States it refers to the constellation of symptoms discussed above. The term as used in Australia refers to the acute form of psittacine beak and feather disease; various Japanese, Canadian, and German aviculturists have described lesions that they state were caused by *Papovavirus* (implicated in budgerigar fledgling disease) as French molt (Harrison, 1986a).

Causative Agent   The cause or causes of French molt are not known. It may be a multifactorial disease. Taylor (1982) feels that anything adversely affecting the supply of the feather pulp of a growing feather with oxygen and nutrients may potentially cause French molt.
Several suggested (but unconfirmed) causes of French molt are:

Bacterial or viral infection: The viral etiology is particularly favored. Taylor (1982) hypothesizes that an antibody-antigen reaction could cause changes in feather pulp capillaries, leading to hemorrhage in the pulp cavity and death of the feather. Viruses suggested as being implicated include mutant *Poxvirus, Herpesvirus,* and *Papovavirus* (Harrison, 1984).

Nutritional problems: Taylor feels that an excess of vitamin A in relationship to other fat-soluble vitamins (particularly E and D_3) may be part of the problem. The reason for this is that abnormally high amounts of vitamin A cause red blood cell fragility and capillary hemorrhage, thus causing feather pulp damage.

Environmental problems: This theory is based on the occurrence of French molt toward the end of the breeding season.

Parasitic problems: This would not seem to be a likely cause in view of the findings of Schofield, as cited by Taylor.

Hereditary factors

Autoimmune disease: This possibility is suggested by Taylor, also. In such a condition, the body's immune system does not recognize its own tissue proteins and fights them as if they were invading bacteria or viruses. Needless to say, such a vicious and protracted war with the bird as the battleground leads to extensive body organ damage.

Transmission   There is some feeling that the disease may be transmitted to the egg by affected parents (Taylor, 1982). Whether this is due to an infectious or a hereditary process is unknown. It is known, however, that eggs produced by affected parents, and fostered by healthy birds, still produce diseased babies.

Symptoms Loss of primary flight and tail feathers in young budgerigars at or about the time of fledging. In severe to extreme cases, secondary flight or body feathers may be lost.

Laboratory Work Laboratory work may be done to help the veterinarian rule out other feather disorders such as psittacine beak and feather disease. Such tests may include hematology, serum chemistries, microscopic examination of feathers and feather pulp (in growing feathers), and feather follicle biopsy. Gram stains of cloaca, choana, and feather follicles may also be warranted.

Treatment There is no treatment for French molt. Good husbandry is doubly important for a bird that has lost some or all of the insulating qualities of its plumage.

Prognosis The bird affected with French molt will never regain normal feathering. It is not, however, a fatal disease. Such birds may be prone to the disorders caused by lack of adequate feather insulation, such as infection and hypothermia.

Because of possible hereditary factors, the breeder may wish to consider the wisdom of breeding birds with French molt.

GIARDIASIS: Giardiasis is the parasitic infection of the lining of the intestine by *Giardia*, a protozoan. Protozoa are of the phylum *Protozoa*, which contains the simplest animals in the animal kingdom. These wee beasties are usually one celled, and they usually reproduce asexually. *Giardia* is capable of infecting dogs, cats, horses, and humans, as well as birds.

Giardia occurs in two forms: the motile trophozoite that lives in the gut of its host, and the nonmotile cyst that is produced by the trophozoite. The trophozoite die quickly outside the host's body. The cysts, which are shed in the feces, can survive for several months in a cool, moist environment (Willard et al., 1987).

The life cycle of *Giardia* is important to understand from the standpoint of control. First, cysts are ingested by the bird (or other animal or human host) via contaminated food or water. They produce trophozoites that attach themselves to the lining of the bird's intestine, where they in turn produce more cysts. These new cysts are then excreted in the feces, where they await ingestion by other potential victims, thus beginning the whole cycle again.

Both cysts and trophozoites reproduce asexually. Alan Fudge and Loni McEntee (1986) believe this to be the reason that avian giardiasis is sometimes difficult to cure. Cysts are highly resistant to drying, boiling, and freezing. However, certain disinfectants such as phenols (Lysol, for example), household bleach, and quaternary ammonium products (Roccal-D) are effective against them.

According to Fudge and McEntee, the problems experienced by birds infected with *Giardia* seem to be related to two factors:

1. The parasite interferes with the absorption from the gut of fat-soluble vitamins, riboflavin, and essential fats and proteins.

2. Birds (especially cockatiels) develop an allergy to *Giardia* that leads to severe itching.

Causative Agent   *Giardia* species, a protozoan intestinal parasite.

Transmission   *Giardia* is transmitted in food and water contaminated by feces containing its cyst form. Overcrowding of birds and poor sanitation are important contributory factors.

Symptoms   While it is not rare for an afflicted bird to be completely asymptomatic, a bird with giardiasis usually presents at least some of the following symptoms:

> Diarrhea
> A yellowing of the urates
> A history of partial or nonresponse to antibiotic therapy in a bird thought to have bacterial gut infections
> Lethargy
> Weight loss
> Unthriftiness ("poor doers")
> Death

In addition, a particular syndrome reported by Fudge and McEntee (1986) seems to be specific to cockatiels. It is called cockatiel feather syndrome and is associated with giardiasis in cockatiels. The symptoms include:

> Persistent feather picking—especially of wings, flanks, and legs—often accompanied by screaming, as if the bird were in pain
> Wasting of the breast muscles
> Dry, flaky skin
> Patchy feather loss
> Loss of appetite
> Shifting leg lameness
> Bleeding due to self-trauma, particularly during the molting season when blood feathers may be involved

Laboratory Work

> *Microscopic examination*: May be performed on feces for evidence of *Giardia* organisms.
> *Serology*: Not commonly done at present, but a test has been developed in England for the detection of *Giardia* antigen in human feces (Fudge and McEntee, 1986). This test may be adopted for birds in the future.
> *Hematology*: This will often show an increase in a special type of white blood cell called an eosinophil; it is also common for birds with giardiasis to have low serum protein levels.

Treatment   There are several medications available from which the veterinarian can choose when treating giardiasis:

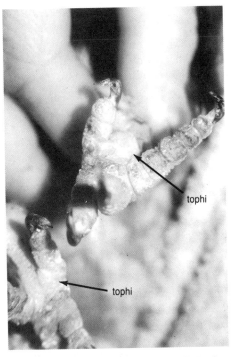

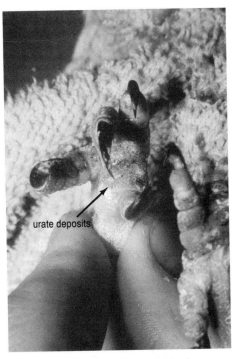

The feet of an Amazon Parrot affected with gout. The whitish swellings (tophi) are caused by deposits of urates on and in the toe joints. *Peter Sakas, D.V.M.*

Gout in the foot of a conure. Swelling on sole of foot is caused by urates.
Peter Sakas, D.V.M.

Visceral gout. Note deposit of white urates on surface of heart and part of liver.
Peter Sakas, D.V.M.

163

Metronidazole (Flagyl), given as an injection

Ipronidazole (Ipropran), given orally

Dimetridazole (Emtryl), given orally (this medication is placed in the drinking water; in warm weather when the bird drinks more, there is some danger of overdose and toxicity)

Good husbandry is necessary both in the cure and prevention of giardiasis:

Consistent daily cleanup of fecal matter and items soiled by feces
Prevention of overcrowding
Good nutrition
Clean food and water at all times
Management of environment to reduce physical and psychological stress
Control of rats and other animals that can spread *Giardia* in aviaries

In addition, any bird suspected of having giardiasis should be isolated until completion of treatment, at which time a two- to four-week follow-up CBC and fecal examination should be done.

Prognosis   The occurrence of a relapse following treatment is a fairly common phenomenon. This is thought to be due to the fact that both life forms of *Giardia* (trophozoite and cyst) can reproduce asexually. A second course of treatment will usually eliminate the problem, provided husbandry is good.

Fudge and McEntee (1986) state that relief from itching can occur only hours after medication has been given. They have also noted cessation of feather picking and rapid weight gain.

GOUT: Gout is a condition in which uric acid and urates are not excreted normally by the kidneys, resulting in the deposition of these substances in the bird's body. Articular gout refers to the form in which urates and uric acid are deposited in joint spaces. It is generally a chronic ailment. Visceral gout is the form in which these substances are deposited in body tissue other than the joints. This form is usually acute, with rapid onset, and frequently ends in death. Occasionally, the two forms occur together.

Uric acid is the result of protein metabolism in birds. It is produced in the liver and kidneys, and excreted by the kidneys. In humans, disease processes (such as pneumonia and leukemia) causing the breakdown of body proteins lead to an increased production of uric acid, resulting in increased uric acid serum levels. This is also true in birds (Minsky and Petrak, 1982).

It is unclear at the time of this writing whether gout is caused by malfunctioning kidneys, or whether abnormal amounts of uric acid are produced for some other reason, with result that the kidneys—though they may be normal—cannot excrete the uric acid rapidly enough.

Causative Agent   The cause (or causes) of gout are unknown. Various ideas have been put forth:

Chronic vitamin A deficiency (results in cellular changes in the kidney tissue, which renders the kidneys incapable of normally excreting uric acid and urates into the urine)

Infectious diseases (such as nephritis—an infection of the kidneys that so damages the kidneys that they cannot excrete urates and uric acid normally)

Chemical poisoning

Inactivity

Water deprivation

Stress (such as shipping or exposure to cold)

Dietary excesses of protein, vitamin D, or calcium

Renal tumor

Transmission Gout is not infectious and cannot be transmitted from bird to bird.

Symptoms The symptoms of visceral gout are nonspecific and may include the following:

Decreased appetite

Mood changes

Inconsistent droppings

Weight loss

Weakness

The symptoms of articular gout are more specific, since individual joints are involved, and such changes are more easily visualized:

Restlessness (due to the discomfort of bearing weight for prolonged periods of time on the affected joint or joints)

Frequent shifting from one leg to the other

Difficult perching

Toes extended in a rigid position; swollen, tender, warm to the touch

Small, rounded, light-colored spots called tophi, adjacent to one or more toe joints (they consist of uric acid and urates being deposited around the joints)

Drooping wings (due to joint involvement in these extremities)

The progression of articular gout is usually from toe joint to heel joint, then knee joint. Often, tendons and tendon sheaths are involved. The bird suffers great pain.

Laboratory Work

Murexide Test: This test consists of placing a tiny amount of material taken from tophi onto a white porcelain plate. A drop of nitric acid is added, and the mixture dried carefully over a small open flame. When this has been accomplished, a drop of ammonia is added. If the mixture then turns reddish-purple in color, the presence of uric acid is confirmed (Minsky and Petrak, 1982).

Serology: Uric acid levels are measured.

Radiographs: Will rule out the possibility of arthritis.

Microscopic examination: Material from tophi or joint fluid will reveal whether urate crystals are present in the bird with articular gout.

Diagnostic laparotomy: Will sometimes allow the veterinarian to visualize urate and uric acid deposits in abdominal tissues.

Kidney biopsy: May allow diagnosis of gout based upon changes seen microscopically in kidney tissues.

Treatment   Treatment of gout is directed toward relief of pain and prolongation of life.

1. Good husbandry must be practiced: perches should be flat, broad, and soft, as the bird's feet are frequently swollen and unable to grip. The use of padding on perches, such as lamb's wool, is recommended. Several layers of paper toweling wrapped securely around the perch may also be used. Such material should be kept scrupulously clean. Food and water bowls should be placed within easy reach of perches, so the bird does not have to climb to reach them.

2. Dietary changes may be required, to a diet with low protein content, especially of animal protein sources. This helps decrease uric acid production by the bird's body. The diet should include increased amounts of fruits and vegetables, especially those high in vitamin A, and a plentiful supply of clean, fresh water.

3. Avoid exposure to cold and other stressors.

4. Medication may be prescribed: aspirin for pain relief (*the dosage must always be prescribed by the veterinarian*); allopurinal (Zyloprim), to decrease uric acid synthesis and cause the tophi to shrink.

5. Large tophi may need to be excised. This procedure is accomplished by electrocautery. According to Lothrop et al. (1986) extreme hemorrhage often results; therefore it is not recommended in most cases.

Prognosis   Gout cannot be cured, only controlled somewhat. The bird frequently suffers great pain, with the result that its owner often elects euthanasia. This decision must be evaluated carefully in each individual case by the owner, with the guidance and counsel of the bird's veterinarian.

HAEMOPROTEUS: *Haemoproteus* is a protozoa that infects the red blood cells of birds. It is quite common in cockatoos and macaws, and has been associated with stress and feather picking (Barnes, 1986). According to Gordon Bennett (1987), at times of high intensity infection, 60 to 90 percent of the bird's red blood cells may be involved. He further states that the parasitic involvement can become quiescent, only to intensify during breeding season.

The parasite requires two hosts: the intermediate host in which sexual

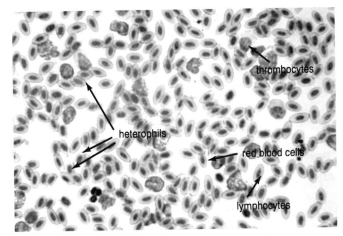

Microscopic view of red blood cells and two types of white blood cells—heterophils and lymphocytes. Thrombocytes are also shown.

Peter Sakas, D.V.M.

A group of African Grays (*Psittacus erithacus erithacus*).

Peter Sakas, D.V.M.

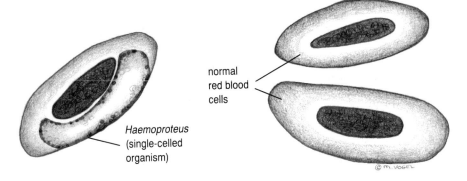

Haemoproteus organism

167

reproduction take place; and the avian host, in which asexual reproduction takes place (Bennett, 1987; Campbell, 1988).

When a blood stain of an affected bird is examined microscopically, the gametocyte form of *Haemoproteus* can be seen inside the red blood cells. Asexual reproduction of this parasite takes place in the linings of those blood vessels supplying the lungs, liver, spleen, and bone marrow (Campbell, 1988). Infection by any of the over two hundred species and varieties of *Haemoproteus* is not considered serious, as these organisms do not seem very pathologic (Bennett, 1987).

Causative Agent *Haemoproteus* species.

Transmission *Haemoproteus* is transmitted by the bite of either one of the intermediate hosts to *Haemoproteus* (house fly or midge). J. Barnes (1986) states that it is very difficult to establish and maintain a *Haemoproteus* infection in a potential avian victim by inoculating it with the blood of another bird already infected.

Symptoms *Haemoproteus* infections do not generally produce symptoms; the infection is usually discovered on routine blood smear examination being done for another purpose. When symptoms are present, they are general and nonspecific, and include anemia, loss of appetite, and depression (Campbell, 1988).

Laboratory Work Microscopic examination of a blood smear.

Treatment Because *Haemoproteus* does not usually cause disease or symptoms, and the medication used to rid the bird of this parasite is very toxic, treatment is usually not attempted (Bennett, 1987; Barnes, 1986).

Prognosis No difficulties are usually encountered in the bird with a *Haemoproteus* infection. They will usually remain healthy and live a normal life-span.

HYPOCALCEMIA SYNDROME IN AFRICAN GRAY PARROTS This is a condition in which an African Gray Parrot's serum calcium level falls below acceptable physiological levels. As a result, the bird convulses.

Calcium is necessary for many body functions, among which are proper muscle contractions and the transmission of nerve impulses (see the discussion on serum calcium in Chapter 3). Lack of adequate serum calcium creates seizuring activity because nerve impulses and muscle contractions are improperly controlled. It is thought that African Grays lack the ability to mobilize calcium from their bones when their serum calcium levels drop, unlike other parrots that will exhaust their stores of body calcium to maintain normal serum calcium levels (Rosskopf and Woerpel, 1985a).

Birds that suffer this problem and do not survive always show enlarged parathyroid glands upon necropsy, according to Rosskopf and Woerpel. The parathyroid glands are located next to the thyroid glands in the chest cavity, close to the syrinx, the jugular veins, and the carotid arteries. These tiny glands are responsible for regulating calcium levels in the blood serum. When this level decreases, the parathyroid glands secrete parathyroid hormone (PTH). They continue to secrete this hormone in a futile attempt to raise serum calcium levels. This "overwork" leads to the enlargement of the parathyroids.

Another factor that may prove to be of significance in this syndrome is the role the kidneys play (Rosskopf and Woerpel, 1985a). The kidneys, in response to PTH, excrete higher than normal amounts of calcium (Kenny, 1986). It may be possible that the African Gray not only does not respond to PTH by mobilizing bone calcium, but actually excretes what little serum calcium it has, in the urine, in response to continued PTH secretion. This would tend to compound the bird's already precarious calcium situation. At the time of this writing, this possibility has not been explored, but it may prove an interesting area of research in the future.

In a recent article by Marjorie McMillan (1988) it was stated that in studying the radiographs of African Grays, numerous small deposits of calcium have been found in the kidneys. These birds evidenced no change in the size or shape of their kidneys, nor were any signs of illness noted. However, as McMillan points out, it is intriguing that such deposits have been found in the one species that not uncommonly suffers abnormally low serum calcium levels. The significance of this finding is not yet apparent.

Hypocalcemia syndrome is most frequently found in young birds, aged two to five years. One case of a ten-year-old bird has been reported in the literature (Rosskopf and Woerpel, 1985a).

Causative Agent The cause (or causes) of African Gray hypocalcemia syndrome is not known. It may be an hereditary problem involving parathyroid and kidney function in specific individuals, as not all Grays are affected. Viral disease of the parathyroid gland has also been suggested (Rosskopf and Woerpel, 1985a).

Transmission At this time, hypocalcemia syndrome is not believed to be infectious, and is therefore not transmissible to other birds.

Symptoms Signs of hypocalcemia syndrome consist of tremors and/or convulsions, frequently stimulated by excitement.

Laboratory Work Serum calcium levels must be determined. In addition, the veterinarian may order a CBC and a complete panel of serum chemistries to rule out other disease states that may be present concurrently or exacerbating the problem.

Treatment Treatment is aimed at stopping the seizures and preventing their recurrence. To these ends, in the bird that is having convulsions, some or all of the following will be done:

Intravenous injections of a calcium and phosphorus preparation
Intramuscular injections of Injacom (vitamins A, D, and E)
Intramuscular injections of Valium
Supportive therapy, such as antibiotics and fluid therapy

For the bird that has recovered from the acute, seizuring phase of hypocalcemia syndrome, a strict regimen of prevention must be adhered to for the rest of the bird's life:

1. Adequate dietary calcium supply: Foods high in calcium, such as low-fat cheese, yogurt; supplementation with a high-quality avian mineral supplement containing vitamin D_3 and phosphorus (D-Ca-Phos, for example); soluble calcium, such as Neocalglucon, added to the drinking water.
2. Periodic blood tests to determine serum calcium levels. This allows the veterinarian to determine the bird's response to therapy and allows adjustments to be made accordingly.

Prognosis   This is dependent upon the amount of parathyroid damage that has occurred. If damage is minimal, a successful therapeutic outcome is likely. If, however, parathyroid damage is such that the bird is no longer able to regulate calcium metabolism, regardless of treatment, the outlook is very poor.

MACAW WASTING SYNDROME: This is a serious disease, affecting not only macaws but also cockatoos, conures, African Grays, Amazons, *Eclectus*, and cockatiels; the death rate is nearly 100 percent. It was first brought to the attention of the veterinary community by Woerpel and Rosskopf (1984a). In this article, the authors hypothesize that the disease was introduced into the United States through southern California via imported birds newly out of quarantine. Many of the affected birds were young, and their country of origin was Bolivia.

The disease was first described in macaws, but as more case evidence was gathered, it became apparent that other species were also susceptible. To reflect this, other names for the problem are used in addition to the original name. These include proventricular dilatation syndrome, myenteric ganglioneuritis and encephalomyelitis of psittaciformes, and infiltrative splanchnic neuropathy. These names are actually descriptive in nature and refer to the major symptoms found in macaw wasting syndrome—namely, gastric (digestive) and neurological (nervous system) disturbances.

Whatever the causative agent of the disease—and this is yet unknown—it has an affinity for avian nervous tissue, particularly the digestive tract function, and those of the brain stem (that portion of the brain controlling such activities as motor coordination relative to sight, breathing, cardiac function, regulation of various digestive activities, sleep/arousal mechanisms, and various muscle coordination functions).

The hallmark of macaw wasting syndrome is the loss of ability to digest food, with subsequent wasting of body tissue and severe weight loss. It is also not uncommon for the bird to show signs of central nervous system damage, such as imbalance and uncoordination.

Causative Agent   The cause is unknown. Studies with electron microscopy by A. Mannl, Helga Gerlach, and Rose Leipold (1987) have demonstrated foreign

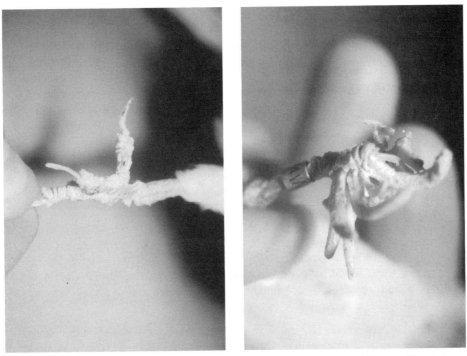

Two views of tassel foot infestation in a canary. The causative organism of this condition is the *cnemidokoptes* mite.   *Peter Sakas, D.V.M.*

The *cnemidokoptes* mite is also responsible for the condition known as "scaly face," shown by this infested budgerigar.   *Peter Sakas, D.V.M.*

particles in nerve cells supplying the proventriculus, ventriculus, and the duodenal portion of the small intestine. The authors state that these particles are similar to a *Paramyxovirus* (PMV). There are several groups of viruses in this category of viruses. PMV Group I causes Newcastle disease. However, according to Woerpel and Rosskopf (1984c), if one of the *Paramyxoviruses* is proven to be the cause of macaw wasting syndrome, it will *not* be the same group causing Newcastle disease. Gerlach (1986d) cites studies by other workers that have demonstrated viruslike particles in kidney tissue of affected birds, resembling *Adenovirus*, as well as virallike particles in cells of the spinal cord.

Whatever the cause, it is important to note that at the time of this writing no causative agent has been isolated, experimentally reproduced, and subsequently reintroduced into a susceptible host bird to cause disease. Until this has been done, no definite infectious agent can be said to be the cause of macaw wasting syndrome.

Transmission   Macaw wasting syndrome is thought to be infectious, but does not appear to be highly contagious (Woerpel and Rosskopf, 1984c). Nevertheless, any bird suspected of having this disease should be separated from other birds and strict isolation procedure initiated until the diagnosis of macaw wasting syndrome can be confirmed or denied.

Symptoms   Symptoms fall into those having to do with digestive tract problems and those related to central nervous system damage. Symptoms may be very sudden in onset, with little time elapsing between their appearance and the death of the bird, or symptoms can be more intermittent in nature, with a greater period of time elapsing before death.

Digestive system–related symptoms include:

Regurgitation (may be sudden in onset and very persistent, or may be intermittent)
Passage of whole seed or other obviously undigested food, in the feces
Diarrhea
Loss of appetite (although the bird may continue feedinglike behavior)
Wasting muscle tissue, especially of the pectoral muscles
Severe weight loss
Depression
Gut infection, especially by *E. coli*

Symptoms related to central nervous system damage include:

Leg weakness
Imbalance
Lameness

The final and irrevocable symptom is death. Important necropsy findings (which definitely confirm the presence of macaw wasting syndrome) include:

Grossly dilated, thin-walled proventriculus
Dilated gizzard (although this is a less common finding)

Proventriculus impacted with seed or other food (can sometimes cause the proventriculus to rupture)

Severe wasting of muscles, with very little body fat present

Flaccid crop (an occasional finding)

Microscopic findings: severe inflammation and disruption of the smooth muscle layers of the proventriculus and ventriculus; inflammation and degeneration of the brain stem; destruction of the ganglia (that is, the collection of nerve cells supplying a specific area of the body, such as a muscle, or a particular body organ) that supply the digestive organs

Laboratory Work   Three tests are normally used to rule out other coexisting disease: serum chemistries, hematology, and cultures, especially of the cloaca.

Radiographs are used for further diagnosis: the plain X ray will often reveal a dilated, thin-walled proventriculus and/or gizzard; a barium series will demonstrate a delayed transit of food through the digestive tract, consistent with nerve damage and compromised digestive system function.

Treatment   Treatment will consist of supportive measures such as fluid therapy, antibiotics if indicated, and tube feedings. These are usually given frequently and in small amounts. Mannl et al. (1987) suggest that the feeding of soft food may prolong survival time somewhat.

Prognosis   The prognosis for macaw wasting syndrome is very poor. The disease carries a virtually 100 percent mortality rate, regardless of treatment. If the bird does not first succumb to starvation, then a secondary infection, central nervous system damage, or autointoxication will cause its death (Mannl et al., 1987). (Autointoxication is a state of "self-poisoning" in which the body is overwhelmed and succumbs to poisons produced by infection or the waste products of its own metabolic processes.)

MALARIA: Avian malaria is an infectious disease caused by *Plasmodium* species, which are protozoa. *Protozoa* is the phylum in the animal kingdom including the simplest animals. They are one celled, and usually reproduce asexually by cell division. Occasionally, asexual reproduction occurs. Protozoa are free living in fresh or salt water and in damp terrestrial environments. They may also live as parasites in other living organisms. *Plasmodium* species are an example of the latter.

Avian malaria is very rare in parrots. I. F. Keymer (1982b) reports it in Greenwing Macaws and Blue-headed Parrots. It has also been reported in Moluccan Cockatoos (Barnes, 1986).

Plasmodium causes damage to liver, spleen, and red blood cells. Once *Plasmodium* enters the bird's body, it moves to the liver, where it multiplies and returns to the bloodstream. Some penetrate red blood cells, and some return to body tissues such as the liver, spleen, kidney, and lungs. The parasite multiplies in the red blood cells, causing them to burst and release their increased numbers of *Plasmodium* to begin a new cycle of invasion, multiplication, and rupture.

The initial infection causes the most severe illness. Thereafter, if the host survives, symptoms rapidly decrease in severity. Eventually, a chronic, low-level parasitemia is created. However, stress can bring about a flareup of malarial symptoms. If a bird with no evolutionary experience with *Plasmodium* becomes infected, the results are rapid and fatal (Bennett, 1987).

Causative Agent More than fifty species of *Plasmodium* have been identified as a cause of avian malaria. Interestingly, this disease is not limited to tropical birds. Keymer (1982b) reports a study in which many wild birds of North America have been shown to be infected with *Plasmodium*. It appears to be common in raptors, for example.

Transmission Avian malaria is transmitted, as in humans, by the bite of mosquitoes. The red or roost mite (*Dermanyssus gallinae*) is also reported to transmit *Plasmodium* through its bite (Sthelik, 1987).

Once infected, a bird is not able to infect another bird. This is because *Plasmodium* must pass part of its life cycle in its insect host before it can be infective to birds and mammals.

Symptoms Bennett (1987) lists the following symptoms of avian malaria:

Listlessness
Loss of appetite
Swelling of the eyelids
Emaciation
Sudden death

Laboratory Work

Stained blood smears examined microscopically: Will demonstrate *Plasmodium* within the red blood cells.
Hematology: Will demonstrate anemia.
Serum chemistries: Will indicate organ damage, the bird's overall health status, and response to treatment.

Treatment Treatment is with antimalarial medications such as chloroquine, primaquine, proguanil, and quinacrine (Bennett, 1987; Keymer, 1982b; Barnes, 1986). Carl Clark (1986) states that tetracyclines may be of use in treating avian malaria. Some of these drugs act to kill *Plasmodium* in the red blood cells. Some act to kill the organism in tissue such as the liver, thus preventing their eventual migration to red blood cells.

Prognosis: Avian malaria can be an acute, fatal disease. Success of treatment probably depends upon the bird's overall health status and response to therapy. In order to achieve a complete cure, both forms of *Plasmodium* must be killed: those in body tissues and those in the red blood cells.

MUCORMYCOSIS (PHYSOMYCOSIS, ZYGOMYCOSIS): This is a very serious and usually fatal fungal disease, most often caused by *Absidia corymbifera* (Patgiri,

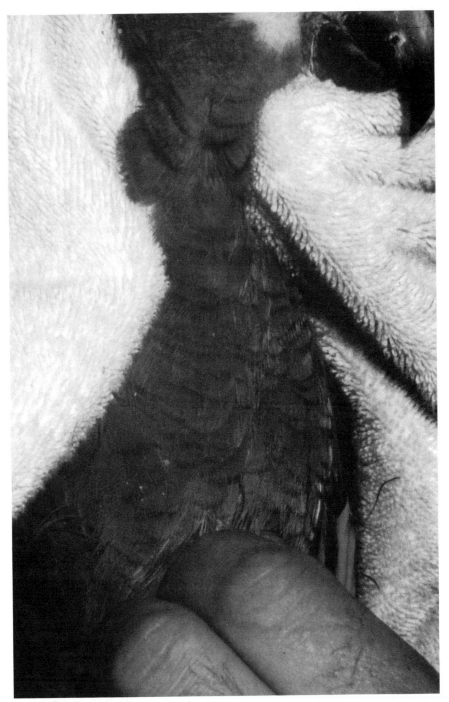

The avian veterinarian will palpate the bird's breast muscle to determine nutritional status and the presence of any chronic, wasting disease.   *Peter Sakas, D.V.M.*

1987; Keymer, 1982a). It often appears in combination with aspergillosis (Clubb, 1983a). It is quite rare in birds, but it has been reported to have been found in the budgerigar and African Gray Parrots (Keymer, 1982a).

Fungal growth may be confined to the respiratory system (trachea, syrinx, lungs, and air sacs) or affect the heart or kidneys. It also may be spread in the blood to any part of the body. Susan Clubb (1983a) feels that the brain is a not uncommon site for mucormycotic invasion.

Causative Agent Members of the fungal class Zygomycetes, most commonly *Absidia corymbifera*.

Transmission The causative fungal agents are ubiquitous, being found in soil and in decaying organic matter, such as feces and food (Smith, 1980). Inhalation of airborne spores from such sources is probably the main route of infection.

Keymer (1982a) suggests that prior antibiotic therapy may be a predisposing factor in the development of mucormycosis. Presumably, normal body flora are altered by such drugs, allowing the pathologic growth of the causative fungus.

Symptoms

> Sores in mouth, with subsequent difficulty eating in some cases
> Depression
> Ruffled feathers
> Resting on breastbone
> Rapid, labored breathing
> Twisted neck
> Sudden death

Although the author finds no mention in the available literature of symptoms associated with central nervous system damage, it is reasonable to assume that if there is brain involvement (as Clubb believes), signs such as imbalance, difficulty perching, disorientation, convulsions, and the like are possible.

Laboratory Work Firm diagnosis of mucormycosis can be made only at necropsy, according to Keymer (1982a), due to the fact that microscopic examination of affected internal tissues must be made. However, when the veterinarian is first presented with the affected bird, routine serum chemistries, hematology, scrapings of any mouth lesions, radiographs, and cloacal and choanal cultures will no doubt be performed in order to establish a presumptive or "working" diagnosis. As the reader will be able to ascertain from the list of foregoing symptoms, such signs are general and do not reflect anything more concrete than that the bird is gravely ill. Also, a thorough history revealing an environment favorable to the growth of, and exposure of the bird to, fungi will be of help.

Treatment Currently, amphotericin-B is the drug of choice in combating mucormycosis (Clubb, 1983). It has its problems, though, the main one being that it is highly toxic to the kidneys.

176

Prognosis The outlook for recovery is extremely grave. This disease is most often fatal, regardless of treatment (Clubb, 1983).

Prevention of mucormycosis, and indeed other fungal infections, is easily achieved if good sanitation practices are adhered to in the maintenance of a collection or aviary. Fungi require adequate nutrients, warmth, humidity, and subdued light in order to grow and flourish. Therefore, scrupulous removal of feces and uneaten food, fresh air, and the avoidance of a dank, ill-lit environment will go far in the prevention of such avian scourges.

MYCOPLASMOSIS: This is an infection caused by an organism known as *Mycoplasma*. It is a chronic, multifactorial disease.

Mycoplasma used to be classified as a bacterium, but because of several unique attributes it possesses, it has now been placed in the category *Mollicutes*. *Mycoplasma* differs from bacteria in that it has no cell wall, only a cell membrane, surrounding the cell contents. This has two important implications. The first is that antibiotics that act upon an organism's cell wall to effect its death are not effective against *Mycoplasma*. This makes mycoplasmosis somewhat difficult to treat. The second implication involves disinfection. Because the organism lacks a cell wall, it is susceptible to most of the commonly used disinfectants, provided surfaces have been cleaned of organic debris first, in order to allow direct contact between disinfectant and organism.

Mycoplasma is extremely small—so small, in fact, that 8,000 could fit inside a human red blood cell (Smith, 1980). It is the smallest known single-celled organism able to live and reproduce independently of its host, according to Smith. Even so, the organism can survive for only approximately five hours in the environment, except in water, where it may exist for two to four days, depending upon its specific strain (Gerlach, 1986c).

Mycoplasma can be found in colonies on the mucous membranes of the respiratory and urogenital tracts of normal birds. It is basically a commensal organism—that is to say, it lives in a close, nonparasitic relationship with its host, causing no illness. The problem arises when *Mycoplasma* gains entry to the bird's internal body through damaged mucous membranes. It then travels via the bloodstream to various organs, where it grows and flourishes, causing disease (Gerlach, 1986c). Organs frequently targeted are joints, egg follicles in the hen, oviduct, and brain. It can also involve the bird's nasal passages, sinuses, and eyes.

Mycoplasma causes mutations of the cells from which white blood cells evolve. This renders such cells unable to function properly in their job as recognizers of, and producers of antibodies against, bacteria, fungi, and viruses. Thus the bird's ability to protect itself against infection is seriously compromised. Mycoplasmosis sets the stage for secondary bacterial infections. It also mimics psittacosis in many of its symptoms (Gerlach, 1986c; Woerpel et al., 1987). This situation can complicate diagnosis.

Causative Agent *Mycoplasma* species.

Transmission   Very close contact between infected and susceptible birds is necessary for the transmission of mycoplasmosis. This is because of the limited survivability of *Mycoplasma* outside its host. Such contacts include infected crop contents fed to nestlings by parents, respiratory spread via aerosolized droplets containing the organism, and venereal spread by contact between breeding birds. It is also possible for the hen to infect her eggs. Rodney Reece (1987) states that an infected left abdominal air sac can spread the pathogen to the fertilized yolk as it first begins to pass down the oviduct. He further states that *Mycoplasma* is commonly isolated from hens with salpingitis, an infection of the oviduct.

Symptoms   Symptoms are dependent upon the organs affected and include the following:

Sneezing
Coughing
Discharges from eyes and/or nose
Breathing problems
Lameness and/or reluctance to bear weight on the affected foot or leg
Difficulty perching

In addition, reproductive failure such as decreased fertility, hatchability, and increases in neonatal deaths may indicate mycoplasmosis (Gerlach, 1986c).

Laboratory Work

Serology: This may or may not be of help in determining the presence of *Mycoplasma*. The problem lies in the fact that as yet we have no reliable way of differentiating between the harmless, commensal strains and those that cause disease.

Culture: This remains the best way to determine the presence of *Mycoplasma* (Gerlach, 1986c). Culture of the organism is done via sterile swabs from affected birds; these are then inoculated into chicken embryos or cell cultures for isolation and identification.

In addition, the veterinarian will probably do routine serum chemistries, hematology, and culture of choana and cloaca to determine the bird's general health status and the presence or absence of secondary bacterial or fungal infections.

Treatment   Treatment is directed toward eliminating any secondary infection, as well as the *Mycoplasma* organism. Because of this, antibiotics as indicated, supportive care such as fluid therapy, and dietary changes may be instituted. In addition, various antibiotics known to be effective against *Mycoplasma* may be used.

Prognosis   Mycoplasmosis is a difficult disease to eradicate. Even with the use of antibiotics, relapses are apt to occur when medication is discontinued (*Avian Disease Manual*, 1983). In commercial poultry operations, complete depopulation of an infected flock is recommended to eliminate the problem.

A malignant fibrosarcoma on the wing of a cockatiel. This type of tumor arises from the connective tissue cells.   *Peter Sakas, D.V.M.*

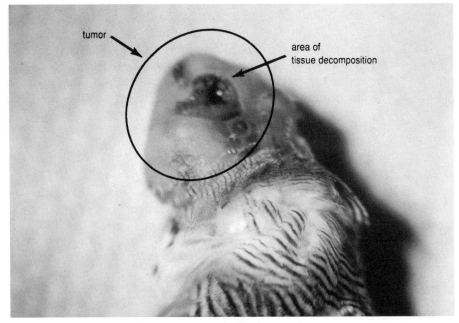

A malignant head tumor on a budgerigar. The center of the tumor has begun to rot and decompose (tissue necrosis).   *Peter Sakas, D.V.M.*

Improved husbandry and nutrition are the best ways of preventing mycoplasmosis. Reduction of the dust content in the air and eliminating stress are also important control measures (*Avian Histopathology*, 1987).

MYCOTOXICOSIS: This is a general term describing the disease condition that results when a bird comes in contact (by eating, inhalation, or skin contact) with the poisons produced by a fungus (Campbell, 1986b). It is important to note that this is a completely different ailment than a disease caused by the actual growth of a fungus within the bird's body (for example, aspergillosis or mucormycosis). In mycotoxicosis, the damage is caused by the poisonous byproducts of fungal growth. The most common place for the fungi to reproduce and thereby manufacture their toxins is in food products, especially grains or cereals. Other foods that are excellent growing media for fungi are peanuts and peanut products, nuts, bread, cheese, beans, fruit juice, and meats.

Not all fungi are capable of producing toxins. And for those that have this ability, the conditions must be conducive: moisture, stagnant air, the right temperature (25°C to 30°C; or 77°F to 86°F), and darkness. Of these, moisture seems to be the most critical factor.

There are three fungi best known to create mycotoxicosis in birds. *Aspergillus flavus* and *parasiticus* cause a mycotoxicosis called aflatoxicosis. *Fusarium* fungus species cause a mycotoxicosis called fusariotoxicosis. *Aspergillus ochraceous* causes the mycotoxicosis known as ochratoxicosis. As avian research progresses, other fungi capable of causing mycotoxicosis may be discovered.

There are certain characteristics of a mycotoxicosis outbreak that may allow the veterinarian to identify the disease:

1. The disease outbreak is often associated with a newly introduced food source. This source may show signs of fungal contamination.
2. The disease does not pass from bird to bird.
3. The disease often shows a seasonal pattern, because fungal growth is dependent upon seasonal climatic conditions.
4. There is no apparent infectious cause of the disease outbreak.
5. Sick birds do not get better when treated with antibiotics or other standard medications.

It is easier to identify mycotoxicosis if it manifests as a sudden, acute outbreak. This is because the symptoms are more dramatic than in a chronic, ongoing situation. Another factor is that the introduction of a new food source may be more easily associated with outbreak due to the shorter passage of time between the two incidents. The suspected food source is also more readily available for testing.

In chronic cases of mycotoxicosis, the symptoms are more subtle and less easily attributed to possible feed contamination. A greater period of time elapses between the source of infection and the disease manifestation. Indeed, the food will probably not even be available for testing. If the food is available, all evidence of fungal growth may be gone, leaving only the toxins behind, which are not visible to the eye and which may be identified only at great expense. Because mycotoxicosis impairs the bird's immune system, secondary infections may hide the primary disease problem.

Causative Agent   The toxins produced by *Aspergillus flavus, Aspergillus parasiticus, Fusarium* species, and *Aspergillus ochraceous.*

Transmission   The toxins may be inhaled or eaten. Skin contact with the toxin may also produce symptoms. Mycotoxicosis is not contagious and cannot be passed from bird to bird.

Symptoms   Symptoms vary, depending upon the fungus involved. Aflatoxicosis is most damaging to the liver. It causes widespread death of liver cells and also seems to have some cancer-causing (carcinogenic) properties. Among the various signs and symptoms are the following:

Decreased reproductive success
Poor growth
Digestive tract hemorrhage (due to blood-clotting abnormalities induced by liver disease)
Increased susceptibility to infection (due to an impaired immune system)
Weight loss
Loss of appetite
Depression
Death, in some cases

Fusariotoxicosis appears to affect the mucous membranes of the mouth, the nervous system, and the circulation in the bird's extremities. The following symptoms may be noted:

Sores in the mouth that are raised and yellowish-white in color (these may seriously interfere with the bird's ability to eat)
Lesions similar to the above on legs and feet
Rashes on unfeathered skin areas that have been in contact with *Fusarium* toxin
Abnormal feathering
Altered growth
Dry gangrene of the toes due to severely impaired blood circulation
Convulsions or imbalance (due to nervous system damage)

Ochratoxicosis affects the liver, kidneys, bone marrow, and lymphoid system (which is responsible for white blood cell and antibody production). The following symptoms may be seen:

Increased susceptibility to infection
Visceral gout
Wasting
Convulsions, imbalance, or other symptoms indicative of nervous system lesions
Breathing difficulties (due to infection of respiratory system)

Laboratory Work The causative fungus must be isolated from the suspected food source. Gross and microscopic necropsy findings can confirm organ damage consistent with mycotoxicosis in affected birds. The presence of fungal toxins in suspected food source, digestive tract, and/or organ tissues of dead birds can be confirmed through chemical testing.

In addition, a thorough history is extremely important in making the diagnosis of mycotoxicosis. The veterinarian will also need to perform serum chemistries, hematology, cultures, and possibly radiographs to determine the extent of damage and presence of secondary infections.

Treatment There is no specific treatment for mycotoxicosis. Treatment may include supportive therapy such as fluids, antibiotics if indicated, tube feedings, aerosol and/or oxygen therapy when severe respiratory distress is present.

An important aspect of therapy is the use of substances or chemicals that will absorb toxins in the gut and thus prevent absorption into and damage to the bird's body. An example of one such substance is activated charcoal.

Prognosis The outcome of treatment is dependent upon the individual bird: the length of time elapsed before treatment was sought, the specific toxin involved, and the bird's response to therapy.

Prevention of mycotoxicosis involves the purchase of only high-quality food products and their proper storage. Store food in *small* amounts in a refrigerator. This includes grain and peanuts. Maintain a dry environment in food storage areas. Do not store food in airtight plastic. This seals in moisture. When the container is opened, fungus spores gain access to the food, are trapped inside, and are thus provided with perfect conditions for growth.

Never give a bird food that is moldy. Throwing away suspect food is much cheaper financially and emotionally than treating a sick bird or experiencing its death.

NEOPLASM: A neoplasm is defined as a new and abnormal formation of tissue—in other words, a tumor or growth. Neoplasms may be benign (noncancerous) or malignant (cancerous). "Neoplasia" refers to the development of a neoplasm.

Campbell (1986c) states that companion birds have a higher incidence of neoplasms than wild birds, and gives the following reasons:

1. Companion birds usually live longer than wild birds. Since neoplasia is a problem of aging organisms, it is therefore seen more commonly in an older population of birds.
2. Companion birds are more likely to come into contact with the carcinogens produced in abundance by "civilization."
3. Companion birds are more affected by important cofactors in the production of neoplasms, such as dietary imbalances, genetic selection, hormonal problems (presumably encountered because of their captive state), and infectious agents to which they have developed no evolutionary immunity.

Tumor on the upper eyelid
of a Blue-fronted Amazon.
Peter Sakas, D.V.M.

Malignant kidney tumor.

A fatty tumor (lipogranulo-
ma) in a Mealy Amazon.
Peter Sakas, D.V.M.

4. The opportunity to study the process of neoplasia in wild birds is much less than in a captive population of birds, thereby biasing the study sample.

Why are neoplasms so dangerous? When we address this question, we are speaking primarily of malignancy. However, even a benign tumor can be potentially dangerous in certain situations—if it presses on nerves or blocks a portion of the intestine, for example.

Malignancies cause severe disability and/or death for the following reasons. First, they grow in an uncontrolled fashion, directly extending into normal tissue and interfering with essential body functions. Second, many malignant tumors can spread throughout the body, forming secondary tumors. Third, diffuse systemic involvement can occur in some types of cancers, such as those involving the blood system (leukemia, for example). In any of these three cases, serious problems arise that are directly attributable to the tumor:

Destruction of normal, essential body tissue

Hemorrhage, as when the tumor invades a major blood vessel

Obstruction, as may occur in the digestive tract (in such instances, the bird may be unable to use the food it eats or, in the case of respiratory tract involvement, it may be unable to breathe)

Infection of the tumor or the tissue surrounding it

Increased susceptibility to infection, as in cancers involving the white blood cells

Heart failure due to the increased stress that chronic, debilitating illness places on the heart and blood vessels

Malfunction of the central nervous system (brain, spinal cord), or peripheral nervous system (nerves supplying all other parts of the body)

The reader is apt to be confused by the various terms used in any discussion of neoplasms: "adenoma," "carcinoma," "sarcoma," and the like. To understand why these terms are used in specific situations, it is necessary to know a bit about embryo tissues and how they differentiate to form various mature body tissues. Neoplasms are classified according to this system.

A chick in the egg (or any mammal in the uterus) begins from a collection of three kinds of cells: ectoderm, mesoderm, and endoderm.

From the tissues of the ectoderm arise the external skin cells, and all the cells forming the nervous system—brain, spinal cord, and peripheral nerves. These tissues are supported and nourished by cells arising from the mesoderm.

The mesoderm not only produces cells supporting the nervous system, but also fibroblasts (which form connective tissue such as cartilage and collagen). It also produces cells that line lymph vessels, blood vessels, the heart, and other body cavities. Such cells comprise what is known as endothelium (internal skin cells). Other cells arising from the mesoderm include muscle cells, fat cells, red blood cells, and white blood cells (which are important to the immune system). While by no means an inclusive list, this gives the reader a general idea of the diversity of cells arising from the mesoderm.

The endoderm gives rise to tissues of the digestive tract, respiratory tract, and glands such as the thyroid, parathyroids, and thymus. Again, this is not an exhaustive list.

Cancers are classified in the following manner, based upon their embryonic cells of origin (King et al., 1983):

Carcinoma: A malignant tumor arising from the skin cells, whether on the inside or outside of the body (see Avitaminosis A in this chapter for a further discussion of epithelial cells).

Sarcoma: A malignant tumor arising from cells of mesodermal origin.

Leukemia, lymphoma: Malignant tumors arising from cells in the bone marrow and white blood cell-producing tissues (lymphoid tissues, such as those found in the spleen and liver, for example).

Carcinosarcoma: A malignant tumor containing both cells of epithelial and mesodermal origin.

Teratocarcinoma: A malignant tumor containing tissues arising from all three primitive cell types: ectoderm, endoderm, and mesoderm.

In addition to the basic classification of malignancies, benign tumors also have a characteristic classification (see Table 5-1).

The following is a list of several neoplasms found in birds. We will first look at the more commonly found benign (noncancerous) neoplasms. This is by no means a complete list:

Adenoma: An ordinarily benign tumor of cells that form glands or glandlike structures. They are usually well defined and tend to compress surrounding tissues, rather than invade them.

Fibroma: A benign tumor arising from fibrous connective tissue (the tissue that forms the supportive framework of any organism's body, such as cartilage).

Goiter: A chronic enlargement of the thyroid gland arising from the en-

TABLE 5-1. Characteristic Classification of Tumors

Neoplasm Arising from a Specific Cell Type	Benign Terminology	Malignant Terminology
External skin cell (squamous cell)	Papilloma	Squamous cell carcinoma
Glandular cell (as, for example, in a salivary gland)	Adenoma	Adenocarcinoma
Fibroblant (cells that form connective tissues of the skeleton)	Fibroma	Fibrocarcinoma
Fat cells	Lipoma	Liposarcoma
Endothelial cells (such as those that line blood vessels)	Angioma	Angiosarcoma
Cartilage cell	Chondroma	Chondrosarcoma
Bone cell	Osteoma	Osteosarcoma

largement of individual thyroid cells. It is not a true neoplasm. It is caused by a lack of iodine in the diet and is correctable by dietary adjustment. (The reader is referred to Thyroid Problems in this chapter for further discussion of goiter.)

Hemangioma: A benign tumor of the endothelial cells that line the blood vessels. It is not a true neoplasm, in that it is usually present from birth (congenital). It is most frequently seen in the skin and subcutaneous tissues. The "strawberry" birthmark is an example of a hemangioma.

Leiomyoma: A benign tumor of smooth muscle tissue, which lies in the walls of tubes or other hollow structures, such as the intestine or oviduct.

Lipoma: A benign tumor arising from fat cells and the cells (lipoblasts) from which mature fat cells arise. It is felt that these tumors may be a result of altered fat storage metabolism, rather than true neoplasms (Turrel et al., 1987a, b).

Neurofibroma: A benign tumor arising from the connective tissue that supports nervous tissue.

Papilloma: A benign tumor of the skin. The external skin may be affected, as in a cutaneous papilloma. The mouth and cloaca are also common sites for such neoplasms. Papillomas are thought to be viral in origin (Turrel et al., 1987a, b). It is not uncommon for a bird with oral papillomas also to have them in its larynx, crop, esophagus, and internal nares. It is also common to find cloacal papillomas in birds with oral papillomas, and vice versa. Cutaneous papillomas often regress without treatment; however, surgery may be required for those occurring in the mouth and cloaca. Some success has been obtained with the use of autogenous vaccines (Turrel et al., 1987a, b), a preparation derived from the affected bird's papillomatous tissue, then administered by injection. If successful, the bird's immune system is stimulated to produce antibodies against the virus causing the papilloma, thereby conferring immunity against recurrence of the neoplasm.

Pituitary Adenoma: Although benign, this tumor is very serious due to its location—the pituitary gland in the brain. Its symptoms are produced for two major reasons. First, its location in the brain makes pressure on surrounding tissue inevitable as the tumor grows and expands. Second, the pituitary is the "master" endocrine gland and controls all other endocrine glands in the body. Symptoms, therefore, may be related to pressure on surrounding brain tissue, or endocrine changes in one or more endocrine glands in the body. Commonly associated with either of these sets of symptoms are behavioral changes. According to Louise Bauck (1987), this tumor primarily affects budgerigars, and little is known about its treatment.

Rhabdomyoma: A benign tumor of skeletal muscle tissue.

Thymoma: A tumor arising from thyroid tissue. It is usually benign, but it may occasionally invade surrounding healthy tissue. However, it rarely metastasizes.

A barium X ray of a bird with a kidney tumor. Note displacement of abdominal contents forward, especially in a side view (left).
    Peter Sakas, D.V.M.

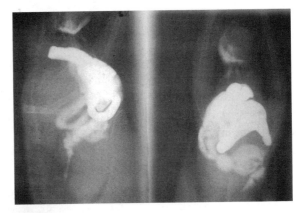

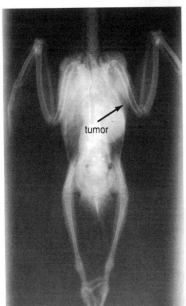

tumor

An X ray of a cockatiel with a spinal tumor (front view).   *Peter Sakas, D.V.M.*

A front and side view of a stomach (proventriculus) tumor, which prevents barium from outlining stomach in its entirety.
    Peter Sakas, D.V.M.

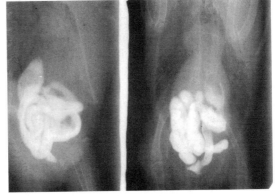

Uropygial gland adenoma: A tumor arising from the glandular tissue of the uropygial gland (preen gland). According to Turrel et al. (1987a, b), complete removal is usually curative.

Xanthoma: A tumor composed of large amounts of fat. It is not a true neoplasm (Campbell, 1986c; Turrel, et al., 1987a, b). They are seen as thick, yellowish masses on the skin surface, and often overlie lipomas.

The following is a list of malignant tumors found in birds. Some are rare; others are more commonly found. Again, this is not a complete list:

Chondrosarcoma: A malignant tumor arising from the cartilage cells.

Fibrosarcoma: According to Turrel et al., this is the most common external malignancy seen in companion birds. It arises from fibroblasts (those cells that give rise to connective tissue).

Hemangiosarcoma: A malignant tumor arising from the cells that form the lining of blood vessels (endothelium).

Hepatoma: A malignant tumor of the liver.

Leukosis: A malignancy arising from the tissues that form white blood cells. As such, tissues in various parts of the body may be affected in such diverse areas as the liver, spleen, lymph nodes, certain areas of the intestinal tract, and so forth. In leukosis, there is an abnormal increase in the number of white blood cells. However, these cells are not functional and result in an overall decrease in the effectiveness of the immune system.

Liposarcoma: An infrequently found malignancy of fat cells and the cells that give rise to mature fat cells. It may also be called lipoblastoma.

Lymphosarcoma: A malignancy affecting the tissue that produces lymphocytes, a type of white blood cell. They are produced in huge numbers. The lymphocytes are abnormal and do not function properly. The tissue where the lymphocytes are produced becomes enlarged and infiltrates surrounding tissue.

Nephroblastoma: Also known as Wilm's tumor, this is a malignancy of the kidney. It arises from embryonic kidney tissue and is rarely seen in species other than budgerigars (Turrel et al., 1987a, b).

Osteosarcoma: A malignancy of the bone. It usually occurs in long bones such as the upper wing and thigh bones. The bird may pick at feathers and skin overlying the tumor. It may also exhibit an inability to fly or perch, or may be lame.

Ovarian tumors: These tumors often secrete hormones. Some of the types encountered are stromal cell tumors, arising from the stroma (or connective tissue network) of the ovary. These tend to be the most commonly found ovarian tumors in birds (Turrel et al., 1987a, b). Other more rare tumors include cystadenocarcinoma and leiomyosarcoma. The former is a cyst-forming malignancy of the epithelial and glandular tissue of the ovary. The latter is a malignancy of the smooth muscle tissue of the ovary.

Reticular cell sarcoma: Reticular cells appear in the spleen, bone marrow, and lymphatic tissue. Normally, they develop into macrophages (a type of white blood cell responsible for ingesting harmful foreign matter such as bacteria) and several kinds of connective tissue cells. When a malignant condition affects these cells, they are produced in abnormally high numbers and are deformed, thus unable to perform their various functions.

Seminoma: A malignant tumor of the testicle. It is relatively rare, occurring mostly in older budgerigars and Amazons (Turrel et al., 1987a, b).

Sertoli cell tumor: A malignancy arising in the testicle. It is not common. However, when it occurs, it is fairly easily diagnosed, because this tumor secretes estrogen. Estrogen, being a feminizing hormone, will cause female characteristics in male birds. A classic example of this is the change of cere color in the male budgerigar from blue to brown.

Squamous cell carcinoma: A malignant skin tumor, usually occurring on the surface of the body. According to *Stedman's Medical Dictionary* (1976), it may also occur where glandular cells are present. Many times it occurs at the site of chronic skin irritation, and may appear as a nonhealing wound or sore. It is not a common malignancy in birds, although it has been observed in cockatiels.

Uropygial adenocarcinoma: A malignant tumor arising from the glandular and skin cells of the uropygial, or preen, gland. Self-trauma is frequently seen in connection with this tumor.

Causative Agent There are many causative agents in the production of neoplasms. They are roughly classified into two groups: primary factors and cofactors. There is much interplay between the two, the end result being the production of a neoplasm. Primary factors (or carcinogens) include radiation, viruses, and chemical agents. Radiation to which a bird might be exposed is limited, but proximity to an old, improperly shielded television might conceivably be one source. Viruses such as some types of *Herpesvirus* have been implicated in certain avian neoplasms. Examples of chemical agents include dyes, hydrocarbons, and aflatoxins produced by certain species of *Aspergillus* fungi (see Mycotoxicosis in this chapter). Donald King et al. (1983) mention the high incidence of liver cancer in humans who have ingested grain so contaminated. This problem has also been noted in birds with aflatoxicosis. He also cites the production of stomach cancer in humans from the habitual ingestion of smoked foods, which contain hydrocarbons. This has implications for a bird's diet—obviously, it would be wise to avoid offering such foods.

Cofactors (or cocarcinogens) that interact with primary factors include hormones, genetic predisposition, physical factors such as trauma, dietary problems, and environmental factors. It is felt that hormonal imbalances may help promote gonadal tumors. Genetic predisposition of tumor formation can be observed in budgerigars, with their propensity for kidney and pituitary adenomas; and the Rose-breasted Cockatoo, which has an abnormally high incidence of lipomas. A bird living near a major highway will be exposed to an unacceptably high level of hydrocarbons from automobile exhaust. Self-trauma may play a role in uropygial gland adenocarcinoma and squamous cell carcinoma. A high-fat diet has been found to increase the incidence of colon cancer in rodents (King et al., 1983). It may be that such diets have some cofactor effect on birds also, although to the author's knowledge no research has been done on this.

Transmission In general, neoplasms are not contagious, and are not transmissible to other birds.

There is one exception to this, however. Birds with tumors thought to be of viral origin should be kept isolated. It is felt that treatment of such birds may create viral shedding and thus create a source of infection for other birds. Campbell (1986c) feels that such birds should not be used for breeding because of the danger of transmitting the virus to the egg.

Symptoms The symptoms produced by tumors are dependent upon the location of the tumor, and whether it is benign or malignant. Although benign tumors can produce symptoms by pressing on a vital structure or blocking a hollow structure, *generally speaking* their symptoms are less distressing and somewhat more easily curable than those of a malignancy.

When dealing with a malignancy, many symptoms are seen. Pressure on vital structures, invasion of healthy tissue that renders it nonfunctional or destroys it altogether, rupture of blood vessels, disruption of the nervous system, infection, undue stress on the heart, disfigurement, loss of function of the limbs—all of these may appear. Cancer manifests itself in a vast, ugly panorama of symptoms. Many times the symptoms observed are not immediately recognizable as being caused by a neoplastic process. In Bauck's (1987) paper on pituitary tumors in budgies, she cites a case in which one of the presenting symptoms was poor feather condition. In another paper the same author found that many pet birds with a white blood cell malignancy were presented with skin tumors or abnormal feathering (Bauck, 1986).

Rather than list the various types of tumor with an enumeration of their symptoms, it will be more helpful to discuss a range of symptoms commonly found by body system—in other words, symptoms caused by the location of the tumor. These locations include the integument (skin); the respiratory system (nares, sinuses, trachea, bronchi, lungs, air sacs); the hematopoietic system (those tissues forming both red and white blood cells); the gastrointestinal system (mouth, esophagus, crop, proventriculus, ventriculus, intestines, cloaca, liver, pancreas); the urinary/reproductive system (kidneys, testes, ovaries, oviduct); nervous system (brain, spinal cord, peripheral nerves); and muscoloskeletal system. The endocrine system will not be discussed as a whole because such glands occur throughout the body. Not only do these glands produce hormones that have "body-wide" effects, such that a tumor in any one of them may cause widespread symptoms, but depending upon location they may also cause symptoms due to pressure on, or invasion of neighboring structures.

The reader must understand that the following discussion of symptoms is

A Spectacled Amazon with Newcastle disease. Typical symptoms are the fluffed-out feathers and half-closed eyes. This unfortunate bird, like so many others, was smuggled out of Latin America. The head feathers have been bleached so the bird could be sold as a more expensive Double Yellow Head Amazon. *Peter Sakas, D.V.M.*

A confiscated smuggled Amazon displaying seizuring normally associated with Newcastle disease. *Peter Sakas, D.V.M.*

by no means exhaustive. It is designed to help the reader gain a general knowledge of the range of effects caused by neoplasms, whether benign or malignant. It is also necessary to understand that any of the symptoms discussed below *may not necessarily indicate a tumor*, but may be due to other disease processes. *Your avian veterinarian is the only person qualified to make such a differentiation.*

Integument

Lumps or swellings on the body
Excessive scaliness of feet
Nonhealing sores
Feather picking confined to a specific area, or accompanied by vocalizations
    of discomfort
Abnormalities of the beak, such as excessive cracking, peeling, overgrowth
Abnormal coloration of the skin
Crusty sores
Thickening of the skin
Bleeding from skin

It is fairly common for a bird to pick at any body surface abnormality they notice. In addition, birds may also pick at skin surfaces overlying tumors or other disorders deep in the body that cause pain or discomfort. This behavior is probably an instinctual response aimed at attempts to alleviate pain.

Respiratory System

Labored breathing
Rapid breathing
Difficulty swallowing
Regurgitation (due to tumor pressure on crop and/or esophagus)
Weakness (due to lack of adequate oxygen to body cells)
Tail-bobbing (due to lack of adequate oxygen to body cells)
Discharge from eyes and/or nose
Open-mouthed breathing
Unusual respiratory noises, such as wheezing or squeaking

Hematopoietic System

Abdominal swelling (due to growth in organs such as spleen and liver)
Abnormal droppings
Skin thickening (occurs when abnormal growth takes place in the white
    blood cell–producing tissues of the subcutaneous areas of skin)
Poor or abnormal feathering
Weakness and depression (due to anemia caused by abnormal or inadequate
    number of red blood cells, leading to inadequate oxygen delivery to
    body tissues)
Breathing difficulty (due to decreased numbers of red blood cells, leading
    to decreased oxygen supply to body tissues)
Increased susceptibility to infection (due to abnormal white blood cells
    that can no longer protect against germs)

Lameness or paralysis of one or both legs (due to pressure on nerves supplying legs, by tumors in liver, spleen, bone marrow)

Gastrointestinal System

Difficulty eating and/or swallowing (due to obstruction to passage of food by tumor)

Regurgitation

Breathing difficulty (due to pressure of tumor on lungs, air sacs)

Abnormal droppings (due to inability of digestive tract to process food normally; may also have blood in droppings because of ulceration of intestine)

Weight loss (due to body's inability to utilize the food it ingests)

Swelling of crop area or abdomen

Protrusion of tissue from cloaca

Changes in appetite, either increased or decreased (a feeling of fullness may occur because of the presence of a space-occupying tumor in the digestive tract, in which case the bird will not have a desire to eat; on the other hand, if an organ such as the pancreas is affected, a secondary diabetes mellitus may develop, causing a ravenous appetite)

Lameness or paralysis of one or both legs (due to pressure on nerves supplying legs by abdominal tumor)

Increased thirst (may be related to secondary diabetes mellitus)

Urinary/Reproductive System

Abdominal swelling

Lameness or paralysis of one or both legs (due to pressure on nerves supplying legs by abdominal tumor)

Changes in cere color in budgerigars (due to abnormal production of estrogen by tumor)

Behavioral changes (due to abnormal hormone production by tumor)

Weight loss

Abnormal droppings (may be due to pressure on or invasion of intestine by the tumor; if the kidneys are involved, their inability to excrete normal urine is a factor)

Breathing difficulty (due to pressure of tumor on lungs and/or air sacs)

Weakness

Bloody droppings (due to kidney involvement)

Nervous System

Blindness (a common symptom with pituitary tumors, which place pressure on ophthalmic nerves)

Behavioral changes (due to a multiplicity of hormonal imbalances caused by the tumor; may also be caused by direct pressure of the tumor on the areas of the brain controlling behavior)

Lameness (due to failure of proper function of brain, spinal cord, or peripheral nerves)

Paralysis of legs or wings
Abnormal head position
Convulsions
Abnormal droppings (may be due to abnormal secretion of a hormone that
    controls urine production by kidneys)
Abnormal thirst
Lethargy

Musculoskeletal System

Swellings on wings, legs, or shoulders
Feather and skin picking or mutilation
Loss of ability to fly
Lameness
Paralysis
Inability to perch
Bone fractures with no history of trauma, or minimal trauma (due to
    abnormal bone tissue, which is much less strong than normal bone)

Many systems overlap relative to the symptoms that may be exhibited. In addition, a bird with a neoplasm will frequently show the general symptoms of illness: fluffed feathers, weakness, somnolence, loss of appetite, and decreased vocalization.

Laboratory Work

Blood serum chemistries: Abnormalities in various serum chemistry findings will alert the veterinarian to problems in specific areas. For example, an elevated serum alkaline phosphatase might indicate abnormal bone growth activity associated with osteosarcoma. Elevated liver enzyme levels may indicate a neoplastic condition in the liver.

Hematology: Abnormalities in the appearance and number of red and white blood cells may indicate a neoplastic process in the hematopoietic system.

Radiographs: These will, in many cases, allow the veterinarian to visualize abnormal masses in bone and soft tissue.

Biopsy: Microscopic examination of tissue from tumorous masses will allow the practitioner to identify cancerous or other abnormal cells.

Characteristic changes in the nuclei and cytoplasm of cells, as well as mitotic figures (those nuclear changes indicating an abnormally high level of cell division and growth) are some of the things a veterinary pathologist looks for when examining suspect tissue.

Tissue may be obtained for biopsy in one of two ways. An excisional biopsy consists of the removal of the entire suspected mass. It is usually done where such a mass is easily accessible surgically. A small piece of the whole is then submitted for diagnosis. A needle biopsy is done when the suspected mass is inaccessible surgically, such as the kidney or liver. A needle is introduced

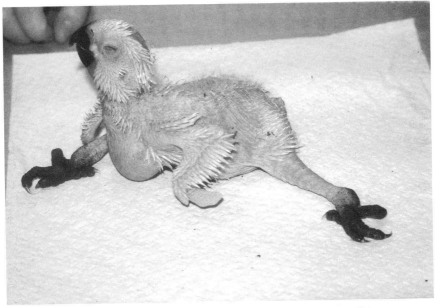

The splayed legs in this baby cockatoo are the result of a severe calcium deficiency.

Peter Sakas, D.V.M.

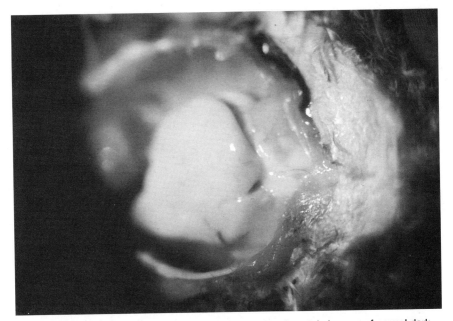

The liver of a bird that died of Pacheco's disease. Note the total absence of normal dark color in this liver. Also, this organ no longer has any functional cells.

Peter Sakas, D.V.M.

into the biopsy site and a small portion of tissue is removed. The contents are then placed on a microscope slide for examination.

Treatment   There are several methods of treatment for neoplasms. They may be used alone or in combination. The location of the tumor, its accessibility or lack thereof to surgery, and its potential for metastasis (spread throughout the body) all play a role in treatment choice. Treatment may aim at complete cure and restoration of function, or it may have as its aim palliation—relief of symptoms and some return to minimal function—in those cases where cure is not possible.

Surgery: The first treatment to be discussed is surgery. It may be done to remove completely the offending tissue. It may also be performed to "de-bulk" a tumor that cannot be entirely removed, but which partial excision thereof may bring relief of pain or restore lost function to a degree. Either electrosurgery or cryosurgery may be performed.

Conventional surgery using a scalpel is not as commonly used with birds as in the past. Rather, electrosurgery, using an electrosurgical unit, is used. This allows the surgeon a much more delicate touch and far greater control of potential hemorrhage. According to Turrel et al. (1987a, b) surgery is recommended for most benign and many small cancerous tumors. The limitation of this approach concerns the location of the tumor and the bird's size.

Cryosurgery is "the use of controlled local application of cold to destroy abnormal tissue and yet spare adjacent normal tissue" (Turrel et al., 1987a, b). It is most often used to remove small skin tumors, and oral and cloacal tumors. It can also be used to "de-bulk" a very large tumor. Liquid nitrogen is the most commonly used substance for cryosurgery.

Irradiation, or radiation treatment: Can be employed in combination with surgery or used alone. The implantation of a radioactive substance in cockatiels with abdominal tumors has been tried experimentally (Turrel et al., 1987). In this study, seeds of radioactive iodine encased in stainless-steel capsules were implanted in the kidneys of cockatiels. The authors concluded that this mode of therapy was a relatively simple, safe treatment for such birds. Irradiation, used in conjunction with surgery, can destroy cancerous cells "missed" by the initial surgery.

Chemotherapy: Often used as a follow-up to surgery. Chemotherapeutic drugs kill cancerous cells. Unfortunately, they are also destructive to healthy cells. This accounts for symptoms such as nausea, loss of appetite, and hair loss seen in humans undergoing such treatment. In birds, these drugs have not been widely used at the time of this writing. Therefore, knowledge of safe, therapeutic doses and side effects is as yet not established. It is to be expected that much work will be done in this field in the future.

Immunotherapy: Consists of the use of certain medications that will boost the bird's immune system and help its body attack and destroy cancer cells, just as the antibodies it is able to make will attack and destroy bacteria. Nonspecific medications such as levamisole have an overall effect on the immune system. Specific medications, such as autogenous vaccines, are designed to destroy a particular invader, such as virally caused papillomatosis (see Papillomatosis in this chapter).

Hyperthermia: May be used to treat neoplasms, especially small skin tumors. This treatment consists of applying heat greater than 43°C (109.4°F) to the tumor. Such heat naturally kills the tumor cells, but does a minimal amount of damage to surrounding healthy tissue. There are special machines designed for such use.

Prognosis It is not possible to make blanket statements concerning prognosis when discussing a field as broad as that of neoplasms. Your avian veterinarian will be able to discuss this with you, based upon your bird's individual problem. Many factors will be taken into consideration: whether or not the neoplasm is benign or malignant, its potential for local invasion and metastasis, the location of the tumor, and the bird's age, size, species, general health, and individual response to treatment.

In general, most benign tumors have a better prognosis than malignant ones. Malignant tumors that are small and localized have a better prognosis than those that are large, have spread throughout neighboring tissue, and are surgically inaccessible. Each case must be considered individually on its own merits, before a judgment can be made regarding probable outcome.

NEWCASTLE DISEASE (VELOGENIC VISCEROTROPIC NEWCASTLE DISEASE, VVND):   This is a grave, virally caused disease, with virtual 100 percent death rate. The disease takes its name from Newcastle-on-Tyne, England, where it was first identified in 1926. It was identified in the United States in 1944. Today it is found in many countries worldwide. The origin of the virus is unknown. This disease is also known by such names as avian pneumoencephalitis, Ranikhet disease, avian pest, avian distemper, and Asiatic Newcastle disease.

Newcastle disease, caused by *Paramyxovirus (PMV) Group I*, is a disease all bird owners should be aware of. Although rarely a problem in companion birds, it does occur—mainly in young, smuggled psittacines. The disease spreads rapidly and is a serious threat to the domestic poultry industry. Because VVND can destroy poultry flocks in just days, causing billions of dollars' worth of loss to the industry, the United States government is heavily involved in the prevention, control, and eradication of the disease. It is for this reason that imported, exotic birds (known to be sources of VVND) are subject to a thirty-day quarantine in the United States.

When veterinarians become involved in cases where birds (whether pets or poultry) are dying in numbers, are exhibiting symptoms associated with VVND, and have a history of recent acquisition, they are required by law to notify the United States Department of Agriculture (USDA). Diagnosis is made based on tests done in government-controlled laboratories. If VVND is confirmed, all sick birds are killed. The USDA Animal Disease Eradication Branch performs this task. The USDA also regulates the cleanup and disinfection of contaminated premises. No private person, poultry farmer, or company is immune to these regulations.

Although parrots have been identified as one of the most likely sources of VVND, it has been found in a wide variety of wild birds: quail, pheasant, partridges, waterfowl, pigeons, ravens, crows, falcons, hawks, eagles, owls, penguins, pelicans, toucans, ostriches, woodpeckers, finches, and hummingbirds.

VVND outbreaks seem to cycle every ten to twelve years. The virus has an affinity for red blood cells, allowing it to reach all parts of the body very quickly (Gerlach, 1986e). It is able to survive for long periods of time outside its host, given the proper conditions of heat and humidity (Cavill, 1982).

There are several forms of Newcastle disease, which may involve the respiratory system, central nervous system, digestive tract, or a combination of these systems (Gerlach, 1986e). There may be sudden death, with few or no preceding symptoms. The acute respiratory form may include nasal discharge, respiratory distress, lethargy, and anorexia. The acute visceral form may involve diarrhea, depression, anorexia, and cyanosis. The acute mixed form may include respiratory and gastrointestinal symptoms. The chronic form affects the central nervous system. There may be persistent infection with no evident symptoms. Such birds shed the virus via respiratory and fecal routes and are carriers of Newcastle disease.

Symptoms related to central nervous system damage may occur in any form. They may also occur without visceral and respiratory symptoms (Fowler, 1987). Birds that survive invariably are left with permanent neurological damage.

Because VVND is highly contagious, and its symptoms are so general, it spreads through entire flocks before confirmation of its presence is made.

Causative Agent Paramyxovirus Group I.

Transmission VVND is highly contagious. It is transmitted through oral and respiratory routes, through normal breathing, as well as exudates (Fowler, 1987). The virus is also shed in feces, which may contaminate food, water, perches, and bedding material. Penetration of the egg by the virus via feces soiling may also occur, thus infecting the embryo (Gerlach, 1986e). However, this rarely happens because egg laying ceases very quickly if the hen has developed VVND.

Symptoms The severity of symptoms varies with the virulence of the particular strain of PMV involved, the host species, the ambient temperature, the individual bird's resistance, and the virus dosage to which the bird was exposed. In resistant birds, early signs are anorexia and depression, and the course of the illness may be prolonged, rather than acute (Fowler, 1987).

The following may be seen in VVND, either separately or in any combination:

198

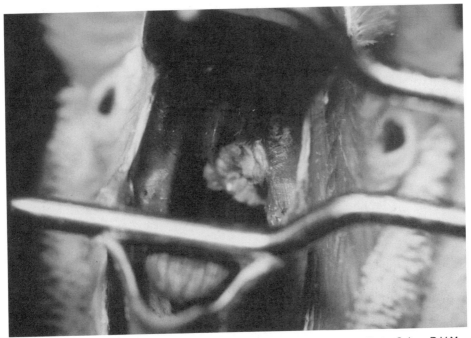

A close-up view of an oral papilloma in an Amazon Parrot. *Peter Sakas, D.V.M.*

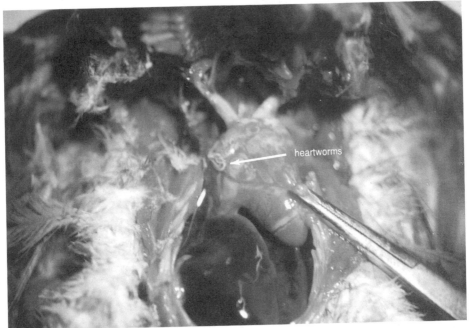

heartworms

Heartworm infestation. *Peter Sakas, D.V.M.*

Nasal and/or respiratory discharges

Diarrhea, sometimes bloody

Cyanosis

Anorexia

Depression

Breathing difficulty

Seizures

Backward-walking movements

Muscle twitching

Head and/or eye twitching

Neck bent and head drawn to the side (torticollis, due to muscle spasms in the neck)

Head bent backward, touching the tail, with body arched outward (opisthotonos, due to muscle spasms in the body torso)

Laboratory Work   In live birds, virus samples collected by means of swabs taken from throat and/or cloaca are inoculated into chicken embryos. When the embryo dies, it is tested for the presence of Newcastle disease antibodies. If these are found, the diagnosis is confirmed. Such testing is done in government-controlled laboratories. This same procedure may also be used employing tissues from dead birds to inoculate the chicken embryos.

Treatment   None. All sick and exposed birds are euthanized once the diagnosis of VVND has been confirmed.

Prognosis   Nearly 100 percent death rate.

NUTRITIONAL SECONDARY HYPERPARATHYROIDISM (NSHP):   This is a disorder of the parathyroid glands caused by inadequate calcium in the bird's diet. The parathyroid glands, which lie behind the thyroid gland at the base of the neck, become greatly enlarged.

The parathyroid glands are primarily responsible for regulating the blood serum levels of calcium in the bird. As discussed in Chapter 3, calcium has many important body functions, so the maintenance of normal levels of this mineral is of prime importance to the well-being of the bird. To maintain the proper levels the pituitary glands secrete a hormone called PTH (parathyroid hormone). PTH has as its main function the following, all designed to promote normal serum calcium levels:

1. Mobilization of calcium from the bone and into the bloodstream (reabsorption).
2. Increased loss of phosphorus by its excretion in the urine.
3. Reabsorption of calcium from the urine by the kidney, from whence it is returned to the bloodstream.

In addition to the above three functions, PTH also:

1. Enhances the synthesis of vitamin D_3 by the kidney (Kenney, 1986).

2. Causes a lowering of the blood pressure (hypotension) by causing the smooth muscles of the blood vessels to relax.
3. Promotes the replacement of calcium taken from the bone by fibrous connective tissue. This is called osteitis fibrosa. It causes weakened bones and is a classic radiographic finding in birds with secondary nutritional hyperparathyroidism (Harrison and Harrison, 1986).

NSHP develops through a chain of events. First, the bird does not receive adequate dietary calcium, which in turn causes the serum calcium level to drop. This drop signals the parathyroids to secrete PTH in an effort to raise calcium levels. For a time, this works because calcium is removed from the bone and diverted to the bloodstream. However, that source eventually becomes exhausted. Nevertheless, when calcium levels continue to drop, the parathyroids once more secrete PTH. And they keep on doing it, even though it is an exercise in futility. Eventually, the parathyroids *enlarge* in an effort to produce more and more PTH and thus try to return serum calcium to normal levels. At this point the bird is stricken with nutritional secondary *hyper*parathyroidism.

Causative Agent   Inadequate dietary calcium.

Transmission   NSHP is not contagious and therefore not transmissible from bird to bird.

Symptoms   Symptoms are related to the actual physical size of the parathyroid glands and their subsequent impingement on neighboring anatomical structures; they are also related to the effects of low serum calcium levels on various body functions. They are as follows:

Difficulty swallowing
Regurgitation
Breathing problems
Anorexia
Abnormal droppings, especially with regard to feces content (Brugère-Picoux and Brugère, 1987)
Polydipsia (excessive thirst) and polyuria (related to the excretion of phosphorus in the urine: the increased amount of phosphorus in the urine causes an increased excretion of water, which in turn creates thirst as the body's fluid content decreases)
Difficulty walking, flying, or perching (due to muscle cramps and spasms, and bone pain)
Legs and feet swollen and inflamed
Toes clenched or twisted over each other
Dull feathers
Slow feather growth
Feather picking
Sleepiness
Mental dullness

Involuntary wing flapping
Seizures
Deformed eggs or eggs with no shell
Cardiac arrest and death

Laboratory Work In addition to the physical examination and history, it is helpful to obtain the serum calcium level and take radiographs in making a diagnosis of NSPH.

Treatment The aim of treatment is to return serum calcium levels to normal.

1. Adequate diet calcium must be made available to the bird.
2. Calcium/phosphorus/vitamin D_3 must be supplemented in the proper ratio. These three components, in the proper amounts, work together to provide normal use of calcium in the body.
3. Calcium given intravenously can be used in an emergency, when the bird is having frequent and extended convulsions.

Prognosis In the early stages of NSPH, recovery should be good providing the bird has ongoing, consistent dietary calcium supplementation in proper combination with phosphorus and vitamin D_3. In advanced cases in which the parathyroid glands have sustained much damage, the outlook is grave.

PACHECO'S DISEASE: Pacheco's disease is a virally caused hepatitis in psittacines, affecting primarily the liver and spleen. In some cases, the disease may last as long as five days to several weeks, but it is usually rapidly fatal, with few or no symptoms other than listlessness, which occurs a few hours before death. Up to this point, most birds are active, and eat and drink normally.

The disease seems to have a seasonal incidence, with the months of November and February being the peak relative to disease outbreak (Gaskin, 1987b). This is because of the reversal of seasons between the northern and southern hemispheres. Young birds are captured in South America during their summer and then shipped to the United States, where it is midwinter. Stresses associated with shipping and quarantine encourage outbreaks of Pacheco's disease. The stress of cold ambient temperatures is also a factor.

Other potential causes are courtship/mating stress and socialization stress brought about by the introduction of new birds into an established collection (Gaskin, 1987a). In fact, according to Gerlach (1986e), "The common factor in all reports [of Pacheco's disease outbreaks] is a distinct change in the environment."

Some species of conures, such as the Nanday, Patagonian, and Red-bellied Conure, seem to be resistant and have been often implicated as carriers of the disease (Harlin, 1985). Other species of parrots have varying resistance to the disease, although in most cases the mortality rate is 100 percent. In general, macaws, cockatoos, Amazons, and the smaller parrots such as the *Pionus* species, parakeets, and lovebirds die with minimal symptoms (Gaskin, 1987a). African Grays are also highly susceptible. In a 1978 Florida outbreak of Pachecho's

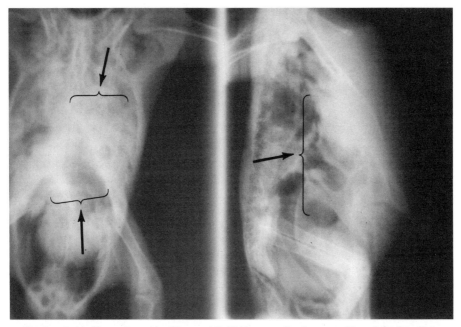

Front and side X ray views of a Blue and Gold Macaw with air sac and lung infection. Note extreme cloudiness throughout affected organs. *Peter Sakas, D.V.M.*

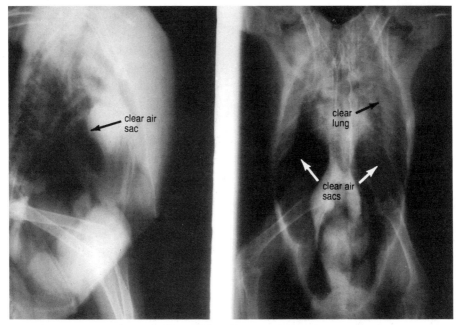

clear air sac

clear lung

clear air sacs

Front and side X ray views of a Blue and Gold Macaw with normal air sacs and lungs.
Peter Sakas, D.V.M.

disease, Gaskin reports that White-eyed Conures had an 80 percent survival rate; Blue and Gold Macaws and cockatiels had a survival rate of approximately 20 percent. He also reports an outbreak in 1987 in which Mitred Conures were only mildly affected, while among the Peach-fronted Conures mortality was very high.

It is interesting to note that until 1975, when the causative viral agent of Pacheco's disease was isolated and identified, this illness was thought to be an atypical form of psittacosis.

Causative Agent   A member of the *Herpesvirus* group is responsible for Pacheco's disease. Stress due to one or several causes is capable of precipitating the disease in birds that have latent, or subclinical, *Herpesvirus* infections.

The virus is thought to be very susceptible to drying (Gaskin, 1987a). It is also killed by heat (10 to 15 minutes at 56°C or 132.8°F) and most commonly used aviary disinfectants (Gerlach, 1986e).

Transmission   Transmission is very rapid and is thought to be caused by both direct and indirect routes. Direct routes include the aerosolization of throat secretions from infected birds, such as occurs with coughing and sneezing. Food and water can be contaminated by feces, in which the virus is also shed.

It is thought that stress causes carrier birds to shed large numbers of the virus, thus starting an outbreak among susceptible birds with which it comes in contact. Roger Harlin (1985) feels that the carrier state may last as long as two and one-half years.

Symptoms   In the peracute form (sudden and virulent), birds may eat, drink, and carry on all activities in a perfectly normal fashion for up to a few hours before death.

Symptoms of the acute form may include:

Regurgitation
Lethargy
Increased thirst
Diarrhea
Orange-colored urates

Gaskin feels this may happen particularly with birds such as macaws and cockatoos. He further states that birds with these symptoms may sometimes recover.

In either the peracute or acute form, Pachecho's disease usually results in death.

Treatment   Some clinical success is being experienced with the use of acyclovir (Zovirax).

Prognosis   Among exposed, susceptible birds, with the exception of some conures and possibly cockatiels and Blue and Gold Macaws, the death rate is virtually 100 percent. Because Pacheco's disease is so highly contagious and lethal, every precaution should be taken to prevent its spread throughout an exposed flock.

Laboratory results may take several weeks, and one cannot afford to await confirmation of Pacheco's before preventative steps are taken. Any sudden, unexpected death in the flock or collection should be followed immediately by these precautions:

1. Cage all birds individually or in small, species-specific groups to prevent spread by fecal contamination of food and water.
2. Remove all cagemates of stricken birds to another area, preferably another room. Care for these birds last, after the "healthy" birds have been cared for. Use protective clothing and strict hand-washing procedure with a good aviary disinfectant such as Environ-One Stroke or Roccal-D.
3. A solution of Nolvasan (chlorhexadine) in the drinking water may help prevent water contamination (Gaskin, 1987b). Use according to the manufacturer's directions for dilution, and for no more than ten days.

It goes without saying that the corpses of dead birds should be taken immediately to the avian veterinarian for necropsy. (See Chapter 7 for a discussion of how to prepare *properly* a corpse for this purpose.)

After the outbreak has been contained, the following precautions *must* be observed:

1. The aviary or bird room must be thoroughly cleaned and disinfected, including all food bowls and feeding utensils. Discard *all* wooden items. The use of an effective disinfectant is mandatory.
2. Allow no contact among survivors and new birds brought into the collection.
3. Surviving birds should have cloacal and choanal cultures periodically for several months to make sure they have not become carriers.

A word should be said about the use of a "sentinel" bird. This is an inexpensive bird, such as a cockatiel or Grey-cheeked Parakeet, which is kept with a group of birds suspected of carrying a disease such as Pacheco's. The sentinel should remain with the suspected group for at least a month, during which they should all be kept in complete isolation. If the sentinel dies, it is necropsied immediately. This precaution is not 100 percent foolproof, but it may save entire collections that might otherwise be unsuspectingly exposed to Pacheco's.

PAPILLOMATOSIS: See also Neoplasm. This is the condition that exists when a bird has one or more papillomas. A papilloma is a benign neoplasm of the skin, oral cavity, digestive tract, or cloaca.

Skin (cutaneous) papillomas may occur virtually anywhere on the body: neck, wings, feet, legs, eyelids, or uropygial area. Papillomas are fairly common on the feet of macaws and cockatoos. In African Gray Parrots they are often found on the face, especially around the eyes and beak. Papillomas are commonly seen at the beak margins of budgerigars and cockatiels.

Cutaneous papillomas vary in appearance. They may appear as hard, white or gray horny growths on the feet. They can appear as crusty sores or reddish, cauliflower growths. Papillomas of the skin are not associated with those of the oral cavity or cloaca (Turrel et al., 1987a, b).

Cloacal papillomas appear as tissue extrusions from the vent. They are moist, red in color, and "warty" or cauliflowerlike in appearance. They are frequently misdiagnosed as cloacal prolapses (Campbell, 1986c).

Oral-cavity papillomas resemble those of the cloaca in appearance. They may be confined to the mouth, being often seen in the choanal slit, or they may extend to the larynx, esophagus, crop, and proventriculus. Papillomas of the oral cavity are often associated with cloacal papillomas, and vice versa.

Petrak and Gilmore (1982) cite a case in which a papilloma was found in the choroid plexus of a male budgerigar. The choroid plexus is an area in the eye, rich in blood supply, and located between the white of the eye and the retina. It extends into the optic nerve. The symptoms seen in this case were blindness, protrusion of the eyeball (exopthalmos), and seizures.

Macaws, cockatoos, African Grays, and Amazons seem to be particularly susceptible to papillomatosis. Any papilloma may bleed very easily and copiously when traumatized, as they have an extensive blood supply.

Causative Agent The origin of all papillomas is thought to be viral. Viruses have been identified positively by electron microscopy in cutaneous papillomas. They have been of three types: *Papovavirus*, *Herpesvirus*, and *Papillomavirus*.

Transmission Because papillomas are thought to be viral in origin, there is some possibility that they may be transmissible to other birds. How long this process may take is not known. Cribb (1984) notes an instance involving two Blue-fronted Amazons that had been cagemates. One bird was seen and treated for cloacal papilloma. At a later time, its cagemate was presented for the same problem.

Symptoms Besides the actual visualization of a papilloma, various symptoms may be seen.

In cloacal papillomas:

Blood in the droppings
Difficulty passing droppings (tenesmus)
Chronically pasted vent
Foul odor to droppings

In oral or digestive tract papillomas:

Retching
Regurgitation
Difficulty swallowing (dysphagia)
Wheezing

In cutaneous papillomas, especially those obscured by feathers:

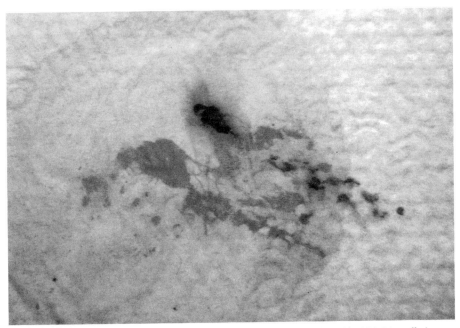

The blood that was excreted with the urine here indicates that the subject bird is suffering from lead poisoning. *Peter Sakas, D.V.M.*

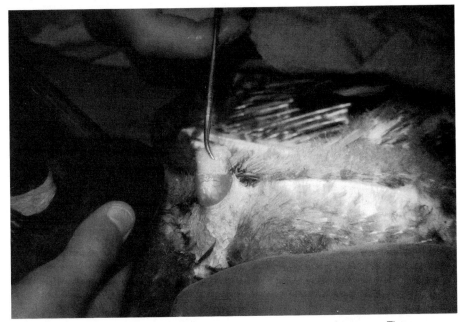

In this procedure, wood shavings are being removed from the crop of a macaw. The surgery is known as a cropotomy or ingluviotomy. *Peter Sakas, D.V.M.*

207

Picking
Screaming
Hemorrhage

Laboratory Work   Diagnosis is usually made by physical examination. Radiographs may be used to confirm the presence of papillomas in the digestive tract. Examination of the diseased tissue under the microscope is the only way to confirm positively that it is papillomatous and not of different origin, such as a malignancy.

Treatment   Electrosurgery and cryosurgery are the treatments of choice in instances where the papillomas are causing lost function or physical distress. Even after surgery, papillomas tend to recur, probably because it is extremely difficult to remove all of the neoplastic tissue. Some success in preventing recurrence of papillomas postsurgery has been reported using autogenous vaccines (Cribb, 1984; Turrel et al., 1987a, b).

Prognosis   Recurrence following treatment is common. Some types of cutaneous papillomas may become smaller or disappear spontaneously, according to Turrel et al.

PAPOVAVIRUS: See Budgerigar Fledgling Disease.

PARASITES, INTERNAL (ENDOPARASITES):   There are many microscopic organisms (other than bacteria, fungi, and viruses) that can live in a bird's body. Strictly speaking, any organism that depends upon another living creature for its sustenance can be called a parasite. However, the study of parasites (parasitology) deals only with those *animal* parasites that cause disease.

There are several terms used with reference to parasites that the reader should be familiar with:

Host: The animal within which the parasite lives. In some cases, all stages of the parasite's development may take place in a single host.
Intermediate host: In some cases, a parasite may have two or more hosts. The larval stage of the parasite is often spent in the intermediate host. The adult stage will then be spent in another host called the definitive host.
Vector: An animal or insect in which the disease-causing parasite multiplies and/or develops prior to becoming infective for a susceptible individual.
Transport host: An organism that is capable of carrying the parasite, but is not required in order for it to complete its life cycle.
Direct life cycle: One in which only a single host is required by the parasite for its entire life-span.
Indirect life cycle: One in which two or more hosts are required by the parasite for the completion of its growth, development, and reproduction.

In this section, protozoa, hematozoa, helminthes, and arthropods will be discussed.

Protozoa: These are one-celled animals. The reader is referred to the entry for Malaria in this chapter for a discussion of the characteristics of protozoa.

Hematozoa: A type of protozoa that live in the blood.

Helminthes: These are worms, some free living, others parasitic. Several types of worms can infect birds: nematodes, cestodes, microfilariae, trematodes, and ascarids. Nematodes are commonly known as roundworms. An ascarid is a particular type of roundworm. Microfilariae (microfilaria, singular) are the immature forms of filariae, which are also a type of nematode or roundworm. Cestodes and trematodes are types of flatworms. Cestodes are commonly known as tapeworms; trematodes are also called flukes.

Arthropods: Included are mites, spiders, ticks, flies, lice, and fleas. Such insects may in themselves cause illness, as with *Sternostoma*, which causes respiratory problems, or they may be vectors or transport for the spread of disease, as with the flies and lice that cause *Leucocytozoan*.

Some of the parasites discussed in this section are common. Others are not, but remain significant for certain psittacine species. We will depart from the format adopted for most disease entities in this chapter. Instead, a brief paragraph will be given for each parasite included. Name, method of transmission, symptoms, method of identification, treatment, and prevention will be outlined.

Ascarids: These roundworms, also known as proventricular and gizzard worms, live in the intestine. Their life cycle is a direct one. They are especially a problem in Australian Parakeets. They may become so numerous in the bird's intestinal tract that they may cause complete blockage and death. Eggs of the ascarids are passed in the feces and ingested by other birds. Symptoms may include weight loss, pasty diarrhea that fouls the vent, weakness, paralysis, and death. Occasionally, adult worms will be passed in the stool. Diagnosis is made by examination of the feces for ascarid eggs. Treatment is by thiabendazole (Clubb, 1986b). Levamisole administered in the drinking water, and injectable ivermectin may also be used (Rosskopf, "The Diagnosis of Parasitism"). Prevention includes good sanitation. It is important to keep food and water containers clean. Dirt floors in aviaries are to be avoided.

Capillaria: These nematodes, also known as crop worms or threadworms, frequent the esophagus and crop, where they burrow into the lining of these structures, causing inflammation and thickening. The worms are difficult to see with the naked eye because they are thin and threadlike. The life cycle is direct, with eggs being passed in the feces and ingested by other birds. Symptoms include regurgitation, weight loss, emaciation, anemia, listlessness, decreased food and water intake, inflammation of the mouth, drooping head, penguinlike stance, and frequent attempts to swallow (Shanthikumar, 1987). Treatment is by levamisole. Prevention includes good hygiene and the avoidance of dirt-floored aviaries.

Coccidia: This protozoa has its environment in the intestines of its bird host. The bird sheds eggs of this parasite. With a warm environment, these eggs hatch and become infective. They are then ingested by other birds and recommence the cycle. Elisha Burr (1987) states that *Coccidia* causes enteritis (inflammation of the intestinal tract) with blood-tinged feces and polyuria. Death may follow a heavy infestation of several months' duration. Barnes (1986) lists wasting and mucoid/hemorrhagic diarrhea as symptoms of coccidiosis. Extreme lethargy, anorexia, ruffled feathers, and insatiable appetite for grit can be seen in heavy infestations (Keymer, 1982b). Diagnosis is by fecal examination. Treatment is with amprolium and nitrofurazone (*Avian Disease Manual*, 1983). Bactrim and Tribrissen can also be used (Rosskopf, "The Diagnosis of Parasitism"). Treatment is not always satisfactory, so prevention is very important, especially good hygiene. The maintenance of a dry, clean floor in the cage or aviary is extremely important.

Cryptosporidia: This protozoa affects the epithelial cells of the respiratory and intestinal tracts. When the intestinal tract is involved, a severe enteritis with diarrhea and high death rate is caused. The respiratory-tract form manifests itself in nasal and ocular discharge, sinusitis, coughing, and decreased activity levels (Ley, 1987). Eggs of *Cryptosporidia* are shed in the bird's feces and create infection in other birds when they are ingested. It is somewhat difficult to diagnose cryptosporidiosis in the live bird. Ley suggests the use of special fluorescent stains applied to fecal smears and then examined microscopically. To date, there is no effective treatment available. Prevention through good hygiene and husbandry practices is therefore very important. Although some strains of *Cryptosporidia* can infect man, most strains that infect birds do not seem to be infective for humans.

Leucocytozoan: Infection in parrots of this hematozoa is rare, but fatal infections have been reported in parakeets (Barnes, 1986). The parasite is transmitted by the bite of the black fly and penetrates the bird's red and white blood cells. Birds with *Leucocytozoan* infection may have depression, anorexia, thirst, loss of equilibrium, weakness, anemia, and rapid, labored breathing. The disease course is often short, with either death or improvement within a few days (*Avian Disease Manual*, 1983). Bennett (1987) mentions a watery eye discharge and severe convulsions before death. Diagnosis is by microscopic examination of blood smears. Although there is no effective treatment at present, clopidol (Coyden) is thought to have good potential as a prophylactic medication (Fite, 1984). Control of the black fly vector represents the best method of prevention.

Microfilariae: These immature forms of filarial roundworms (nematodes) are transmitted to the bird by mosquitoes, biting flies, and lice (Bennett,

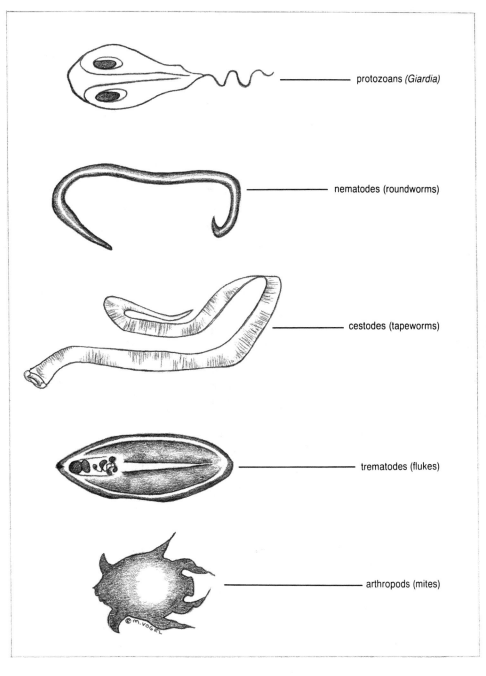

protozoans *(Giardia)*

nematodes (roundworms)

cestodes (tapeworms)

trematodes (flukes)

arthropods (mites)

Avian parasites

1987). Once having gained entry into the bird's body, they inhabit various tissues (eyelids, arterial and lymph walls, and connective tissue), grow to maturity, and release more microfilariae into the bloodstream. Although many microfilarial infections produce no symptoms, when adult worms infect areas such as joints, muscles, and the eye itself, symptoms may certainly occur. Joint and muscle infections may cause pain, swelling, and loss of function. Surgery may be necessary for their removal. These worms may also wrap themselves around kidneys and ovaries. A case of ocular involvement by microfilariae is cited by Lorraine Karpinski (1987). The parasite was found in the anterior chamber of the eye and required surgical removal. Although some authorities do not recommend treatment of asymptomatic microfilarial infection, Rosskopf feels that they do indeed warrant treatment. He recommends levamisole in the bird's drinking water (Rosskopf, "The Diagnosis of Parasitism"). Clubb (1986b) states that Panacur (fenbendazole) may also be used. Control of insect vectors is very important in the prevention of microfilarial disease.

Sarcocystis: Infection of parrots by this protozoa is not common. However, it can cause acute, fatal disease in some birds, particularly Old World psittacines (cockatoos, cockatiels, African Grays, *Eclectus*) (Clubb, 1986a). The lungs seem to be the primary target of *Sarcocystis*. Clubb reports a case where this parasite was transmitted to the affected birds via droppings of infected opossums that had gained access to the aviary. It was also found that infected cockroaches eaten by the birds caused illness. Clubb hypothesizes that Old World birds were more susceptible to *Sarcocystis* than New World species (Amazons, macaws, *Pionus*, conures, and caiques) because Old World birds evolved in an area of the world where this parasite does not exist, thereby allowing the birds no evolutionary experience in dealing with them effectively. The disease was most often peracute, with no symptoms until immediately prior to death. In the few birds found ill prior to death, severe breathing difficulty, yellow-pigmented urates, and depression were noted. Diagnosis of *Sarcocystis* infection is difficult with living birds, and can be usually confirmed only with necropsy. In living birds, cysts containing *Sarcocystis* may sometimes be seen in the muscles. There is no known treatment at this time. Prevention consists of the control of carrier animals and insects. Good hygiene and husbandry are also important.

Sternostoma: This mite, a member of the arthropod group, is also known as the air sac mite. It infests the trachea, air sacs, body cavities, and kidneys. Passerines are more commonly affected by *Sternostoma*, such infections being unknown in large parrots and rare in the smaller ones (Stehlik, 1987). It is transmitted to other birds in the respiratory secretions of infected individuals. Such secretions may contaminate food and water. Infected adults may infect their nestlings when feeding them. Symptoms include difficulty breathing, wheezing, voice change or loss, sucking and/or clicking noises, coughing, sneezing, nasal discharge, open-beaked breathing, and failure to thrive. Diagnosis is by examination of respiratory secretions. Alternately, transillumination may be used. This consists of shining a powerful light through the bird's neck. When viewed from the side opposite the light, mites can often be visualized in the trachea. Tracheal washes may also be used to demonstrate the presence of the mites. Ivermectin is the drug of choice used in treatment. Prevention consists of good hygiene and husbandry practices.

Syngamus: Also known as gapeworm, this nematode lives in the trachea and bronchi and causes a characteristic neck stretching and beak gaping. Other symptoms include shortness of breath, head shaking, anorexia, emaciation, and anemia. Heavily infected victims may die due to suffocation. Young birds are the most susceptible to *Syngamus* (Shanthikumar, 1987). The eggs of this parasite are coughed up and onto the ground, or passed in the bird's feces. The larva hatch are eaten by other birds or by an intermediate host such as earthworms, slugs, or snails. These in turn are eaten by birds. Diagnosis is by examination of respiratory secretions or feces. They can sometimes be directly visualized in the trachea. Transillumination may also be used. Treatment is with use of ivermectin (Barnes, 1986). Thiabendazole may also be used (Clubb, 1986b). Sometimes, manual removal of the gapeworms may be possible. Prevention consists of good hygiene and husbandry, including the avoidance of dirt-floored aviaries.

Tapeworms: These cestodes, a type of flatworm, require a secondary host, such as insects, worms, and molluscs (snails). Birds eat these creatures and thus become infested with tapeworms. (It is interesting to note that such organisms provide animal protein for birds, indicating that these birds are *far* from strict vegetarians in the wild.) Tapeworms infest the intestinal tract. Their eggs are passed in the feces of their definitive hosts, but are not infective to these hosts at this point in the worm's life cycle. They require an intermediate host in which they can develop before becoming infective to other birds. Although it is believed that tapeworms can live in their bird host without causing a great deal of damage, Rosskopf reports that they are a common cause of death in southern California (Rosskopf, "Diagnosis of Parasitism"). Some of the tapeworms seen on necropsy by Rosskopf filled the entire gizzard and kidney. Symptoms of tapeworm infestation include weakness, weight loss, diarrhea, and general unthriftiness. Owners may occasionally see ricelike particles in the bird's droppings. These are the worm segments that contain its eggs. Rarely, a whole worm may be passed by the bird. These can be quite large. Diagnosis is by observation of worms or segments in the dropping, or by fecal examination. The drug of choice in the treatment of tapeworms is Droncit (praziquantil). It is not uncommon to see whole worms passed thirty minutes after a Droncit injection has been given (Rosskopf, "Diagnosis of Parasitism"). Clubb

(1986b) states that Yomesan (niclosamide) can also be used to treat tapeworms.

Trematodes: These flukes, a type of flatworm, infest the bird's liver, bile duct, pancreatic duct, and gall bladder (in those species that possess a gall bladder). Trematodes require a secondary host such as fish, snails, insects, and tadpoles. The bird eats these organisms and subsequently becomes infested with flukes. They are particularly a problem in cockatoos (Quesenberry et al., 1986). Symptoms include anorexia, diarrhea, depression, vomiting, and acute death. S. Shanthikumar (1987) states that flukes may also infest the reproductive system, eye, skin, and blood vessels. Symptoms will be dependent upon which body systems are affected. Weight loss, bloody diarrhea, and malformed eggs are some of the symptoms observed when these various systems are involved (Shanthikumar, 1987). Since eggs are shed in the feces, fecal examination is used for diagnosis. As with tapeworms, the eggs shed are not infective to other birds until they have hatched and matured in a secondary host. No treatment is available for trematode infestation (Quesenberry et al., 1986). However, Rosskopf feels that use of injectable Droncit may be effective, at least in some cases (Rosskopf, "Diagnosis of Parasitism").

Trichomonas: This protozoa causes caseous (cheeselike) plaques in the bird's mouth, esophagus, and crop. Transmission is by contamination of food and water by infected birds. Parents with trichomonas can infect their nestlings when they feed them (Burr, 1987). Symptoms include labored breathing, weight loss, regurgitation, and failure to thrive. Young birds are most susceptible and have a high mortality. Clubb (1986b) recommends Emtryl (dimetridazole) and Ipropran (Ipronadazole) for treatment of trichomoniasis. Diagnosis is by examination of scrapings of accessible lesions and crop washings. Prevention consists of good husbandry and sanitation.

PODODERMATITIS: See Bumblefoot.

POISONING: See Chapter 4: Poisoning. A poison is defined as any substance taken into the body by ingestion, inhalation, infection, or absorption that interferes with normal physiological functioning. Virtually any substance can be poisonous if taken into the body in sufficient quantity. Therefore, the term "poison" more often implies an excessive degree of dosage, rather than a specific group of substances (*Taber's Medical Dictionary*, 1985).

Birds, with their extremely efficient respiratory system, high metabolic rate, and relatively small body mass, are more easily affected by very small quantities of injurious substances than are most other warm-blooded creatures. The ways in which birds react to potentially injurious substances is dependent upon age, body weight, breeding status, and species-specific characteristics (Harrison, 1986f). Harrison states that the bird's ability to detoxify such substances is dependent upon the health of the liver (the organ primarily responsible for this function) and the kind and numbers of bacteria in the bird's intestinal flora.

214

The topic of poisoning is a broad one, and can be discussed here in only a general way. The reader is urged to review the discussion on poisoning in Chapter 4, and on safety precautions in Chapter 2.

Causative Agent   There are many toxins that have been documented in cases of avian poisoning.

> *Food toxins*: These include botulism (see Clostridium Infection in this chapter), aflatoxicosis (see Mycotoxicosis in this chapter), and table salt (sodium chloride).
>
> *Fertilizers containing nitrates*: Nitrate poisoning causes a change in hemoglobin, resulting in the decreased oxygen-carrying capacity of the red blood cells. It also causes an abnormal relaxation of the blood vessels, resulting in lowered blood pressure (*Merck Veterinary Manual*, 1985).
>
> *Insecticides*: The two main classifications are chlorinated hydrocarbons (DDT, dieldrin, gammexene, lindane, and heptachlor) and organophosphates (Dimpylate, malathion, parathion, and dichlorvos). These insecticides accumulate in fat cells and are stored in the bird's body. In this way, their effects become cumulative over time if the bird is constantly exposed to them. According to Butler (1987), if fat deposits are then mobilized due to stress (starvation or infection, for example), the poison is released into the bloodstream and causes signs and symptoms of toxicity.
>
> *Rodenticides*: Arsenic, strychnine, and warfarin are rarely used now, and do not pose much of a threat to birds unless placed where they can gain access to them. Arsenic can affect all body systems, but in birds the main effect seems to be on the digestive system (Butler, 1987). Strychnine has its effect on the central nervous system. Warfarin is an anticoagulant that causes hemorrhage of various body tissues.
>
> *Household poisons*: Alcohol, nicotine from ingested cigarette butts and loose tobacco, hexachlorophene (an ingredient in facial soaps and deodorants), ammonia, naphathalene (found in mothballs), spray starch (contains fluoropolymers), and nonstick cookware (contains polytetrafluoroethylene, or PTFE). The hazard from nonstick cookware is particularly dangerous. Sakas (1986) states that under normal cooking conditions, such utensils are safe. Problems (which are invariably lethal) arise when they are overheated. When PTFE is heated above 280°C (530°F), it breaks down and emits toxic fumes. Examples of normal cooking temperatures are: water boils at 100°C (212°F), deep frying occurs at 210°C (410°F). When a nonstick cooking utensil is left empty on a high flame, it quickly reaches 400°C (750°F). An extreme hazard to birds are PTFE-coated drip pans. *Even with normal use, they rapidly reach unsafe temperatures.* Tests have shown that when a burner is turned to high setting for five minutes, the drip pan reaches a temperature of 684.5°F, with a range of 620° to 745°F. All bird owners have a responsibility to see that their homes are free of PTFE in any form.
>
> *Plants*: See Poisoning in Chapter 4.

Heavy metals: Lead, zinc, mercury, some paints, solder, and some types of galvanizing can all be sources of heavy metals. Most homes have at least one source of lead. Mercury is often used as a preservative with stored grains (Butler, 1987). Birds should never be fed preserved grain.

Autointoxication: According to Harrison (1986f), this source of poisoning is not often considered. Autointoxication (endotoxemia) can be a result of metabolic waste products absorbed from the intestine. This may occur because of the occlusion of the vent due to pasting, with subsequent obstruction. Obstruction of the intestine by foreign objects or neoplasms may also be a cause. Any condition that causes slowed transit time of food through the gut may cause autointoxication. Examples of such conditions are pansystemic illness, crop stasis, or macaw wasting syndrome.

Iatrogenic poisons: These are toxicities caused by treatment with medication. According to *Tabor's Cyclopedic Medical Dictionary*, an iatrogenic condition is "any adverse mental or physical condition induced in a patient by the effects of treatment by a physician or surgeon." It is probably safe to say that most iatrogenic toxicities occur because of the well-meaning, but uninformed, use of drugs by lay owners on their birds—not at the hands of avian veterinarians. According to Butler (1987), the following medications *should never* be used in avian subjects: procaine, lidocaine, procaine penicillin, streptomycin, and dihydrostreptomycin. If the aviculturist has occasion to use Emtryl (dimetridazole) or Panacur (fenbendazole) it should only be done with an avian veterinarian's supervision. These drugs are used for various endoparasites and can cause severe toxicity. Levamisole phosphate is another drug, sometimes used for endoparasites and sometimes as an immune system booster, that should never be used without the supervision of the avian veterinarian because of possible toxicity (Butler, 1987).

Transmission   Poisoning is, of course, not contagious and is therefore not transmissible to other birds.

Symptoms   The following is a list of the common symptoms grouped according to the causes listed above. It is not exhaustive. It should go without saying that if the owner suspects that any bird has been poisoned, appropriate steps should be taken immediately to obtain care for the bird.

Food toxins: For symptoms of *Clostridium* and fungal poisoning, refer to Clostridium Infection and Mycotoxicosis in this chapter. Symptoms of salt poisoning include depression and thirst, followed by excitement, tremors, severe muscle spasms, "backward walking," complete incoordination, coma, and death (Petrak, 1982).

Fertilizers containing nitrates: Depression, weakness, cyanosis of mucous membranes, subnormal body temperature, incoordination, difficulty breathing, convulsions, and death (*Merck Veterinary Manual*, 1979).

Insecticides: Chlorinated hydrocarbons—apprehension, muscle twitching, incoordination, and respiratory paralysis, with symptoms appearing twelve to twenty-four hours postexposure (Butler, 1987); organophosphates—vomiting, diarrhea, salivation, tearing of the eyes, breathing problems, and muscle twitching.

Rodenticides: Arsenic—vomiting, diarrhea, anorexia; strychnine—severe muscle spasms, twitching, respiratory muscle paralysis, and resulting death; warfarin—bruising, bleeding from vent, mouth, nose, blood in droppings.

Household poisons: As this list is virtually limitless, it would be impossible to list signs and symptoms for each potential toxin. The reader is referred to the list of general signs and symptoms of poisoning in Chapter 4. Special mention should be made of the symptoms of PTFE poisoning. These fumes are very irritating to the lungs, resulting in lung congestion and hemorrhage. The bird is usually found dead or gasping for air, later dying.

Plants: Poisoning from various plants is a broad topic, and space does not allow for a detailed discussion of symptoms. The reader is referred to the list of general symptoms of poisoning mentioned above, as well as Table 4–4, Plants Considered Harmful to Birds, found in Chapter 4.

Heavy metals: The symptoms revolve around effects of the poison on the digestive tract and the central nervous system. Regurgitation, weakness, depression, ruffled feathers, abnormal droppings, muscle twitching, convulsions, incoordination, odd and unusual head positions may all be seen. In Amazon Parrots, blood in the urine is a frequent finding in lead poisoning.

Autointoxication: Digestive tract and central nervous system symptoms may be seen.

Iatrogenic toxicities: These symptoms are dependent upon many variables, not the least of which is the medication involved. The avian veterinarian will be the authoritative source of information in each individual case.

Laboratory Work   In cases such as heavy metal poisoning, radiographs may demonstrate metal particles in the gut or other body tissues. If lead is involved, serum lead levels will be helpful. Other laboratory work will be necessitated, depending upon the toxin. The single most useful aid to diagnosis of poisoning is a complete history. Things such as the bird's environment, diet, behavior, type and source of food, chemical and/or volatile compounds recently in use, amount of ventilation available, and materials used in the bird's cage are all very important points in pinning down the source of the injurious substance.

Treatment   Treatment varies with the individual case and the poison involved. In general, supportive care is used: warmth, gentle restraint if necessary, oxygen if indicated, and fluid therapy.

Removal of the toxin from the skin or the interior of the bird's body is essential, if at all possible. To this end, lavage of the crop may be done.

Lubricants may be given orally to aid in passage of metal particles through the gut. The use of calcium EDTA will chelate (render nontoxic) the heavy metal particles that are in tissues other than the gut. A slurry of crushed, activated charcoal given orally may help absorb poison in the digestive tract.

Preparations such as milk of magnesia, mineral oil, Pepto-Bismol, and Kaopectate may be used to soothe irritated gastrointestinal tissues.

In the case of respiratory tract irritation, antibiotics and steroids may be used for alleviation. Inhaled irritants may require treatment with controlled oxygen, temperature, and humidity.

When treating salt poisoning, Butler (1987) recommends the use of diuretics to enhance excretion by the kidneys, fluid therapy, and plenty of fresh water orally if the bird is able to drink. Water can also be given by gavage.

Toxins that cause excessive central nervous system stimulation may require sedative-type medication (Butler, 1987). Butler mentions the use of atropine in organophosphate poisoning, where severe digestive tract symptoms may be present. Atropine has a marked effect in decreasing gut hypermotility, thereby alleviating symptoms such as vomiting and diarrhea.

Prognosis Prognosis varies with the individual case. Many times, the bird dies so suddenly that veterinary intervention is not possible. To reiterate, recovery depends on the following variables:

Amount of toxin absorbed
Time elapsed before care is sought
Proper identification of poison involved
Properities of the toxin
Age of bird
Body weight
Breeding status
Species
Health status of bird "prepoisoning"
Individual response to therapy

PSITTACINE BEAK AND FEATHER DISEASE (PBFD): This disease is also known by a variety of other names: cockatoo rot, beak rot, White Cockatoo disease, cockatoo feather loss and malformation syndrome, feather maturation syndrome, cockatoo apterylosis, and keratodysgenesis. PBFD is actually a far more apt name, as this devastating disease is not limited to cockatoos alone. Other species that have been documented as having PBFD are budgerigars, cockatiels, lovebirds, African Grays, Vasa Parrots, *Eclectus*, Malle Ringnecks, Bourke's Parrots, King Parrots, lorikeets, and rosellas. The very young bird is primarily affected by this disease and is especially at risk.

PBFD has two major effects. The first is a severe depression of the bird's immune system, making it susceptible to the most minor of infections, often with devastating results—including death. The immune system depression found in birds with PBFD is very severe. For this reason, it is sometimes referred to as avian AIDS.

The mechanism that causes this immune system malfunction is the destruction of certain cells found in the thymus and the bursa of Fabricius (Johnson, 1987c). The thymus is a structure located alongside the trachea. It produces T-lymphocytes. The bursa of Fabricius is located in the intestinal wall, close to the vent. It produces B-lymphocytes. Both types of lymphocytes are very important in fighting infection. With the destruction of the body's ability to produce such cells, the immune system is severely compromised. The bird's susceptibility to infectious disease skyrockets.

Both the thymus and bursa reach their maximum size and productivity while the bird is young, between six months and one year of age (Johnson, 1987c). Thereafter, the thymus and bursa shrink and become much less susceptible to the causative agent of PBFD. The damage done in PBFD to these lymphoid tissues occurs during their growth period.

The second major effect of PBFD is on the beak, feathers, and skin. Extensive feather loss is a hallmark, with little or no feather replacement. The feather loss of PBFD is body wide, *including* the feathers of cheeks and head. This is in marked contrast to feather loss occurring for reasons other than PBFD (see Feather Picking, in this chapter). Those feathers that do regrow are abnormal. This exposes the victim to the dangers of hypothermia. The beak and nails overgrow. They are subject to fracturing and subsequent hemorrhage. Birds often have difficulty eating because of beak involvement.

Affected birds experience considerable skin, beak, and nail pain due to such abnormalities. They become withdrawn, irritable, and intolerant of handling because of their physical distress. Risa Teitler (1985) feels that these birds commonly suffer disturbances in equilibrium, causing them to feel imbalanced and insecure in their surroundings. Teitler notes that preening in PBFD-afflicted birds she studied was modified to the point that such birds became careful to refrain from pulling out or displacing down feathers. The birds resisted bathing strenuously. This is a marked deviation from the behavior of a normal cockatoo, which usually adores a bath. A marked decrease in physical activity was also found. Birds were content to sit quietly on the perch. There was no beak clicking, wing flapping, dancing or prancing to and fro on the perch. In fact, none of the normal cockatoo activity behavior was present. At the same time, Teitler noticed an increase in the defensive swaying activity of those birds she observed.

As the birds' beak problem increased, they eschewed all their former preferred foods in favor of soft food. A change in vocal quality was also observed: The clear, ringing cockatoo vocalization was replaced by those characterized as "rough and gritty." Teitler states that those birds with PBFD she observed were overall less adventurous, mischievous, and playful. She noted that preening activities became incessant.

Trudy Rosenthal (1986) has written an article about caring for her PBFD-affected cockatoo. She makes the point that most people with chronic illnesses, especially those in which body image is altered, experience "situational" depression. She feels this occurs in birds with PBFD as well. This point has implications for the nursing care of such birds. This will be discussed later in this section, relative to the treatment of PBFD.

Causative Agent PBFD is virally caused. The virus responsible has been named *Diminuvirus* because of its extraordinarily small size (Ritchie, 1988). This virus was isolated from birds diagnosed as having PBFD. It was then made into a preparation containing 100 trillion virus particles per milliliter and administered to susceptible birds. These birds then developed PBFD, with the typical feather follicle lesions.

Transmission PBFD is contagious. Wild-caught adults having no apparent symptoms, obviously infected adults and chicks, and contaminated aviaries and rearing areas have all been implicated in the infection of susceptible nestlings. It is important to realize that PBFD *does* exist in the wild. Estimates of prevalence in wild flocks run as high as 5 percent, according to Silva (personal communication). This fact has great implication for those who wish to see Australia legalize the export of its wild birds.

Although breeders have reported PBFD in offspring of "healthy parents," Johnson feels that upon close examination, such parents either exhibit very mild symptoms of PBFD or may be harboring the virus (Johnson, 1987c).

Material from beak, feathers, skin, and feces is considered to transmit infection. Any bird of any age, without apparent symptoms, could be shedding the viral agent of PBFD. Therefore, any such bird is a possible source of infection for any young bird present at the same time and place.

Richard Smith (1986) cites a cluster outbreak of PBFD in a hand-fed psittacine nursery. Seven nestling umbrella cockatoos were pulled for hand rearing before one week of age. All but two had different parents, and these parents appeared free of PBFD. The babies were housed in the same nursery, but all were kept in individual brooding containers. All the babies developed bacterial and fungal problems before the first signs of feather abnormality were noted. Smith concludes that the youngsters contracted PBFD after hatching, and probably after removal from the nestbox.

Any bird up to the age of four to five years, when thymal and bursal regression has been completed, should be considered at risk of contracting PBFD. It would be of great help to have a test that would indicate the age when maximum thymal and bursal development has occurred and regression has begun. These events occur at different ages for different species, so no such test is currently available.

It is not known at this time if a carrier state exists in PBFD (Johnson, 1987b).

Symptoms

Delayed or abnormal molt
Lost feathers, if replaced at all, are replaced with progressively abnormal
    feathers: retained feather sheaths, clubbed feathers, curling feathers,
    feathers "pinched" midway along shaft, marked stress lines, blood
    vessel remnants retained in quill, changes in feather pigmentation
Loss of powder

Psittacine beak and feather disease in a lovebird (*Agapornis* sp.). There is a total absence of feathers on the head and face.   *Peter Sakas, D.V.M.*

Psittacine beak and feather disease in an Umbrella Cockatoo.

Peter Sakas, D.V.M.

Feathers, beak, skin tender and painful
Feathers break and bleed easily
Changes in pigment and growth rate of beak and nails
Necrosis or "rot" of beak and nails
Fracturing of beak and nails
Skin wounds may heal slowly
Variable appetite and poor growth rate
Discomfort, pain, and irritability during grooming and handling
Personality and behavioral changes
Difficulty clearing infections with appropriate antibiotic or antifungal
   therapy

Laboratory Work   At present, there are two newly developed diagnostic blood tests available for the detection of PBFD. One test detects antibodies for the PBFD virus. The other can be used to identify birds that have the PBFD virus circulating in the bloodstreams. Both of these tests have been developed by Branson Ritchie, D.V.M., and his colleagues of the University of Georgia. Diagnosis must be confirmed by excisional biopsy of ten or more affected feathers, along with their follicles (Johnson, 1987c). Some veterinarians feel one good sample should be adequate for diagnosis. Graham (1984) points out that the best biopsy material contains the "intact, actively regenerating, yet obviously affected, follicle and its contained, developing feather."

The object of examination of such biopsy material is to demonstrate the presence of BGCS (basophilic, granular, or globular cells). These cells contain a granular substance that, when viewed with an electron microscope, appears to be viral particles. These BGC cells are found not only in affected feather follicles, but also in samples of bursal and thymal tissue at necropsy.

A negative biopsy report does not necessarily mean that the bird is free of PBFD. Such a result may occur because of an inadequate sample submitted for examination. It may also occur due to a problem with the preservation of the sample, or staining techniques employed in examination. If the bird is definitely suspected of having PBFD, another biopsy sample should be submitted again in thirty to sixty days, especially if the bird is showing no signs of improvement with symptomatic treatment (Johnson, 1987c).

In addition to biopsy, the veterinarian will run serum chemistries and a CBC to assess the bird's response to secondary infections and the overall status of the immune system. Physical examination and a good history are very important in helping to establish the diagnosis.

Treatment   At present, PBFD cannot be cured. Treatment is aimed at stimulating the immune system and providing symptom relief and supportive care in order to provide the bird with improved quality of life.

Stimulation of the immune system may be obtained with the use of such medications as levamisole, avian interferon, and avian interleukin I. Avian interferon, a product of lymphocytes, is a powerful antivirus agent. Avian interleukin I is a lymphokine, also produced by lymphocytes. These substances help

223

produce immunity to viruses and bacteria by stimulating white blood cells such as macrophages and monocytes. These cells attack and digest foreign invaders.

Autogenous vaccines have had some success in causing a remission of the disease (Johnson, 1986). It is not known at present whether vaccine-induced remissions are temporary or permanent. The autogenous vaccine used is made individually for every bird. It consists of a preparation made from all flora (both abnormal and normal) cultured from cloacal and choanal material, feather pulp, beak and skin lesions, plus any viruses grown from cell cultures of feather, skin, and beak material. The vaccine is usually administered at gradually lengthening intervals for one year, or as long as symptoms are present. In addition to use of autogenous vaccines, secondary infections are treated, as are any parasite infestations. Great attention is given to diet and proper nutrition.

According to Sakas (personal communication), in his experience with sixty-five birds receiving autogenous vaccine, only three showed regrowth of normal feathers. He states that if beak lesions had already appeared, the prognosis was much poorer, the birds worsening regardless of the vaccine.

Because of the severe feather loss experienced with PBFD, care must be directed to the prevention of hypothermia. Warm room temperatures help. The use of infrared lamps is also very beneficial. Safe placement of such a lamp above one end of the perch allows the bird to move toward or away from the heat, as its comfort level dictates (Rosenthal, 1986).

Good husbandry and careful monitoring of the bird are of paramount importance in the treatment of PBFD. Such care is a long-term project, requiring absolute commitment by the owner. Patience and much love are prime requisites if progress is to be made. Improvements are very gradual, and may take as long as a year to emerge. While the treatment is in progress, observe for:

> Decreased beak and feather pain
> Decreased growth rate of beak and nails and return of normal pigment
> Appearance of normal feathers
> Changes in personality and activity levels to pre-illness levels
> Return of powder down
> Return of reproductive behaviors

Careful laboratory monitoring of the bird's progress is necessary during treatment. Repeat feather-follicle biopsies are recommended every six weeks while the vaccine is given on a weekly basis. When the vaccine schedule is reduced to every two weeks or monthly, such biopsies should be done every two or three months (Johnson, 1986). The desired results are those in which no BGCs are found, and there is no evidence of secondary infections or abnormal bacterial flora in the sample.

Bacterial cultures and sensitivities will be run on the same schedule as the feather-follicle biopsies, or as needed if an unexpected infection occurs. T4 level should be checked every eight weeks to make sure the thyroid is functioning optimally.

Hematology and serum chemistries are done every six to twelve weeks to

destruction of
upper beak

severe overggrowth
in lower beak

A striking example of the effects of psittacine beak and feather disease. There is extensive destruction in the upper beak of this cockatoo and severe overgrowth in the lower beak.

Peter Sakas, D.V.M.

monitor the bird's overall response to therapy, and the status of its immune system. Weights are checked at every vaccine injection, and beak and nails trimmed as needed.

Even if great clinical improvement is made, it is not known if such birds can be reinfected with PBFD, or if they can become carriers.

The author feels that the bird's mental attitude is an important area that needs to be addressed. Any long-term illness invariably brings with it depression. This is especially true when body image is severely and negatively affected. Birds, and cockatoos in particular, are vain creatures. They seem to delight in the loveliness of their plumage and thoroughly enjoy showing it off. Can you imagine their horror when they look at themselves and see, instead of shining, smooth plumage, naked skin and objects that are barely recognizable as feathers? This may seem farfetched and anthropomorphic, but the author has personally observed in years spent working professionally with cats that have had to be shaved to the skin for fur matting the anxiety this procedure engendered—and the cats' pitiful attempts to hide themselves from view. I can hardly imagine that a highly intelligent psittacine would feel less or differently when faced with the loss of all that makes it unique and exquisite.

Coupled with the loss of feathers and its possible emotional consequences, there is pain, a sense of imbalance, and discomfort eating—all things that may make a bird with PBFD depressed. It seems that measures to lift the bird's spirits and help it to feel more positive about itself and life would be of immense benefit in the struggle for health and wholeness. These needs should be taken into account in any long-term health plan for the PBFD bird.

In her article, Rosenthal discusses such concerns and their implementation in the care of Magnolia, her eighteen-month-old Umbrella Cockatoo with PBFD. It is an article filled with great love and insight and should be read by all who own birds afflicted with this disease. Magnolia was treated with autogenous vaccine. Her medical regimen was very similar to the one discussed above. The unique aspect of Magnolia's care revolves around Rosenthal's recognition of her bird's emotional needs and her special efforts to address those needs. Half-hour "cuddling" sessions were a twice-daily routine, in which the bird was loved and petted, and told how pretty and special she was. These sessions were in addition to all the other attention she received daily. Magnolia was given much supervised freedom outside her cage daily. Special efforts were made to provide her with chewable perches, so she could indulge this favorite pastime at will. Nutritious treats were placed on a plate on top of the bird's cage, so she could exercise some control over inspecting them and nibbling in her own time, and under her own terms. A tape recording made by a physician for cancer patients, emphasizing health and wholeness, was played often for the bird. Rosenthal felt the soothing delivery of the speaker and the positive concepts expressed on the tape "might help Magnolia imagine herself well, the effect it has on humans." Much of Magnolia's care was carried out at home because of Rosenthal's background as a nurse. This helped ensure that the bird was spared the stress of endless visits to the veterinary clinic.

Abnormal crest feathers in a cockatoo affected with psittacine beak and feather disease.

Peter Sakas, D.V.M.

Does all this sound farfetched? Upon reflection, it shouldn't. All creatures thrive on loving care, especially sick ones. Rosenthal says, "I am blessed with a loving bird who appreciates every effort on her behalf. . . . After sixteen weeks of treatment, my efforts have shown some improvement in her condition. She has grown twenty normal feathers, is no longer plagued by foot warts, and is clear of psittacosis. She is so active that I believe her anemia has disappeared, too. Just last week, Magnolia danced and entertained our guests in great style. As I write this article, she sits on my shoulder, coos, and gently preens my hair. I am getting back more love than I'd ever imagined."

Prognosis The prognosis for a bird with PBFD is always grave. The younger the bird, the more doubtful the outcome. In older birds that have been treated and have experienced a regression of symptoms, we are not able to predict a carrier state. Nor do we know if a latent and slower phase of the disease exists, to which the regression could be attributed, rather than to the effects of treatment. Johnson feels that such birds cannot be considered cured and are probably a source of infection to young birds. Transmission of PBFD to older birds whose thymal and bursal growth and regression have already occurred is improbable.

As to how long a PBFD bird can live with treatment, each case is highly individual. Magnolia, referred to earlier, is still alive and functioning well as of this writing. She has developed beak lesions but remains active and free of infections. At this point, she has been in treatment almost two years (Rosenthal, 1988). Rosenthal states, "I value each day that I have her, and love her as if every day is her last."

From a preventive standpoint, there is much that can be done to prevent PBFD. The following are suggestions taken from Cathy Johnson's article in *Bird World* (1987c), so often cited in the foregoing material:

1. Close aviary and rearing facilities during breeding season to new birds and to people.
2. Strictly quarantine new stock.
3. Do not mix different age groups of birds.
4. Do not house nestlings with adults.
5. Chicks of different age and species should not be mixed together.
6. Don not incubate and hatch eggs from different clutches in the same tray.
7. Keep eggs from touching during incubation.
8. Clean and disinfect incubators, brooders, and other equipment between clutches. (Environ-One-Stroke, Roccal-D, and Chlorox are good, but rotate monthly as it has not yet been determined which disinfectants are best for the PBFD virus.)
9. Keep chicks from different clutches separate when feeding, rearing, caging, and shipping.
10. Do not expose youngsters to other birds until they are at least six months to one year of age.
11. Observe strict personal hygiene between care of chicks from different clutches.

12. Observe strict isolation of known affected birds and contaminated material from young birds of any species.

Branson Ritchie, D.V.M., and his colleagues at the University of Georgia are making great strides in the research of PBFD. Perhaps within the near future a vaccine will be available to prevent this disease.

PSITTACOSIS (PARROT FEVER, CHLAMYDIOSIS, ORNITHOSIS): This highly contagious disease is caused by *Chlamydia psittaci* (*Chl. psittaci*). It creates damage to the liver and kidneys and often manifests a combination of respiratory and digestive tract symptoms.

"Psittacosis" is the term commonly used to denote infection by *Chl. psittaci* in parrots. "Ornithosis" denotes chlamydial infection in birds other than parrots. The term "chlamydiosis" is often used interchangeably with "psittacosis." The reader may also see "chlamydiasis" in various literature. This term indicates infection by *Chl. psittaci*, but without apparent illness. Such birds are often carriers.

Chl. psittaci infection in psittacines is relatively common. Manifestations of infection range from symptomatic to acute and sudden death. According to *The Avian Diseases Manual*, published by the American Association of Avian Pathologists, mild disease may go unnoticed because of lack of symptoms; alternately, there may be only mild and transient respiratory symptoms and diarrhea.

Birds other than parrots can become infected with *Chl. psittaci*. These include poultry, such as turkeys and chickens, as well as wild and migratory birds. In addition, cats, dogs, humans, cattle, sheep, and goats can become infected. According to Gerlach (1986b), cats, dogs, and humans are unable to transmit this disease to others of their own kind. However, cattle, sheep, and goats can transmit psittacosis to those of their own species, and other mammals as well. David Alderton (1988) points out that domestic cats are commonly infected by *Chl. psittaci*. In a British study cited by this author, 45 percent of cats tested showed evidence of previous *Chl. psittaci* infection or were actively shedding *Chlamydia* at the time of testing. Alderton states that *Chl. psittaci* is one of the most common causes of abortion in sheep in the United Kingdom.

Alan Fudge (1984) mentions various diseases in animals other than psittacines caused by *Chl. psittaci*. These include feline pneumonitis; food animal polyarthritis; sheep and cattle abortion; cattle enteritis; conjunctivitis of cats, dogs, and sheep; and septicemia of hares.

It can be seem from the foregoing that *Chl. psittaci* is a problem in many more species than merely parrots. For a discussion of psittacosis in humans, the reader is referred to the Zoonoses entry in this chapter.

Chl. psittaci has several strains. These strains vary in their ability to infect and cause mild, moderate, or serious disease. Therefore, the degree of illness experienced by a bird infected by *Chl. psittaci* is dependent upon the strain with which it is infected, the amount of exposure to which the bird was subjected, the bird's immune system status, and environmental factors. Highly infectious strains of *Chl. psittaci* have an accelerated rate of growth and a wide host spectrum (that is, they are able to infect a large number of species). Stress is a very important factor in triggering shedding of the agent in carrier birds (Clipsham, 1988c).

Chl. psittaci is unique in that it possesses the characteristics of both bacteria and viruses. For many years, it was thought to be a virus and was classified as such. Recently, it has been reclassified as a very small bacteria, and it occupies a place midway between bacteria and viruses. *Chl. psittaci* is an obligate intracellular pathogen, meaning that in order to live and reproduce it must gain entry into the cells of its host. In this, it shares one of the characteristics of viruses. The method in which this organism matures within the cell also gives it a property similar to that of viruses. Its size and method of replication are similar to those of bacteria.

The infectious particles of *Chl. psittaci* are called elementary bodies. Once inside a host cell, they enlarge. These enlarged infectious agents are called reticulate bodies. (The reticulate body was formerly known as an initial body, and this term is still common in avian literature.) These reticulate bodies reproduce by dividing in two (binary fission) and forming clusters of daughter cells. These daughter cells reduce in size and become elementary bodies, ready to infect still more host cells and begin the entire process once more.

In a study using turkeys, cited by Fudge (1984), the following "schedule" of *Chl. psittaci* spread was found. Within four hours following exposure, the agent was found in abdominal air sacs. Twenty-four hours after exposure, large numbers of *Chl. psittaci* were recovered from lungs, air sacs, and pericardial membranes (those delicate tissues encasing the heart). After forty-eight hours, *Chl. psittaci* was found in the blood, spleen, and kidneys. After seventy-two hours, large numbers were found in the nose and cloaca, and viral shedding from feces and respiratory secretions started. Soon after these last events, the bird began production of antibodies against *Chl. psittaci*.

Opinions as to incubation time vary. According to Gerlach (1986b), forty-two days following naturally occurring infection (not experimentally induced infection) is the shortest incubation time. Gerlach further states that incubation times of up to one and one-half years have been observed. Fudge (1984) feels that incubation time may be as short as five days, and as long as several weeks.

Many parrot species susceptible to psittacosis have been reported. Young birds with immature immune systems are generally more susceptible than adults. According to Gerlach (1986b), South American species such as Amazons and macaws are more at risk than birds from South Asia, Australia, and related islands; African Grays are less susceptible than the two foregoing groups. Amy Worrell (1986b) indicates that macaws are highly susceptible to psittacosis and are often presented to the veterinarian literally "at death's door."

Severity of symptoms as well as susceptibility can vary with species. Exposure to *Chlamydia* does not guarantee illness in the bird (Clipsham, 1988c). Clipsham states that cockatoos and cockatiels are fairly resistant to psittacosis and remain alert during prolonged illness. Gerlach (1986b) feels that the factor

All parrot species and a number of other kinds of birds are susceptible to psittacosis.

Photo courtesy Richard Schubot,, Avicultural Breeding and Research Center

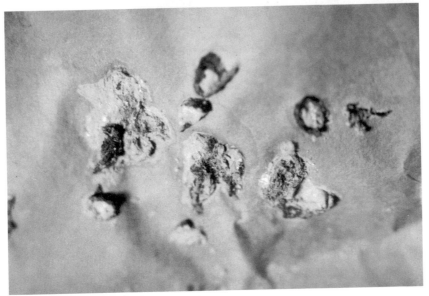

The unmistakable look of the droppings of bird affected with psittacosis.

Peter Sakas, D.V.M.

231

of primary importance in whether or not a bird develops psittacosis as result of contact with *Chl. psittaci* is that individual's overall health status.

Psittacosis is found in all wild parrot populations, but does not seem to cause serious disease (Gerlach, 1986b). It seems that serious illness is precipitated by man's intervention in these birds: the taking of nestlings, transport of wild-caught birds, drastic changes in food and environment, and exposure to other disease. Fudge (1984) emphasizes that pet stores are often responsible for the continued transmission of psittacosis in that they gather together birds from quarantine, smuggled birds, and domestically bred birds.

Psittacosis is a disease that can be transmitted to humans, with attendant medical and legal problems. As such, it is a reportable disease, of which public health authorities wish to be informed. According to R. Mohan (1987), "Anyone who deals with pet birds is a potential target of a liability case involving psittacosis. . . ." This category includes breeders, sellers, importers, veterinarians, pet owners, and even parents of minor children owning a bird that has infected a person with psittacosis. Because of the risk of litigation relative to psittacosis, all bird sellers should insist that the purchasers of their birds have that bird examined by a qualified avian veterinarian within a few days of purchase. This should be done regardless of any examination made on the bird while it was still in the possession of the seller or breeder.

Causative Agent *Chlamydia psittaci* (*Chl. psittaci*) is the pathogen responsible for psittacosis. There are several strains of *Chl. psittaci* that differ in their abilities to cause disease, ranging from mild illness to acute and sudden death. According to the *Avian Disease Manual*, concurrent infection with another organism, such as *Salmonella*, greatly enhances the disease-producing capacity of *Chl. psittaci*. *Chlamydia* was discovered to be the cause of psittacosis in 1929. This obligate intracellular parasite can survive in the environment for up to one month under the proper conditions (Gerlach, 1986b). However, bacterial decomposition of feces or tissues kills *Chl. psittaci* within hours. For this reason, transport of the organism to a laboratory for testing is often unsuccessful due to bacterial overgrowth of the specimen sample and the subsequent death of the organism.

Gerlach states that most modern disinfectants are of unreliable efficacy in killing *Chl. psittaci*. Formalin in 5 percent strength still is the most effective disinfectant agent against it. Gerlach cautions that formalin loses its effectiveness with decreasing room temperatures and that a minimum of 20°C (68°F) is necessary for its use. A temperature range of 30°C (86°F) to 40°C (104°F) gives the best chlamydicidal effect.

Graeme Eamons and M. J. Cross (1987) give the disinfection schedule recommended by the United Kingdom Public Health Laboratory Service for use in contaminated premises. According to this protocol, an iodophor (such as Betadine) should be used on cages, 5 percent formalin for surfaces, and phenolic compounds (such as Environ-One-Stroke) on waste products.

Transmission The two routes of transmission for psittacosis are respiratory and oral. Respiratory transmission includes the inhalation of infected particles of fecal, ocular, nasal, and respiratory discharges, and feather dust. Oral transmission includes the ingestion of food and water contaminated with *Chlamydia*-bearing feces.

Parents that are carriers can infect their nestlings via the regurgitated food they feed the babies. Transmission of psittacosis via insects is possible, though not a big problem in caged birds owing to the rarity of ectoparasites in such birds (Fudge, 1984). The disease is thought to be transmitted through the bite of blood-sucking insects such as spiders, lice, and simulid flies. Such insect transmission is mainly a problem with domestic poultry. Egg transmission of psittacosis has been proven in ducks, but there is no evidence for this in caged birds at present.

Having experienced psittacosis does not render the bird immune from reinfection. This is because *Chl. psittaci* lives inside the cells of its host and therefore does not stimulate high production of antibodies by the bird against *Chlamydia*.

A carrier state does exist with psittacosis. Birds that survive an initial infection may shed the organism intermittently in their feces for at least several months, and possibly longer, according to Gerlach (1986b). Clipsham (1988c) feels carriers may remain so for life, but may not always be a danger to other birds. Worrell (1986b) cites one case in which a bird with asymptomatic (latent) psittacosis developed overt psittacosis after a period of ten years, during which time exposure to other birds had not occurred.

The presence of latent psittacosis in a breeding flock may only be discovered when nestlings of apparently healthy parents die suddenly and inexplicably. The diagnosis of psittacosis in the human caretaker is also an indication of subclinical psittacosis in the aviary. Exposure to *Chl. psittaci* by birds or humans does not guarantee that either will actually develop psittacosis. At this point in time, it is not believed that humans can become carriers.

An avian carrier of *Chl. psittaci* develops a state of mutual tolerance with the particular strain with which it is infected. Under ordinary circumstances, the bird's immune system keeps the organism under control. However, this same strain may not be of such "benign temperament" in other birds. If stress causes the carrier to shed *Chl. psittaci* or to break with a full-blown case of psittacosis, other birds with which it comes in contact will be exposed to an organism that for them may be very virulent.

Symptoms The symptoms of psittacosis are variable. They depend upon the strain of *Chl. psittaci* with which the bird is infected, the bird's immune system status, species, age, and the presence of other concurrent infections. It may be difficult to separate the bacterial and chlamydial components relative to symptoms in a sick bird.

Mild outbreaks of psittacosis may go unnoticed because there will be very few symptoms. Alternatively, there may be very mild respiratory symptoms and diarrhea (*Avian Disease Manual*, 1983).

Symptoms vary with the species of bird involved. Worrell (1986b) has observed that budgerigars often present with chronic respiratory problems and diarrhea. She further notes that with cockatiels chronic respiratory problems, diarrhea, and poor reproductive records are common. Amazons may generally appear as "poor doers," with chronic weight loss and the classic lime green urates of psittacosis (due to liver involvement). *Pionus* parrots may have respiratory problems, poor reproduction, and high nestling mortality rate. Macaws are often affected with sudden, acute onset and are frequently near death when first seen by the avian veterinarian. It is common for any sick bird to stop talking or otherwise vocalizing. This is the case with psittacosis, also.

The symptoms of psittacosis are usually related to respiratory and digestive system involvement. During the acute phase, the following symptoms may be seen (Gerlach, 1986b):

Respiratory problems (shortness of breath, noisy breathing, "runny nose," sinus infection)
Diarrhea
Polyuria
Lethargy
Dehydration
Ruffled feathers
Loss of appetite
Yellowish, grayish, or lime green urates

Subacute or chronic psittacosis may show the following symptoms (Gerlach, 1986b):

Tremors
Unusual head positions
Convulsive movements
Opisthotonos
Partial or complete paralysis of the legs (the bird may be found lying helpless on the cage floor).

Gerlach states that survival, especially in a young bird, may leave the bird with chronic feather problems. This is due to thyroid and/or adrenal damage during the period of active illness.

In addition to the above manifestations, other symptoms may be noted (Fudge, 1984):

Weight loss
Unusual tameness
Lack of normal molt
Poor condition in beak and nails
Sneezing
Swollen, infected eyelids
Wasting of breast muscles

Laboratory Work   The diagnosis of psittacosis in a live bird is problematic because there is no one test that will give 100 percent reliable results. Usually, at least two laboratory tests will be used in combination to verify the presence of *Chl. psittaci*. Kevin Flammer (1987) feels that the most reliable results are obtained using a combination of serology and culture/isolation/identification. The reader is urged to review the Psittacosis Testing entry found in the Laboratory Work section of Chapter 3.

The three commonly used methods for laboratory confirmation of chlamydial infection are:

Isolation: Infected material from the bird is inoculated into cell cultures or live chicken embryos, allowing for isolation and identification of *Chl. psittaci*.

Serology: Tests such as latex agglutination, direct complement fixation, and indirect complement fixation are performed on blood serum samples. The purpose is to demonstrate the presence of antibodies to *Chl. psittaci*.

Stained smears: Material such as eye and nasal discharge or feces is placed on a microscope slide, stained with *Chlamydia*-specific stains, and examined for the presence of elementary bodies in the bird's cells.

There are problems and disadvantages with each of the diagnostic tests listed above. They will be discussed briefly because the reader should understand why results can be negative even in a bird that obviously has clinical psittacosis. In any of the tests used, a positive result is confirmatory of the presence of *Chl. psittaci*. However, a bird that is actually positive may have negative test results for a number of reasons. A negative test result does not carry with it the same degree of validity that a positive result does. In other words, one can be certain that a bird that tests positive is indeed positive; one cannot be so certain that a bird testing negative is *Chlamydia*-free.

Isolation: *Chl. psittaci* is shed only intermittently in body secretions. For this reason, several serial samples are needed for this procedure, to guarantee reasonably that the organism is present in material used for inoculation of cell cultures or embryonated eggs. In addition, bacterial overgrowth of the sample may kill the *Chlamydia* during transport to the laboratory, resulting in false negative results. Worrell (1986b) states that with this method there is only a 30 to 40 percent growth and retrieval rate for *Chl. psittaci*; a positive result, when obtained, is unquestionably positive. Flammer (1987) remarks that isolation is the standard by which other diagnostic methods are compared.

Serology: Some serological methods work better for some species and age groups than for others. Serological tests such as latex agglutination and direct complement fixation do not work well with small parrots (cockatiels, parakeets, and lovebirds) and some juvenile birds such as African Grays and macaws. (Flammer, 1987; Harrison, "Avian Diagnostic Dilemma"; and *Avian Disease Manual*, 1983).

Stained smears: Problems with this method include possible inadequate sampling so that elementary bodies are not apparent on examination.

The stain itself may not be sensitive enough to allow demonstration of elementary bodies (Flammer, 1987). Another difficulty lies in the fact that *Mycoplasma* organisms can be mistaken for *Chl. psittaci* (Clipsham, 1988c).

In addition, false negative results may occur because medication has been given to the bird before testing is done.

Although isolation, serology, and stained smears are invaluable in establishing a diagnosis of psittacosis, other tests are used to augment these techniques:

Radiographs: These will often show the enlarged liver and spleen, and diseased air sacs frequently found in psittacosis.

Hematology: A common finding is a greatly elevated monocyte (a type of white blood cell) count. Often an anemia is present, reflecting the chronicity of psittacosis.

Serum chemistries: LDH, SGOT, and CPK will often be elevated, reflecting tissue damage; serum protein and blood sugar may be depressed; and serum potassium and globulins (the portion of blood serum involved in antibody production) may be elevated (Fudge, 1984).

The physical examination and history are invaluable in aiding correct diagnosis. These tools, together with all the above techniques, will allow the avian veterinarian to confirm the diagnosis of *Chl. psittaci* infection.

Treatment   Treatment of psittacosis is most successful with use of tetracyclines. Chloramphenical and erythromycin can also be used. However, the tetracyclines remain the drugs of choice. If a bird is acutely ill, supportive care such as heat, intravenous fluids, oxygen, and tube feeding may be used.

There are three forms of tetracycline that can be used in the treatment of psittacosis. All forms work to inhibit the growth and reproduction of *Chl. psittaci*. However, these drugs are bacteriostatic—they can control and stop the infection, but they *cannot* kill the organism.

Chlortetracycline: The only type in this family of drugs approved by the USDA in the treatment of psittacosis, chlortetracycline has several serious drawbacks. The first is its unpalatability to the majority of birds. It is nearly always delivered in medicated seed or pellets. Needless to say, if the bird refuses to eat it, it will not establish the constant blood levels needed to control *Chl. psittaci*. Second, it interferes with normal bacterial gut flora, creating a situation conducive to fungal overgrowth, especially *Candida*. Third, it can be injurious to the bird's kidneys. Fourth, it can interfere with the absorption of dietary calcium from the gut.

Oxytetracycline: The second type of tetracycline commonly used, oxytetracycline can be given as an injection. Its side effects are the same as for chlortetracycline.

Doxycycline: This, the third type of tetracycline available for treatment of

236

psittacosis is far and away the best of the three in terms of effectiveness and lack of unwanted side effects. Depending upon the pharmaceutical preparation, it can be given as an intramuscular injection or intravenously (a real advantage in a deathly ill bird). It maintains an effective blood level much longer than chlortetracycline and oxytetracycline. This means that the bird can be medicated less often—a definite advantage in reducing stress. It is much less injurious to the kidneys and liver. The incidence of digestive tract upsets is less, and it does not interfere with normal gut flora. The binding of dietary calcium is not as great, either.

Medication is continued for a minimum period of forty-five days, and longer if necessary. Any bird on prolonged tetracycline therapy should be checked carefully and frequently for the presence of *Candida* or other fungal infection.

Prognosis The outcome of treatment varies, depending upon the individual bird's species, age, immune status, length of illness before treatment was sought, the virulence of the strain with which it is infected, mode of treatment, and its response to that treatment. In general, the sooner treatment is sought, the better the outlook.

Following treatment and apparent recovery the bird may become a carrier. For this reason, any bird that has "recovered" from psittacosis absolutely needs follow-up posttreatment. Fudge (1984) recommends that the bird be reexamined one to two weeks after the completion of the medication regimen. At this time, a CBC and serum chemistries should be done. Two to three weeks following the completion of treatment, another fecal culture should be done, using several day's worth of droppings. This is to confirm that the bird is free of *Chlamydia*. Paster (1983b) recommends fecal cultures at intervals of three and six months posttreatment.

Prevention of the spread of psittacosis throughout a collection or aviary is of paramount importance, as is the protection of human caretakers.

1. Isolate all sick birds.
2. Isolate incoming (new) birds for thirty to forty days.
3. Test suspicious birds (those with loose droppings, weight loss, or respiratory problems).
4. Treat all incoming birds with tetracyclines for thirty days, if feasible and safe for the birds (Clipsham, 1988c).
5. Treat all breeding birds for thirty days with tetracyclines, if the aviary is not a totally closed one (that is, an established collection of several years' duration, with *no* problems and *no* new birds) (Clipsham 1988c).
6. Thoroughly clean and disinfect cages, surroundings, and equipment used for a psittacosis bird. Worrell (1986b) recommends Roccal-D. Likewise, formalin, Betadine, and Environ-One-Stroke may be used (Eamons and Cross, 1987).
7. Keep circulation of feather dust to a minimum.
8. Droppings from an infected bird should be soaked with disinfectant and placed in a sealed plastic bag prior to disposal (Gallerstein, 1984).

9. Contact with birds by humans should be kept to an absolute minimum. Strict isolation technique should be used (see Chapter 2).

The symptoms of *Chlamydia* infection in humans are similar to flu: headache, fever, respiratory problems, and fatigue. Any person with a psittacosis-positive bird, and having such symptoms, should see a physician without delay. The doctor should be aware of the patient's exposure to psittacosis. With proper treatment, complete recovery is usually made.

REOVIRUS INFECTION: The *Reovirus* has been proven to cause disease in African Grays and has been implicated in other multifactorial diseases of parrots (Graham, 1987b; Clubb, 1984; and Gaskin, 1988). In other species of parrots, it is often found at necropsy in birds that have salmonellosis, *E. coli* infections, and chlamydiosis (psittacosis). In such cases, it is not known if *Reoviruses* are incidental findings or part of the overall disease problem. Clubb has found *Paramyxovirus Group 3*, *Aspergillus*, and *Salmonella* as well as *Reovirus* in cases she has examined. Clubb and Gaskin feel that *Reoviruses* may serve as triggering agents that activate otherwise minor or inactive infections.

Although the study of *Reovirus* infections in psittacines is in its infancy, a great deal of work has been done with this virus in domestic poultry. Such things as infectious stunting have been documented in young chickens (*Avian Histopathology 1987*). In this situation, poor growth and a grossly abnormal intestinal tract are hallmarks. *Reovirus* has been recovered from the gut contents or feces of such poultry. Other problems associated with *Reovirus* in domestic poultry include juvenile arthritis, respiratory problems, abnormal feathering, heart disease, and ulcerative enteritis.

It will be interesting to see if any of the poultry *Reovirus*-caused problems will be found in psittacines as study of *Reoviruses* continues in these birds.

Causative Agent   *Reoviruses* are members of the virus classification *Reoviridae*. These viruses are so named because of their presence in the respiratory and enteric systems, and because of *o*rphan status. Orphan status refers to the fact that (at least until recently) these viruses were not known to produce disease. *Reoviruses* replicate in the cell cytoplasm (as opposed to cell nucleus).

The strains that produce disease in birds seem to be infective for birds only and do not possess characteristics in common with those strains infecting mammals and man (Gerlach, 1986e).

Transmission   Transmission is by the oral-fecal route, and involves contamination of food and water by feces of infected birds, in which the organism is shed. Egg transmission has been proven for poultry and it may be proven to occur in psittacines (Gerlach, 1986e; Gaskin, 1987a). Presumably, infected parents would be able to transmit *Reovirus* to their nestlings during the feeding process.

Gaskin (1987a) feels there is good evidence for a carrier state with *Reovirus*.

Symptoms   The following are taken from Clubb (1984). She observed that the

238

course of clinical disease was approximately four days from the time symptoms were first seen until death. The first sign was as "abnormal appearance in the eyes." This was followed by depression, weight loss, and weakness. Many birds developed a unilateral or bilateral leg paralysis. In many birds with paralysis, swelling of the legs and head was seen. Skin in these areas was "weeping and cool to the touch." Often, a dark brown or bloody nasal discharge occurred. Breathing problems were noted prior to death. Death occurred within several hours to one day after leg paralysis was noted. Feces were normal but urates were frequently yellow.

Mohan (1984) observed emaciation, labored breathing, weakness, diarrhea, incoordination, and pale beak and toes (in the Gray-cheeked Parrot), and death.

In Graham's (1987) experimentally induced *Reovirus* illness, using two African Gray Parrots, the course of disease postinfection was somewhat longer than that observed by Clubb in the natural infections she described. The birds in Graham's study lived between eight and nine days following their experimental infection with *Reovirus*. In the bird inoculated intramuscularly, lethargy, anorexia, and yellow-orange urates were noted. The second bird was inoculated orally. It appeared somewhat lethargic, but could be easily aroused. It, too, was anorectic.

Laboratory Work   Because *Reovirus* infections usually occur in conjunction with other pathogens, standard culture and sensitivity tests are performed with choanal and cloacal specimens, as well as other body secretions present at the time of examination. Serum chemistries and hematology are also appropriate. If the avian veterinarian has reason to suspect a *Reovirus* infection, several serological studies are available that may confirm such an infection. Of those available, the agar gel immunodiffusion test is most commonly used (Gaskin, 1988). This test will indicate if antibodies to *Reovirus* are present in the bird's blood. Such antibodies will appear seven to ten days postinfection and will persist for several months. After this time, the serum antibody level will decline and eventually become undetectable. As with many other serological tests, it would probably be most helpful to run serial tests so that a determination could be made regarding whether the infection was new or of less recent origin.

Treatment   There is no known treatment for *Reovirus*. Supportive care will be given. If concurrent infections are present, these will be treated.

Prognosis   This can be a lethal disease, made more so by the presence of other concurrent bacterial, viral, and fungal infections. Clubb (1984) lists mortality rates for four lots of imported African Grays and Jardine's Parrots as varying from 2.3 to 40 percent.

There is no available vaccine for *Reovirus* infection. As always, prevention is the best cure. Precautions include mandatory isolation of new stock, good hygiene and husbandry practices, and thorough cleaning and disinfection of the bird room or aviary following any *Reovirus* outbreaks. The disinfectant agent used should be capable of killing nonenveloped viruses such as the *Reovirus*. Clipsham (1988a) states that sodium hypochlorite (Chlorox), iodophores (Betadine), and glutaraldehydes (Wavecide-01) are all capable of killing such viruses, used at the proper dilution and conditions.

RICKETS: This is the condition in very young birds caused by the failure of calcium to be deposited normally in bone and cartilage. This may also occur in adult birds for a variety of reasons. In the adult, the condition is known as osteomalacia. The reader is referred to the Hypocalcemia and Nutritional Secondary Hyperparathyroidism entries in this chapter for further discussion of calcium-D_3-phosphorus metabolism, and the treatment rationale.

There are three causes of rickets according to Brugère-Picoux and Brugère (1987). The first is inadequate dietary calcium. This may occur simply because the diet lacks adequate calcium, or it may occur because the gut is unable to absorb the calcium present in food ingested. This can occur if the bird is on long-term tetracycline therapy, as this medication is known to bind calcium in the gut, thus preventing its utilization. It can also happen when the bird has been fed quantities of uncooked or sprouted beans (kidney or pinto beans, for example). These, too, bind calcium in the gut, making it impossible for the bird to absorb the calcium properly (Stoodley and Stoodley, 1983).

The second cause of rickets is inadequate vitamin D_3. Again, there are several possible causes for this. There may not be adequate D_3 content in the diet, or the vitamin D_3 may be available in the diet but not utilized due to a gut malabsorption problem. The bird may not receive adequate sunlight. This in itself is not a problem in birds supplemented with D_3. However, in those that have neither dietary supplementation nor access to ultraviolet light, problems can become severe. Bruce Watkins (1987) warns against dependence on artificial light sources such as Vita-Lites to provide enough ultraviolet radiation to allow birds to produce their own D_3. In a study conducted by him, it was found that birds exposed to twelve hours daily of Vita-Lite illumination, without D_3 supplementation, did very poorly. Of all the study groups, those birds in this group showed the poorest weight and bone mineralization.

Diseases of the kidney and liver can interfere with the bird's ability to make and utilize the biologically active form of D_3. David McCluggage (1987) has seen problems with metabolic bone disease in very young birds with hepatitis, as well as in birds with renal failure.

The third cause of rickets may be a severe imbalance in the calcium-D_3-phosphorus ratio. Excess calcium binds with phosphorus in the gut and is excreted. Excess phosphorus also binds with calcium and follows the same fate. Excess vitamin D_3 can actually result in abnormal resorption of calcium from the bone and deposition of calcium in soft tissue.

Causative Agent Those factors (discussed above) that interfere with normal calcium-D_3-phosphorus metabolism.

Transmission Rickets is not a communicable disease and is therefore not transmissible from one bird to another.

This dove is suffering from a severe lack of dietary calcium. Its deformed scissor beak is rubbery in consistency. *Peter Sakas, D.V.M.*

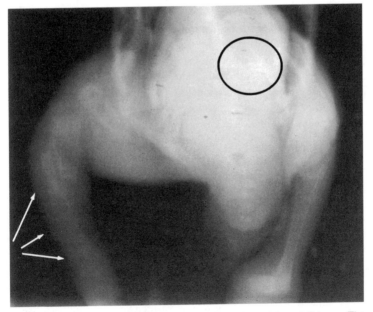

Pathological fractures in a young macaw with severe calcium deficiency. The fracture at the bottom of the left femur is healed at a right angle while the right femur is fractured in three places. *Peter Sakas, D.V.M.*

Symptoms First signs include a softening of the beak, claws, sternum, and vertebrae. These will be soft when palpated. The keel may assume an S shape. As the problem progresses, the following may be seen:

Leg weakness, becoming progressively more severe
Joint swelling
Bowing of long bones (thigh and upper wing bones)
Stunting of growth
Reluctance to perch, walk, or fly
Pathological bone fractures

Brugère-Picoux and Brugère state that these poor little birds frequently rest on their hocks and appear "to wait for death."

Laboratory Work The diagnosis of rickets can often be made by history and physical examination. However, rickets may have as its etiology something other than simple lack of calcium in the nestling. For this reason, the following may be done:

Radiograph: Will confirm poorly mineralized bone.
Serum chemistries: Will help rule out systemic problems such as liver or kidney disease that may be contributing to the problem. Abnormally low serum calcium levels can also be confirmed.
Hematology: Will indicate the presence of anemia or infection.

Treatment The treatment objective is to restore a normal calcium-D_3-phosphorus ratio in the bird's dietary intake. This may be accomplished by dietary changes and/or supplementation with medications such as D-Ca-Phos or Neocalglucon. If there are underlying disease processes (such as malabsorption) contributing to the calcium-D_3-phosphorus problem, these should be treated.

Birds that have suffered pathologic fractures will need orthopedic care. According to Harrison and Harrison (1986), many of these fractures exhibit abnormal or impaired healing.

Breeding birds should be supplemented for two reasons:

1. The hen needs extra calcium for egg laying, and to prevent her from exhausting her own body stores in the process.
2. Adequate calcium intake by the hen will assure normal bone and cartilage formation in the embryo.

Precautions must be taken once the chick is hatched to assure that a balanced calcium-D_3-phosphorus ratio is maintained while it is being fed. If the parents are to perform this task, their diet must contain adequate amounts of these elements. If hand feeding, the breeder needs to ascertain that the formula meets these requirements.

Prognosis Rickets caused by a simple lack of the necessary dietary components should respond well to supplementation, provided the problem is identified early. Long-standing rickets, once full growth and development has been attained, is irreversible. Chicks with early bone deformities may benefit from orthopedic splinting or surgery. The outcome of such cases depends on the individual's age and response to therapy.

SINUSITIS: See Colds in this chapter.

SOUR CROP: See Crop Emptying Problems in Chapter 4.

STAPHYLOCOCCUS: This is a Gram-positive bacterium. It is one of the pyogenic bacteria, so called because of its ability to produce pus. There are many species and strains of *Staphylococcus*. Many do not cause disease. The type most commonly producing disease in birds (and man) is *Staphylococcus aureus* (*S. aureus*). However, the human and avian strains of *S. aureus* are rarely transmitted from bird to man and vice versa (Gerlach, 1986a).

Those types of *Staphylococcus* that cause disease produce one or more metabolic products that have serious effects on body tissues. These products include those that destroy red blood cells (hemolysins), destroy white blood cells (leucocidins), cause tissue death (necrotizing exotoxins), and produce death of the entire host organism (lethal factor) (Smith, 1980).

In birds, as in man, *Staphylococcus* produces two major types of problems:

1. Skin and/or superficial tissue infection (exogenous infection)
2. Systemic infection (endogenous infection)

Staphylococcus is a ubiquitous bacterium. It is everywhere in the environment. It is also a normal inhabitant of the bird's skin. Furthermore, birds are extremely resistant to skin infection. Therefore, two conditions must be present in order for *Staphylococcus* to cause disease in a bird. First, there must be a break in the skin, however small and minor. Second, a "triggering" agent must be present. Such agents would include prior illness, a poorly functioning immune system, environmental stressors, or long-term antibiotic therapy (Gerlach, 1986a).

Exogenous infections affect the bird's skin in a localized fashion, but may not remain at this primary site. The bacteria may gain access to the blood via the skin lesion, thus creating a septicemia and multiple organ involvement. Examples of exogenous *Staphylococcus* infections include vesicular dermatitis, gangrene, bumblefoot, and naval/yolk-sac infection in the newborn. Endogenous infections include septicemia, arthritis-synovitis, and osteomyelitis. In addition, *Staphylococcus* can cause high embryo mortality rate.

Causative Agent   The various species and strains of *Staphylococcus*. These bacteria form characteristic grapelike clusters or broad sheets when they divide. They grow best in the presence of oxygen, but are able to grow without it (Smith, 1980). All species of *Staphylococcus* are readily able to develop antibiotic resistance. Smith states that nearly 80 percent are resistant to penicillin.

S. aureus (from the Latin, meaning "gold") has been so named because of the characteristic golden color of its colonies when grown on blood agar culture plates.

Transmission   Transmission of *Staphylococcus* may be directly through secretions of infected birds, or through contamination of food, water, perches, and other articles in common use. Egg transmission is also possible and is a cause of embryo death. Egg infection may occur because of an infected hen. It may also be the result of poor hygiene in the incubation process, as in the use of a contaminated incubator or the handling of an egg by a person with *Staphylococcus*-contaminated hands.

Staphylococcus may remain alive in dried pus for several weeks or months (Smith, 1980).

Symptoms   Because *Staphylococcus* may cause infection anywhere on the inside or outside of the bird's body, symptoms are dependent on the location of the infection. Gerlach (1986a) has reported the following as symptoms for some of the more common manifestations of *Staphylococcus* infection:

> *Vesicular dermatitis*: A skin infection characterized by small blisters containing a yellowish exudate. These blisters eventually break and form brownish or blackish crusts.
>
> *Gangrenous dermatitis*: The actual death of tissue, which follows a skin inflammation characterized by redness, swelling, and bleeding into the deep skin layers. The dead tissue appears black, smudgy, and is devoid of feathers.
>
> *Bumblefoot*: *S. aures* is frequently cultured from bumblefoot lesions. The bacteria may gain access to the bloodstream, causing other lesions or death (see the Bumblefoot entry in this chapter).
>
> *Navel and/or yolk-sac infection*: Seen in newborns up to approximately ten days of age. The navel region may appear dry, brownish, or smudged, or it may appear red and swollen. The yolk sac is not absorbed normally and may begin to deteriorate, causing further bacterial problems for the chick.
>
> *Septicemia*: The condition in which the blood contains many bacteria, often in overwhelming numbers. Symptoms include lethargy, anorexia, ruffled feathers, a humped-back posture, and sudden death. If the bird survives the initial septicemia, it may develop metastatic abscesses in various parts of its body, including the central nervous system. Symptoms of nervous system involvement can appear suddenly, and include such things as tremors, unusual head positions, and incoordination. An interesting condition that may result from *Staphylococcus* septicemia is the sudden death of the end parts of the toes. It occurs because of clots formed in the small blood vessels supplying the extremities. When deprived of oxygen, the end portions of the toes simply die. They change in color to brown or black and become somewhat shriveled in appearance. At the outset of the process, there is much pain and the bird shows extreme reluctance to perch or bear weight.

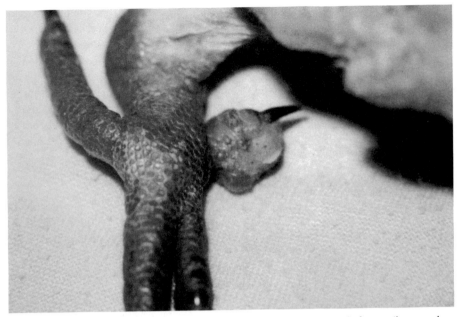

Toe necrosis (complete tissue death) in a baby macaw. This condition is frequently caused by *Staphylococcus* infection.   *Peter Sakas, D.V.M.*

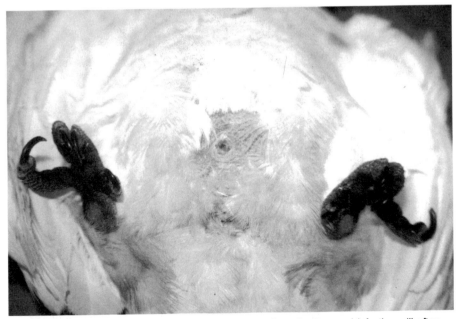

Umbilical abcess in a young cockatoo. Staphylococcal or streptococcal infection will often result in this condition.   *Peter Sakas, D.V.M.*

Arthritis-synovitis: The inflammation of the bone and membranes of a skeletal joint. The *Staphylococcus* organism may gain access through a local skin lesion or via septicemia. Symptoms include lameness, inability to perch or fly, reluctance to bear weight, and a general loss of function in the involved extremity.

Osteomyelitis: The infection of a bone. Any bone may be affected, but the head of the thigh bone, the "shin" bones, the bones of the foot, and the vertebrae are often involved. Severe involvement of the spinal cord may occur, resulting in pain, semi- or complete paralysis of the extremities, and other central nervous system symptoms.

Laboratory Work   Aside from toe necrosis, which is a good indication of *Staphylococcus* infection, culture and sensitivity tests of skin lesions and/or body exudates and secretions must be done to establish the diagnosis.

Treatment   Treatment is with appropriate antibiotic therapy as determined by culture and sensitivity testing. If concurrent disease is present, treatment will also be directed to its eradication. Supportive care, a change in diet, and improvement of husbandry practices may also be indicated.

Prognosis   The outcome of treatment of *Staphylococcus* infection is dependent upon the location of the infection and its response to appropriate antibiotic therapy. The bird's age and general state of health are also important. Thus, no generalizations can be made concerning so individual a disease process.

Prevention includes good husbandry and hygiene, good nutrition, and the bird's freedom from stress. If the breeder is experiencing a high proportion of embryos dead in the shell, it would be worthwhile to submit such eggs (*unopened*) for culture and sensitivity testing. A thorough review of the hatching protocol is also in order. If the problem is due to *Staphylococcus* egg transmission by an infected hen, her treatment and temporary removal from the breeding program is indicated.

STREPTOCOCCUS: This is a Gram-positive bacterium. Relative to its disease-producing capabilities, it is similar to *Staphylococcus*. It can cause localized skin lesions. It can also cause systemic illness, such as septicemia. Also, like *Staphylococcus*, *Streptococcus* is not ordinarily a primary cause of disease in the bird. It is most likely to cause disease if there is a concurrently existing illness such as viral or chlamydial infection, or if environmental stressors such as excessive heat or cold, exhaustion, or starvation are present (Gerlach, 1986a; Arnall and Petrak, 1982). Many species of *Streptococcus* are found normally on the bird's skin and upper respiratory tract, becoming disease producers only in the above-mentioned circumstances.

Examples of problems caused by *Streptococcus* are septicemia, arthritis, valvular heart disease, and embryo/neonate death. Problems such as arthritis and heart disease are the result of an acute septicemia that the bird has survived. Because *Streptococcus* can invade any part of the body, any part so affected may be chronically and permanently damaged.

246

Causative Agent   Species and strains of the genus *Streptococcus*. These organisms are ubiquitous, found everywhere in the environment, as well as part of the bird's normal body flora. The ability to produce disease varies tremendously with the specific strain or species of *Streptococcus*. Some are deadly in any circumstance; some produce disease only under certain conditions. Quite a few do not produce disease at all (Smith, 1980). Some need oxygen in which to grow, while others are able to grow without it. A few species of *Streptococcus* are strict anaerobes (that is, they can grow only in the absence of oxygen). These organisms can survive for several months in dried blood and pus.

The reader may hear such terms as *alpha hemolytic* or *beta hemolytic* used in reference to *Streptococcus*. These terms refer to the organism's abilities to destroy red blood cells in blood agar culture plates. Alpha hemolytic strains are able to accomplish this to a slight of incomplete degree. Beta hemolytic strains are powerful destroyers of red blood cells when grown on blood agar plates. There is a third type of *Streptococcus*, called *gamma*, which does not cause red blood cell destruction.

The significance of these terms is in the classification of virulence of *Streptococcus*. In general, beta hemolytic strains are associated with acute and overwhelming infection; alpha hemolytic strains are most often implicated in chronic, low-grade infections; while most gamma strains do not cause disease (Smith, 1980).

Like *Staphylococcus*, *Streptococcus* produces various substances harmful to living tissue. These include red and white blood cell destroyers (hemolysins and leucocidins), substances that interfere with normal blood clotting (streptokinase), substances that help destroy connective tissue (hyluronidase), and substances that produce rashes (erythrogenic toxin).

Transmission   The port of entry into the bird's body is most often a break in the skin, although entry may be via respiratory or other contaminated body secretions of infected birds. Contaminated food, water, and perches may also spread *Streptococcus* infections.

Egg transmission is caused by an infected hen. It may also occur through unhygienic brooding practices by the breeder. Newly hatched chicks may contract streptococcal infection through the umbilical cord.

Symptoms   As in staphylococcal infections, symptoms vary with the body system affected, the strain of *Streptococcus* involved, the number of organisms introduced into the bird's body, their mode of introduction, and the bird's age and state of health.

Gerlach (1986a) states that streptococcal infections are usually peracute or acute, the hallmark being sudden loss of consciousness and death. It is also possible to see great depression and somnolence followed by death in two to three days.

If a chronic streptococcal infection exists, it may manifest itself as arthritis, heart disease, or any number of other problems. The reader is referred to the *Staphylococcus* entry in this chapter for a more complete discussion of such symptoms.

247

Laboratory Work   Culture and sensitivity testing is the only way to confirm streptococcal infection. If the bird is suspected of suffering from other concurrent problems, serum chemistries and a CBC will probably be done.

Treatment   Treatment consists of appropriate antibiotic therapy as indicated by culture and sensitivity testing. Supportive therapy may be needed. Treatment of any concurrent illness is also a necessity. Gerlach suggests that chronic joint and tendon sheath problems may be treated with injections directly into these areas. Antibiotics and corticosteroids are also possibilities in these cases. Corrective surgery may also be a treatment alternative in such instances.

Prognosis   Outcome of treatment is dependent on the same factors discussed relative to prognosis of staphylococcal infections. Prevention is also identical.

SUBCUTANEOUS EMPHYSEMA: See Air Sac Rupture in Chapter 4.

THYROID PROBLEMS: The disease entities relative to thyroid dysfunction fall into four categories:

1. Hypothyroid function
2. Hyperthyroid function
3. Goiter (thyroid dysplasia)
4. Neoplastic disease of the thyroid

The thyroid glands in birds are paired. They lie on either side of the trachea, just within the opening to the thoracic (chest) cavity. It is for this reason that an enlarged avian thyroid gland is difficult to detect by palpation until it is greatly enlarged (Lothrop, 1984).

The thyroids are responsible for many extremely important bodily functions. These functions are mediated by the hormones it produces: thyroxine (T_4) and triiodothyronine (T_3). Thyroxine is the major product of the thyroid gland and is the precursor of triiodothyronine. The latter is the active intracellular hormone largely responsible for the various body functions the thyroid controls.

According to A. King and J. McLelland (1984), the thyroid gland has a major role in the following:

1. The stimulation of general metabolism, to regulate heat production in response to changes in environmental temperature.
2. The regulation of the growth of the body as a whole and the reproductive organs in particular. Moderately increased availability of thyroid hormone accelerates growth and increases egg production.
3. Control of molting. An increase in thyroid hormone precipitates molting, possibly by stimulating the growth of new feathers.

Studies of the effects of thyroid hormones on various avian species have been done and their results enumerated by Wentworth and Ringer (1986):

1. A decrease in thyroid hormones has been found to decrease metabolic rate and increase the deposition of body fat. It sometimes depresses

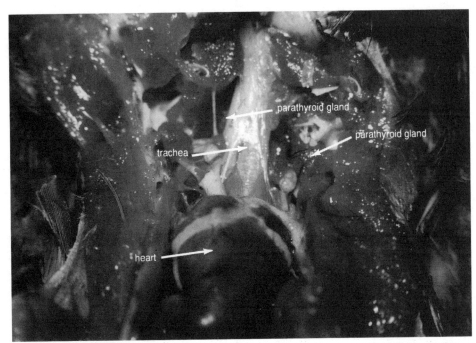

Enlarged parathyroid glands

Peter Sakas, D.V.M.

growth rate and the effectiveness of the immune system. Decreases in thyroid hormones result in a slight reduction of body temperature. In the hen, decreased egg production, egg weight, shell thickness, and ovarian weight can occur. In the male, testicular size decreases as does semen quality. Occasionally, a cock will entirely cease producing sperm.

2. An increase in thyroid hormones has been found to increase slightly body temperature.
3. An increase in thyroid hormones has been found to increase the metabolic rate of chicks at the time of pipping and hatching.
4. Thyroid function is intimately related with the chick's development of thermoregulatory ability.

The thyroid gland itself is regulated by the secretion of thyrotropin (also known as TSH). When blood levels of T_3 and T_4 are lower than those levels needed by the body, the pituitary gland secretes TSH, which stimulates the thyroid to produce more T_3 and T_4.

Other factors appear to have some influence on the thyroid gland. Season, temperature, photoperiod, gonadal hormones, and the molt itself appear to be involved to some degree (Wentworth and Ringer, 1986). Thyroid activity was greater in winter than in summer in a study using domestic poultry. It has been found that when environmental temperature is high, thyroid size may decrease, along with hormone secretion. Cold temperatures increase thyroid hormone secretion. Long days appear to stimulate thyroid activity initially, until the gonads become active and begin producing their own hormones. When this happens, thyroid activity decreases. With regard to the molt, it appears that in some birds, an increase in thyroid activity precedes the molt by several weeks or may occur at the onset of molt.

The above studies were carried out using a variety of domestic poultry and wild birds. It remains to be seen if psittacines parallel these findings. Nevertheless, it can be readily realized that the thyroid in psittacines and other birds is an important and complex organ. Its dysfunction, for any reason, will have profound effects on the entire body.

Hypothyroidism   In this condition the thyroid functions at below normal levels. Symptoms include the following:

Weight gain and obesity with normal caloric intake
Decreased fertility
Lethargy
Depressed mental alertness
Obvious sensitivity to cold temperatures, with heat-seeking behavior; may feel cool to the touch
Recurrent lipomas
Abnormal molt

Lackluster feathers that are dry and brittle; alternately, they may have a
    greasy feel due to abnormally high production of body oil
Predisposition of bacterial and fungal diseases

Diagnosis is by TSH stimulation test (see Chapter 3). Another indication of hypothyroidism may be bacterial and fungal problems that clear with appropriate medication, only to recur when the bird is off medication. Treatment consists of thyroxine replacement therapy. Any coexisting bacterial and/or fungal diseases should be treated, also. The thyroid medication can be placed in the bird's drinking water, but the preferred method is to give it directly into the mouth. Improvement of plumage and other symptoms can usually be seen in four to six weeks. Complete return to normal feathering usually takes about six months (Lothrop, 1984). Birds with hypothyroidism must remain on medication throughout their life.

Hyperthyroidism In this condition the thyroid functions at higher than normal levels. Although it has not yet been reported in companion birds, it is well within the realm of possibility. Any bird exhibiting weight loss, voracious appetite, voluminous droppings, hyperactivity, and nervousness should be evaluated for hyperthyroidism. Diagnosis is by TSH stimulation test. It has been suggested that treatment should consist of either surgical removal of the thyroid gland or suppression of its hormone secretions by medications such as [131]Iodine or propylthiouracil (Lothrop, 1984). [131]Iodine is radioactive iodine. It is taken up by the thyroid just as is normal iodine, but it destroys thyroid gland tissue with ionizing radiation. Propylthiouracil interferes with the synthesis of thyroid hormones. Although there are no reports in the literature at the time of this writing as to the time required for symptom abatement with these drugs, this is well documented for people. A few days to two or more weeks usually elapse before improvement is seen. Then, over a period of two to three months symptoms gradually abate (Gilman et al., 1985).

Goiter In this condition the thyroid is massively enlarged due to a lack of dietary iodine. The thyroid gland is unable to produce its hormones without iodine, so blood levels of T_3 and T_4 are low. This signals the pituitary to produce TSH, which stimulates the thyroid to step up its production of thyroid hormones. However, without iodine, it cannot do so regardless of TSH's influence. Instead, the thyroid becomes larger and larger in a futile effort to maintain normal function. This condition is most often reported in budgerigars, but can occur in any parrot species. Diagnosis is by physical examination and TSH stimulation test. Treatment is with iodine supplementation, usually with Lugol's solution added to the drinking water. Improvement should be seen in three to five days.

Neoplastic Thyroid Disease Benign or malignant tumors of the avian thyroid are very rare, although there are reports of a few such cases in the literature (Blackmore, 1982). These include a thyroid neoplasia in a Scarlet Macaw, a budgerigar with thyroid carcinoma, and a budgerigar with thyroid adenoma. In addition, Blackmore states that a few such lesions have been reported in various species of birds kept in zoo collections. The reader is referred to the Neoplasm entry in this chapter for a discussion of diagnostic tests, treatment, and prognosis.

TRAUMA: See Bleeding, Burns, Convulsions, Crop Burns, Foreign Object in the Eye, Fractures, Heat Stroke, Leg Band Problems, Poisoning, and Shock in Chapter 4.

TUBERCULOSIS (TB): This is a chronic infection caused by various species of *Mycobacterium*. All birds are susceptible to tuberculosis, but some species especially so. Among these are the *Brotogeris*, Amazons, and *Pionus* parrots. Nicole Van der Heyden (1986a) feels that export and quarantine stations and wholesale outlets are common sources of tuberculosis for psittacines. Arnall and Petrak (1982) state that the incidence of tuberculosis sharply increases in captive birds that are subjected to poor nutrition and kept in aviaries that are cold, wet, crowded, poorly ventilated, and dirty. Tuberculosis seems to be uncommon in wild birds, so we must assume that this is yet another "benefit" conferred upon captive birds by "civilization."

There are three species of *Mycobacterium* that can cause tuberculosis in birds. The first is *M. avium*, the most common causative agent in birds. It rarely infects man, but when it does it is often resistant to treatment (Gerlach, 1986a). The second species is *M. tuberculosis*. This is the common causative agent of TB in man, and it is fully capable of infecting birds. The third species is *M. bovis*. This species is largely specific to cattle, but can infect both birds and man via contaminated milk products. Because of pasteurization, this organism is not the problem it has been in centuries past.

It is interesting to note that W. T. Greene, in his classic nineteenth-century work *Parrots in Captivity*, often cautions against giving milk products to birds, as he had observed it often made them ill. Although birds lack the enzyme to digest milk products, which could account for some of the illness observed by Greene, it is probable that much of the disease seen was due to tuberculosis caused by *M. bovis*.

Tuberculosis in birds is primarily a disease of the digestive tract, at least during the initial period of infection. This is in direct contrast to man, in which TB is overwhelmingly a respiratory disease.

The effects of any *Mycobacterium* species are caused by the formation of that characteristic tuberculosis lesion, the tubercle. These modules range in size from very tiny to pea-sized. They are formed by aggregates of white blood cells (specifically, macrophages) that have engulfed the tuberculosis organism as the body's first defense against it. Unlike many bacteria "eaten" by macrophages, the *Mycobacterium* organism is not killed by this process. It continues to live on in these cells, walled off from the body by the tubercle.

Early in the disease, the tubercle may be soft, consisting only of the macrophages with their pathogen burden. Later on, the cells at the center of the tubercle may die and form a cheesy substance, giving rise to the term "caseonodular tubercle." As the tubercle grows older, the body will form a dense fibrous capsule around it. The tubercle becomes hard and is known as a fibrocaseous tubercle. Eventually, the fibrous capsule surrounding the tubercle becomes impregnated with calcium and is then known as a calcified tubercle.

Tubercles can be found in the bird's intestinal wall, liver, spleen, and bone marrow. The skin is also often involved. They occur after the initial infection, in which the organism is ingested by the bird. From here, it migrates into the intestinal wall and on to the liver via the portal circulation. It is then carried all over the bird's body via the general circulation. As macrophages in various organs remove the organism from the blood, tubercle formation begins. At this point, the lungs and air sacs may become involved. Skeletal joints may also become a site of secondary infection. Birds lack an efficient lymph node, and this helps in the early and widespread dissemination of *Mycobacterium* throughout the body (Gerlach, 1986a).

Avian tuberculosis, like human TB, is a chronic disease with a slow onset and long disease course. The incubation period may be from weeks to years. The length of incubation varies with the individual, based upon the frequency and dose of exposure, and the general health status of the host (Gerlach, 1986a; Petrak, 1984). Initial infection is seldom accompanied by clinical symptoms. This slow, insidious onset makes avian tuberculosis difficult to diagnose.

Causative Agent   *Mycobacterium avium, tuberculosis*, and *bovis*. These organisms are remarkably tough and can live in dried respiratory secretions or dust in a dark place for weeks or months. They are capable of living in moist secretions for six weeks or more. Direct sunlight will kill these organisms within two hours (Smith, 1980).

These organisms are very resistant to most disinfectants. Only those proven to be effective *specifically against Mycobacterium* should be used. Such disinfectants are usually phenols, such as Environ-One-Stroke; or glutaraldehydes, such as Wavecide-01 (Clipsham, 1988a).

Transmission   The *Mycobacterium* organism is excreted in the urine and feces. Because tubercles in the intestinal wall are never completely closed, but maintain an opening into the lumen of the gut, an infected bird will shed *Mycobacterium* continuously (Gerlach, 1986a).

Most often the bird is infected by ingestion of contaminated food or water, or through contact with contaminated perches, cage wires, and so on. Arthropods such as ticks, mites, and spiders can act as mechanical transmitters of TB. Egg transmission is thought possible but has little impact because *Mycobacterium* causes an almost immediate cessation of egg laying. It is also possible for the bird to contract TB through a skin wound that has come in contact with contaminated articles.

Respiratory spread of TB caused by *M. avium* is rare (Gerlach, 1986a). However, it is entirely possible for a human with TB to transmit it to a bird in this way, as respiratory secretions in humans with TB are highly contagious if the person is not on medication.

The bird owner or aviary attendant may unwittingly spread TB via fecal or urine soil on the hands or clothing. This is especially likely when handling pet parrots that enjoy mouthing their owner's fingers and clothing.

Symptoms Symptoms are not diagnostic for tuberculosis, as they are fairly general in nature. They are, of course, dependent on the parts of the body affected:

> Masses under the skin, often mistaken for lipomas or cancer (Perry [1987] states that such masses may appear wartlike, and there may also be dry flaking of skin masses or ulcers, especially on the head.)
> Chronic wasting, in spite of good appetite
> Recurrent diarrhea
> Polyuria
> Dull feathers
> Intermittent lameness or favoring of a leg (due to bone pain)
> Arthritis in wings (may have a thickening of skin or ulceration over affected joint)
> Breathing problems
> Swollen joints
> Bumblefoot (Van der Heyden [1986b] feels this may occur due to increasing inactivity, loss of body weight, and decreased vitamin A intake; however, it is possible that a compromised immune system may be at fault here, as well.)
> Bright red blood in droppings
> Cloacal prolapse
> Lethargy and depression
> Abdominal enlargement (due to enlarged liver and fluid-gas-filled bowel)

Laboratory Work Various laboratory tools may aid in the diagnosis of avian tuberculosis. Some are more helpful than others.

> *Microscopic examination*: Slides of material taken from biopsies or tissues taken at necropsy can be specially stained and examined microscopically for the presence of *Mycobacterium*. Such material may include feces, tracheal washes, and biopsy of liver, spleen, bone marrow, intestines, or skin lesions.
> *Culture of feces*: This method takes three to six weeks.
> *Tuberculin test*: This test consists of injecting a small amount of test material containing the TB antigen into the bird's skin. If the bird has been infected with the TB organism, a localized reaction consisting of redness, swelling, and tenderness will occur at the site of injection forty eight hours postinjection. However, false negatives often occur very early or very late in the disease, due respectively to an immature immune system or one that is "worn out."
> *Serology*: This entails the use of the slide agglutination test. A small amount of the bird's blood serum is placed on a slide with test material containing *Mycobacterium* antigen. If the bird has tuberculosis, a clumping reaction will be observed when the two substances are mixed together.

CBC: This will reveal a greatly increased white blood cell count.

Radiographs: These may reveal indications of tubercular bone infection in thigh, skin, and upper wing bones. They may also show a bowel filled with gas and fluid, a frequent finding in avian tuberculosis. An enlarged liver and/or spleen may be visualized.

Barium series: This may demonstrate delayed transit time of the barium meal, a crop lacking in normal muscle tone, and gaseous distention of the bowel.

Endoscopy: May reveal various abdominal organ abnormalities, and/or tubercle formation at these sites.

Fecal stains: A fresh fecal specimen is placed on a microscope slide and stained with acid-fast stain, which will reveal *Mycobacterium*.

Treatment   There are two opposing schools of thought concerning the treatment of avian tuberculosis. The first school advocates euthanasia. The rationale is that avian tuberculosis may be transmitted to humans, that there are no drugs that have been specifically tested for use with intestinal tuberculosis typical of birds, and that the *M. avium* strain is often refractory to treatment if transmitted to man (Gerlach, 1986a; Fudge et al., 1986).

The second school advocates the treatment of avian tuberculosis, using medications found to be effective for tuberculosis in humans. The rationale appears to be that avian TB is seldom transmitted to humans, and that fair success has been achieved with treatment of this problem in birds (Van der Heyden, 1986b).

Nevertheless, the reader should understand that there are risks associated with close contact with a bird having tuberculosis, even if the bird is on medication and being properly monitored. Anyone in such a situation should arrange to see a physician immediately for a tuberculin test and/or chest X ray. Certain people are at much greater risk than the general population in contracting avian tuberculosis. These include the very young and the very old, or anyone who is immunocompromised in any way. Examples would be persons receiving chemotherapy for cancer or medication to prevent the rejection of an organ or skin transplant, or a person with AIDS (Forster and Gerlach, 1987).

If the avian veterinarian recommends treatment and the owner concurs, a very strict medication regimen must be adhered to, as well as periodic monitoring of the bird's response to therapy. A long-term commitment by the owner is required in this situation, not only for the bird's sake, but for the sake of the health and safety of the owner and family members.

Medications currently recommended for use with avian tuberculosis include a combination of isoniazid (INH), rifampin, and ethambutol. Isoniazid is bacteriostatic for mature, nonreproducing *Mycobacterium* organisms. However, in rapidly dividing organisms, it is bacteriocidal. It has very few side effects, but can occasionally cause liver problems (Gilman et al.,1985). Rifampin is an antibiotic that inhibits the growth of *Mycobacterium*. It does not generally produce side effects if the bird's liver is normal. If there is liver damage, however, side effects may occur. Rifampin turns the urates, as well as the skin and feather shafts, a red-orange color (Van der Heyden, 1986b). This is not serious and is not a cause for alarm. Ethambutol is a medication that also inhibits the growth of *Mycobacterium*. Its method of action is unknown. In cases where kidney damage is present, the medication can build to toxic levels, causing side effects.

A combination of the above medications is administered daily for a period of eighteen months. Van der Heyden states that clinical improvement usually occurs two to six weeks following the initiation of therapy. While a bird is on medication the owner should observe for any lethargy, digestive tract symptoms, or abnormal droppings that could indicate medication reaction.

These medications are usually ground into a powder, then mixed with dextrose powder. This preparation is then sprinkled in the prescribed amount over the bird's favorite soft food. This is offered to the exclusion of other food in the morning. When the bird finishes its medicated food, other foods can then be given (Van der Heyden, 1986b).

After medication therapy has been completed, the bird should be monitored at least twice yearly to ensure that it remains noninfective.

Van der Heyden recommends the surgical removal of tuberculosis granulomas (tubercles) when feasible, in addition to medication therapy. Treatment of any concurrent infection is necessary, in addition to any supportive care and/ or dietary adjustments that may be needed.

Prognosis   Some birds respond very well to the above treatment protocol. This is largely dependent upon the individual, the status of its immune system, the amount of permanent organ damage sustained (if any), and the owner's commitment to the bird's therapy.

Prevention consists of good hygiene and husbandry. In situations where TB has been diagnosed, it is imperative that thorough cleaning and disinfection be carried out. All dirt, gravel, and wood in the bird room or aviary must be replaced.

Van der Heyden (1986a) recommends that birds that have been exposed to the index case should be isolated for two to three years and tested periodically to ascertain whether they have remained free of infection.

Gerlach (1986a) recommends that those birds diagnosed as having tuberculosis be euthanized, as well as all birds with which it has come in contact. She states that if such contact birds are too valuable to euthanize, they should be isolated and caged singly. Such birds should be retested at six-week intervals for one year. If they remain negative and are in good body condition at that time, they can be considered tuberculosis free.

When owners have such birds in their collections, strict isolation procedures should be observed in their care (see Chapter 2).

VITAMIN A DEFICIENCY: See Avitaminosis A.

ZOONOSES: A zoonosis (pl., zoonoses) is a disease that can be transmitted from animals to man. "Although birds are not a major source of zoonotic infections in humans, the list of zoonoses is continuously increasing and the potential hazards that accompany the ownership of pet birds cannot be overlooked. . . . Although zoonotic infections may have only minor clinical manifestations in humans, they are nevertheless of particular concern to the affected person'' (Turner, 1987).

There are, indeed, some diseases that can be transmitted from birds to their owners. Bird owners need to be aware of this, and their physicians need to be informed of the presence of birds in the home or aviary, especially if an infectious disease is suspected.

There are several zoonoses involving birds that are of longstanding documentation. Examples include chlamydiosis (psittacosis) and salmonellosis. Several diseases are emerging as potential zoonoses where man and bird are concerned, including campylobacteriosis and giardiasis.

There are several reasons why these ''new'' zoonoses are being discovered. The first is that the number of pet birds in the United States is very large and will no doubt continue to increase. The second is that advances in epidemiological methods and diagnostic technology have resulted in an increased awareness of potential zoonoses involving companion birds (Turner, 1987). A third reason is that more human diseases having a depressed immune system as at least part of their effect are being discovered and diagnosed. AIDS is a good example of this. Such people are far more susceptible to possible infection by organisms present in *any* pet (bird, cat, dog), even if these organisms are normal to that pet and do not ordinarily cause illness in human owners.

Another factor contributing to the transmission of disease from animal to man is the intimacy of contact between a pet and its owner. It is generally recognized that the human-animal bond is very beneficial to the physical, emotional, and mental well-being of the owner. This bond is manifested in a variety of ways, from regular conversation with the pet, to actually sharing one's plate and bedding with the pet. Hugs, kisses on the beak, parrot ''poop'' on the shoulder—all these normal acts may, under certain circumstances, enhance the spread of disease organisms from bird to owner.

It is sometimes difficult to diagnose accurately the presence of a zoonosis in pet bird owners because birds can be asymptomatic carriers of various disease organisms. However, intelligent use of the principles of avian husbandry and hygiene, and of personal hygiene, will go a long way in reducing the bird owner's chances of contracting potential avian zoonoses.

A number of avian zoonoses will be discussed. Some are well known; others are newly emergent, or thought to have potential as zoonoses, depending upon individual circumstances and the bird owner's general state of health.

Avian tuberculosis   The causative agent is *Mycobacterium avium*. (See the Tuberculosis entry in this chapter.) This organism causes a gastrointestinal form of tuberculosis in humans. However, man is regarded as extremely resistant to *M. avium*. Factors such as prior illness or depressed immune response are probably necessary to predispose one to infection by this pathogen (Evans and Carey, 1986).

Transmission is by ingestion of *M. avium* in avian feces, food or water contaminated by infected feces, or inhalation of fecal aerosols.

Symptoms in man may be absent or minimal. Those having symptoms may experience one or more of the following: fever, loss of appetite, nausea, abdominal gas and distention after eating, various food intolerances, abdominal pain, constipation, mild to severe diarrhea, and weight loss (Krupp and Chatton, 1974).

Diagnosis is by radiograph, tuberculin test, sputum cytology, and serology.

Treatment is with use of antituberculosis medications such as isoniazid, ethambutol, and rifampin.

Anyone previously infected with tuberculosis must avoid reexposure to infectious material to prevent reinfections. The pros and cons of treating tubercular birds is discussed elsewhere in this chapter. In this matter, an owner who has contracted avian tuberculosis *must* be guided by the advice of a physician and avian veterinarian. If treatment for a tubercular bird is sought, treatment protocol should be *rigidly* adhered to. Great attention to personal hygiene is necessary, as is attention to overall avian husbandry. It is probably not too cautious to suggest that another person in the household should care for such a bird, until such time as both owner and bird have *fully* recovered.

Campylobacteriosis The causative agent of this zoonosis is *Campylobacter jejeune*, an enteric pathogenic bacteria. (See the Enteric Organism–Caused Infections entry in this chapter.) This bacteria is found in the reproductive organs, intestinal tract, and mouths of human beings and animals (Smith, 1980). It has only recently been implicated as a cause of gastroenteritis in humans and is thought by some to be a greater cause of this disorder than *Salmonella* (Turner, 1987). *C. jejeune* has been isolated from chickens, ducks, migratory waterfowl, sparrows, starlings, blackbirds, and finches as well as mammals (Evans and Carey, 1986). At the time of this writing, no documentation exists of its isolation from parrots.

Transmission is by ingestion of infected poultry or contaminated water, by direct contact with infected birds, or person-to-person by the fecal/oral route.

Symptoms in humans closely resemble those of salmonellosis, shigellosis, or acute appendicitis (Evans and Carey, 1986). They may be self-limiting or very severe. The disease causes inflammation of the large and small intestines, and once started tends to spread to healthy bowel tissue. Moderate to severe diarrhea occurs, with or without a fever (Smith, 1980). This diarrhea is characterized as watery, with mucus present. Abdominal pain may last several days. Deaths have been reported in the elderly or debilitated.

Diagnosis can be made by examination of a fresh fecal sample, serology, or blood culture. Treatment is by use of appropriate antibiotics. Good personal hygiene and avian husbandry should prevent this disease.

Candidiasis The causative agent is *Candida albicans*. (See the Candidiasis entry in this chapter.) Transmission is by exposure to the secretions of an infected bird (Evans and Carey, 1986). However, mere exposure is not enough to cause infection in the healthy human. A predisposing factor such as long-term antibiotic therapy or an already existing disease state must be present.

Humans may contract the gastrointestinal form of candidiasis, just as birds do. Symptoms include loss of appetite, difficulty swallowing, inflammation of the intestines with resulting diarrhea, and ulcers (Evans and Carey, 1986). It is more common for humans to manifest candidiasis as an infection of the mouth (thrush), nails (paronychia), skin folds (intertrigo), or vulvovaginal area.

Diagnosis is made by microscopic examination of skin-lesion scrapings or body exudates. Treatment is with medications such as Nystatin (mycostatin). The prevention of candidiasis includes good avian husbandry, adequate ventilation in bird room or aviary, and the avoidance of damp, moldy material that encourages fungal growth.

Giardiasis   The causative agent is the protozoa *Giardia*. (See the Giardiasis entry in this chapter.) It is spread through direct contact with an infected bird's feces, or indirectly through food or water contaminated with such feces.

Symptoms in humans include abdominal pain, weakness, diarrhea, and weight loss.

Diagnosis is by examination of fresh fecal material. Treatment is with antiprotozoal medications such as Flagyl (metronidazole). Prevention includes good avian husbandry and personal hygiene.

Newcastle Disease   The causative agent is *Paramyxovirus Group I*. (See the Newcastle disease entry in this chapter.) This disease is not as severe in man as it is in birds. It is most common in laboratory workers and poultry pathologists who handle tissue infected with Newcastle virus (Evans and Carey, 1986). Transmission is by direct contact with infected birds, or inhalation of aerosols of infected birds' respiratory secretions, which are subsequently inhaled by humans.

Newcastle disease in humans causes a mild to severe infection of the linings of the upper and lower eyelids (conjunctivitis). It may also cause sinusitis. Recovery is usually uneventful and occurs within seven to twenty days.

Psittacosis (Chlamydiosis)   The causative agent is *Chlamydia psittaci*. (See the Psittacosis entry in this chapter.) Transmission is by ingestion of material contaminated by the feces of an infected bird, or inhalation of aerosols of its feces or respiratory secretions. Transmission may also occur by direct contact with an infected bird. It is also possible to contract psittacosis through bites of infected birds, or through skin abrasions when handling infected tissues without gloves (Turner, 1987).

The time elapsing from first contact with the organism to first symptoms can be as short as forty-eight hours or as long as five days to two weeks (Evans and Carey, 1986). Onset of psittacosis may be very abrupt, or slow and insidious.

In humans, psittacosis resembles ''flu'' and usually lasts seven to ten days. Symptoms can range from mild or inapparent to very severe. Symptoms include fever, chills, weakness, headache, muscle pain, chest pain, loss of appetite,

259

nausea and vomiting, shortness of breath, and extreme sweating. Age (very young or very old), stress, or previously existing disease can greatly influence the course of psittacosis in humans. Death has been caused in some cases by *Chlamydia psittaci*. In some cases, the infection can spread from its usual respiratory site and cause damage to the liver and heart (Grimes, 1987).

Diagnosis of psittacosis in humans is by serology, using paired blood samples taken at the beginning of illness and during the convalescent period (Grimes, 1987). The reader may wish to review the discussion of psittacosis testing in Chapter 3.

Treatment of psittacosis in humans is with tetracyclines, as is done with birds. Supportive care such as intravenous therapy for those suffering dehydration, or pain relievers such as aspirin, may be indicated. Recovery is usually uncomplicated.

Prevention includes good avian husbandry, good personal hygiene, and prompt veterinary care for any bird suspected of having psittacosis. In addition, all newly acquired birds should be tested for psittacosis so that carriers may be identified and treated.

Rabies　The causative agent is the rabies virus, a member of the *Rhabdovirus* group. There has never been a reported case of rabies in birds, although all warm-blooded mammals are theoretically susceptible to rabies virus. Antibodies to rabies virus have been recovered from wild birds (Evans and Carey, 1986). Fatal rabies has been produced experimentally in birds. Evans cites an interesting case in which a Great Horned Owl was exposed to rabies by being allowed to eat a dead, rabid skunk. The owl did not become ill, but did develop antibodies to rabies. The bird then shed rabies virus in its oral secretions for several months postinfection.

Ringworm　The causative agent is fungi of the group *Trichophyton*. Both Turner (1987) and Keymer (1982a) believe that avian ringworm is transmissible to man. These fungi can be isolated from the skin and feathers of infected birds. Transmission is by direct or indirect contact.

The symptoms of ringworm in birds and man are similar, except that birds lose feathers and people lose body hair. Ringworm lesions are distinctive: concentric, ring-shaped sores that are scaly and reddened. These lesions are accompanied by intense itching.

Treatment is with oral antifungal medications and topical salves and ointments. Any salve or ointment must be used cautiously, and *only* as the veterinarian prescribes it.

Veterinary treatment should be sought for birds having skin problems. As always, good avian husbandry and personal hygiene should help prevent spread of this disease from bird to man.

Salmonellosis　The causative agents are bacteria of the *Salmonella* group. These are enteric bacteria notorious for causing food poisoning and gastrointestinal disease. (See the Enteric Organism–Caused Infections entry in this chapter.)

260

According to Smith (1980), *Salmonella* and its enteric relatives "are probably responsible for more human misery than any other group of bacteria."

Transmission is classically by ingestion of food contaminated by *Salmonella*. However, in the case of its transmission from bird to man, direct contact with the feces of an infected bird, or ingestion of food and water so contaminated, is largely responsible. One of the difficulties with salmonellosis in the zoonotic situation is that birds may be asymptomatic carriers of *Salmonella*, shedding the bacteria in their feces.

The incubation period may be eight to forty-eight hours. Symptoms include headache, fever, chills, abdominal pain, nausea and vomiting, and diarrhea. This disease is often severe, resulting in collapse of its victims due to dehydration.

Diagnosis is made by culture of blood and/or feces. Treatment is with appropriate antibiotics. Intravenous fluid therapy may be necessary to correct dehydration.

Prevention includes good personal hygiene and good avian husbandry. Prompt veterinary treatment for any sick bird, particularly those with digestive tract symptoms, should be sought. Newly acquired stock should have fecal cultures to rule out asymptomatic carriers of *Salmonella*.

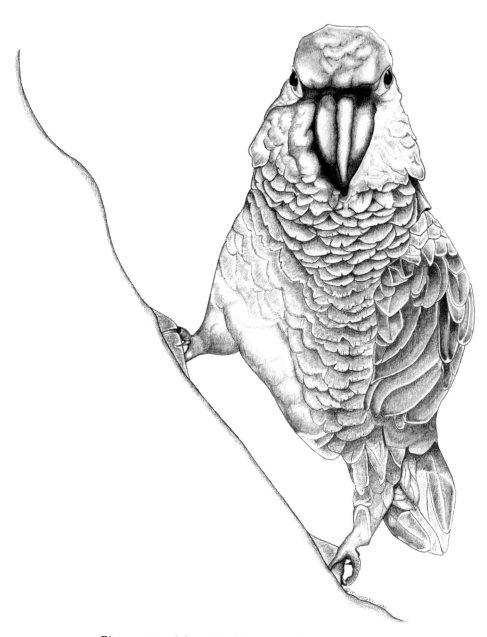

Blue-crowned Amazon *(Amazona Farinosa guatemalae)*

6

Avian Surgery

SURGERY IS OFTEN THE TREATMENT of choice for a number of conditions. It may be performed for tumor removal, to correct a condition not responsive to medical management, as an exploratory procedure to confirm a diagnosis, for repair of a fracture, or for surgical sexing. A hysterectomy may be the appropriate treatment for a chronically egg-bound hen.

Whatever the reason for surgery, success is much greater now than in years past, "when too often the surgery was successful but the patient died." The advent of new and safer anesthetic agents; techniques such as microsurgery, electrosurgery, and cryosurgery; and a better understanding of avian anatomy and physiology have all contributed to the increasing success of avian surgery.

There are several differences between birds and mammals that the avian surgeon must take into account (Martin and Dufficy, 1987). The first is the unique nature of avian skin. It is very thin, with little subcutaneous fat such as is found in dogs, cats, humans, and other mammals. This means that great care must be taken to avoid cutting through vessels in the skin and structures that lie directly beneath the skin. The absence of subcutaneous fat leaves a much smaller margin for error than in mammals.

The second feature unique to birds is their possession of special muscles that allow them to walk, perch, and fly. The surgeon must be aware of their anatomical position and be careful to avoid damaging them during the surgical procedure. This difficulty is overcome by using a technique known as "blunt dissection." This means that rather than cutting through muscle tissue at the surgical site, the muscle fibers are teased apart with a blunt instrument such as forceps. This preserves the muscle's integrity and allows a return to full function postsurgically.

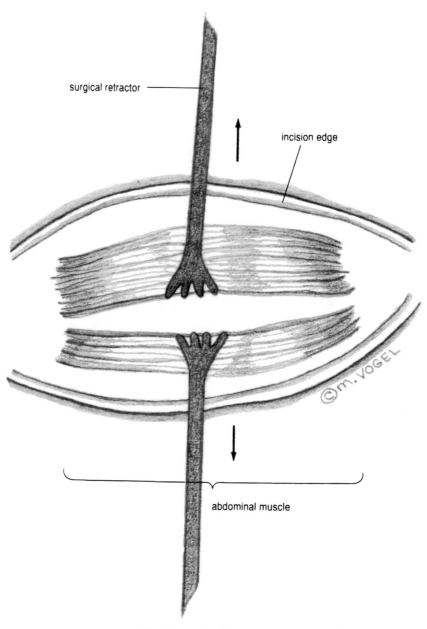

surgical retractor

incision edge

abdominal muscle

Blunt muscle dissection

The third special consideration is especially important in the surgical repair of bone fractures. If a fracture is to be successfully repaired, allowing full use of the affected limb when healing is complete, great attention must be paid to the blood vessels and nerves supplying the injured bone. Merely setting the bone and allowing it to heal will not ensure full return to function. Careful repair of the nerves, blood vessels, and surrounding muscle tissue is also required. This is particularly important for birds such as raptors, which will be unable to return to the wild unless they are able to fly and perch well. Microsurgical techniques are particularly helpful in this respect.

The fourth area of special consideration are the air sacs. Although the air sacs themselves are relatively poor in blood supply, the ligaments that suspend and support them in the bird's body are very well supplied—not only with blood vessels, but nerves as well. The surgeon must be careful not to sever these when performing abdominal surgery.

THE PRESURGICAL WORK-UP

There are basically three "surgical conditions": elective surgery, non-elective surgery, and emergency surgery. Elective surgery is surgery that the bird's owner chooses to have performed, but which is not necessarily done to correct a potentially life-threatening condition. Examples of this would be wing pinioning or the removal of a small lipoma that is not interfering with the bird's ability to locomote or breed. Nonelective surgery is surgery that is performed to correct conditions that are serious but not immediately life-threatening. Emergency surgery is performed immediately to prevent the bird's death.

These three surgical categories have relevance to a very important part of surgery: the presurgical work-up. Naturally, the avian veterinarian wishes to have the greatest possible amount of information about a patient's overall health status before surgery takes place. This helps the surgeon to select the most appropriate anesthetic agent and to care for the bird surgically and postsurgically in the way that best assures the bird's full return to health and wholeness.

It is necessary, for example, to know if the bird's liver is healthy. Liver problems could lead to clotting problems and the possibility of hemorrhage. Impaired liver and kidney function will compromise the bird's ability to metabolize and excrete some anesthetic agents leading to a possible anesthetic overdose and subsequent death. A bird with a subclinical bacterial infection will often react to the stress of surgery by developing a full-blown illness that will decrease its chances for a full and uneventful recovery.

Clipsham (1988e) states that the minimal presurgical work-up should include a physical examination, CBC, whole-body X ray, and cultures of choana and cloaca. Darryl Heard (1988) feels that a PCV, total serum protein, and blood glucose should also be performed. Harrison (1986b) states that the basic work-up should include a complete physical examination, an estimate of the bird's general condition, Gram stains of feces and choana, a fecal parasite examination, and an estimate of the bird's respiratory recovery rate. The respiratory recovery rate is defined as the amount of time it takes the bird to return to its normal breathing rate after being captured and handled for at least two minutes. The normal time for this to occur is estimated at three to five minutes.

According to Harrison, optional tests might include hematology (with a PCV and total serum protein), an EKG, X rays, cultures and sensitivities if indicated by the results of the Gram stains, serum chemistries, and body temperature. Clipsham lists as optional tests a barium series, if indicated, and urinalysis.

A thorough work-up is possible when the surgery contemplated is elective or nonemergency. If emergency surgery is necessary, time and the bird's debilitated and precarious condition do not allow this. Nevertheless, most avian veterinarians will attempt to get a PCV and total serum protein, as this will give a general idea of the bird's state of health and the adequacy of the oxygen-carrying capacity of its blood.

SURGICAL PRECONDITIONING

If a surgical procedure is elective or nonelective but not an emergency, there is time to correct (or at least ameliorate) any problems discovered as a result of the presurgical work-up. Conditions such as bacterial and fungal infections can be treated with appropriate medications. Necessary dietary changes can be instituted. Severe vitamin A deficiencies can be treated with oral or injectable vitamin A preparations. The bird can be freed of intestinal parasites. If dehydration is present, fluid therapy can be instituted. A bird with clotting problems will be given vitamin K injections to help prevent hemorrhage during surgery.

Many avian veterinarians prefer to give their patients a course of antibiotic therapy prior to surgery to help decrease the risk of postsurgical infections and/or septicemia. If surgery on the digestive tract is being planned, the bird is often treated presurgically with antibiotics to "sterilize" the gut (Harrison, 1986c).

These measures are all aimed at giving the bird the best possible chance of surviving surgery and making a good recovery. Even in emergency situations, the bird will be given the presurgical support of fluid therapy, antibiotics, and steroids, if at all possible. Often, such birds will receive vitamin K injections.

If the avian veterinarian recommends presurgical conditioning of any kind, the bird owner is well advised to follow through with the suggestions made. Such treatment is important to the bird's ultimate recovery.

ANESTHETIC AGENTS

The choice of anesthetic agents is an important one. There are two groups of these drugs: inhalation agents and parenteral agents. Within these two groups,

Anesthetic machine with oxygen tank and bottle of isoflurane—the anesthetic of choice for avian surgeries.

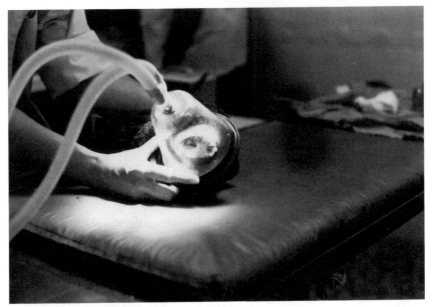

Anesthetic induction in Blue-fronted Amazon. The face mask covers the bird's entire head, and tubes connected to face mask permit delivery of oxygen and anesthetic in measured, precise amounts.

M. Vogel

267

there are a number of possible choices, each having advantages and disadvantages. The choice of the agent right for the individual bird will be made based on its overall health status and the type of surgery being considered.

Inhalation Agents

Often called gaseous anesthetics, these are anesthetics that the patient inhales to produce the desired level of anesthesia.

ISOFLURANE (AERRANE): Of such agents available, this is the best available for use with birds. It is safe for use with baby and adult birds, as well as those birds that are sick and debilitated. It does not have the potential for liver damage (both to operating personnel and the bird itself) that other inhalant anesthetics have (Harrison, 1986a; Heard, 1988; and Rosskopf et al., 1987). This is very important to the surgeon and assistants, who are exposed to the anesthetic day after day, year in, year out. Isoflurane produces no anesthetic hangover—that groggy period of anesthetic recovery that often produces disorientation and fatigue. Recovery is extremely rapid, with birds awake and alert in a matter of a few seconds. This agent allows the surgeon or assistant to make rapid changes in anesthetic level when needed. It provides good muscle relaxation, which is imperative in order to allow the surgeon unimpeded access to the surgical field. Disadvantages of isoflurane include a somewhat depressed body temperature, a lowered blood pressure, some respiratory depression (although not as much as with other available gaseous anesthetics), and the tendency of some birds to vomit on recovery if they have not fasted prior to surgery.

METHOXYFLURANE (METAFANE): Another gaseous anesthetic, this is the least expensive of the inhalation agents and gives excellent muscle relaxation, but it has several disadvantages (Harrison, 1986a; Heard, 1988; Rosskopf, et al. 1987). It produces recovery hangover. It takes a long time to reach anesthesia level, and can also cause respiratory depression, with cardiac arrest sometimes occurring at the same time. Prolonged depressed body temperature is another side effect. This anesthetic agent is not safe for debilitated birds, and unexplained deaths have been attributed to it. In addition, it possesses the potential for causing liver damage in operating room personnel.

HALOTHANE (FLUOTHANE): The advantages of this inhalation anesthetic include a rapid return to consciousness, good muscle relaxation, and rapid return of normal body temperature. However, it can cause liver and kidney damage, produces a prolonged hangover, is a respiratory and cardiac depressant, and has been associated with death in birds thought to be "healthy" (Harrison, 1986a).

ETHER: An anesthetic familiar to most readers, it is no longer used because of its explosiveness. This is a real drawback in operating theaters packed with sophisticated electrical equipment.

Parenteral Agents

These are anesthetic agents administered via intravenous or intramuscular injection. Indications for their use include situations in which inhalation agents and the equipment for using them are unavailable (as in a field situation) or when surgery of the head and neck is to be done, making use of a face mask impractical. All parenteral anesthetics have one great disadvantage: once given, they cannot be "called back." When using a gaseous anesthetic, the surgeon or assistant can control the amount of inhalant delivered to the patient from minute to minute. If the bird shows signs of lowered respiratory rate or heartbeat, the dose of anesthetic can be reduced immediately. With a parenteral agent, this is an impossibility. Nevertheless, there are some parenteral anesthetics possessing a wide safety margin and providing good anesthetic effect.

KETAMINE (KETASET OR VETALAR):   Strictly speaking, this is not an anesthetic in the sense that it does not prevent the bird's perception of pain. It does, however, effect immobilization of the bird and possesses a wide safety range. Ketamine does not produce good muscle relaxation. Anesthetic recovery can be very violent, with thrashing and flapping of wings. There is great potential for the bird to injure itself if proper postanesthetic monitoring is not done. It is not recommended for use in birds with poor kidney or liver function (Harrison, 1986a).

Ketamine is most often used in combination with xylazine (Rompun), and less often with diazepam (Valium). These combinations produce analgesia as well as immobilization. There is a wide safety margin relative to dose. The recovery period, like that of ketamine when used alone, can be prolonged and violent. It can cause lowered body temperature and depressed respiration. A few unexplained deaths have been associated with this combination of anesthetic agents. Ketamine/xylazine or ketamine/diazepam are also contraindicated for use in birds with kidney and liver damage (Harrison, 1986a).

Some medications are never recommended as anesthetic agents for birds. These include chlorohydrate, xylazine when used alone, and barbiturates. Barbiturates may be used for treatment of convulsions, however. Harrison cautions against the use of local anesthetics, as the possibility of dosage error is very great.

The bird owner should be aware that no matter how safe the anesthetic agent used, no matter how skilled the surgeon and anesthesiology assistant, no matter how minor the surgical procedure, no matter how healthy the bird—anesthetic "accidents" (death) do happen. Such events have been attributed to possible allergy to the agent, or idiosyncratic reaction to it, when cats, dogs, and humans have been involved. It is likely that these same factors may be operative when birds experience anesthetic-related deaths. Such sad events cannot be predicted or prevented. Anesthesia always carries with it an inherent risk.

PREOPERATIVE MEDICATION

The use of preoperative medication is no doubt familiar to many readers who have experienced surgery themselves, or have helped friends and relatives through the experience. The use of preoperative medication for mammals has several purposes. It helps relax the patient, making the induction of anesthesia proceed more quickly and smoothly. It reduces the patient's anxiety about the surgical experience. Preoperative medication also acts to reduce respiratory and gastrointestinal secretions, thereby reducing the risk of aspiration while the patient is unconscious or recovering from anesthesia. In birds, however, preoperative medication is not routinely used. It is thought that such medication prolongs anesthetic recovery time. Preoperative medication has variable effects from one bird to the next, making effective use difficult. Occasionally, when digestive tract surgery is planned, a preoperative medication will be used to dry secretions.

Some minor surgical procedures do not generally require the use of an anesthetic agent. If such procedures can be completed quickly, successfully, and with a minimum of discomfort to the bird, it is generally thought to be wise not to expose the bird to anesthetic risk—even those anesthetics with a wide margin of safety. Examples of such surgery are the removal of foreign objects, such as thorns, from the eye; uncomplicated cropotomy; or the removal of a damaged toe.

TYPES OF SURGICAL TECHNIQUES

There are several surgical techniques available to the avian veterinarian, who will choose among them after taking into consideration the type of surgery to be performed, familiarity with the technique, and the bird's overall health status.

State-of-the-art avian surgery requires state-of-the-art equipment, experience, and training on the part of the veterinarian. The bird owner is advised to seek such an avian veterinarian if surgery for the bird is anticipated. The possible extra travel and expense are more than justified by the bird's enhanced chances of survival and recovery.

Electrosurgery

Electrosurgery is sometimes referred to as radiosurgery because this technique utilizes high-frequency radio waves in the same frequency range as those used in amateur and maritime radio (Harrison, 1986e). Such sound waves are produced by a specially constructed electrosurgical unit. Various attachments in the form of fine, needlelike operating tips can be used with the unit. These tips transmit the energy waves to the surgical site and can be used for cutting, blood coagulation (sometimes referred to as electrocautery), or a combination of both.

270

These functions are created as a result of the high-frequency energy, which generates heat within the individual cell. The intracellular fluids expand and vaporize, causing the cell to explode. This in turn seals capillary cells, preventing bleeding. It also allows cutting of tissue with a minimum of tissue damage.

In addition to the excellent cutting and coagulating capacities of electrosurgery, this method allows easy access to surgical areas not easily reached by the relatively large conventional scalpel. Radiosurgery may be combined with conventional surgical technique in many cases.

Microsurgery

This technique is employed when the surgical field is too small to allow use of conventional surgical tools. It is particularly useful when repair of tiny nerves and blood vessels must be effected. When the veterinarian uses this method, an operating microscope is necessary, as well as high-intensity lighting and very small instruments such as those used in eye surgery. Electrosurgery may be used in conjunction with microsurgery, depending on the type of surgery being done.

Cryosurgery

This method employs refrigerants, such as liquid nitrogen, to destroy tissue. It is often used to remove cloacal papillomas, mouth lesions, and other granulomas. It has also been used to effect enucleation of the eye.

Medical Acrylics

Medical acrylics are gluelike substances, originally developed for use in human dentistry. They are often called surgical glue or cement. These substances can be used in beak and bone repair, and for splinting in some situations. A soft, flexible type of medical acrylic can be used for surgical bandaging and closure of incisions (rather than conventional suture technique). Michael Krinsley (1988) has reported the use of this type of medical acrylic to fill in the holes left when lesions have been removed from a bird's mouth. This has the triple advantage of preventing hemorrhage, promoting rapid healing, and lessening postoperative pain, therefore making it much easier for the bird to eat. Soft acrylics can be used as bandages for very small areas, such as that of an amputated toe or on the wing stump left after amputation, where there is very little skin and tissue with which to cover the exposed bone end.

THE DAY OF SURGERY

The day of surgery for your bird has arrived. The preoperative work-up has been completed, preconditioning has been prescribed and carried out in a faithful manner, and the bird has been admitted to the avian veterinary hospital.

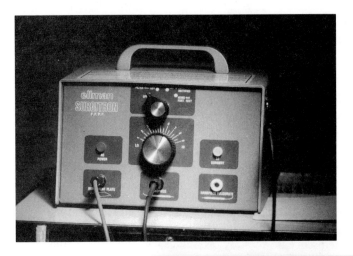

The surgical electrocautery instrument allows much more finely controlled cutting along with cautery of blood vessels as incision is made.

Peter Sakas, D.V.M.

The cutting tip used with the electrocautery instrument.

Peter Sakas, D.V.M.

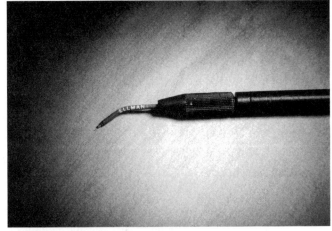

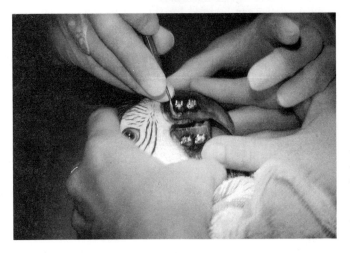

The orthodontic repair of the malformed beak of a young Blue and Gold Macaw. The technique uses dental acrylics to hold the device in place.

Peter Sakas, D.V.M.

What occurs as your bird is prepared for surgery, while the surgery is taking place, and during the recovery period?

The first thing that will be done (if the owner has not been instructed to begin at home, before the bird has been admitted) is to fast the bird. Veterinarians differ slightly in the amount of fasting time they require prior to surgery. The range is usually between one to three hours for medium and large birds, with regard to solid food. Water may be offered up to one hour before surgery in most cases. Small birds are usually fasted a shorter amount of time due to their higher metabolic rate and the faster transit time of food through the gut. The purpose of the presurgical fast is to prevent regurgitation or vomiting with subsequent aspiration while the bird is anesthetized.

After an appropriate fast has been achieved, the bird will be placed under anesthesia. This process is referred to as the induction period of anesthesia. This is done with gaseous anesthetics by placing a face mask over the bird's beak and nostrils. Once a satisfactory plane of anesthesia has been effected, the face mask may be left in place or it may be replaced with an endotracheal tube. This device is a specially constructed tube that is attached to the anesthetic delivery hose of the anesthetic machine. The other end of the endotracheal tube is placed directly into the bird's trachea. The advantages of using an endotracheal tube are several:

1. It allows a more precise dose of anesthetic to be delivered, due to the reduction of dead air space found in the face mask, mouth, and throat.
2. It allows the surgeon or assistant to suction mucus from the lower airways, if necessary.
3. It allows the bird to be "breathed" artificially, if natural respirations should cease.

After the bird has been anesthetized, the surgical site is prepared. Feathers over the site will be plucked. The skin is then scrubbed with a surgical disinfectant. When this has been done, the area is covered with a sterile drape, to keep the surgical site free of contamination. Many veterinarians use transparent surgical drapes, thus allowing them to observe the entire bird during surgery.

Once the surgical site has been prepared, the surgeon will make an initial skin incision. An electrosurgical tip or a conventional scalpel may be used. Either way, great care will be taken to make this incision relative to the feather tracts. In so doing, the type and direction of feather growth will not be altered postsurgically.

During the surgical procedure, loss of the bird's body heat will be prevented by the use of a heating pad or a warmed, circulating water blanket placed under the bird's body. The bird will be very carefully watched by the assistant responsible for anesthesia.

The bird's breathing rate and heartbeat will be monitored. If changes occur, the dose of anesthetic can be altered immediately to prevent complications. Breathing rate can be monitored visually. Heart rate can be monitored by an EKG machine or an esophageal stethoscope. This is a sound-sensitive device that is encased in a small, flexible tube and inserted in the bird's esophagus. It produces an audible tone with each heartbeat.

In addition to the monitoring of respiratory and heart rates, blood pressure may also be monitored. The bird's body temperature may be checked by means of a temperature probe inserted into the cloaca. Some avian veterinary surgeons may use blood gas analysis while the bird is anesthetized, in order to check the blood for the relative amounts of oxygen and carbon dioxide present (Harrison, 1986c). This is yet another, very sophisticated way of making sure that the bird's cardiorespiratory status remains adequate during surgery.

Often, the bird will be further supported by intravenous fluids during surgery. This ensures that dehydration does not occur. It also helps the kidneys remain functional by ensuring that adequate amounts of fluid are passing through them.

Occasionally, a bird will require a blood transfusion. This can be accomplished by using blood from another parrot, preferably of the same species. It is also possible to use chicken or pigeon blood for this purpose (Altman, 1985a; Harrison, 1986c). This works very well, if the bird needs only one transfusion. If a second one is needed, chicken or pigeon blood should not be used, as there is the danger of inducing a blood reaction. This same phenomenon occurs in humans who have been given the wrong blood type during a blood transfusion. Basically, what happens is that the bird reacts to the foreign proteins in the chicken's or pigeon's blood by attacking them with antibodies against them; these antibodies have formed as a result of the first transfusion (known as the sensitization phase). Every effort must be made to obtain parrot blood, if by some unlikely chance a second transfusion is required.

It is very common for the veterinarian to give the bird a dose of corticosteroid at some point during surgery. This helps the bird avoid a shock reaction to the anesthetic/surgical experience.

POSTSURGICAL SUPPORT

The surgery has finally been completed, and the bird is now recovering from the anesthetic. Careful monitoring is continued during this period to assure a rapid and smooth return to consciousness. The bird will be kept warm. Intravenous fluids may continue during this time. Its breathing and level of consciousness are carefully watched. If it has been given an anesthetic that creates an excitatory phase during recovery, it will be loosely wrapped in a towel or placed in a padded recovery cage to prevent injury due to wing flapping and thrashing about. If anesthetic recovery is prolonged, the bird's position will be changed frequently to ensure that mucus does not pool in its airways, and that circulation remains unimpaired to all parts of the body.

In the days following surgery, supportive care will continue. Tube feeding, medications, and fluid therapy may be part of the postoperative treatment plan.

In some instances, the veterinarian may wish to monitor the bird's recovery process by use of serial hematologies (which will include a CBC, PCV, and total serum protein).

If orthopedic surgery for repair of a wing, leg, or foot has been done, a program of rehabilitation may be instituted to help the bird's limb return to full function. This is especially important for breeding birds and for raptors that will be returned to their natural habitats. A graduated program of return to flight can be used, if a wing is involved. Ambulation can be managed in the same way.

Stuart Porter (1988) relates his experiences working with a physical therapist in the rehabilitation of some of his avian patients that had undergone orthopedic surgery. He points out that birds having fractures that occur close to a joint have great difficulty in regaining full use of the affected limb. In such cases, friction massage, range of motion exercises, and ultrasound therapy were suggested by the physical therapist and implemented by Dr. Porter and his staff. He reports "dramatic results" relative to return of function, due to the use of these techniques.

SURGICAL PROCEDURES

Some of the more commonly performed avian surgical procedures will be discussed in this section. It is convenient to group these according to the body area involved.

Surgery of the Skin

Primary surgery of the skin may be done to remove feather cysts, to repair traumatic wounds, and to remove superficial tumors.

TRAUMATIC SKIN WOUNDS: These must first be carefully cleaned of all dirt, dead tissue, and feather debris. The wound can then be flushed with an antibiotic solution and left open to heal. If healing fails to take place, it may become necessary to trim away dead tissue again, then suture the wound closed. In some cases, medical acrylics may be used for skin closure or to strengthen conventional sutures.

FEATHER CYST REMOVAL: This can be accomplished in one of two ways. One method employs the use of an electrosurgical instrument tuned to the current that will give complete destruction of tissue (fulguration). The cyst is incised, and the entire feather follicle, including its attachment to the bone, is destroyed. The other method employs conventional surgical technique to cut away the entire feather cyst. With either method, a tourniquet is placed between the surgical site and the bird's body to prevent excessive bleeding. Sutures may be used to close the wound if the veterinarian deems this necessary (Harrison, 1986d).

Feather cyst on the wing of a canary. Such cysts are caused by the feathers growing in on themselves, much like ingrown hairs on mammals.

Peter Sakas, D.V.M.

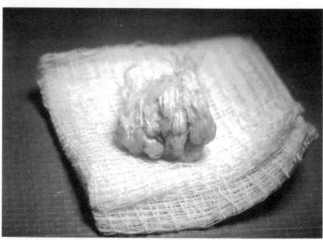

The same feather cyst after surgical removal.
Peter Sakas, D.V.M.

Severe swelling in the right eye of a budgerigar due to a chronic sinus infection.
Peter Sakas, D.V.M.

REMOVAL OF SUPERFICIAL SKIN TUMORS: Such procedures often employ electrosurgery coupled with the use of traditional instruments. Such tumors often have a rich blood supply. The veterinarian uses great care to avoid excessive bleeding and tissue damage, while removing the skin growth.

Surgery of the Head

This may be done for the removal of oral and periopthalmic (in the area surrounding the eye) abscesses or tumors, sinus flushing, sinus trephination, enucleation of the eye, or cataract removal.

REMOVAL OF THE ORAL ABSCESSES OR TUMORS: This may be done with electrosurgery or conventional instrumentation. Rosskopf et al. (1985) suggest the use of ferric subsulfate-soaked cautery sticks to remove oral abscesses by blunt dissection. Pus may be removed in this way, while at the same time controlling bleeding. Cryosurgery is also used at times for the removal of oral lesions.

Harrison (1986d) recommends the use of electrosurgery and magnification for the removal of mouth tumors and foreign bodies that have penetrated the tongue. Such situations may result in severe hemorrhage, which electrosurgery can greatly reduce or eliminate.

Medical acrylics are often used to close mouth wounds.

REMOVAL OF PERIOPTHALMIC ABSCESSES: This procedure, also known as curettage, is sometimes necessary in the bird with chronic sinusitis that does not respond to antibiotics. These abscesses are the result of small pockets of infection in the bone sinuses around the bird's eye. Owners sometimes mistake these swellings for eye infections; in fact, they are the direct result of a longstanding sinus infection. If the abscess is directly behind the bony eye socket it may actually cause the eye to bulge (exopthalmos).

An incision is made over the bone underneath the eye, if the abscess is located in this area. The eye itself may be gently lifted up and away from the area of investigation with the use of cotton-tipped swabs or special eye instruments. The veterinarian then carefully explores the exposed sinus to reveal and remove any caseous pus. If the abscess borders the eye on the side nearest the beak, an incision is made over this aspect of the bony socket that supports the eye. Harrison (1986d) recommends the use of magnification and electrosurgery to decrease the risk of hemorrhage and make visualization better in these very tiny surgical fields.

SINUS FLUSHING: This technique is used to instill medication into the areas of sinus infection. It is accomplished by the insertion of a needle, to which a syringe is attached, into the bird's sinus. This allows the antibiotic to reach areas of infection where it would not ordinarily have access, due to a relative lack of blood supply in the sinus cavities.

SINUS TREPHINATION: This is the process of creating a temporary opening in the bird's sinuses so that antibiotic solution can be instilled over a period of time. Such openings usually remain open for at least one week (Rosskopf et al., 1985). This procedure is not often performed, but may be necessary in those situations in which sinus infection has not responded to sinus flushing and systemic antibiotic therapy.

An incision is made between the bird's eye and nostril. The bone is exposed, and an opening is made into the sinus with a small drill such as the Dremel tool. Electrocautery or an anticoagulant such as ferric subsulfate is used to control bleeding. Gel-Foam packing may also be used for this purpose if necessary. On the days following surgery, the trephination sites are used as routes to flush the sinuses. Rosskopf et al. state that healing of the surgical wounds is rapid and leaves a minimum of scarring. The trephination procedure is performed on both sides of the bird's head to allow for maximum delivery of the medicated flushing solution.

ENUCLEATION OF THE EYE: This procedure may be necessary because of severe trauma, destruction by a cancerous growth, or a chronic and nonresponsive infection. The surgical technique is somewhat more difficult in birds than mammals. One reason is that the eye is much larger with relationship to its bony orbit. Another reason is that the optic nerve is short. If too much tugging should occur during the procedure, the optic nerve supplying the healthy eye may be damaged.

To perform an enucleation, the surgeon first sutures or clamps the eyelids together. An incision is then made around the margins of the eyelids. When this has been done, the eye is loosened in its bony socket by blunt dissection. The optic nerve is then clamped and severed. Because the surgical site is so small and cramped, and great care must be taken to prevent traction on the optic nerve, the surgeon will sometimes find it necessary to collapse the eye in order to make more working room. This is done by removing the contents of the eye. After the enucleation has been completed, the incision around the eyelids is sutured (Altman, 1984; Leon, 1989).

Cryosurgery has been used for destruction of the eye, as an alternative to enucleation (Harrison, 1986e).

CATARACT REMOVAL: Cataracts must occasionally be removed. However, it is usually not recommended unless the bird has cataracts in both eyes. A cataract is actually the clouding of the lens of the eye. It seems to be a problem in older birds, no doubt due to the general aging process.

Removal of a cataract may be accomplished in one of two ways. The first method employs an ultrasonic device that disintegrates the cataract, which is then aspirated and removed from the eye. This is known as phacoemulsification. Another method utilizes aspiration of the lens contents alone. This method is possible due to the very soft nature of the bird's lens (Murphy, 1985).

BEAK REPAIR: Beak repair becomes necessary when the bird has suffered severe damage that prevents it from eating. Prevention of infection in exposed beak germinal tissue or nasal sinuses require that the beak be repaired. Exposure of such traumatically damaged soft tissue provides a direct route for infection. Cosmetic appearance is also a consideration. Problems involving severe beak damage are commonly seen in breeding cockatoos.

Success of the beak repair is dependent in many cases upon whether the germinal layer of the beak remains intact. If so, the damaged beak will grow out, and the beak repair will function as a temporary prosthesis until the beak has fully regrown. If this is the case, the artificial beak will require reshaping from time to time. If the germinal layer of the beak has been damaged, the repair, if it can be effected at all, will function as a permanent prosthesis. In such cases, it may become necessary to repair or replace the prosthesis as it wears over time.

Repair of the beak can be made to appear so natural that the beak cannot be distinguished from the bird's own, in many cases. Rosskopf reports in "Avian Obstetrics" that some dishonest individuals may sell such a bird, without informing the new owners that the bird has a prosthetic beak. The new owners then have to grapple with any follow-up care the bird may need several months into the future.

The beak repair is made with medical acrylic, tinted to match the color of the bird's natural beak. If cracks or fissures have occurred, the damaged area may be reinforced with surgical steel wire, around which the acrylic will be molded. An alternative consists of drilling a series of small holes into the beak on either side of the injury. These are angled in toward the injury from top to bottom. Acrylic is then placed in these holes as well as in the actual repair site. This method achieves stabilization of the repair in two ways. First, the extra holes increase the surface area to which the acrylic can adhere. Second, the angle at which the holes are drilled helps prevent the margins of the damaged area from pulling apart under the stress of normal beak use (Altman, 1985b; Harrison, 1986e).

If the whole beak has been lost, prosthetic repair is effected by driving wires into the beak remnant. These act as a framework around which the prosthesis can be molded.

Sometimes, crush wounds of the beak can expose the nasal sinuses. Such wounds must be filled in while the beak regrows, in order to prevent infection.

Surgery of the Neck Area

REPAIR OF RUPTURED AIR SACS IN THE NECK (CERVICOCEPHALIC AIR SACS):   (See Chapter 4, Air Sac Rupture, for a further discussion of this problem.) Many times, ruptured cervicocephalic air sacs will heal themselves. When they do not, air continues to leak out and form pockets under the skin. Some of these can be quite large and cause the bird to assume very peculiar head postures. Such posture may interfere with head and neck mobility, making eating and preening difficult.

One approach to repair utilizes a small surgical opening in the skin, which is sutured open to allow air to escape. In many cases, the damaged air sac will eventually heal by itself (Rosskopf et al., 1985).

Harrison (1986d) uses a method whereby the damaged air sac is repaired by means of sutures. The skin over the air sac is incised. The air sac itself is then sutured. The skin is closed, and any remaining air is aspirated with a syringe and needle.

There are reports in the literature of the use of medical acrylics to repair torn air sacs.

SURGERY OF THE CROP (CROPOTOMY, INGLUVIOTOMY): This may be done to remove foreign bodies, to repair a crop that has been burned and sloughed to the outside as a result of feeding too-hot formula to baby birds (fistula), or to repair injuries due to trauma (such as punctures resulting from tube feeding). Some crop repairs in the very young may be done without anesthesia.

The skin over the crop is incised, and then the crop itself. If a foreign body is present, it is removed with forceps or a surgical spoon. The crop is then closed, followed by skin closure. If the cropotomy is being done to repair trauma or a fistula, the crop is cleansed of all food material and dead tissue. Overlying skin and muscle must also be freed of such matter. When this has been done, the crop is sutured closed, checking for possible leaks. The skin is then closed. Postoperative care includes frequent, small, liquid meals, with a gradual return to the bird's normal diet.

Surgery of the Abdomen

Surgery of the abdomen is done for many reasons, ranging from surgical sexing to hysterectomy.

There are three commonly used approaches for opening the abdominal cavity. In the first, the bird is placed on its back (dorsal recumbency), and the incision is made over the abdominal midline, from the tip of the sternum to the pubic bones.

In the second method, the bird is also placed in dorsal recumbency, but a "flap" is created by making a horizontal incision across the abdomen. At either end of this incision, additional incisions are made, extending upward toward the bird's upper abdomen. The resultant incision resembles a square envelope flap. This flap is then peeled back (reflected) to allow for a better view of the abdominal contents and more working space for the surgeon.

The third method places the bird on its right side. The initial incision is made on the left side of the abdomen, beginning directly beneath the last rib and continuing diagonally down to the pubic bone. This approach is the one used for surgical sexing, with the exception that a very tiny incision is made, rather than the large one described above. It is also the preferred approach by Harrison for examining air sacs and the lower lungs for evidence of disease; exploratory surgery involving the ovary, testicle, and kidney; for biopsy or

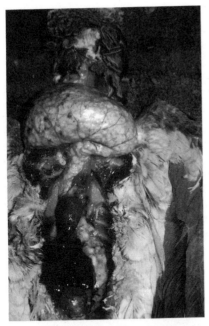

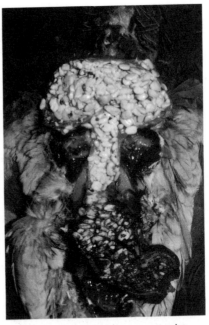

Extensive seed impaction of crop and entire digestive tract of an African Gray Parrot. In this photo, crop and digestive tract have not yet been opened. *Peter Sakas, D.V.M.*

Seed impaction after crop, esophagus, proventriculus and ventriculus have been opened.
Peter Sakas, D.V.M.

The electrocautery cutting tip in use during the hysterectomy of a cockatiel.
M. Vogel

Saran Wrap has proven a very effective material for use as a drape in avian surgery. The transparent nature of the material allows more accurate visual monitoring. *M. Vogel*

surgery of the kidney or liver, or spleen; hysterectomies; and surgery of the proventriculus and ventriculus. With this particular approach, the surgeon may find it necessary to remove one or two ribs to allow better visualization of the surgical field (Harrison, 1986d).

After the initial skin incision has been made, the surgeon carefully moves through the muscle layer and underlying fat pad to expose the contents of the abdominal cavity. Blunt dissection is usually used for this part of the surgery.

AIR SAC EXPLORATORY SURGERY: This is done to aid diagnosis in birds with chronic respiratory problems. Gram stains, impression smears, and cultures and sensitivities may all be done in this way. It is also possible to remove air sac lesions or parasites such as air sac mites during such a procedure.

EXPLORATORY ABDOMINAL LAPAROTOMY: A laparotomy is merely the surgical opening of the abdomen. It is done for diagnostic reasons and to obtain diagnostic tests such as Gram stains and impression smears. It is also done to locate ectopic eggs or to clean up the abdominal cavity in a hen with egg-yolk peritonitis.

PROVENTRICULOTOMY: This is the surgical opening of the proventriculus. It may be done to remove pieces of lead or other heavy metal, foreign bodies such a small pieces of jewelry, or pieces of feeding tube that have been bitten off and swallowed. Because the proventriculus, or "true stomach," contains acid to aid food digestion, great care must be used to prevent the contents of the proventriculus from spilling into the abdominal cavity. If this were to happen, peritonitis would result. In order to prevent this, the proventriculus, esophagus, and ventriculus are flushed with sterile saline or lactated Ringer's solution, then gently vacuumed out with a surgical suction pump (Harrison, 1986d).

Once the surgery has been completed, liquid foods are given to the bird after a suitable number of hours have elapsed. Harrison suggests the incorporation of grape juice into the formula. This dyes the feces, making it much easier to confirm that food is passing normally through the digestive system.

VENTRICULOTOMY (GIZZARDOTOMY): This is the surgical opening of the ventriculus, or gizzard. This may be done to retrieve foreign bodies or to relieve an impaction of some sort. Rosskopf (1985a) also states this has been done in work with birds suffering macaw wasting syndrome. The same precautions to keep the abdominal cavity free of ventricular spillage must be observed as for a proventriculotomy.

Harrison states that there are several difficulties to be encountered when performing surgery on the ventriculus. The ventriculus has a rich blood supply and excessive bleeding may occur. It is also rather firmly attached to the liver by membranes, again making the avoidance of excessive bleeding a problem. The ventriculus is partially covered by the lower end of the sternum, making access difficult. Suturing the gizzard may also present problems, because it is difficult to roll gizzard tissue inward while suturing—a technique that must be

282

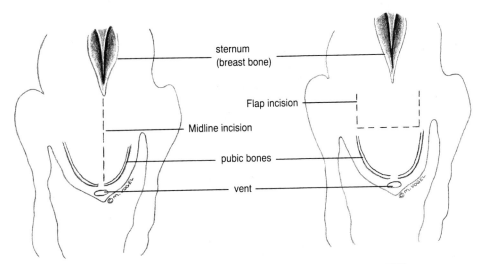

sternum
(breast bone)

Flap incision

Midline incision

pubic bones

vent

Dorsal recumbency (after Harrison & Harrison, p. 587)

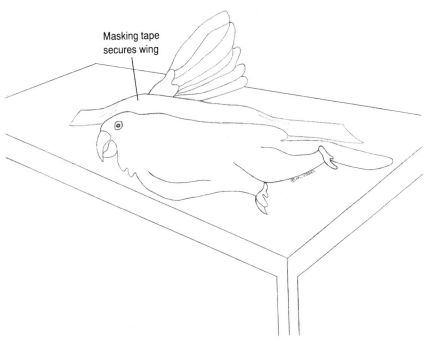

Masking tape
secures wing

Lateral recumbency

283

used to produce a good surgical seal and prevent leakage of gizzard contents into the abdominal cavity.

HYSTERECTOMY: This is the removal of the oviduct in a hen with egg-laying problems. It is not routinely done in healthy, normal hens, as is a "spaying" procedure for dogs and cats. It may be performed to prevent further egg laying in those birds that have experienced chronic egg-binding episodes. The removal of the oviduct prevents the formation of eggs, even though the ovary is not removed. Some hormonal control over ovulation is exercised by the oviduct. When this organ is removed, the ovary becomes dormant and ovulation ceases, for a time, at least.

Peter Sakas (personal communication) states that he has seen many birds on whom he performed hysterectomies subsequently recommence reproductively related behaviors, such as nesting activities. Such activities are caused by the reestablishment of ovulation. This increases the risk of ectopic eggs and egg-yolk peritonitis.

One technique that may be of help in preventing such occurrences is the implant of a small silicone bead impregnated with methoxyprogesterone acetate (Depo-Provera). This has been tried experimentally by Harrison and the results are encouraging (Harrison, 1989). Methoxyprogesterone given by injection is commonly used in avian practices to prevent ovulation, control unwanted egg laying, and control reproductively related unwanted behaviors such as aggression, screaming, and biting. An implant containing this drug provides a slow, constant delivery of the medication over a long period of time, thus decreasing the need for frequent injections. It also decreases unwanted side effects such as weight gain, polyuria, increased water consumption, and diabetes. This is because a smaller dosage can be used with this method. Harrison feels that such implants, especially with the addition of testosterone to the methoxyprogesterone, may virtually eliminate the need for hysterectomies done to prevent egg laying. More work needs to be done to determine how consistently effective this technique will be, but it appears very promising.

A hysterectomy may also be done in conjunction with exploratory laparotomy to clean up egg-yolk peritonitis or to remove ectopic eggs.

A lateral surgical approach is sometimes used; in other cases, a midline incision may be done. If it is suspected that fluid is present in the abdominal cavity, as in peritonitis, Harrison recommends the midline approach, as it is easier to prevent the drainage of such material into the air sacs once the initial incision has been made. Magnification and electrosurgery are used when a hysterectomy is done.

SURGICAL SEXING: This procedure is done by means of endoscopy (see Chapter 3). Although a minor surgery, it should always be performed under sterile conditions. If the bird shows any signs of ill health, the procedure should be postponed until all problems have been corrected.

The bird is anesthetized and placed on its right side with its left leg extended as far back as possible. Feathers over the site are plucked. Alternately, they may be dampened with alcohol and pushed away from the incision site. The skin is then cleaned with a disinfectant soap. A very small incision is always made on the bird's left side because if the bird is a hen, her one functioning ovary will be on this side. Only the skin is incised, not the underlying muscle. Care is exercised to avoid cutting through a feather follicle, which can cause bleeding problems (McDonald, 1987).

After the initial skin incision has been completed, a small, hollow tube containing another smaller hollow tube is introduced into the abdominal cavity by means of gentle rotational pressure. This arrangement of a tube within a tube is called a trocar-cannula. The outside tube, or trocar, has a sharp end to facilitate its introduction into the abdominal cavity. The inner tube, or cannula, provides the "tunnel" through which the laparoscope will be introduced. The trocar is withdrawn once it has served its purpose of introducing the cannula into the abdomen.

Once the laparoscope is in place, the gonads can then be visualized and identified as to sex. The testicle appears cylindrical or elliptical and has a smooth surface well supplied with blood vessels. The ovary in an adult hen appears like a cluster of grapes due to the maturing egg follicles on its surface.

Clubb (1986b) states that a skilled veterinarian can determine the sex of a bird very accurately, even before the bird fledges. The testicle of a sexually immature male does not have the rich surface blood supply of the mature male's testicle. The immature ovary is usually flat, with many surface folds, making it appear, in McDonald's words, "brainlike." It may also resemble a small piece of fat tissue.

While the laparoscope is in place, the veterinarian also has an excellent opportunity to view the abdominal air sacs, kidneys, and adrenal glands. When the procedure has been completed, the bird is tattooed in the wing web, using a small amount of ink such as India ink. A hen is tattooed in the left wing web, a male in the right wing web.

Sutures are usually not required, as the incision site seals itself when the bird's leg is released from restraint. Antibiotics are not routinely given postsexing. Surgical sexing is highly accurate and very safe when done by an experienced avian veterinarian.

Surgery of the Cloaca

Surgery of the cloaca may be performed to replace a prolapsed cloaca. It may also be done to remove papillomatous growths of the cloaca.

CLOACAPEXY: This is the repair of the prolapsed cloaca. It is done using an abdominal midline incision. The prolapsed portion of the cloaca is gently placed in position by an assistant wearing a finger cot. The cloaca is then sutured to the cartilaginous tip of the sternum, using suture material or surgical steel wire (Rosskopf, "Avian Obstetrics").

If abdominal surgery should again become necessary for the bird at some time in the future, the surgeon should be made aware that a cloacapexy has been previously performed.

REMOVAL OF CLOACAL PAPILLOMAS: This is done using electrocautery, cryosurgery, or ligation on the growth, followed by excision. Even with surgery, these growths may recur. This probably happens because it is difficult to destroy or remove 100 percent of the abnormal cells. Any cells left intact carry the potential for regrowth.

Orthopedic Surgery

This is done for purposes of wing pinioning, amputation, or fracture repair.

WING PINIONING: This procedure is done to remove the end portions of metacarpals I and II, on one of the bird's wings. These bones are analagous to a human's hand. Wing pinioning is itself an amputation, and renders the bird permanently flightless. It is seldom performed on companion birds.

AMPUTATION: This may be done when a bird has sustained damage to an extremity that cannot be surgically repaired. Gunshot wounds are often a cause of such injuries in raptors. Amputation may be performed when a cancerous growth is present, or in the case of bone infection (osteomyelitis) refractory to conservative treatment with appropriate antibiotics.

When amputation of a pneumatic bone is done, care must be taken to close the soft tissue overlying the stump in a very thorough manner. If this is not done, air may leak into surrounding tissue, creating swelling. It is also possible that pathogens could gain access to the inside of the unhealed bone, and then the air sacs and lungs, creating bone and respiratory infection.

When an amputation is performed, all surrounding muscle is dissected away from the bone. Blood vessels are located and tied off or coagulated using electrocautery. Only then is the bone actually severed. Muscle and skin are then drawn over the stump and sutured. Bandaging will further protect the surgical site until healing has taken place. Because birds have little subcutaneous tissue, it is sometimes difficult to cover the amputated stump adequately. In such cases, medical acrylics may be used to reinforce the sutures.

SURGICAL FRACTURE REPAIR: This becomes necessary when a fracture is complicated by crushing or shattering of the bone and the skin is broken. (See Chapter 4, Fractures, for a discussion of the types of fractures.) Such fractures result in damage to surrounding nerves, muscles, blood vessels, ligaments, and tendons. In these cases, it is not enough to set the bone. Soft tissue damage must be repaired if the bird is to regain function of the injured limb. Microsurgery techniques are very helpful in these instances.

Orthopedic surgery of this nature is referred to as internal fixation of the

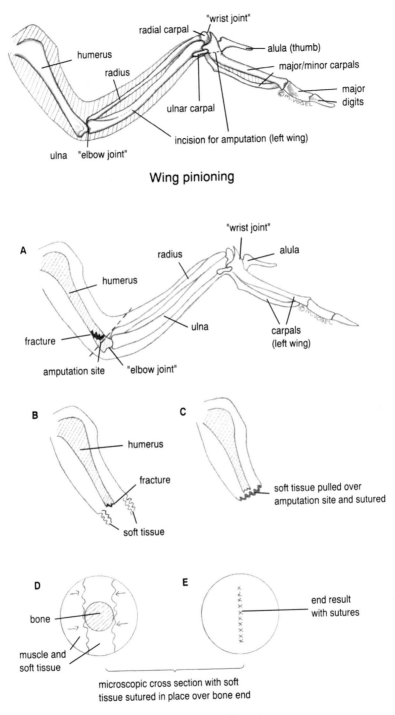

Wing pinioning

Amputation with skin flap closure

287

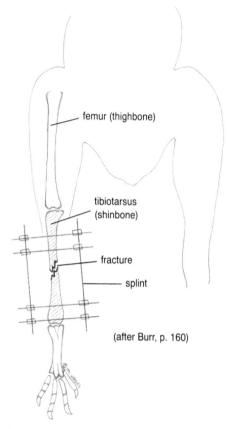

femur (thighbone)

tibiotarsus (shinbone)

fracture

splint

(after Burr, p. 160)

Fracture repair with Kirschner-Elmer splints

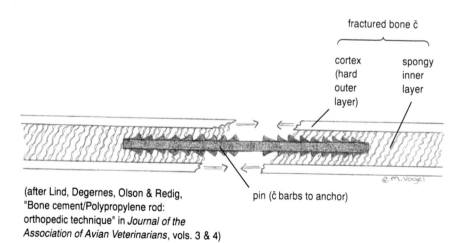

fractured bone c̄

cortex (hard outer layer)

spongy inner layer

pin (c̄ barbs to anchor)

(after Lind, Degernes, Olson & Redig, "Bone cement/Polypropylene rod: orthopedic technique" in *Journal of the Association of Avian Veterinarians*, vols. 3 & 4)

Fracture repair with intramedullary bone splints

fracture, as opposed to external fixation by means of casts and splints. According to Hannis Stoddard (1987a), the principles of internal fixation include accurate alignment of the bone ends or fragments, rigid fixation, and prevention of infection. Advantages of internal fixation are several. It allows the surgeon to see the bone fragments and to align them as carefully as possible. It permits a much more rigid fixation of the bone fragments than does external splinting or casting, and helps prevent their displacement during the healing process. Because the bones have been fixed into position internally, the bird can often return to use of the limb more quickly.

Devices used in internal fracture repair include bone pins, Kirschner-Ehmer splints, and bone plates. Bone pins are inserted into the bone marrow space at the end of each fragment. The bone ends are then gently brought into correct anatomical position as the pins are worked further into the marrow cavity, providing a very rigid repair. This procedure is also known as intramedullary pinning.

A Kirschner-Ehmer splint is an external splinting device that utilizes the principle of transfixation splinting. Rather than placing the bone pin within the actual bone cavity (as in intramedullary pinning), the pins are driven through the bone at more or less right angles to it. Once this has been done, the bone ends are aligned. (In actuality, the pins are usually driven through the bone at a slight angle to prevent them from working loose.) A portion of each pin actually extends through the skin to the outside of the bird's injured limb. The external parts of the pin are inserted into a rigid splint that runs the length of the limb on the outside. This external splint serves to keep the pins from working out of the bone and provides extremely rigid fixation of the fracture while it heals.

Advantages of using a Kirschner-Ehmer splint include good bone fixation, minimal soft tissue damage when pins are placed, relatively short surgery and anesthetic time, ease of application, quick return to function, and removal of the device with little or no anesthesia. Disadvantages include greater weight of the device as compared to that of the intramedullary pin, risk of infection, damage to the external splint, and risk of bone shattering at the point where the pins have been inserted.

Bone plating is seldom used on small birds such as parrots. This method of fracture repair is more appropriate to large birds, and then is usually confined to fractures of the leg (Blass, 1987). The procedure consists of aligning the fractured bone ends, then fixing them in place by screwing a metal plate over the fracture site to prevent bone movement. Birds can usually regain function of the limb as soon as surgery has been completed. However, as with any open fracture repair, the danger of infection is present. There is also the risk that the bone may splinter at the site where the plate is affixed. Other disadvantages include a large surgical opening, which means that a great deal of soft tissue will be exposed and manipulated with the inherent risk of damage. A prolonged anesthetic time is also usually required to effect the repair.

Blue and Gold Macaw (*Ara ararauna*)

7

Necropsy

WHY DO A NECROPSY?

A pet store owner begins to experience sudden, unexplained deaths in a mixed species group of South American Parrots recently out of quarantine.

A Hyacinth Macaw dies after a short illness characterized by regurgitation, scant droppings, and a diagnosis of digestive tract obstruction of unknown origin.

A dear family pet, a Yellow-naped Amazon, dies after a debilitating illness of several weeks' duration. The bird has never been exposed to other birds in the ten years it resided with its family. The tentative antemortem diagnosis was chlamydiosis and the family wishes to know if it will be safe to bring a new bird into their home once the mourning process has been completed.

A breeder begins to experience high hatchling mortality during the current breeding season. This has never before occurred in the aviary.

A cockatiel is found dead in its cage the morning after its owner has used her brand-new kitchen range for the first time.

In all the above cases, the owners ask, "Why?" The veterinarian asks the same question. Although antemortem diagnostic techniques can supply many answers and play a tremendous role in allowing the veterinarian to select an appropriate treatment plan, there are times when a definitive diagnosis cannot be made on the living bird. This happens for many reasons. Sometimes the bird is presented when too ill to allow blood work and other diagnostic tests to be done without causing lethal stress. At times, specimens submitted for diagnostic tests are not suitable. This is a common problem with samples submitted for

Chlamydia psittaci culture (see Chapter 5, Psittacosis, for a discussion of this problem). Perhaps the bird has died suddenly, with no discernible symptoms.

When such situations occur, with the result that a bird dies and the veterinarian is still not able to identify with absolute certainty the cause of death, both the veterinarian and the owner are left with many unanswered questions. It is at such times that a necropsy is indispensable.

A necropsy is the veterinary equivalent of a human autopsy. Indeed, the terms "autopsy" and "postmortem examination" are used interchangeably with "necropsy." They mean the same thing: the examination of a dead organism in order to determine with precision the cause of death.

The necropsy serves several purposes. It answers definitively, in most cases, why the bird died. This is very important to bird owners because it helps them begin to work through the loss of their pet and put their feelings of grief behind them. Often, if the question "Why?" is not answered, pet owners may spend unnecessary time grieving, because they will continue to wonder how the bird's death came about. Emotional energy then becomes invested in useless conjecture, rather than in coping with the fact of the bird's death and the healthy normal mourning process. In addition, knowing a pet's cause of death will relieve any lingering guilt feelings owners may have. Knowing that they "did not do anything wrong" to cause the bird's death can be a tremendous comfort.

Besides the emotional benefits they derive from necropsy, owners will obtain valuable information about the nature of the disease that killed their bird. If it was infectious, they will know how to go about treating and protecting other birds in their care. This is extremely important economically, also, especially if a large and valuable collection or a breeding operation is at risk. Indeed, in a flock situation, where several deaths have already occurred, it is wise to sacrifice one or two sick birds for the purpose of necropsy. This will greatly increase the chances of finding the cause of illness. Once this has been determined, the veterinarian has much better information on which to base a treatment and prevention plan for the remaining birds. And, of course, there are important ramifications if only a single bird is involved. If another bird is being considered as a replacement, an owner will know the answers to such pragmatic questions as how to go about disinfection, what products to use, and how long a period must elapse before it is safe to bring another bird into the household.

There are several benefits of performing a necropsy for the veterinarian as well. In many cases, the veterinarian will be able to find out what really did kill the bird, and whether this confirms or disproves the antemortem diagnosis. In either case, valuable knowledge and experience has been gained that can then be used for the benefit of future avian patients. If the veterinarian is involved in research and publication, these findings may find their way into the professional avian literature, and in turn benefit many other veterinarians and their patients. It is in this way that knowledge about new and emerging diseases is compiled and disseminated, thus helping all aviculturists in a very real way.

In addition to confirming or disproving a diagnosis, necropsy helps the veterinarian to see and better understand the disease process and how it affected that *particular* bird. The veterinarian may also discover that the bird had other problems that had gone undetected. These may or may not have contributed to the bird's death. Such findings are referred to as incidental or secondary findings. Examples include tapeworm infestation in an African Gray Parrot in which *Reovirus* infection was the cause of death, or subclinical chlamydiosis in a hen in which egg-binding complications were the primary cause of death. Often, thyroid and parathyroid hyperplasia will be a secondary finding in birds that had been maintained on all-seed diets.

If a bird dies and the veterinarian requests permission to perform a necropsy, it is wise to do so. Sometimes the first reaction is to refuse, because of a feeling of repulsion at having one's beloved pet "cut up." But mature and informed reflection should overcome such hesitancy, because giving permission for necropsy will confer benefits on all involved.

HOW IS A NECROPSY DONE?

There are two major parts in the performance of a necropsy: the gross portion (gross in the sense of "whole," as opposed to microscopic) and the microscopic, or histopathologic portion. In addition, special laboratory procedures such as serology or toxicology may be done.

Gross Portion of Necropsy

During this part of the necropsy, the pathologist will examine the bird's body internally and externally for signs of disease by looking at body structures in their entirety. The pathologist will first observe the bird externally, before opening its body cavities. The general condition is checked for signs of obesity, tumors, thinness, good or poor muscular development, and evidence of fractures. The condition of the skin and plumage will be noted, as well as evidence of external parasites. All body orifices—eyes, ears, nose, and mouth—will be checked for discharges. The vent is examined for evidence of pasting or soiling. The soles of the feet are checked for the presence of callouses, which could indicate a chronic vitamin A deficiency. Once all of this has been accomplished, the body cavity is opened.

When the body cavity is opened, all organs are first observed in their natural anatomic position for signs of disease and infection. If the pathologist sees such signs, impression smears or material for culture will be taken at this time. Heart blood is withdrawn into a sterile syringe for blood smears and culture. (All material used for the purpose of making slides, cultures, or other special tests are sterile. This ensures that no accidental contamination occurs that might lead to inaccurate results.)

Thyroid and parathyroids are observed for evidence of enlargement. The liver and spleen are observed, and frequently impression smears are taken of these organs. It is often possible to find evidence of bacterial, viral, chlamydial, and protozoal infections on such slides. The proventriculus and ventriculus are observed and opened. They provide good clues as to whether or not the bird was eating at the time of death. Foreign bodies and obstructions are often identified in these organs. Pale muscle walls can indicate a vitamin E deficiency. The intestines are observed, and their contents aspirated with a syringe and needle before they are opened. Gonads, adrenals, kidneys, and pancreas are checked, as are the air sacs and lungs. The heart is opened and all four chambers observed.

After the contents of the abdominal and chest cavities have been examined while still in place in the body, opened up and checked further, and all tissue, blood, and exudate samples obtained, the pathologist then examines the head and neck. Sinus cavities, mouth, esphogus, crop, trachea, and syrinx are all observed.

If there is reason to believe that central nervous system disease has occurred, the skull is opened and the brain examined. Examination of the spinal cord may also be carried out. The major nerve centers supplying the wings and legs are checked (the brachial and sciatic plexi, respectively). The intercostal nerves (which lie between the ribs) and sciatic nerves may be examined.

The joints will be opened and observed for signs of disease, such as infection, arthritis, and gout. Samples of bone marrow may be obtained by cracking a bone and doing an impression smear or aspirating a portion of the marrow with a syringe and needle.

Microscopic Portion of Necropsy

This portion of the necropsy consists of the examination of various tissues and smears under the microscope. They may be stained with various preparations to make identification of cellular structures and pathogens easier.

When examining such specimens, the pathologist is looking for many things that will reveal the identification of the disease, its progressive course in the bird's body, and how its effects are manifested at the level of the individual cell. The pathologist looks for evidence of whether the disease was acute or chronic and checks for the physical presence of fungi, bacteria, and viruses (often manifested by the presence of inclusion bodies inside various cells).

In order to facilitate the microscopic examination and postmortem diagnosis of disease, the pathologist routinely examines tissues removed from the heart, lungs, liver, spleen, kidneys, gonads, and intestines. Additional tissue from virtually every body organ (including those already sampled), skin and breast muscle, and bone marrow may be preserved so further study may be done if indicated by the results of the initial microscopic examination of tissues routinely submitted.

Occasionally, in situations where hatchlings or very small adults are involved, the whole bird may be preserved and submitted for histopathologic examination.

Special Laboratory Procedures

In addition to the gross and microscopic aspects of the necropsy, special tests may be done. These may include (depending on the pathologist's findings and the clinical history of the bird) bacterial, fungal, and viral cultures of body secretions and exudates; toxicological examination; serology; parasitology examination; and cytological examination of various body fluids and secretions.

PREPARING A SPECIMEN FOR NECROPSY

Probably more ambiguous or poor necropsy findings result from incorrect preparation of the carcass than from any other reason. The owner is frequently the person responsible for preparation of the carcass, as many birds die unexpectedly at home. Failure to do this properly will waste the owner's money and the veterinary pathologist's time.

The cardinal rule is *never freeze a carcass*. When tissue is frozen, the fluid inside each cell freezes and expands, rupturing the cell and destroying its contents. Such material is useless for examination.

The second rule is that the carcass ideally should be submitted for necropsy within twelve hours of death. Helpful results can probably be obtained within twenty-four to forty-eight hours after death (if the carcass has been properly prepared), but after that time the natural decaying process that takes place (autolysis) decreases the chance of obtaining useful information.

The third rule is that the bird's body should be cooled *rapidly*. To accomplish this, the feathers should be thoroughly wetted with soapy water to destroy their insulating properties. After this has been done, immerse the bird in *very cold* water for thirty minutes (longer if the bird is large). When the body is cold to the touch, sponge off the excess water and place it in two layers of air-tight plastic bags. Place the carcass in the coldest part of the *refrigerator* and keep it there until it can be transported to the veterinarian. *Do not store the body in the freezer!*

The bird owner's care in the unhappy but necessary preparation of the body for necropsy will be rewarded by accurate, meaningful information that will help the owner, veterinarian, and other birds alike.

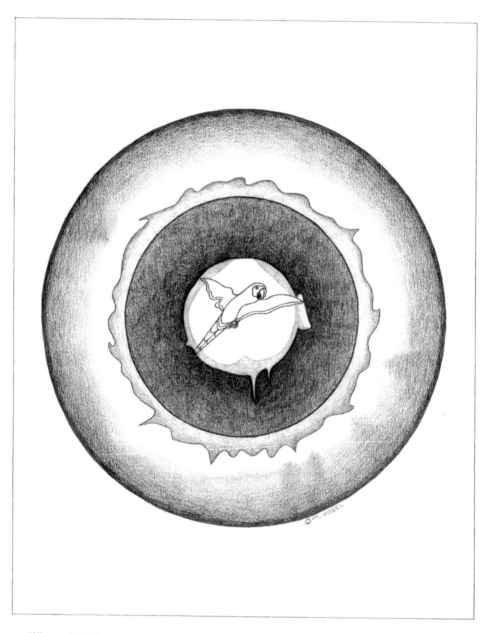

When a bird dies, its physical manifestation is gone from us and we see it only in memory through the mind's eye. Surely, the loss of a much-loved pet bird is traumatic for the owner and his or her family. The normal grief response helps us come to terms with such a loss and to eventually remember a special bird for the happiness it gave us during its life rather than the sadness we experienced at its death.

296

8

When a Bird Dies

<hr>

THIS BOOK deals almost exclusively with what we as bird owners should know about the care of our birds. To discharge faithfully our responsibilities to them is our privilege. To receive their love is an honor of which to be humbly proud. Their lives enrich and enhance our own in ways we may not even be fully aware.

When their lives end, our inheritance is grief. Just as our birds have deserved our informed and loving care in life, their bereaved owners deserve care and attention in the period of grief when those birds die. It is with the hope that grief can be understood and eased, even a little, that this chapter has been written.

Grief, like all other human emotions, has various shadings and intensities. The feeling of loss and bereavement will vary from person to person, situation to situation. An owner of a dear pet with whom he has spent twenty or thirty years; a breeder who has just lost a baby bird, whose loss is compounded because it was one of a rare and endangered species; an elderly widow who has lost her budgerigar, the only living creature with whom she had the opportunity to relate on an ongoing, daily basis; a young child's cockatiel that has provided a meal for the family cat—no matter what the relationship, the death of that pet results in a feeling of loss. It may be brief and transitory, or it may be deep and prolonged. The important thing to know is that grief for the death of a pet is very real; it is genuine and should be respected as such. In the past few years, it has become acceptable to grieve for a dead pet. Prior to this time, people were often make to feel ashamed of the depth of their grief when a pet died. It has now been recognized that the animal-human bond is of great significance and that grief for its severance is necessary and acceptable. Grief for one's dead pet is probably the finest epitaph one could give. It symbolizes a meaningful relationship in which both owner and pet shared something that was precious and unique.

WHAT BIRDS MEAN TO US AS COMPANIONS

It seems to the author that the death of a parrot may possess extra dimensions that are not present when a cat or dog dies. The first of these factors is that we expect our birds to live long lives—after all, the life expectancy of many species approaches that of humans. When such a bird dies, it seems doubly tragic and unexpected in relationship to the time we thought we would have with the bird.

The second factor is that many birds that die are members of an endangered species, or one that may become so in the foreseeable future (and this includes many psittacines). So the death of a bird may represent a very real blow to the preservation of a given species, as well as a personal loss for the owner.

The third factor involves the origin of many of our companion birds—whether caught wild or domestically bred. (After all, even hand-raised babies are at *most* only a few generations removed from the hundreds upon thousands of generations of their wild genetic inheritance.) The fact is, that *any* parrot is *not* a domestic animal. The love and friendship offered by *any* parrot to its owner is a free gift, a gift that the bird *consciously* makes. The ability to give easily the gift of love and devotion is *not* a part of its genetic makeup, is *not* automatic, as it is with domestic dogs and cats. This bond with its owner is an especially poignant one, as anyone who has gentled a wild-caught bird will testify. The giving of trust and love to its owner on the part of a parrot, especially one that was caught wild, is like no other animal-human bond. Its loss, through death, is doubly heartbreaking.

The fourth factor involves the parrot's speech. Many parrots use cognitive speech, and have a well-defined sense of cause and effect with respect to the use of human language. Lest there are still those who pooh-pooh the fact that a parrot does anything but indulge in mindless mimicry, let them be advised that when a bird learns that to make a certain sound will bring a specific and particular result, it is using the same method that a human infant does when it learns the human tongue. To associate on a daily basis with an animal that to some degree can actually communicate with its owner using human speech can be an almost eerie experience. It is certainly one that cannot be had with other animals. It becomes a bonding enhancement, one that reaches out to us in our essential human isolation, and gives a very special dimension to the bird-human relationship.

In addition to all the special aspects of parrot ownership discussed above, the parrot serves the same purposes for its owner that a cat or dog does. It can become a wellspring of unconditional love and acceptance for its owner. All of us crave such love. This is the legacy of our infancy and childhood, when our parents—however much they loved us, and however excellent they were as parents—in the task of rearing and socializing us had the unhappy but inescapable task of punishment, discipline, and temporary withdrawal of affection from us. Later in life, as adults, we have experienced the betrayal of friends; perhaps the loss of a spouse through divorce, with all its bitterness and acrimony; perhaps the faltering of religious convictions and the void that often follows; possibly the alienation of family. But a pet never rejects, never ceases to love. It loves without reservation.

A pet can be a playmate, a child, a parent. A pet can be a guardian of one's hearth. Many parrots excel at this. We all know the squawking and shrieking a stranger can elicit from a possessive parrot. Greene, in his book *Parrots in Captivity*, tells an anecdote about a Moluccan Cockatoo that surprised and repulsed a midnight housebreaker by yelling, ''Who are you? What do you want?'' Can you imagine the poor burglar, confronted by a huge bird with every feather on end, demanding in no uncertain terms what the burglar's business was? It brings a smile to the lips and a glow to the heart.

Pets serve many times as an incentive to keep to a routine, particularly for those who might otherwise have a great deal of unstructured time on their hands. Birds must be fed, cages must be cleaned, babies must be cared for, health needs must be attended to, and emotional needs must be met. Ongoing attention to these needs provides a reason to get up in the morning, to interact with others, to turn one's concerns outward rather than inward. Such caring and giving, directed toward a companion animal, can be for many a bulwark against loneliness and depression.

Pets provide an acceptable, positive outlet for our very human need to nurture. The woman whose children are grown and gone, the retired man whose lifetime habit was to provide for others, the child who seeks to gain maturity and competence in demonstrating his ability to be responsible for another living creature—all share the need to care. Even if there is not another human soul who needs us, our pets do. They allow us to give—something very necessary in maintaining our humanity.

Pets, especially birds, can be the stimulus for intellectual challenge and creativity. Anyone involved in the art and science of aviculture can attest to this. People breed birds, do research about them, write books, give lectures. A whole host of such activities revolve around parrot keeping and breeding, for those who wish to learn and grow in their avocation. The opportunities to meet people of like interest, to share information and friendship, are numberless, for those who would reach out.

Pets can help people adjust to the loss of health and physical function. Their complete and unquestioning acceptance of us when we are no longer as we were can be a tremendous comfort, an anchor during the times when we are changing in frightening ways. Pets can give comfort and help even as death approaches. In the March 1989 issue of *Bird Talk* magazine, a letter from Marion Belden described such a case. Cookie, a Citron-crested Cockatoo, was devoted to her husband and actually saved his life by shrieking and alerting Mrs. Belden when her husband suffered a heart attack. He recovered from this event, only to become a victim of incurable cancer some months later. Mrs. Belden describes touchingly Cookie's visit to the hospice where her husband spent his last days, and the comfort he derived from the presence of his beloved bird.

There has been much research done on the benefits to one's health deriving from pet ownership. One study demonstrated that pet ownership actually increased one-year survival rate postcoronary heart disease (Friedman et al., 1984). The percentage of those who did not own a pet and did not live to see the first anniversary of their heart attacks was significantly higher than for those who owned pets. Touching and stroking a pet has been shown to alleviate anxiety and lower blood pressure. To be involved in caring for a pet may trigger physiological changes that increase one's resistance to disease. The activity involved in caring for pets also encourages exercise and the benefits it provides.

When one loses to death a companion such as a parrot, one loses many precious things. Under the circumstances, it is natural to grieve. It is not abnormal or neurotic in any sense. Not only does the person grieve for all *he* has lost. He grieves for the loss of his dear pet—the pleasures of life that are no longer the animal's to enjoy. We know that our birds' lives matter to them, that those lives possess a significance, an intrinsic value over and above their relationship with us. And we mourn the loss of such lives.

THE STAGES OF GRIEF

It is helpful to know that there are identifiable stages of grief. A person who has lost a pet will travel through all the stages, sometimes going back to a previous stage or experiencing an overlap between stages. One's progression through grief is not clear cut or distinct at each stage. Human emotions are not so easily pigeonholed. But a knowledge of the various grief phases will help bereft owners recognize the signs in themselves so that they may better cope with them. It also provides the much needed reassurance that there is an end to grief. The length of time needed for any given individual to move through grief and finally to achieve peace of mind varies a great deal. Days, weeks, or several months may be required.

The first stage of grief consists of shock and numbness. During this period, the fact of death has no reality. One may be unable to realize that death has occurred, or one may recognize intellectually that death has occurred but on an emotional level it seems not to have happened. The author recalls the death of a much-loved fourteen-week-old Blue and Gold Macaw. He had been hospitalized for a week for a gastrointestinal problem. On the sixth day of hospitalization, he underwent exploratory abdominal surgery to rule out the possibility of a foreign object. None was found, and he seemed to rally. The night of the seventh day, the veterinarian called to tell me he had died. I was so calm, so able to cope. My husband and I stayed up late, talking about Maury, how sick he had been, about our expectation that he would not live, our relief that he was now no longer experiencing pain. I went to bed and slept, feeling that I was well in control. This state of affairs lasted two or three days.

Then came the second stage of grief: reality and its attendant pain. At this time, the pet owner may experience several distressing feelings: guilt, anger, loneliness, depression, overwhelming sadness, or fantasy that the pet still lives. In my situation, it gradually dawned emotionally that Maury was really gone. Music that he had enjoyed brought terrible feelings of sadness and loss. When I disposed of his frozen formula, I felt I had thrown Maury away. Putting away his toys, his playpen, cleaning his cage the final time were almost unbearable acts. I occasionally thought I could see him out of the corner of my eye, toddling across the family room floor. I was bewildered and angry that his death should have occurred, regardless of all the care and the love we had lavished on him. I blamed myself for possibly having missed some early sign of illness.

The feelings of guilt and anger that often happen at this stage are very difficult, compounded as they are by loneliness and sadness. We may feel that we were in some way responsible for our pet's death. We may feel that if only the veterinarian had tried harder, the pet would be alive. Although these things may have been the case in a very few instances, by and large they have no real basis. Such feelings are the products of a mind in turmoil and change, attempting to come to grips with the death. Mercifully, they pass with time and the chance to think about them and discuss them with friends and family.

Another common reaction during the second stage of grief is depression. This may be marked by an overwhelming sense of fatigue, loss of appetite, inability to sleep, or a lack of desire to interact with other people. Bouts of crying and restlessness, possible hyperactivity, may be present. The things that usually give us great pleasure and satisfaction become meaningless. Sometimes, we become frightened by the intensity of our feelings and fear that we may be losing our minds. However, with the passage of time, these distressing feelings lessen and finally abate altogether. In their midst, it is difficult to believe that this is so. Nevertheless, it is.

How do we know when recovery has begun? Someone says "Remember when . . . ?" You grin and chuckle, and the familiar sense of loss does not make an appearance. You come across a photograph of the departed pet and say to yourself, "I think I'll put this on the refrigerator door. He was so lovely, and I want to remember that." You wake up one morning and think to yourself how welcome the sun is. Food begins to taste better. Peace of mind begins to return with stealth, almost unnoticed at first. To be sure, there will be times of relapse. I recall a period about three months after Maury's death. My husband and I were shopping and came across a pet store with which we were not familiar. We went in, and right in the front was a cage with several baby Blue and Gold Macaws. They had just been weaned and were waiting to go to new homes. I had to leave immediately—it was suddenly and unexpectedly painful. I am happy to say that I am once again able to view baby macaws with equanimity; then, it was miserably hard.

COPING WITH GRIEF

How does one go about "getting well" after the death of a pet? Knowing the stages of grief and how they manifest themselves is the first step. Realizing that grieving for a pet is natural and normal is a great comfort. It becomes easier to do the hard work of grieving when you know that you are not losing your mind, that your reactions are appropriate to your loss. This brings us to a very important point: Do not try to ignore your grief. It is there. If you do not allow yourself to deal with it at the appropriate time, you can be sure it will come back to haunt you at the least expected time, with sometimes devastating results. Do not deny grief; do not hide it from yourself. Live with your feelings, day to day, however painful, allowing your mind to follow the natural course of grief. If this is not done, grief will sink into the subconscious mind. With the passage of time, you may not consciously think of your loss, but your subconscious does not forget. The unresolved grief will show itself in various ways. There may be unexplained insomnia or anxiety. Irritability may be present. A fatigue out of proportion to energy expenditure may linger. Because the original grief was denied and not resolved, subsequent deaths may be doubly hard to handle. Because, in effect, you are then dealing with two losses—the original loss that you denied and were unable to accept, and the loss that has recently occurred.

Depression may appear for no obvious reason. All these things may take place weeks, months, or even years after the original loss. When they occur, the individual is usually at a loss as to why they are happening—for he is unable to connect them with any current situation in his life.

Another important point is to give yourself time to get over your bereavement. It is tempting to say, "It's been three weeks now and I ought to feel better." Well-meaning friends and family may indicate the same thing. This advice, whether self-administered or proffered by others, is absurd. No one, lay persons and experts alike, truly know the course of a person's grief—what one should feel, how long the process takes. One feels what one feels. Providing you are not hiding from your feelings, you will, however slowly, move from denial and shock, through pain, and on to acceptance and peace of mind.

An extremely helpful thing to do is learn to forgive yourself, if guilt about your pet's death is present. This is especially important if euthanasia has been involved. It helps to realize that *you* did not cause your pet's demise because you opted to give it a painless, dignified, peaceful death. The *disease* was the cause of the pet's death. In providing the last loving act of euthanasia to your suffering pet, you have behaved with courage and responsibility. The loved animal no longer experiences pain; no longer suffers the indignities brought by loss of bodily function; no longer gazes with patient, endless, incomprehensible pain. There is nothing for which one needs to feel guilty about having made the choice of euthanasia.

Perhaps, though, you were in some way responsible for your pet's death. Perhaps a thoughtlessly open window allowed the bird to take flight from which it never returned. Perhaps you did notice that things "were not quite right" but

302

Most bird enthusiasts will share their homes with more than one bird. Many have found that it helps to take comfort from the others when one bird dies.

you were busy, maybe a little low in funds—for some reason you did not get to the veterinarian on time. One needs to realize that all of us do our best in any given situation, and so did you. We do what we can, and that is all we can do. Our very humanity makes us vulnerable to occasional poor judgment, illness, worry, and any number of things that may interfere with the best interests of our pets. The solution is to look at the situation honestly, decide what culpability you bear, and resolve to take whatever steps are necessary to see that it does not happen again. And—remember to be kind to yourself. Mistakes happen with best of intentions. Learn and go from there. Guilt that you refuse to let go can keep you mired in grief and sadness for many long, weary, unnecessary days.

In addition to the mental attitudes discussed above, there are other and very practical things you can do to help get through the work of grieving. Find sympathetic friends who are themselves pet owners and talk with them about what you are going through. If you are feeling guilty or angry, express these feelings and explain why you feel as you do. It is surprising what balm it is to have a friend gently correct you and point out that you did all that could possibly have been done. If you bear some responsibility in the death of your pet, admitting this to a sympathetic listener can be the beginning of exorcising the guilt. Share your memories of your pet with your listener. Mental pain is somehow magically lightened and made more bearable through the offices of a kind listener. There may be those few unfortunate souls who have never owned a pet and who do not understand your grief. Avoid talking about your feelings with such people. If those in the workplace notice that you are not yourself and inquire, a good response can be "I've recently lost a very dear friend," and let it go at that (New, 1987).

Another thing that can be very comforting is to spend time with your remaining pets. (Did you ever know anyone who had only *one* bird?) Will yourself to be consciously grateful for their continued good health. Give them time and attention. It is entirely possible that those birds remaining are feeling a sense of loss also. Birds are very observant. They will notice that one of their fellows is absent. They will notice your distraction, tears, and sadness. So by loving them, talking with them, taking extra pains with their care, you will comfort and reassure them. And you will receive comfort, love, and reassurance in return.

Sometimes grief produces acute restlessness. If this is the case, work of some kind can be miraculous therapy. This urge to "do something" probably has its roots in the desire to reassert control over one's life and surroundings in the face of great mental turmoil and emotional upheaval. If you are experiencing such restlessness, get busy. I am by no means advocating mindless activity as a means of not thinking about your loss and grief. But a morning spent scrubbing the floor, cleaning out a closet or garage, baking a cake, or straightening the mess on the desk can do a great deal to help alleviate the helpless, restless feelings. First, you will have imposed some sort of structure on your time (which can sometimes seem endless and empty). Second, you will have the reassurance that you are still functioning. Third, you will have the satisfaction of seeing the positive results of your work. Fourth, physical activity will induce the gentle fatigue that is healthy and natural—not the mental exhaustion that is so draining and still leaves one sleepless. You will rest better at night, and a rested mind is much better able to cope with the demands of grief.

Finally, at some point in your mourning, after a period of time has elapsed, let yourself think of a new bird—not as a replacement, for one bird can *never* replace another, just as one child can never replace another; but as a new relationship in which friendship and love can happen once again. To risk love again is to risk loss again. It is, it seems, part of the human condition. But love must be given away, especially if one possesses a special feeling for all creatures, and birds in particular. Somewhere, there is a bird that needs you. Somewhere there is a bird whom you need. Leave yourself open to this possibility. When you feel able, with your lost bird secure in your heart, go out and find that new little fellow. Love is like matter and energy. It may change form, but it is never lost. For the grieving pet owner, love has for a time been changed to grief and turned in upon itself. But eventually, that grief begins to look outward and transforms itself once more into the need to love. Healing and recovery have taken place and there is once more room in the "country of the heart" for yet another occupant.

WHEN GRIEF DOES NOT GO AWAY

Sometimes, grief does not go away. This happens because at some point the mourning process has been blocked, or it has become tangled up in some other emotional turmoil the pet owner is experiencing. This can happen for many reasons. In some instances, the pet has been beloved by the entire family and it falls to one person to "be strong" and shoulder the comfort and consolation of other family members. When this happens, the consoler sometimes does not have a chance to mourn.

Jamie Quackenbush (1984) reports instances where several pet owners' responses to the death of their pet were especially intense. In some cases, the pet owner had experienced the death of someone close to him within the past two years of the pet's death. In other cases, the owner himself, or someone close to him, is experiencing the same illness that caused the pet's death (heart disease, diabetes, or cancer, for example). People who had looked upon their pets as genuine child substitutes experienced very deep grief reactions. In other instances, the owner and pet had shared significant events in the owner's life— the pet had been an anniversary gift (this was the case with the author's bird, Maury), the pet had been a close companion through an illness or divorce experienced by the owner, or the pet had been an especial favorite of a deceased spouse or child. The loss of a pet by an elderly person can be terribly painful if the owner has led a socially isolated life.

There are many circumstances surrounding a pet's death and its intrinsic meaning that can intensify and heighten the mourning process and prolong it past reasonable length. How, then, does one determine if one's grief has passed reasonable limits, especially if no one really knows how long grief could or should last? It is probably safe to say that if *acute* grief is still being experienced six weeks to two months after the pet's death, there may be some difficulty that needs to be addressed. If such a period of time has elapsed and *you* are beginning to question the freshness and intensity of grief, this is a strong indication that help in getting through the process should be sought.

Such prolonged grief reactions may include chronic loss of appetite, difficulty functioning at work or home, chronic insomnia, aches and pains (including difficulty breathing, chest pains, intestinal cramping, and diarrhea), accident-proneness, forgetfulness, chronic tiredness, panicky feelings, withdrawal from people, lack of interest in things that have always given pleasure, and intense feelings of grief and loneliness whenever reminded of the lost pet.

If such difficulties are plaguing you even months after the death of your pet, you should seek help from your physician, religious adviser, or a mental health counselor. Your veterinarian may be aware of programs or services in your area designed to help the grieving pet owner. Do not be ashamed or afraid to seek such help. Just as the human body sometimes needs medical assistance to recover from illness, the mind sometimes needs the wise counsel and support of a trained counselor in order to recover peace. You have a right to be free of grief and achieve serenity and acceptance. Seek whatever assistance you need to obtain this for yourself. People are not meant to live in perpetual mourning, but to turn eventually to light and life, to the condition in which they are once more able to give and receive love and happiness. Every effort you make to secure this state for yourself will be well worth it. You have only to make the decision to reach out. You will be comforted and reassured to find that there are many who will hear and help you in the ways you most need help.

WHEN A CHILD GRIEVES

Helping a child deal with the sorrow he or she feels when a pet dies is a task that most parents face at one time or another. If one is grieving oneself, it can be very hard to give the support and help the child needs. A conscious effort must be made to do this, however. For the way the child learns to handle the fact of death and grief will in large part be predicated upon how you, the parent, show the child how to cope with it.

It is necessary to understand that at various ages children view death in different ways. This has a major impact on what the parent should say to the child. To include a lengthy discussion of what to tell a child about the death of a pet, based upon the various stages of development, is beyond the scope of this book. However, no better advice can be had than that contained in Herbert Nieburg and Arlene Fischer's *Pet Loss: A Thoughtful Guide for Adults and Children* (1982). The author earnestly hopes that parents in every home possessing young children and pets will avail themselves of this book. The book's information will be of immense help to the parent in handling the situation in an honest, open, and supportive way. If parents are able to avail themselves of this information before it becomes necessary, a difficult situation will be made much less stressful for the entire family.

This perhaps may seem to be an unusual topic to include in a book which deals almost exclusively with objective material relating to the keeping of parrots. It is not, however, an inappropriate topic for a chapter dealing with the death of one's birds and the grief that follows. It is probably safe to assume that when some people lose a beloved animal companion, they hope in their hearts that their pets will experience an afterlife, free of pain and death, and full of happiness. It is hard to believe that the love, loyalty, intelligence, and beauty encompassed in the creature who was our friend will be forever obliterated by that event we call "death" in all its stark finality.

It may interest the reader to learn that some of our very notable church fathers, from the early days of Christianity up to modern times, have held that there is the possibility of an afterlife for our animal companions. The reader referred to *Animals and Christianity*, edited by Andrew Linzey and Tom Regan, published by Crossroad Publishing Company in 1988. This book provides a very full discussion of the topic for those who wish to investigate it further.

Whatever the readers's religious/theological beliefs, it is important to know that shared love is tremendously creative. It matters not whether it was shared with an animal or another person. It widens and spreads from its source, just as ripples on a pond. It never ceases to exist, but touches many lives in many ways, whether those lives be human or animal, and with results of which we often will never be aware. The far-reaching quality of love is almost incomprehensible, and as such, achieves a measure of immortality for itself by the sheer fact of its existence.

A Prayer for Animals

Hear our humble prayer, O God, for our friends, the
animals, especially for animals who are suffering;
for any that are hunted or lost or deserted or
frightened or hungry; for all that must be put to
death. We entreat for them Thy mercy and pity, and
for those who deal with them we ask a heart of
compassion, and gentle hands and kindly words. Make
us ourselves to be true friends to animals and so to
share the blessings of the merciful.

Albert Schweitzer

A magnificent Green-wing Macaw (*Ara chloroptera*)
Photo courtesy Richard Schubot, Avicultural Breeding and Research Center

APPENDIX I

Medications

Acyclovir (Zovirax): Used to treat certain *Herpesvirus* infections. It interferes with the synthesis of the virus's DNA. It can be applied topically in ointment form, orally, or intravenously.

Aerrane: See Isoflurane.

Allopurinol (Zyloprim): Used to treat gout. Its action inhibits uric acid production. It is given orally, usually in the drinking water.

Amphotericin-B (Fungazone): An antifungal antibiotic used to treat fungal infections that do not respond to other antifungal drugs, especially *Aspergillus*. It may be applied topically as a lotion, creme, or ointment. It may also be given intravenously, injected directly into the trachea, or delivered to the respiratory tract via nebulization. This drug can cause bone marrow and kidney toxicity.

Amprol: See Amprolium.

Amprolium (Amprol, Corid): Used, in combination with other drugs, to treat *Coccidia*. It is administered in the drinking water.

Ancobon: See Flucytosine.

Aralen Phosphate: See Chloroquine.

Atabrine: See Quinacrine.

Calphosan: Injectable form of calcium used to treat convulsions due to low serum calcium level. Also used as a dietary supplement during egg laying, periods of rapid growth, or bone healing. May also be used in the treatment of egg binding and soft-shelled eggs.

Chloroquine (Aralen Phosphate): Used to treat avian malaria. It acts to destroy *Plasmodium* in the red blood cells. It is administered orally.

Clopidol (Coyden): Used to treat *Coccidia*.

Corid: See Amprolium.

Coyden: See Clopidol.

D-Ca-Phos: A balanced vitamin D_3-calcium-phosphorus nutritional supplement.

Depo-Provera: See Progesterone.

Diazepam (Valium): Used to treat convulsions. Its action is to relax skeletal muscle. It can be given intravenously or intramuscularly.

Dimetridazole (Emtryl): Used to treat giardiasis and trichomoniasis. It should not be used when birds are breeding, as males feeding hens in the nest may consume enough to reach toxic levels. The drug is administered in the drinking water. Prolonged use may result in toxicity or development of candidiasis.

Droncit: See Pranziquantel.

Emtryl: See Dimetridazole.

Ethambutol (Myambutol): Used to treat avian tuberculosis. It acts to suppress the growth of the tuberculosis organism. The drug is given orally.

Ether: An inhalant anesthetic agent no longer in use due to its inflammatory and explosive qualities at concentrations needed to induce anesthesia.

Ferric Subsulfate: Used as a coagulant to stop bleeding. Available in liquid and powder forms.

Flagyl: See Metronidazole.

Flucytosine (Ancoban): Used to treat aspergillosis. Its action is to inhibit certain biochemical reactions necessary to the life of the fungus cell, thereby killing it. It can be toxic to the bone marrow. It is administered orally.

Fluothane: See Halothane.

Fungazone: See Amphotericin-B.

Halothane (Fluothane): An inhalant anesthetic. It gives moderately good muscle relaxation but has the potential for kidney and liver damage.

Injacom: An injectable preparation of vitamins A, D_3, and E used to treat vitamin A deficiency, to promote bone healing, and in the treatment of egg binding, soft-shelled eggs, and soft bones.

[131]Iodine (Iodotope Therapeutic): The radioactive form of iodine, used to treat hyperthyroidism, and in the diagnosis of thyroid disorders. It is administered orally.

Iodotope Therapeutic: See [131]Iodine.

Ipronidazole (Ipropran): A medication used to treat giardiasis and trichomoniasis. It is administered in the drinking water.

Ipropran: See Ipronidazole.

Isoflurane (Aerrane): An inhalant anesthetic agent, rapidly becoming the anesthetic of choice for avian anesthetic procedures due to its safety, effectiveness, and rapid recovery period.

Isoniazid: Used to treat avian tuberculosis. It is bacteriostatic for bacilli that are not growing, and bacteriocidal for bacilli that are dividing rapidly. It is given orally.

Ivermectin (Ivomec): A medication used to treat intestinal roundworms, *Coccidia*, gapeworms (*Syngamus*), and *Knemidocoptes* infestations. It is administered orally or as an injection.

Ivomec: See Ivermectin.

Ketamine (Vetalar): A nonbarbiturate anesthetic that produces immobility without analgesia. It can be given intramuscularly or intravenously.

Ketoconazole (Nizoral): An antifungal medication used in severe candidiasis that is unresponsive to other drugs. It is given orally.

Lactated Ringer's Solution: A solution composed of sterile water, sodium, calcium, potassium, chloride, and bicarbonate. These components are in the same amounts and proportions as found in the blood. The solution is used intravenously to treat problems such as shock and dehydration.

Lactobacillus: A preparation of nonpathogenic Gram-negative bacteria that promotes the reestablishment of normal bacterial flora in the gut, without which digestion of food and absorption of nutrients cannot occur. It is given orally.

Levamisole (Ripercol-L): Used to treat intestinal roundworms. Also used to stimulate depressed immune systems. When used for this purpose, it seems to restore certain immune mechanisms in white blood cells. It also stimulates the production of T-lymphocytes. It may be given in the drinking water or administered via feeding tube. It can also be given as an injection.

Lincocin: See Lincomycin.

Lincomycin (Lincocin): An antibiotic that is effective mainly against Gram-positive bacteria, thus limiting its usefulness in parrot species, in which bacterial infections are usually of the Gram-negative variety. It is administered orally.

Lugol's Solution: An iodine solution used to treat certain thyroid conditions such as goiter. It is added to the drinking water.

Methoxyflurane (Metofane): An inhalant anethetic that gives excellent muscle relaxation, but has the potential for liver damage and causes prolonged depressed body temperature.

Metofane: See Methoxyflurane.

Metronidazole (Flagyl): Used to treat giardiasis and trichomoniasis. It is given orally.

Mintezol: See Thiabendazole.

Myambutol: See Ethambutol.

Mycostatin: See Nystatin.

Neocalglucon: An oral preparation of calcium used as a dietary calcium supplement. It is administered in the drinking water.

Niclosamide (Yomesan): Used to treat tapeworms. It is administered orally.

Nitrofurazone: A highly effective antibiotic used to treat Gram-negative bacteria, especially *E. coli* gut infections. It is given in the drinking water.

Nizoral: See Ketoconazole.

Nystatin (Mycostatin): An antibiotic used to treat candidiasis. It is also used as a preventative for this disease in hand-fed baby birds being treated with other antibiotics, or in adult birds on long-term antibiotic therapy, especially of the tetracycline family. It is administered orally.

Oxytocin: A hormone used to aid egg expulsion in egg-bound hens. It acts to stimulate both the frequency and force of smooth muscle contractions in the oviduct. It is given as an injection.

Pranziquantel (Droncit): Used to treat tapeworms. It works in two ways: (1) it causes increased muscular activity in the intestine, causing the worms to lose their grip on host tissue; (2) it destroys the skin of the tapeworm, making it susceptible to host immune mechanisms and destruction. It can be given in the feed, by tube, or as an injection.

Primaquine: Used to treat avian malaria. It is primarily useful in killing the malarial protozoa lodged in body tissues such as the liver, rather than those in the red blood cells. For this reason, it is almost always used in conjunction with an antimalarial drug such as chloroquine, which is effective against the protozoa residing in the red blood cells. It is given orally.

Progesterone (Depo-Provera): A hormone used to inhibit ovulation in hens with chronic egg-laying problems. It is given as an injection.

Proguanil: Used to treat avian malaria. It is given intramuscularly.

Propylthiouracil: Used to treat hyperthyroidism. It acts to inhibit the formation of thyroid hormones. It is administered orally.

Quinacrine (Atabrine): Used to treat avian malaria. It is given orally, usually via feeding tube.

Rifadin: See Rifampin.

Rifampin (Rifadin, Rimactene): Used to treat avian tuberculosis. It inhibits the growth of the tuberculosis organism and enhances the effectiveness of isoniazid, with which it is used in combination. It is given orally.

Rimactene: See Rifampin.

Ripercol-L: See Levamisole.

Rompun: See Xylazine.

Spiramycin: An antibiotic sometimes used to treat botulism.

Thiabendazole (Mintezol): Used to treat ascarid roundworm infestation of the gut, also to treat gapeworm (*Syngamus*). It is given orally.

Valium: See Diazepam.

Vetalar: See Ketamine.

Xylazine (Rompun): An analgesic and sedative used in combination with ketamine to produce anesthesia. This combination is administered intravenously or intramuscularly.

Yomesan: See Niclosamide.

Zovirax: See Acyclovir.

Zyloprim: See Allopurinol.

APPENDIX II

Disinfectants

Betadine: An iodine preparation of the iodophor or "tamed iodine" group. It is effective against some viruses, fungi, and bacteria. It is not effective against all microbes. It is ineffective against *Mycobacterium tuberculosis*. It must be used at full strength to kill organisms that are sensitive to it, which makes it expensive.

Clorox: A sodium hypochlorite solution. As a common household bleach, it is available and inexpensive. It is very effective against bacteria, fungi, viruses, and protozoa. It is ineffective against *Mycobacterium tuberculosis*. It is caustic to the skin and respiratory tract.

Formalin: A 50 percent solution of formaldehyde and water. It is effective against *Mycobacterium tuberculosis*, bacteria, many viruses (single-stranded RNA types), and fungi. It is slow acting (may require several hours or even days to accomplish its germicidal action). It can cause skin and tissue irritation. It is also thought to be carcinogenic. It must be obtained with a veterinary prescription from your veterinarian or pharmacist.

Lysol: A phenol disinfectant. It is effective against many bacteria, including *Staphylococcus*, *Pseudomonas*, and *Mycobacterium tuberculosis*. It is also effective against enveloped viruses. (An *enveloped virus* is one that is wrapped in a protein coat. Such viruses include *Poxvirus*, *Herpesvirus* [Pacheco's disease, Amazon tracheitis], *Coronavirus*, *paramyxovirus* [PMV I causes Newcastle disease]. These viruses do not survive well outside their hosts and are easily killed by disinfectants, especially those having detergent action.) It is ineffective against nonenveloped viruses and will not kill all bacteria. (*Nonenveloped viruses* are those lacking a protein "wrap." They are much more difficult to kill with most standard disinfectants than enveloped viruses. This group includes *Parvovirus*, *Papillomavirus*, *Polyomavirus*, *Reovirus*, and *Adenovirus*.) It is caustic to living tissue in concentrated form, toxic to cats, and may have some potential carcinogenic effects.

Nolvasan: Also known as chlorhexadine. It is effective against fungi, including *Candida* and *Aspergillus*. It is also effective against some bacteria and enveloped viruses (including the causative agent for Newcastle disease). It is ineffective against many Gram-positive and some Gram-negative bacteria, including *Pseudomonas*. It will not kill nonenveloped viruses. Nolvasan may have potential carcinogenic effects.

One-Stroke-Environ: A phenol disinfectant. See the Lysol entry for a discussion of advantages and disadvantages.

Roccal-D: A disinfectant of the quaternary ammonium compound group, or "quat." It is effective against Gram-positive and Gram-negative bacteria, and *Chlamydia psittaci*. It is ineffective against fungi and nonenveloped viruses. It is incompatible with soap and is neutralized by it. It is toxic to birds if swallowed by them.

Wavecide-01: A disinfectant of the glutaraldehyde group. It is effective against virtually 100 percent of all microbes: all viruses, bacteria, fungi, and protozoa. Its disadvantage consists chiefly in skin damage, which may result from prolonged contact with the product.

Glossary

Acute: Sharp or severe; having a rapid onset, severe symptoms, and a short course.

Adsorb: To attract and retain other material on the surface.

Aerosol: A system in which solid or liquid particles are suspended in air or other gas.

Allo-feeding: Mutual feeding behavior.

Allo-preening: Mutual preening behavior.

Ambient: Surrounding, as in the surrounding or "ambient" air temperature.

Amino acid: Any one of a large group of compounds containing the amino (NH_2) and carboxyl group (COOH). They occur naturally in plant and animal tissue and are the "building blocks" of various proteins.

Analgesic: (1) A drug that relieves pain; (2) having the properties of pain relief.

Anemia: A decrease in the number of circulating red blood cells, a decrease below normal in the amount of hemoglobin in each red blood cell, or a combination of both conditions.

Antibiotic: A chemical substance, either natural or synthetic, that has the ability to kill microorganisms (biocidal activity) or inhibit their growth (biostatic activity).

Antibody: A specialized protein contained in the blood serum and formed by a certain type of white blood cell (the B-lymphocyte) in response to an antigen to which an animal has been exposed. The antibody destroys or inactivates certain foreign substances that have gained access to the body, especially microbes and their products.

Antigen: A substance that, when introduced into the body, causes the production of antibodies. Antigens may be substances such as foreign protein, toxins, bacteria, or tissue cells.

Aspirate: (1) To withdraw fluid by means of suction (negative pressure), as in the withdrawal of a blood sample with a syringe and needle; (2) to inhale, especially with regard to the sucking of foreign substances such as vomitus, into the lungs.

Asymptomatic: Showing no symptoms.

Autogenous vaccine: A suspension made from material obtained from the lesions of the animal to be vaccinated, and used for the prevention, amelioration, or treatment of a specific infectious disease.

Bacteriocidal: Having the capacity to kill bacteria.

Bacteriostatic: Having the capacity to halt the growth of bacteria, but without killing them.

Broad-spectrum antibiotic: An antibiotic effective against a large array of microorganisms.

Caseous: Resembling a dry, cheesy material, which is one of the forms of tissue death (necrosis).

CBC: See Complete blood count.

Cellulitis: A diffuse inflammation of solid tissue. Signs include redness, swelling, pain, and loss of function in the affected area.

Choana: The slit in the hard palate of a bird's mouth, connecting the nasal passages with the oral cavity.

Chronic: Designating a disease of long duration, showing slow progression of symptoms.

Cloaca: The lowermost portion of a bird's intestine, into which are emptied urine, feces, and reproductive products (eggs, semen).

Collagen: A fibrous, insoluble protein that forms part of the supportive framework of the skin, bone, ligaments, cartilage, and tendons. It is also found in the vitreous humor of the eye as a stiffening agent.

Commensal: Living on or within another organism and deriving benefit from that organism without harming it.

Compensation: Making up for or counterbalancing any defect of function or structure.

Complete blood count (CBC): A microscopic examination of the blood that includes counts of red and white blood cells, and a report of the relative numbers of specific types of white blood cells.

Corticosteroid: Any of the hormones produced by the cortex (outer layer) of the adrenal glands. These substances may also be produced synthetically. Their action is generally to allow many biochemical reactions to proceed at optimum rates.

Culture: The propagation of microorganisms or living tissue cells in special media conducive to their growth.

Cyanosis: A bluish, grayish, slatelike, or dark purple discoloration of skin and/or mucous membranes. It is caused by a deficiency of oxygen and an excess of carbon dioxide in the blood, as in heart problems, obstruction of the airways, or overdoses of certain drugs.

Cytoplasm: The thick, viscous substance that surrounds the nucleus of a cell. It constitutes the physical basis of all living activities in the body.

Decompensation: Failure of the body to make up for defects of function or structure.

Diabetes insipidus: Disease in which excessive water is excreted in the urine, due to failure of the renal tubes to reabsorb water.

Diarrhea: The rapid movement of fecal matter through the intestine, resulting in poor absorption of water, nutritive elements, electrolytes, and producing frequent, loose bowel movements.

Dysfunction: Abnormal, inadequate, or impaired function of an organ.

Ectoparasite: A parasite living on the surface of its host's body.

Electrocardiography: A graphic recording of the electrical activity of the heart, allowing the action of the heart muscle to be studied.

Electrolyte: A substance that, in solution, conducts electric current and is decomposed by the passage of an electric current. The most important positively charged ions in body fluids are sodium (Na^+), potassium (K^+), calcium (Ca^{2+}), and magnesium (Mg^{2+}). The most important negatively charged particles in body fluids are chloride (Cl^-), bicarbonate (HCO_3^-), and phosphate (PO^{3-}). The concentration gradients of sodium and potassium across the cell membrane produce the membrane potential and provide the means by which electrochemical impulses are transmitted in nerve and muscle fibers.

Endocrine gland: A ductless gland that produces an internal secretion that is discharged directly into the blood or lymph and circulated to all parts of the body.

Endoparasite: A parasite that lives within the body of its host.

Endotoxin: Bacterial toxin confined within the body of a bacterium and freed only when the bacterium disintegrates.

Epidemiology: The study of the relationship of various factors determining the frequency and distribution of diseases in a community of organisms (people, animals, or plants).

Etiology: The origin and cause of a disease.

Exotoxin: A toxin produced by a microorganism and excreted into its surrounding medium.

Extracellular: Situated or occurring outside of a cell or group of cells.

Exudate: Accumulation of fluid, protein, and cellular debris in a cavity; matter that penetrates through vessel walls into adjoining tissue; or the production of pus or serum.

Fecal flotation: A microscopic test in which an animal's feces are examined for the presence of intestinal parasite eggs. Feces are mixed with a chemical solution, spun in a centrifuge, and the fluid lying above the feces at the bottom of the test tube is drawn off, stained, and examined under the microscope.

Feces: The solid body waste discharged from the intestines.

Fibroblast: An immature fiber-producing cell that is capable of differentiating into a cell that can produce collagen, bone, or cartilage.

Flora, intestinal: The bacteria normally residing within the intestine.

Fomite: An inanimate object or material on which disease-producing agents may be conveyed (for example, food bowls or perches).

Gamete: One of two cells, male (spermatozoan) or female (ovum), whose union is necessary in sexual reproduction to initiate the development of a new individual.

Gametocyte: (1) a cell that produces gametes; (2) a stage of the malaria protozoan that reproduces in the blood of the *Anopheles* mosquito.

Gastroenteritis: Inflammation of the lining of the stomach and intestinal tract, the symptoms of which include vomiting and diarrhea.

Glucose: A simple sugar (monosaccharide) in certain foodstuffs, especially fruit, and also found in the blood. It is the major source of energy for most living organisms.

Gram stain: Method of differential staining of bacteria, devised by Hans C. J. Gram, a Danish physician (1853–1938). It is of importance in the identification of bacteria. Gram-positive bacteria stain violet; Gram-negative bacteria stain red or pink.

Granuloma: A tumorlike mass or nodule consisting of actively growing capillary buds, fibroblasts, and several types of white blood cells. A granuloma may be caused by a chronic inflammatory process associated with infectious disease, by invasion by a foreign body, or by the healing process of a large, gaping wound.

Hematology: The science dealing with the structure of blood and blood-forming tissues (such as bone marrow), and with their function in sickness and health.

Hematopoiesis: The production of red and white blood cells and platelets (thrombocytes, in avian species), occurring primarily in the bone marrow.

Hemolysis: The rupture of red blood cells, causing the hemoglobin contained in them to be released into the blood plasma.

Hepatotoxicity: Poisonous to the liver.

Histopathology: The study of disease effects upon the individual cell, or a group of cells.

Hydrogen ion concentration: The relative proportion of hydrogen ions in a solution, the factor responsible for the acidic properties of a solution.

Hypothermia: Abnormally low body temperature.

Immune system: That group of lymphatic tissues that are involved in lymphocyte production, immune responses, or both. Such tissues include the thymus, bursa of Fabricius, lymphatic nodules and nodes, and the spleen.

Immunity: State of being immune, or protected, from a disease, especially an infectious disease. Usually induced as a result of having been exposed to antigenic substances peculiar to the disease, while infected; or by having been immunized with a vaccine that has the capacity to stimulate the production of specific antibodies.

Incised: Having been cut with a sharp instrument such as a scalpel.

318

Incubation: (1) The provision of proper conditions for growth and development, as for bacterial or tissue cultures; (2) the development of an infectious disease, from time of entry of the pathogen to appearance of the first clinical signs; (3) the period of time required for a fertilized egg to develop and hatch.

Index case: The initial individual whose condition or disease led to an investigation of a disease outbreak or hereditary condition.

Intracellular: Within a cell or group of cells.

Ion: An atom or group of atoms that have lost or gained electrons and thus have acquired an electric charge. A cation is an ion that carries a positive charge. An anion is an ion carrying a negative charge.

Keratin: An extremely tough protein substance contained in feathers, beak, nails, hair (in mammals), or other horny body parts. It is insoluble in water, weak acids, or alkalis, and unaffected by most protein-dissolving enzymes.

Leukocytosis (Leucocytosis): An increase in the number of white blood cells.

Leukopenia (Leucopenia): A decreased number of white blood cells.

Lumen: The cavity or channel within a tube or a tubular organ, as in a blood vessel or intestine.

Malaise: Discomfort, uneasiness, or indisposition, often indicative of an infection.

Media (plural form of "medium"): The materials used on which microorganisms are cultured.

Metabolism: The sum of physical and chemical changes by which a living organism is built up and maintained (anabolism), and by which large molecules are broken down into smaller molecules to make energy available to the organism (catabolism).

Microbe: A microorganism, especially one that causes disease.

Microorganism: A microscopic organism such as bacteria, fungi, protozoa, and viruses.

Microsurgery: The repair of minute structures with the aid of a microscope and very small instruments.

Mitotic: Pertaining to "mitosis," the type of cell division in which each daughter cell contains the same number of chromosomes as the parent cell. It is the process by which the body grows and cells (other than reproductive cells) are replaced.

Mollicute: The classification of those microorganisms that are the smallest capable of reproducing in a cell-free media (as opposed to viruses, which can *only* be propagated in living cell cultures). This classification includes *Mycoplasma*, *Acholeplasma*, and *Ureaplasma*.

Neonate: A newborn. In the parrot species, this state probably lasts, for all practical purposes, until the bird has opened its eyes and begins to quill out.

Neoplasm: Any new and abnormal growth. A neoplasm may be benign or malignant.

Nucleus: The spherical body within the cell, surrounded by a membrane, and containing the chromosomes.

Oocyte: The type of gametocyte that produces ova (eggs).

Opisthotonos: A form of spasm in which the head and tail (or heels) are bent backward and the body bowed forward. It can be seen in some types of poisoning (such as strychnine), in certain infectious diseases such as tetanus, in infections of the central nervous system, and in some types of brain lesions.

Organic matter: Animal or vegetable tissues.

Packed cell volume (PCV): The percentage of the volume of whole, unclotted blood occupied by red blood cells.

Parasitemia: The presence of parasites in the blood.

Parenteral: Administered by subcutaneous, intramuscular, or intravenous injection, as opposed to administration by mouth.

Pathogen: A disease-producing agent or microorganism.

Pathology: (1) The study of the nature and cause of disease, which involves changes in structure and function; (2) condition produced by disease.

PCV: See Packed cell volume.

Peracute: Extremely acute, of only a few hours duration.

Plasma: The fluid portion of the blood in which the red and white blood cells are suspended, as well as the thrombocytes. Not to be confused with serum, which is plasma from which the red and white blood cells have been removed, as well as the fibrinogen (a protein involved in blood clotting).

Polycythemia: An abnormally high number of red blood cells.

Polyuria: The formation and excretion of abnormally high volumes of urine.

Portal circulation: The circulation of blood from the digestive tract and spleen to the liver via the portal vein and, subsequently, out of the liver via the hepatic vein.

Precursor: In biological processes, a substance from which another, usually more active or mature substance is formed.

Prosthesis: An artificial substitute for a missing body part.

Protozoa (plural form of "protozoan"): The simplest of all animals, usually having only one cell, though there are species that live in colonies. Reproduction is usually by fission, although sexual reproduction may occur in certain species. Most are free living, but some species may be commensalistic or parasitic.

Psittacine: Pertaining to members of the parrot family.

Psittacosis titer: A test for the presence of *Chlamydia psittaci* (which causes psittacosis) by diluting the suspect's serum in ever-decreasing amounts with a standard solution containing *Chl. psittaci* antigen. When even a very small amount of serum reacts with the standard solution, this is strong evidence that the bird has experienced *Chl. psittaci* at some time in its life. Two tests made three weeks apart, and showing a fourfold increase in titer, indicates active disease.

Radiograph: An X ray.

Reabsorption: The process of absorbing again.

Resorption: To take up, or absorb again.

Saline: A solution of salt (sodium chloride) in sterile water. A physiologic solution of 0.9 percent salt and water contains the same proportions of these components as does the blood.

Septicemia: Presence of pathogenic bacteria in the blood. If allowed to progress, they may multiply and overwhelm the body, resulting in death.

Sequelae (plural form of "sequela"): Conditions following and resulting from a disease.

Serum: The watery portion of the blood that results when the blood has been allowed to clot, the clot then being removed.

Spermatocyte: The type of gametocyte that produces sperm.

Sputum: Mucous secretion from lungs, trachea, and bronchi.

Stain: A pigment or dye used to color tissue for purposes of elucidating cellular structures and aiding identification, using the microscope.

Subclinical: Without symptoms, said of the early stages of disease, or a very mild form of the disease.

Subcutaneous: Beneath the layers of the skin.

Torticollis: A stiff neck caused by spasmodic contraction of the muscles drawing the head to one side, with the chin pointing to the other side. Also called wryneck.

Toxin: A poisonous substance of plant or animal origin.

Ureter: The tube that carries urine from the kidney to the cloaca.

Vaccine: A suspension of infectious agents, either killed or attenuated (weakened), given for the purpose of establishing resistance or immunity to an infectious disease.

Virulence: The competence of any infectious agent to produce disease, and the degree of bodily damage it is capable of producing.

Visceral: Pertaining to any interior organ in any of the great body cavities, especially those in the abdomen.

An adult female Eclectus parrot. Compare this bird with the male of the same species shown on page vi.

Photo courtesy Richard Schubot, Avicultural Breeding and Research Center

Bibliography

Alderton, David. "Psittacosis: A New Perspective," *Parrot-World* 5:5 (March/April 1988).

Altman, Robert B. "Principles of Electrosurgery and Specific Surgical Techniques," in *Proceedings of the First International Conference on Zoological and Avian Medicine*, sponsored by the Association of Avian Veterinarians and the American Association of Zoo Veterinarians, 1987.

———. "Blood Transfusions," in *Proceedings for Seminar #10—Avian Surgery: 13th Annual Veterinary Surgical Forum*, sponsored by the American College of Veterinary Surgeons, 1985a.

———. "Surgery of the Integument, Beak, and Feet," in *Proceedings for Seminar #10—Avian Surgery: 13th Annual Veterinary Surgical Forum*, sponsored by the American College of Veterinary Surgeons, 1985b.

———. "Ocular Surgery," in *Proceedings for Seminar #9—Avian Medicine and Surgery: 12th Annual Veterinary Surgical Forum*, sponsored by the American College of Veterinary Surgeons, 1984.

———. "Disorders of the Skeletal System," in *Diseases of Cage and Aviary Birds*, ed. Margaret L. Petrak. Philadelphia: Lea and Febiger, 1982.

American Medical Association Handbook of Poisonous and Injurious Plants, Chicago: American Medical Association, 1985.

Arnall, Leslie, and Margaret L. Petrak. "Diseases of the Respiratory System" in *Diseases of Cage and Aviary Birds*, 2nd ed., ed. Margaret L. Petrak. Philadelphia: Lea and Febiger, 1982.

Avian Disease Manual, 2nd ed. Philadelphia: American Association of Avian Pathologists, 1983.

Avian Histopathology. Philadelphia: American Association of Avian Pathologists, 1987.

Axelson, R. Dean. *Caring for Your Pet Bird*. Poole-Dorset, England: Blandford Press, 1984.

Barnes, J. John. "Parasites," in *Clinical Avian Medicine and Surgery*, ed. Greg J. Harrison and Linda R. Harrison. Philadelphia: W. B. Saunders, 1986.

Bauck, Louise. "Lymphosarcoma Avian Leukosis in Pet Birds," in *Proceedings of the Annual Meeting of the Association of Avian Veterinarians*, 1986.

―――. "Pituitary Neoplastic Disease in Nine Budgies," in *Proceedings of the First International Conference of Zoological and Avian Medicine*, sponsored by The Association of Avian Veterinarians and the American Association of Zoo Veterinarians, 1987.

Belden, Marion. "Back Talk: More About Cookie," *Bird Talk* 2:3 (March 1989).

Bennett, Gordon F. "Hematozoa," in *Companion Bird Medicine*, ed. Elisha W. Burr. Ames: Iowa State University Press, 1987.

Benzo, E. A. "Nervous System," in *Avian Physiology*, 4th ed., ed. P. D. Sturkie. New York: Springer-Verlag, 1986.

Blackmore, David K. "Diseases of the Endocrine System," in *Diseases of Cage and Aviary Birds*, 2nd ed., ed. Margaret L. Petrak. Philadelphia: Lea and Febiger, 1982.

Blass, Charles E. "Orthopedics," in *Companion Bird Medicine*, ed. Elisha W. Burr. Ames: Iowa State University Press, 1987.

Blood, D. C., and Virginia P. Studdert. *Bailliere's Comprehensive Veterinary Dictionary*. London: Bailliere Tindall, 1988.

Brugère-Picoux, Jeanne, and Henri Brugère. "Metabolic Diseases," in *Companion Bird Medicine*, ed. Elisha W. Burr. Ames: Iowa State University Press, 1987.

Burr, Elisha W. "Digestive Tract Protozoa," in *Companion Bird Medicine*, ed. Elisha W. Burr. Ames: Iowa State University Press, 1987.

Butler, Raymond. "Toxic Conditions," in *Companion Bird Medicine*, ed. Elisha W. Burr. Ames: Iowa State University Press, 1987.

Campbell, Terry W. *Avian Hematology and Cytology*. Ames: Iowa State University Press, 1988.

―――. "Avian Chemistries," *AAV Today* 1:3 (Summer 1987).

―――. "Mycotic Diseases," in *Clinical Avian Medicine and Surgery*, ed. Greg J. Harrison and Linda R. Harrison. Philadelphia: W. B. Saunders, 1986a.

―――. "Mycotoxicosis: A Potential Threat to Captive Birds," in *Proceedings of the Annual Meeting of the Association of Avian Veterinarians*, 1986b.

―――. "Neoplasia," in *Avian Clinical Medicine and Surgery*, ed. Greg J. Harrison and Linda R. Harrison. Philadelphia: W. B. Saunders, 1986c.

Cavill, John P. "Viral Diseases," in *Diseases of Cage and Aviary Birds*, 2nd ed., ed. Margaret L. Petrak. Philadelphia: Lea & Febiger, 1982.

Clark, Carl H. "Pharmacology of Antibiotics," in *Clinical Avian Medicine and Surgery*, ed. Greg J. Harrison and Linda R. Harrison. Philadelphia: W. B. Saunders, 1986.

Clipsham, Robert. "Preventive Health Care for Aviculture: Disinfection and Sanitation," *AFA Watchbird* 15:5 (October/November 1988a).

―――. "Preventing Egg-Binding, Part II," *Bird Talk* 6:5 (May 1988b).

―――. "Psittacosis Update," *AFA Watchbird* 15:2 (April/May 1988c).

―――. "*Caring for an Egg-Bound Hen*," *Bird Talk* 6:4 (April 1988d).

―――. "Avian Anesthesia," *Bird World* (January 1988e).

―――. "Drugs: Theory and Use in Avian Trade," *AFA Watchbird* 14:5 (October/November 1987).

Clubb, Susan L. "An Acute Fatal Illness in Old World Psittacine Birds Associated with Sarcocystic Falcatula of Opossums," in *Proceedings of the Annual Meeting of the AAV*, 1986a.

———. "Sex Determination Techniques," in *Clinical Avian Medicine and Surgery*, ed. Greg J. Harrison and Linda R. Harrison. Philadelphia: W. B. Saunders, 1986b.

———. "Therapeutics: Flock and Individual Treatment Regimens," in *Clinical Avian Medicine and Surgery*, ed. Greg J. Harrison and Linda R. Harrison. Philadelphia: W. B. Saunders, 1986c.

———. "A Multifactorial Disease Syndrome in African Grey Parrots Imported from Ghana," in *Proceedings of the International Conference on Avian Medicine*, sponsored by the Association of Avian Veterinarians, 1984.

———. "Fungal Diseases," address to American Federation of Aviculture Convention, 1983a; Lion Recording Services, 1905 Fairview Avenue N.E., Washington, DC 20002.

———. "Parrot/Avian First Aid," audiotape of speech to American Federation of Aviculture Convention, 1983b; Lion Recording Services, 1905 Fairview Avenue N.E., Washington, DC 20002.

Clubb, Susan, and R. B. Davis. "Outbreak of a Papova-like Viral Infection in a Psittacine Nursery—A Retrospective View," in *Proceedings of the International Conference on Avian Medicine*, sponsored by the Association of Avian Veterinarians, 1984.

Courter, Gay. *The Bean Sprout Book*. New York: Simon and Schuster, 1972.

Cribb, Peter H. "Cloacal Papilloma in an Amazon Parrot," in *Proceedings of the International Conference on Avian Medicine*, sponsored by the Association of Avian Veterinarians, 1984.

Daft, Barbara M.; Leland C. Grumbles; James E. Pearson; Thomas E. Vice; and James E. Grimes. *A Manual of Methods for the Laboratory Diagnosis of Avian Chlamydiosis*. Philadelphia: American Association of Avian Pathologists, 1986.

Davis, Christine. "Avian Housing and Health Care," audio-cassette, produced by Christine Davis, P.O. Box 816, Westminster, CA 92684.

Doyle, James E. "Introduction to Microsurgery," in *Clinical Avian Medicine and Surgery*, ed. Greg J. Harrison and Linda R. Harrison. Philadelphia: W. B. Saunders, 1986.

Eamons, Graeme J., and Garry M. J. Cross. "Chamydiosis," in *Companion Bird Medicine*, ed. Elisha Burr. Ames: Iowa State University Press, 1987.

Evans, Richard H., and Daniel P. Carey. "Zoonotic Diseases," in *Clinical Avian Medicine and Surgery*, ed. Greg J. Harrison and Linda R. Harrison. Philadelphia: W. B. Saunders, 1986.

Fischbach, Frances. *A Manual of Laboratory Diagnostic Tests*, 2nd ed. Philadelphia: J. B. Lippincott, 1984.

Fite, Richard W. "Diagnosis and Control of Leucocytozoonosis in Waterfowl," in *Proceedings of the International Conference on Avian Medicine*, sponsored by the Association of Avian Veterinarians, 1984.

Flammer, Kevin. "Avian Chlamydiosis—Observations on Diagnostic Techniques and Use of Oral Doxycycline for Treatment," in *Proceedings of First International Conference on Zoological and Avian Medicine*, sponsored by the Association of Avian Veterinarians and the American Association of Zoo Veterinarians, 1987.

———. "Aviculture Management," in *Clinical Avian Medicine and Surgery*, ed. Greg J. Harrison and Linda R. Harrison. Philadelphia: W. B. Saunders, 1986.

Forster, Friedereke, and Helga Gerlach. "Mycobacteria in Psittaciformes," in *Proceedings of the First International Conference on Zoological and Avian Medicine*, sponsored by the Association of Avian Veterinarians and the American Association of Zoo Veterinarians, 1987.

Fowler, Murray E. "Velogenic Viscertropic Newcastle Disease," in *Companion Bird Medicine*, ed. Elisha W. Burr. Ames: Iowa State University Press, 1987.

Freud, Arthur. *All About Parrots*. New York: Howell Book House, 1982.

Friedman, Erika; Aaron A. Katcher; Sue A. Thomas; and James J. Lynch. "Health Consequences of Pet Ownership," in *Pet Loss and Human Bereavement*, ed. William J. Kay, Herbert A. Nieburg, Austin H. Kutscher, Ross M. Grey, and Carole E. Fudin. Ames: Iowa State University Press, 1984.

Fudge, Alan M. "Update on Chlamydiosis," in *Veterinary Clinics of North America: Caged Bird Medicine*, ed. Greg J. Harrison. Philadelphia: W. B. Saunders, 1984.

Fudge, Alan M., and Loni McEntee. "Avian Giardiasis: Syndromes, Diagnosis and Therapy," in *Proceedings of the Annual Meeting of the Association of Avian Veterinarians*, 1986.

Fudge, Alan M.; Loni McEntee; and R. E. Schmidt. "Cutaneous and Systemic Tuberculosis in a Grey Cheeked Parakeet (Brotogeris pyrrhopterus)," in *Proceedings of the Annual Meeting of the Association of Avian Veterinarians*, 1986.

Gallerstein, Gary. *Bird Owner's Home Health and Care Handbook*. New York: Howell Book House, 1984.

Gandal, Charles P., rev. Wilbur B. Amand. "Anesthetic and Surgical Techniques," in *Diseases of Cage and Aviary Birds*, ed. Margaret L. Petrak. Philadelphia: Lea and Febiger, 1982.

Gaskin, Jack M. "Avian Reoviruses: Are They for Real?" *AFA Watchbird* 14:6 (December/January 1988).

———. "Considerations in the Diagnosis and Control of Psittacine Viral Infections," in *Proceedings of the First International Conference of Zoological and Avian Medicine*, sponsored by the Association of Avian Veterinarians and the American Association of Zoo Veterinarians, 1987a.

———. "Herpesvirus Infestations," in *Companion Bird Medicine*, ed. Elisha W. Burr. Ames: Iowa State University Press, 1987b.

Gerlach, Helga. "Bacterial Infections," in *Clinical Avian Medicine and Surgery*, ed. Greg J. Harrison and Linda R. Harrison. Philadelphia: W. B. Saunders, 1986a.

———. "Chlamydiosis," in *Clinical Avian Medicine and Surgery*, ed. Greg J. Harrison and Linda R. Harrison. Philadelphia: W. B. Saunders, 1986b.

———. "Mollicutes," in *Clinical Avian Medicine and Surgery*, ed. Greg J. Harrison and Linda R. Harrison, Philadelphia: W. B. Saunders, 1986c.

———. "Update Macaw Wasting Disease," in *Proceedings of the Annual Meeting of the Association of Avian Veterinarisn*, 1986b.

———. "Viral Diseases," in *Clinical Avian Medicine and Surgery*, ed. Greg J. Harrison and Linda R. Harrison, Philadelphia: W. B. Saunders, 1986e.

Gerstenfeld, Sheldon. *The Bird Care Book*. Reading, Mass.: Addison-Wesley, 1981.

Gilman, Alfred A.; Louis S. Goodman; Theodore W. Rall; and Ferid Murad. *The Pharmacological Basis of Therapeutics*, 7th ed. New York: Macmillan, 1985.

Graham, David L. "Necropsy in Birds," in *Proceedings of Basic Avian Medicine Seminar*, sponsored by the Association of Avian Veterinarians, 1987a.

———. "Characterization of a Reo-Like Virus and Its Isolation from and Pathogencity for Parrots," *Avian Disease* 31:2 (April-June 1987b).

———. "An Update on Selected Pet Bird Virus Infections," in *Proceedings of the International Conference on Avian Medicine*, sponsored by the Association of Avian Veterinarians, 1984.

Graham, David L., and Bruce W. Calnek. "Papovavirus Infection in Hand-fed Parrots: Virus Isolation and Pathology," *Avian Disease* 31:2 (April-June 1987).

Grimes, James E. "Zoonoses Acquired from Pet Birds," in *Veterinary Clinics of North America: Small Animal Practice, Zoonotic Diseases*, ed. John R. August and Andrea S. Loar. Philadelphia: W. B. Saunders, 1987.

————. "Serology," in *Clinical Avian Medicine and Surgery*, ed. Greg J. Harrison and Linda R. Harrison. Philadelphia: W. B. Saunders, 1986.

Harlin, Roger W. "Cloacal Problems," *Bird World* (March 1986).

————. "Pacheco's Disease," *Bird World* (November 1985).

————. "Practical Avian Microbiology," *AFA Watchbird* 11:5 (October/November 1984).

Harris, Don. "Errors in Recognition and Identification of Avian Diseases," *Bird World* (July 1986).

————. "The Use and Misuse of Antibiotics," *Bird World* (September 1984).

Harrison, Greg J. "The Avian Diagnostic Dilemma," paper presented at the 54th Annual Meeting of the American Animal Hospital Association, Phoenix, Arizona; Insta-Tape, Inc., P.O. Box 1729, Monrovia, CA 91016-5729.

————. "Methoxyprogesterone Acetate-Impregnated Silicone Implants: Preliminary Use in Pet Birds," in *Proceedings of the Annual Conference of the Association of Avian Veterinarians*, 1989.

————. "Anesthesiology," in *Clinical Avian Medicine and Surgery*, ed. Greg J. Harrison and Linda R. Harrison. Philadelphia: W. B. Saunders, 1986a.

————. "Disorders of the Integument," in *Avian Clinical Medicine and Surgery*, ed. Greg J. Harrison and Linda R. Harrison. Philadelphia: W. B. Saunders, 1986b.

————. "Evaluation and Support of the Surgical Patient," in *Clinical Avian Medicine and Surgery*, ed. Greg J. Harrison and Linda R. Harrison. Philadelphia: W. B. Saunders, 1986c.

————. "Selected Surgical Procedures," in *Clinical Avian Medicine and Surgery*, ed. Greg J. Harrison and Linda R. Harrison. Philadelphia: W. B. Saunders, 1986d.

————. "Surgical Instrumentation and Special Techniques," in *Clinical Avian Medicine and Surgery*, ed. Greg J. Harrison and Linda R. Harrison. Philadelphia: W. B. Saunders, 1986e.

————. "Toxicology," in *Clinical Avian Medicine and Surgery*, ed. Greg J. Harrison and Linda R. Harrison. Philadelphia: W. B. Saunders, 1986f.

————. "Feather Disorders," in *Veterinary Clinics of North America: Caged Bird Medicine*, ed. Greg J. Harrison. Philadelphia: W. B. Saunders, 1984.

————. "New Aspects of Avian Surgery," in *Veterinary Clinics of North America: Caged Bird Medicine*, ed. Greg J. Harrison. Philadelphia: W. B. Saunders, 1984.

Harrison, Greg J., and Linda R. Harrison. "Nutritional Diseases," in *Clinical Avian Medicine and Surgery*, ed. Greg J. Harrison and Linda R. Harrison. Philadelphia: W. B. Saunders, 1986.

Harrison, Greg J.; Richard W. Woerpel; Walter J. Rosskopf, Jr.; and Lorraine G. Karpinski. "Symptomatic Therapy and Emergency Medicine," in *Clinical Avian Medicine and Surgery*, ed. Greg J. Harrison and Linda R. Harrison. Philadelphia: W. B. Saunders, 1986.

Heard, Darryl J. "Overview of Avian Anesthesia," *AAV Today* 2:2 (Summer 1988).

Johnson, Cathy A. "Chronic Feather Picking: A Different Approach to Treatment," in *Proceedings of the First International Conference on Zoological and Avian Medicine*, sponsored by the Association of Avian Veterinarians and the American Association of Zoo Veterinarians, 1987a.

————. "Psittacine Beak and Feather Disease Syndrome," in *First International Conference of Proceedings of Zoological and Avian Medicine*, sponsored by the Association of Avian Veterinarians and the American Association of Zoo Veterinarians, 1987b.

———. "Update and Status of Psittacine Beak and Feather Disease," *Bird World* (November 1987c).

———. "Clinical Improvement in Cockatoos with Psittacine Beak and Feather Loss Viral Syndrome with Use of Autogenous Vaccine," in *Proceedings of the Annual Meeting of the Association of Avian Veterinarians*, 1986.

Karpinski, Lorraine G. "Ocular Disorders in Birds," *AAV Today* 1:5 (Winter 1987).

Karpinski, Lorraine G., and Susan L. Clubb. "An Outbreak of Avian Pox in Imported Mynahs," in *Proceedings of the Annual Meeting of the Association of Avian Veterinarians*, 1986.

Kenny, A. D. "Parathyroid and Ultimobranchial Glands," in *Avian Physiology*, 4th ed., ed. P. D. Sturkie. New York: Springer-Verlag, 1986.

Keymer, I. F. "Mycoses," in *Diseases of Cage and Aviary Birds*, 2nd ed., ed. Margaret L. Petrak. Philadelphia: Lea and Febiger, 1982a.

———. "Parasitic Diseases," in *Diseases of Cage and Aviary Birds*, 2nd ed., ed. Margaret L. Petrak. Philadelphia, Lea and Febiger, 1982b.

King, A. S., and J. McLelland. *Birds: Their Structure and Function*. London: Balliere Tindall, 1984.

King, Donald West; Cecilia M. Fenoglio; and Jay H. Lefkowitch. *General Pathology: Principles and Dynamics*. Philadelphia: Lea and Febiger, 1983.

Kingsbury, John M. *Poisonous Plants of the United States and Canada*. Englewood Cliffs, N.J.: Prentice-Hall, 1964.

Kirk, Robert W., and Stephen I. Bistner. *Handbook of Veterinary Procedures and Emergency Treatment*. Philadelphia: W. B. Saunders, 1969.

Krinsley, Michael. "Surgical Removal of Oral Lesions," *AAV Today* 2:2 (Summer 1988).

Krupp, Marcus A., and Milton J. Chatton. *Current Medical Diagnosis and Treatment*. Los Altos, Calif.: Lange Medical Publications, 1974.

Leon, Arnold. "Visual Impairment," in *Small Animal Ophthalmology*, ed. Robert L. Peiffer, Jr. Philadelphia: W. B. Saunders, 1989.

Lewandowski, Albert H.; Terry W. Campbell; and Greg J. Harrison. "Clinical Chemistries," in *Clinical Avian Medicine and Surgery*, ed. Greg J. Harrison and Linda R. Harrison. Philadelphia: W. B. Saunders, 1986.

Ley, David H. "Avian Cryptosporidiosis—An Emerging Disease," in *Proceedings of the First International Conference of Zoological and Avian Medicine*, sponsored by the Association of Avian Veterinarians and the American Association of Zoo Veterinarians, 1987.

Lothrop, Clinton D., Jr. "Diseases of the Thyroid Gland in Caged Birds," in *Proceedings of the International Conference of Avian Medicine*, sponsored by the Association of Avian Veterinarians, 1984.

Lothrop, Clinton D., and Greg J. Harrison. "Miscellaneous Diagnostic Tests," in *Clinical Avian Medicine and Surgery*, ed. Greg J. Harrison and Linda R. Harrison. Philadelphia: W. B. Saunders, 1986.

Lothrop, Clinton; Greg J. Harrison; David Schultz; and Tammy Utteridge. "Miscellaneous Diseases," in *Clinical Avian Medicine and Surgery*, ed. Greg J. Harrison and Linda R. Harrison. Philadelphia: W. B. Saunders, 1986.

Lowenstine, Linda J. "Necropsy Procedures," in *Clinical Avian Medicine and Surgery*, ed. Greg J. Harrison and Linda R. Harrison. Philadelphia: W. B. Saunders, 1986.

Lyman, Ronald. "Neurologic Disorders," in *Clinical Avian Medicine and Surgery*, ed. Greg J. Harrison and Linda R. Harrison. Philadelphia: W. B. Saunders, 1986.

MacWhirter, Pat, ed. *Everybird*. Melbourne, Australia: Inkata Press, 1987.

Mannl, A.; Helga Gerlach; and Rose Leipold. "Neuropathic Gastric Dilatation in Psittaciformes," *Avian Disease* 31:1 (January-March 1987).

Martin, Howard D. and Carol Dufficy. "Avian Surgery: Applied Anatomy and Surgical Approaches," in *Proceedings: Basic Avian Medicine Seminar*, sponsored by the Association of Avian Veterinarians, 1987.

McCluggage, David. "Metabolic Bone Disease," *AAV Today* 1:5 (Winter 1987).

McDonald, Scott E. "Endoscopic Examination," in *Companion Bird Medicine*, ed. Elisha W. Burr. Ames: Iowa State University Press, 1987.

―――. "Causes of Seizures," *Bird Talk* 4:5 (May 1986).

―――. "Successful Treatment of Mycotic Tracheitis in a Raven," in *Proceedings of the International Conference on Avian Medicine*, sponsored by the Association of Avian Veterinarians, 1984.

McMillan, Marjorie. "Imaging of Avian Urogenital Disorders," *AAV Today* 2:2 (Summer 1988).

Merck Veterinary Manual, 6th ed. Rahway, N.J.: Merck and Co., 1986.

Miller, Michael S. "Electrocardiography," in *Clinical Avian Medicine and Surgery*, ed. Greg J. Harrison and Linda R. Harrison. Philadelphia: W. B. Saunders, 1986.

Milton, J. L. "Pinioning and Amputation," in *Proceedings for Seminary #9: Avian Medicine and Surgery—12th Annual Veterinary Surgical Forum*, sponsored by the American College of Veterinary Surgeons, 1984.

Minsky, Lawrence, and Margaret L. Petrak. "Metabolic and Miscellaneous Conditions," in *Diseases of Cage and Aviary Birds*, 2nd ed., ed. Margaret Petrak. Philadelphia: Lea and Febiger, 1982.

Mohan, R. "Medico-Legal Aspects of Psittacosis," in *Proceedings of the First International Conference of Zoological and Avian Medicine*, sponsored by the Association of Avian Veterinarians and the American Association of Zoo Veterinarians, 1987.

―――. "Clinical and Laboratory Observations of Reovirus Infection in a Cockatoo and a Grey-Cheeked Parrot," in *Proceedings of the International Conference on Avian Medicine*, sponsored by the Association of Avian Veterinarians, 1984.

Murphy, Christopher. "Avian Opthamology," in *Proceedings for Seminary #10: Avian Surgery—13th Annual Veterinary Surgical Forum*, sponsored by the American College of Veterinary Surgeons, 1985.

New, Karyn. "Coping with Grief," *Bird Talk* 5:5 (May 1987).

Nieburg, Herbert A., and Arlene Fischer. *Pet Loss: A Thoughtful Guide for Adults and Children*: New York: Harper & Row, 1982.

Oates, Wayne E. *Your Particular Grief*. Philadelphia: Westminster Press, 1981.

Olsen, Glenn H.; Simon M. Shane; and Kathleen S. Harrington. "Investigation of the Pathology of *Klebsiella pneumoniae* in Psittacine Birds," in *Proceedings of the Annual Meeting of The Association of Avian Veterinarian*, 1986.

Pasco, W. Joel. "Care of the Sick Bird," *Bird World* (September 1983).

Paster, Michael B. "Candidiasis and Sour Crop," *Bird World* (January 1983a).

―――. "Common Avian Diagnostic Tests," *Bird World* (May 1983b).

Patgiri, Guru P. "Systemic Mycoses," in *Companion Bird Medicine*, ed. Elisha W. Burr. Ames: Iowa State University Press, 1987.

Perry, Ross A. "Avian Dermatology," in *Companion Bird Medicine*, ed. Elisha W. Burr. Ames: Iowa State University Press, 1987.

Petrak, Margaret L. "A Possible Case of Mycobacterium Tuberculosis in a Parrot," in *Proceedings of the International Conference on Avian Medicine*, sponsored by the Association of Avian Veterinarians, 1984.

———. "Poisoning," in *Diseases of Cage and Aviary Birds*, 2nd ed., ed. Margaret L. Petrak. Philadelphia: Lea and Febiger, 1982.

Petrak, Margaret L., and Charley E. Gilmore. "Neoplasms," in *Diseases of Cage and Aviary Birds*, 2nd ed., ed. Margaret L. Petrak. Philadelphia: Lea and Febiger, 1982.

Physician's Desk Reference. Oradell, N.J.: Medical Economics Co., 1987.

Porter, Stuart. "Use of Physical Therapy," *AAV Today* 2:2 (Summer 1988).

Prus, S.E., and S.M. Schmutz. "Comparative Efficiency and Accuracy of Surgical and Cytogenetic Sexing in Psittacines," *Avian Diseases* 31:2 (April/June 1987).

Quackenbush, Jamie. "Social Work in a Veterinary Hospital," in *Pet Loss and Human Bereavement*, ed. William J. Kay, Herbert A. Nieburg, Austin H. Kutscher, Ross M. Grey, and Carole E. Fudin. Ames: Iowa State University Press, 1984.

Quesenberry, Katherine E.; James P. Tappe; Jack L. Allen; and Ellis C. Greiner. "Hepatic Trematodiasis: Clinical and Pathologic Considerations," in *Proceedings of the Annual Meeting of the Association of Avian Veterinarians*, 1986.

Redig, Patrick T. "Treatment Protocol for Bumblefoot Types 1 & 2," *AAV Today* 1:5 (Winter 1987).

———. "Basic Orthopedic Surgical Techniques," in *Clinical Avian Medicine and Surgery*, ed. Greg J. Harrison and Linda R. Harrison. Philadelphia: W. B. Saunders, 1986.

Reece, Rodney L. "Reproductive Disease," in *Companion Bird Medicine*, ed. Elisha W. Burr. Ames: Iowa State University Press, 1987.

Rich, Gregory A. "Excessive Egg-Laying in the Female Cockatiel," *Bird World* (May 1987).

Ritchie, Branson W. "Isolation, Characterization, and Experimental Reproduction of the Psittacine Beak and Feather Disease Virus," *AAV Today* 2:3 (Fall 1988).

Rosenthal, Trudy. "Managing Magnolia, A Follow-up," *Bird Talk* 6:2 (February 1988).

———. "Managing Magnolia," *Bird Talk* 4:11 (November 1986).

Rosskopf, Walter J., Jr. "Analysis of Pet Bird Droppings," 58th Annual Meeting of the Intermountain Veterinary Medical Association; Insta-tape, Inc., P.O. Box 1729, Monrovia, CA 91016-5729.

———. "Diagnosis of Parasitism," 58th Annual Meeting of the Intermountain Veterinary Medical Association; Insta-Tape, Inc., P.O. Box 1729, Monrovia, California 91016-5729.

———. "Avian Obstetrics," address to American Federation of Aviculture, 1988; Convention Recordings International, Inc., P.O. Box 1778, Largo, FL 34649.

———. "Surgery of the Avian Digestive System," in *Proceedings of the 13th Annual Veterinary Surgical Forum*, sponsored by the American College of Veterinary Surgeons, 1985a.

———. "Surgery of the Avian Respiratory System," in *Proceedings of the 13th Annual Surgical Forum*, sponsored by the American College of Veterinary Surgeons, 1985b.

———. "Pre-operative Evaluation: Clinical Pathology," in *Proceedings of the 12th Annual Veterinary Surgical Forum*, sponsored by the American College of Veterinary Surgeons, 1984a.

———. "Pre-operative Evaluation: Restraint, Handling, and Physical Examination," in *Proceedings of the Annual Veterinary Surgical Forum*, sponsored by the American College of Veterinary Surgeons, 1984b.

———. "Surgery of the Digestive System," in *Proceedings of the 12th Annual Veterinary Surgical Forum*, sponsored by the American College of Veterinary Surgeons, 1984c.

———., and Woerpel, Richard W. "The Lutino Cockatiel Syndrome," in *The Proceedings of the Annual Meeting of the Association of Avian Veterinarians*, 1988.

———. "Avian Emergency Care," *Companion Animal Practice* 1:7 (December 1987a).

———. "Avian Dietary Addendum," *Bird Talk* (September 1987b).

———. "The Importance of Laboratory Testing in the Veterinary Care of Caged and Aviary Birds," *Bird World* (July 1987c).

———. "Feather Picking," *Bird World* (May 1987d).

———. "Hypocalcemia Syndrome in African Greys: A Clinical Update," *AFA Watchbird* 12:5 (October/November 1985a).

———. "Hemorrhagic Conure Syndrome," *AFA Watchbird* 12:3 (June/July 1985b).

———. "The Veterinarian and the Import and Sale of Pet Birds," *AFA Watchbird* 11:6 (December/January 1985c).

———. "Egg-Binding in Cage and Aviary Birds," *AFA Watchbird* 11:2 (April/May 1984).

Rosskopf, Walter J., Jr.; Richard W. Woerpel; and Sue Reed-Blake. "Pet Avian Surgical Procedures, Selected Soft Tissue," *AFA Watchbird* 12:2 (April/May 1985).

Rosskopf, Walter J., Jr., Richard W. Woerpel; Sue Reed-Blake; and Rosalie Lane. "Feather Picking in Psittacine Birds—A Clinician's Approach to Dx and Px," in *Proceedings of the Annual Meeting of the Association of Avian Veterinarians*, 1986.

Rosskopf, Walter J., Jr.; Richard W. Woerpel; Sue Reed; Karen Snider; and Tony Dispirito. "Avian Anesthesia Administration," in *Proceedings of the Association of Avian Technicians*, 1987.

Sakas, Peter. *Household Dangers to Pet Birds*, Niles Animal Hospital, 7278 N. Milwaukee Avenue, Niles, IL 60648.

———. "The Hazard of Non-Stick Cookware," *Bird Talk* 4:6 (June 1986).

Sayle, Rhonda. "Evaluation of Droppings," in *Clinical Avian Medicine and Surgery*, ed. Greg J. Harrison and Linda R. Harrison. Philadelphia: W. B. Saunders, 1986.

Shanthikumar, S. "Helminthology," in *Companion Bird Medicine*, ed. Elisha W. Burr. Ames: Iowa State University Press, 1987.

Smith, Alice Lorraine. *Microbiology and Pathology*, 12th ed. St. Louis: C. V. Mosby, 1980.

Smith, Richard E. "Psittacine Beak and Feather Disease: A Cluster of Cases in a Cockatoo Breeding Facility," in *Proceedings of the Annual Meeting of the Association of Avian Veterinarians*, 1986.

Squire, Lucy Frank. *Fundamentals of Radiology*, 3rd ed.; Cambridge: Harvard University Press, 1982.

Stedman's Medical Dictionary, 23rd ed.; Baltimore: Williams and Wilkins, 1976.

Stehlik, Milan. "Entomology," in *Companion Bird Medicine*, ed. Elisha W. Burr. Ames: Iowa State University Press, 1987.

Stoddard, Hannis L., III. "Treating Broken Bones," *Bird Talk* 5:8 (August 1987a).

———. "Treating the Avian Cold," *Bird Talk* 5:9 (September 1987b).

Stoodley, John, and Pat Stoodley. *Parrot Production, Incorporating Incubation*. Lovedean, England: Bezels Publications, 1983.

Stunkard, J. A. *Diagnosis, Treatment, and Husbandry of Pet Birds*, 2nd ed. Edgewater, Md.: Stunkard Publishing, 1984.

Sturkie, P. D. "Kidneys, Extrarenal Salt Excretion, and Urine," in *Avian Physiology*, 4th ed. New York: Springer-Verlag, 1986.

Taber's Cyclopedic Medical Dictionary, 15th ed. Philadelphia: F. A. Davis, 1985.

Taylor, T. Geoffrey. "French Molt," in *Diseases of Cage and Aviary Birds*, 2nd ed., ed. Margaret L. Petrak. Philadelphia: Lea and Febiger, 1982.

Teitler, Risa. "Behavioral Changes in Feather Loss Syndrome—Cockatoos," *AFA Watchbird* 12:3 (June/July 1985).

Turner, G. Vincent. "Zoonotic Disease," in *Companion Bird Medicine*, ed. Elisha W. Burr. Ames: Iowa State University Press, 1987.

Turrel, Jane M.; Marjorie C. McMillan; and Joanne Paul-Murphy. "Diagnosis and Treatment of Tumors of Companion Birds," *AAV Today* 3:4 (Fall 1987a).

———. "Diagnosis and Treatment of Tumors of Companion Birds, Part I," *AAV Today* 3:3 (Summer 1987b).

Turrel, Jane M.; Joanne Paul-Murphy; Shirley Harman; Michael W. Leach; and Laura Rosenberg. "Feasibility Study of 125 I Interstitial Implants for Treatment of Small Abdominal Tumors in Pet Birds," in *Proceedings of the First International Conference of Zoological and Avian Medicine*, sponsored by the Association of Avian Veterinarians and the American Association of Zoo Veterinarians, 1987.

T-W-Fiennes, R. N. "Infectious Diseases," in *Diseases of Cage and Aviary Birds*, 2nd ed, ed. Margaret L. Petrak. Philadelphia: Lea and Febiger, 1982.

University of Pennsylvania. *A Manual of Methods for Laboratory Diagnosis of Chlamydiosis*. Philadelphia: American Association of Avian Pathologists, 1987.

Van der Heyden, Nicole. "Avian Tuberculosis," *Bird World* (September 1986a).

———. "Avian Tuberculosis: Diagnosis and Attempted Treatment," in *Proceedings of the Annual Meeting of the Association of Avian Veterinarians*, 1986b.

Wainwright, P.O.; P. D. Lukert; and R. B. Davis. "Update on Papovavirus Infection in Fledgling Psittaciformes," *AFA Watchbird* 14:1 (February/March 1987).

Washington, John A., ed. *Laboratory Procedures in Clinical Microbiology*, 2nd ed. New York: Springer-Verlag, 1985.

Watkins, Bruce. "Artificial Lighting and Vitamin D Synthesis in Birds," *AAV Today* 1:2 (Spring 1987).

Wentworth, B. C., and R. K. Ringer. "Thyroids," in *Avian Physiology*, 4th ed., ed. P. D. Sturkie. New York: Springer-Verlag, 1986.

Willard, Michael D.; Barrett Sugarman; and Robert D. Walker. "Gastrointestinal Zoonoses," in *Veterinary Clinics of North America: Zoonotic Diseases*. Philadelphia: W. B. Saunders, 1987.

Woerpel, Richard W. "Avian Axioms," *Avian/Exotic Practice* 1:1, Audio-Veterinary Medicine, P.O. Box 1729, Monrovia, CA 91016.

Woerpel, Richard W., and Walter J. Rosskopf, Jr. "A New Disease of Psittacines," *AFA Watchbird* 11:3 (June/July 1984a).

———. "Clinical Experiences with Avian Diagnostics," *Veterinary Clinics of North America, Small Animal Practice: Caged Bird Medicine*, ed. Greg J. Harrison. Philadelphia: W. B. Saunders, 1984b.

———. "Proventricular Dilatation and Wasting Syndrome: Myenteric Ganglioneuritis and Encephalomyelitis of Psittacines—An Update," in *Proceedings of the International Conference on Avian Medicine*, sponsored by the Association of Avian Veterinarians, 1984c.

Woerpel, Richard W.; Walter J. Rosskopf, Jr.; and Marilyn Monahan-Brennan. "Clinical Pathology and Laboratory Diagnostic Tools," in *Companion Bird Medicine*, ed, Elisha W. Burr. Ames: Iowa State University Press, 1987.

Worrell, Amy. "Signs of the Sick Bird and Its Emergency Care," *AFA Watchbird* 13:4 (October/November 1986a).

———. "Psittacosis," address to American Federation of Aviculture Convention, 1986b; Recorded Resources Corporation, 1468 Crofton Parkway, Crofton, MD 21114.

Young, Deborah. "Adverse Reaction to Bitter Apple," *AAV Today* 1:5 (Winter 1987).

Acknowledgments

Writing a book is rarely the creation of one person. So many others contribute to its making. Family and friends were towers of support while the writing was in progress. My husband, Bill; my sons, Andy and Michael; our "third son," Rick; my parents, Dorothy and Stuart Munro; and my sister, Jean, all provided help and encouragement when I needed them most. All those near and dear to me were most patient with my frequent moods of distraction and preoccupation.

Peter Sakas, DVM, was a constant source of help. He graciously made time in his heavy schedule to read and critique the manuscript and provided all the photographs illustrating the diseases discussed herein. These photographs greatly enhance the text, so I am grateful to have had access to his large collection of splendid photographs gathered during many years of avian veterinary practice. His support, friendship, encouragement, and boundless generosity helped tremendously to lighten my tasks in the preparation of this book.

Others also furnished photographs of stunning beauty and have my heartfelt thanks. Bill Wegner of Malibu Exotics lent marvelous photos of his spectacular Black Cockatoos. Richard Schubot of the Avicultural Breeding and Research Center provided many beautiful studies of his Eclectus Parrots, Cockatoos, and Macaws. The Animal Welfare Institute (AWI) helped me obtain photographs showing the horrors of the import and quarantine processes, as well as the tragic fate of most smuggled parrots. Many, many thanks are due AWI and similar organizations for assuming the often thankless role of society's collective conscience regarding the welfare of all fauna.

Very special thanks go to John Lazendorf, without whom it would have been difficult for me to find a publisher. If not for him, this book would probably never have come to be. His faith in me and the book mean more than words can say.

For my editor, Seymour Weiss, I have only plaudits. He helped shaped the book to its present form and provided his special expertise in animal husbandry publishing. He has also consistently rejoiced with me in my avicultural accomplishments and was an absolute delight to work with.

For my illustrator, Martha Vogel, again I have no words with which to thank her properly. Much of her work for the book was executed under the most trying personal circumstances, yet she never faltered, never asked for concessions, and fully justified my trust in her talent. Her ornamentals at the start of each chapter and her line drawings, which clarify some rather obscure anatomical points, are works of art, and I feel most privileged to have them in my book.

To Nanette Wells, I express deep thanks and appreciation for typing the first draft of the manuscript and its subsequent revisions. She labored long and cheerfully because she believed deeply in the project. I do not know what I would have done without her.

Any success that accrues to this book I wholeheartedly share with all who have contributed to it. Any errors or shortcomings are entirely mine.

Last, but really foremost, I thank the good Lord who made all this possible.

Index